Dewey Decimal Classification,
19th Edition

DEWEY DECIMAL CLASSIFICATION, 19th EDITION
A Study Manual

By
JEANNE OSBORN

With an introduction
by
JOHN P. COMAROMI

LIBRARIES UNLIMITED, INC.   Littleton, Colorado
1982

LIBRARIES UNLIMITED, INC.
P.O. Box 263
Littleton, Colorado 80160

Library of Congress Cataloging in Publication Data

Osborn, Jeanne.
    Dewey decimal classification, 19th edition.

    Bibliography : p. 349
    Includes index.
    1. Classification, Dewey decimal. I. Title.
Z696.D708 1982   025.4'31   82-21
ISBN 0-87287-293-9   AACR2

Table of Contents

List of Tables

Preface

This work traces recent developments in the Dewey Decimal Classification and points to those characteristics which appear to be shaping its future. Elementary instruction in number building is touched upon, but not emphasized, since the editor's introduction performs that service competently and we have been promised a further instruction manual from Forest Press. Supplementary manuals such as Bloomberg and Weber's *Introduction to Classification and Number Building in Dewey*, although designed for use with previous editions of *DDC*, offer reliable explanation and drill. The present study is more concerned with differences between *DDC 18* and *19*. Structural character and change are examined in chapters 2 and 3. Indexing and terminological comparisons are the gist of chapter 4. Differences in auxiliary tables occupy chapter 5, while specific comments on each successive class are contained in chapters 6 through 15. The eleventh abridged edition is examined in chapter 16. The final chapter surveys related topics such as book numbers, non-print classification, the pros and cons of DDC, and the status of DDC numbers on Library of Congress bibliographic records.

A feature of chapters 2 and 5-15 is the inclusion of numerous exercises in number analysis and synthesis for which Library of Congress assignments provide benchmarks. Library of Congress card numbers are given for ready identification of the full records. LC prime marks are retained to segment DDC numbers for broad classification, and to give users of the eleventh abridged edition opportunities for comparison and drill. Since all cataloging students complain, with reason, about the snares of classifying from a work's title alone, ambiguities are explained in brackets.

The exercises are of three types. A) LC records carry DDC numbers for analysis of intricate constructions. No "answers" are given since the original syntheses proceeded by prescription, and the results are easily checked by a second or third party. B) Topical statements challenge the student to locate or synthesize class numbers approximating those assigned by the Library of Congress to works on the same, or similar, topics. Exemplary LC records are then supplied. C) Problematic situations reveal apparent discrepancies, or give now-discontinued numbers from earlier editions. Possible solutions are suggested, with apologies in advance for any inadvertent misinterpretation. General instructions accompany the exercises in chapters 2, 5, and 6. Users wishing to study only examples in chapters 7-15 should first consult pages 41, 132, and 148.

The illustrative DDC excerpts which dot the text are not always copied in full detail since extraneous material can blur the focus for a particular point at issue. Titles of Dewey editions are usually abbreviated, e.g., "*DDC 19*." Names of abridged editions are similarly shortened, e.g., "*Abr 11*." *Dewey Decimal*

Classification: Additions, Notes and Decisions appears most often as *"DC&."* To save time and space, references to *DDC 19* are usually cited in the text by volume and page number in parentheses.

A word about terminology. All Dewey numbers are decimals, e.g., 621.8 should be read and filed as .6218. DDC editorial usage works from a base 10. The point after the third digit is for reading convenience, not arithmetic computation, we are told. To avoid circumlocutions, however, four-digit or longer numbers will occasionally be termed "decimals," to distinguish them from section numbers. Incidentally, I cannot refrain from a quibble over the neologism "phoenixing," which has crept into recent DDC commentary. It evolves from the metaphorical use of "phoenix" to describe sweeping modular schedule changes, but so far as I can observe, the verb form has never been officially endorsed. Its very mongrelism may give it enough vigor to establish it in the classification lexicon, but I need more time to adjust my sensibilities.

The bibliography is confined to titles cited or briefly mentioned in the text. The text makes heavy use of quotation to give the reader a flavor of general DDC comment and criticism. No claim is made that all bibliography entries are of uniformly high quality, since a few quotations were included for contrast and what was perceived to be their negative contribution. Most carry footnotes and reading lists of their own, which the reader is encouraged to explore.

I want to thank those who enthusiastically and generously helped in the preparation of this study. Bohdan Wynar was most patient and cooperative. John Comaromi read the manuscript and gave valuable suggestions. Forest Press granted permission to include my endless selective excerpts from DDC passages. The University of Iowa gave me a developmental leave and a secluded office at University House. Its School of Library Science staunchly relieved me of teaching and committee responsibilities, while providing valuable secretarial support from Pat Kondora and Joyce Hartford. I should be remiss not to thank the scores of students and colleagues whose evident interest was both encouraging and intimidating. Whatever merit is in these pages is largely theirs. The mistakes are my own.

Jeanne Osborn, Professor
School of Library Science
The University of Iowa

Introduction

Jeanne Osborn's *Dewey Decimal Classification, 19th Edition: A Study Manual* is a welcome addition to the growing literature on the DDC. The first three chapters of her work deal with the DDC in general: its modern history, general characteristics, and the modernization of its notation and schedules. Chapter 4 is a thorough analysis of the modernization of the terminology used, especially with respect to the index and in the light of recent criticism of this aspect of the DDC. The remainder of the work delineates the notable changes in the auxiliary tables and in each main class.

Exercises in the use of a particular class are located at the ends of the chapters. These are plentiful and arranged in a most useful manner. The first set of exercises is devoted to the analysis of DDC numbers. For each problem given one finds the DDC number, author and title of the work, its date of publication or copyright, and its LC card number. The second set of exercises is devoted to the synthesis of DDC numbers. Fifty or so works are characterized sufficiently to enable the student to assign a number. The answers to these are found at the end of the exercises. As in the analysis exercises, actual works have been used and the number given is that assigned by the Decimal Classification Division of the Library of Congress. The third set of exercises deals with reclassification. Reclassification here does not mean conversion from one edition to another or from one classification to another. The author has listed several dozen works in the order of the DDC number assigned from Edition 18. She suggests sound answers for these.

Dewey Decimal Classification, 19th Edition: A Study Manual has something for many of the members of the library community.

1) For the teacher and practicing classifier it is the most thorough study manual on Edition 19 in print. The problems of analysis, synthesis, and reclassification are based on actual works, thus providing ready-made problems and answers for every class. The usefulness of the problems for the teacher and for the person responsible for training classifiers using Edition 18 is obvious. Of course, the discussion of the changes that occurred in the various classes comprises the bulk of the work and presents the greatest amount of information regarding Edition 19 for the teacher and the practicing classifier. This work does not overlap the content of *Manual on the Use of the Dewey Decimal Classification: Edition 19*, even though their titles are similar. The latter work, published by Forest Press in 1982, focuses on the application of Edition 19, on the meanings and relationships of the various numbers of the DDC. Osborn's work, on the other hand, is concerned with introducing Edition 19 to its readers, and with discussing the strengths and weaknesses of the various changes.

2) For the advanced student it is a good introduction to the character of the DDC and can be used without the need for formal instruction.

3) For the beginning student it is a good introduction to the recent history of the DDC and to the general characteristics of the scheme.

4) For the historian of library classification it continues Comaromi's history of the DDC, *The Eighteen Editions of the Dewey Decimal Classification* (Albany, New York: Forest Press, 1976), which delineates the changes through Edition 18. Chapter 1 is a good introduction to the modern history of the DDC (1950 on).

5) For the critic of library classification it provides a nice analysis of the structure of the index and the response of the editors to terminological change. The comparison between the practices of the DDC and those of Hennepin County Library reveals surprising results.

6) For those who appreciate good writing it contains both wit and style.

As a member of several of the above groups, I look forward to subsequent editions of this work and trust that the reader will enjoy it as much as I have.

John P. Comaromi
Editor, Dewey Decimal Classification
Washington, DC

1

DDC: History and Current Status

After producing 18 editions in 100 years, the Dewey Decimal Classification has officially launched its second century with a nineteenth edition which strives, by a judicious mixture of old and new, to be all things to all libraries. Inventive tacking in the face of strong headwinds has run on occasion into storms of criticism from every corner of the classification compass, but practical mariners of cataloging still in impressive numbers rely on DDC.

The Modern History of DDC

The quarter century following Melvil Dewey's death in 1931 was one of "change and uncertainty."[1] After 60 years of close personal interaction, Dewey's loyal editorial team dissolved almost simultaneously with publication of *DDC 13* (1932). That edition continued the trend toward enumerative expansion upon existing number assignments. Nearly one-third larger than its predecessor, vilified for its corpulence, it still missed the equitable growth of all sections which many users wanted.

After considerable jockeying for control, a new editor took charge halfway through preparations for *DDC 14* (1942), but he lasted only until it was published. Questions of copyright, spelling, schedule proliferation, and cooperation with the International Institute of Bibliography shadowed that work. Its express goal was to develop all as yet unexpanded portions. Demand was growing for a "standard" edition that could serve the needs of an average-sized library of fewer than 200,000 volumes. It would bridge the gap between an intricately detailed bibliographic edition for large institutions, or for indexing purposes, and an abridged edition for school and small public libraries. *DDC 14* was intended to provide a comprehensive support for the controlled reductions anticipated in the forthcoming standard edition. It missed its publication deadline by a year, still failing to provide complete and uniform expansion. Nevertheless, it was a popular, unexpectedly long-lived edition.[2]

When the standard edition appeared in 1951 it was, at best, a qualified success. Theorists said it abandoned or obscured the logical principle of development from the general to the specific. Its index was drastically reduced. It had less in common with *DDC 14* than was predicted. On the other hand, it cut out much dead wood, curtailed the troublesome simplified spelling, and introduced welcome modern terminology. A revised *DDC 15* appeared in 1953 with expanded form divisions, a considerably lengthened index, and other modifications. But irreversible antipathy curtailed sales, and accelerated the trend to reclassify from DDC to the Library of Congress scheme.

Caught in acute financial distress, the Lake Placid Club Education Foundation appealed to "outsiders" to help its programs. For instance, it solicited both the American Library Association and the Library of Congress for professional input. In late 1953, the Forest Press, its operational branch, contracted the Library of Congress to do the editorial work on schedule, and according to predetermined criteria. A use survey was made

> ... to determine whether librarians preferred integrity of numbers (fourteenth edition) or keeping pace with knowledge (fifteenth edition) for their basic policy of classification and to see what had been done in the cases of 316 specific relocations.[3]

The result led to putting DDC numbers from both editions on LC printed cards, and set a more or less consistent policy for future development.[4] The resuscitation was partly the work of new editor Ben Custer. However, most basic policy decisions had been made when he assumed charge in September 1956.

The modern history of DDC is generally dated from 1958, with publication of a refocussed edition 16 that emphasized continuity and disciplinary integrity.[5] Changes were kept to a minimum, reflecting only those most urgently needed to accommodate existing knowledge and literary warrant. Wherever possible, specific numbers were left vacant when discontinued. Only the 546-547 (Inorganic and Organic chemistry) sections were fully recast, inaugurating the overhaul in each successive edition of limited portions that were especially inadequate or unpopular.[6] Dewey's idiosyncratic spelling almost disappeared. Instructional notes were polished and multiplied.

Critics, especially in foreign countries, still found fault. The American Protestant bias remained, although the editors had worked to reduce it.[7] Enumeration prevailed over rudimentary faceting for composite subjects. Users had trouble classing comprehensive works, especially where the decimal notation no longer reflected hierarchical subdivision. Nevertheless, the proof of the pudding was in the marketing. *DDC 16* may not have been a classifier's nirvana, but it sold like hot cakes, assuring the solvency of Forest Press and ensuring a systematic production schedule for later editions. A seven-to-eight-year revision cycle was established. *DDC 17* came out in 1965. Its editor's introduction emphasized

> ... new or renewed emphasis on subject integrity and subject relationships, on the fundamental process of classification as distinct from what has been called "slot-ification."

Encouraged by Melvil Dewey's notable preference for practicality over theory in all activities, misled by the common American view of classification as little more than a system for assigning each book a convenient address or "slot" at which it can be stored and from which it can be retrieved, influenst by the failure of earlier editions of the DDC to provide under every discipline an expansion as full as was warranted by the literature acquired by libraries, classifiers of the past many times unwittingly abandoned the most fundamental feature of the system.... Unfortunately ... Edition 16 affirmed for the first time various practices that had grown up contrary to the consistent development of subjects by discipline.[8]

While continuing to call its approach enumerative, *DDC 17* took a long step toward faceted number synthesis by expanding the table of form divisions, renaming it the "Table of Standard Subdivisions," and adding an "Area Table" which freed class 900 from its burden of enumerative detail, liberating geographic and political specifications from their traditional American distortion. "Divide like" and "Add area notation" instructions directed users to number sequences where established patterns of subdivision could be applied to different but related disciplines. The number of relocations was again reduced, although it still exceeded the announced limitation of 500 (see Table 1, p. 36). As for "completely remodeled schedules," the only explicit one was 150 (Psychology), which incorporated much of the material formerly located in class 130. Incidentally, the editor elsewhere cited Sections 614 (Public health) and 616 (Medicine) as areas of major relocation activity.[9]

The index gave trouble. It represented a 40% reduction of class number entries, but an enormous increase in cross-references. The editor later said of it:

> Previous indexes had contained entries chiefly for those topics that were named in the schedules, plus significant synonyms and subtopics, but had supplied numbers only for those aspects where the topics were named, making no effort to guide the classifier to the vast hidden resources of the system.... The new seventeenth index provided full information for only a limited number of broad core concepts, referred to these from more specific topics, and made many "scatter" references to remind the classifier of other aspects.... This procedure called attention to many possibilities often previously overlooked, but frequently it did not supply a precise number that could be used without close scrutiny of the schedules. Because of the scarcity of exact numbers this index proved to be difficult and time consuming to use, and was replaced in 1967 by a conventional index.[10]

Reminiscent of efforts to salvage the old standard edition, the new index was sent free with an apology to purchasers of the original *DDC 17*.

> Preparation of this new index to Edition 17 is an emergency measure designed to meet the objections expressed in reviews, and is without prejudice to the form that may later be decided upon for the index to Edition 18.[11]

Even so, *DDC 17* was thought difficult to use. The editor's introduction, designed to replace the *Guide to Use of Dewey Decimal Classification* that accompanied *DDC 16*, was murky.[12] Instruction notes within the schedules were inadequate. Centered headings, meant to show the hierarchy, were confusing. The use of multiple zeros in synthetic numbers seemed impractical to many. Yet with all its shortcomings, real or imagined, sales topped those of *DDC 16* by 23%.

DDC 18, published in 1971 with an improved three-volume format, introduced the term "phoenix schedule" for its fully revised classes 340 (Law) and

510 (Mathematics). For ready reference, a reworked editor's introduction got its own index, and all relocations and discontinued numbers were tabulated. Five more auxiliary tables materialized. The older "Divide like" and "Add" notes were consolidated and simplified by listing a "base number" to which the extension could be added. Tables of precedence helped users determine citation order when building numbers. The index curtailed its entries with class numbers, and increased its cross-references, but it was better received than the *DDC 17* index.

> Plans for the eighteenth edition included an enlarged index with all the traditional virtues plus a multiplicity of guides to hidden resources, therefore combining the good features and eliminating as far as possible the deficiencies of the two seventeenth edition indexes.[13]

Foreign sales and translations steadily increased, while the flight from DDC to LC moderated. Dewey's brainchild had not yet exhausted its nine lives. Already in 1973, two years after publication, more copies of *DDC 18* had been sold than of any previous edition.

Forest Press and the Editorial Policy Committee

With the erstwhile invalid once again a self-assured, self-supporting, middle-aged part of the American library establishment and a rising star on the international scene, let us pause to examine its managerial structure. The publisher's foreword of *DDC 19* explains the relation of Forest Press to the Lake Placid Education Foundation (formerly the Lake Placid Club Education Foundation). A Forest Press committee sets policies regarding the ongoing publication program. Editorial control resides in the "advisory" Decimal Classification Editorial Policy Committee. Composed largely of experienced library classifiers, it meets annually at the Library of Congress to discuss the whithers and wherefores of future development. Meeting reports are published regularly in *Library Resources & Technical Services*. Deliberations cover basic classification policy, phoenix schedules and other relocations, conversion tables, terminological changes, the size and nature of the new index, instructions and notes, separate manuals for use, abridged editions, segmentation, and related topics.[14] Day-to-day editing is done on contract in the Decimal Classification Division of the Library of Congress Processing Department.

Benjamin A. Custer, chief of the division and editor of *DDC 16* through *19*, with abridged editions 8 through 11, retired in early 1980 after nearly 25 years of involvement in a highly successful rejuvenation project. He firmly opposed the "pigeon-hole" or "slot-ification" approach that Dewey, in his old age, tended to countenance,[15] repudiating its implicit cynicism regarding logical structure and its dependence on verbal indexing. Custer's concept supplemented enumeration with structured citation orders and facet analysis,[16] techniques that had developed chiefly in India and the United Kingdom. Ranganathan's contributions were recognized and adapted to DDC needs. Cooperation from the *British National Bibliography*, as well as from the national libraries of Canada and Australia, was welcomed. Various subject experts, both American and British, received grants, or professional job responsibility, for drafting extensive revisions. The drafts were discussed and adopted, adapted, postponed, or rejected by the Editorial

Policy Committee; foster-care and critical review, however, fell under the editor's purview. Custer, with his strong personality, his practical approach to classification, and his synthesizing genius, was, more than any other single individual, responsible for reviving and maintaining DDC's vitality and prestige.[17]

Dewey Decimal Activities at the Library of Congress

The LC decision in the 1890s not to use the Dewey Decimal system in reorganizing its collections has been well documented.[18] Whether Dewey himself, through his refusal to permit modifications, surrendered the balance of influence to Cutter's *Expansive Classification* is still being debated. At any rate, the shrewd Dewey decided that his scheme should have its numbers printed on LC cards. Early in 1925, he started a campaign to get them there. The officials at first dragged their feet, partly because of financial hurdles. However, Dewey's aversion for "no" and "impossible" finally co-opted the American Library Association, the Carnegie Corporation, and even the Library of Congress to help supply the money.

> The work of assigning class numbers began on April 1, 1930, and cards with numbers on them began to appear by the end of the second week in April. By Aug. 1 a staff of three began carrying out a program even broader than anticipated....
>
> The following classes of books currently cataloged by the Library of Congress are being assigned Decimal Classification numbers:
>
> (a) All books in English, with the exception of city directories, telephone directories, and nearly all current fiction.
>
> (b) Some foreign books, as many as the time of the present staff will permit.
>
> (c) Nearly all serial publications.[19]

But the Federal Connection was still a long way from satisfactory. After Constantin Mazney was dismissed in 1942, the editorship fell between the Decimal Classification Section of LC's Subject Cataloging Division and the Editorial Office, now also located in Washington, DC. Weak financial support was probably a result, rather than a cause, of differences over developing the scheme as a whole, and over the kinds and quantity of materials for which LC would supply DDC numbers. At long last, in 1958, the two units merged.[20] Still, the relatively low percentage of catalog records carrying DDC numbers decreased further during the early 1960s, when book publishing and library budgets accelerated more exuberantly than did the personnel available for processing. A second major influence in the flight from Dewey was the cost of determining DDC class and book numbers locally, as compared to adopting LC's ready-made call numbers. In 1967, an LC Processing Department reorganization elevated the Decimal Classification Office to division status, with a corresponding increase in staff and production.

Adding spectacularly to its direct service to libraries as a central source of DC numbers for specific works, the Division classed 74,335 titles, compared with 59,799 in 1967 and 35,000 in 1966. The 1968 coverage included all titles cataloged for the MARC program, all current (1966-1968) titles cataloged in English, and the more important and difficult current titles cataloged in the other major western European languages, and received through the National Program for Acquisitions and Cataloging.[21]

At a fiftieth anniversary party in May 1980, it was announced that 2,253,731 titles had "received DDC numbers for use by libraries everywhere and of every kind and size."[22] Records with DDC numbers now run consistently over 100,000 per year. Table 6 in chapter 17 gives production figures for the past 10 years.

The editing of all DDC editions after the fifteenth has been contracted to the Library of Congress. The editor holds dual appointment as chief of the Decimal Classification Division. A copy of the agreement for producing *DDC 16* was published in *Cataloging Service*, to make users aware of developments.[23] The library's record of its Dewey assignments is the closest thing to a working shelflist that DDC editors have.

... All editorial development work of the past twenty years, covering Editions 16 through 19, has included a careful check of the Library of Congress's Dewey-classed catalog to see the trends in the literature that require provision, and also, equally important, to see if the textual provisions of earlier editions, i.e., headings, definitions, scope notes, instructions, and the like, have been clearly enough expressed to be fully understood.[24]

Functioning as a national library, LC can exchange information and enter into mutually beneficial agreements with foreign DDC users, as the following report shows.

Because thousands of users from Japan to Israel and Brazil to Mauritius utilize the Dewey decimal classification there is wide interest in its editorial development and in standardizing its application. Since 1969 the Decimal Classification Division has engaged in a lively exchange of information with the *British National Bibliography*, not only through transatlantic mail, which often moves weekly in each direction, but also through a six-week interchange of decimal classification specialists in 1972 as well as others with the *Australian National Bibliography* and *Canadiana*, the national bibliography of Canada. The result has been a common understanding of editorial policy, progress toward standardized interpretation of the schedules, and a vigorous expression of opinion and much give-and-take among four of the most important users of Dewey.

Recently the interchange with Great Britain entered a new dimension when British librarians, including the staff of BNB, undertook development of new schedules, subject to the guidance and review of the Decimal Classification Division. The first undertaking was the schedule for the new local administrative divisions of the United Kingdom that went into effect in April 1974. It will be followed by a revision of the Dewey decimal scheme for music. This type of dialogue has proved most useful and should be extended since through it overseas users obtain a more complete understanding of official Dewey policy and practice. In turn, they provide expertise in the development and application of the classification in fields of major concern to them.[25]

The serially published *Dewey Decimal Classification Additions, Notes and Decisions*, usually called *"DC&,"* continues its supplemental updating services for Edition 19, with a volume 4, number 1 issue dated June 1980.

DDC's International Presence

The early American WASP bias in Dewey classification is well known. It was more or less inevitable, and even justifiable, in view of its clientele and the literary warrant of the time. But social change and the growing use of the system abroad sparked efforts to broaden its outlook. The decade of the mid-1960s to mid-1970s saw three major surveys of the impact of DDC outside North America, plus one on its use in the United States and Canada.[26] These surveys were variously encouraged and partially financed by the Forest Press, the International Relations Office of ALA, the Library Association, the Asia Foundation, and the Council on Library Resources. Among other things they found:

1. Approval of techniques to give preferred treatment to local/national materials

2. Lack of enthusiasm for mixed notation

3. Concern over DDC's indifference to the "Cuttering concept" or the use of book numbers

4. Some dissatisfaction with the order of the main classes

5. Criticism of numbers (usually synthetic) supplied in the index though not in the schedules

6. Lack of familiarity with *DC&* and consequent ignorance of schedule revisions prior to publication of each new edition

7. Desire for more information on DDC policies and revision plans

Concern for the non-English-speaking users dealt the *coup de grâce* to simplified spelling. *DDC 19* announces:

> ... a return to conventional American spelling from the residual simpler spellings of Editions 16-18, e.g., divorst, publisht, which greatly frustrated those whose native tongue is not English.[27]

Celebration of the Dewey Centennial in 1976 stimulated a variety of cross-cultural activities such as the European Centenary Seminar at Banbury, England. British classificationists, who have long been interested in American schemes, have contributed penetrating commentary. The British serial *Catalogue & Index*, the English-language *International Classification* (published in Germany), and various foreign library association journals, particularly those in Canada, Australia, India, and South Africa, carry articles from time to time on DDC. Western European writers are particularly fond of comparing it to its FID-sponsored offspring, the Universal Decimal Classification (UDC). The studies do not usually redound to the praise of DDC, but they show more respect than did those written a decade or two ago.

The appearance of DDC translations, sometimes abridged, or just as often locally expanded, is further evidence of DDC's international headway. Currently sponsored by Forest Press, although not produced by it, are a French edition and a Spanish edition. Both are based on *DDC 18*, and neither is the first in its language. There is a Danish Decimal Classification in its fifth edition that the Danes themselves call "an illegitimate daughter of Dewey's." With or without authorization, editions are available in such non-European languages as Hebrew, Thai, and Vietnamese.

Conclusion

The Dewey Decimal Classification is the protégé of a series of strong personalities who successively poured their energies into its infancy, development, maturity, and perpetuation. Melvil Dewey, Dorkas Fellows, Godfrey Dewey, Milton Ferguson, David Haykin, and last, but certainly not least, Ben Custer, still cast atavistic shadows over *DDC 19*, shaping its inner consciousness and its outer presence. The advisory activities of the Editorial Policy Committee and the contractual services of LC's Decimal Classification Division have not essentially altered this paternalistic aspect. By contrast, the Library of Congress Classification, although originating in much the same social and intellectual climate, is the misshapen but serviceable product of a series of subject specialists. The individual stamp of a Putnam, a Martel, or a Cutter is visible on a few general features and specific schedules, but the total effect of special interests competing for a viable compromise is reminiscent of much American governmental endeavor.

These derivations subtly affect public reaction to the two systems. The LC classification seldom inspires the enthusiastic personal commitment which is frequently accorded DDC. Proponents of the latter absorbed its rudiments in their school libraries, exploring its idiosyncrasies and learning to live with them as public or college library patrons. They are conditioned to its mnemonic, practical comprehensibility, and its broad comprehensiveness. LC advocates are generally more objective and sophisticated. They have likely come to learn the system as a kind of second language. They may know and prefer specific parts, but its sprawling multiplicity, its loose interrelations, and its lack of close integration through a comprehensive index leave them with little feeling of overall familiarity or identification.

The hazards of such close personal supervision as DDC exhibits are many. It fell on hard times because of certain unilateral administrative or editorial decisions. It also had other, splendid times for similar reasons. Today it stands at yet another turning point. Custer's retirement, coupled with rising production costs, means change. Whether the incoming editor can fill the shoes of his great predecessors, whether he opts for more "participation" in policy decisions, or whether his advent will precipitate a transitional search for rejuvenated identity, remain to be seen.

NOTES

[1]John Phillip Comaromi, *The Eighteen Editions of the Dewey Decimal Classification* (Albany, NY, Forest Press Division, Lake Placid Education Foundation, 1976), p. 339.

[2]In a communication to the publisher dated April 29, 1981, Mr. Comaromi says: "Edition 14 has proven to be the most successful edition if you are measuring success by longevity and wide-spread acceptance."

[3]Comaromi, p. 419.

[4]*Cataloging Service*, bulletin 25 (December 1951): 1.

[5]Much classification ink has been spilled over the definition of "subject integrity." DDC prefers "disciplinary integrity" on the ground that it is, or should be, primarily fields of study that are delineated by a library classification scheme, leaving nuclear subjects to be pinpointed in their various disciplinary manifestations by a "relative" index, or by an alphabetical subject catalog.

[6]Melvil Dewey, *Dewey Decimal Classification and Relative Index.* Ed. 16 (Lake Placid Club, NY, Forest Press, 1958), p. 23.

[7]See, for example: Brenda Williams-Wynn, "Nearly 100 and Still Going Strong: A Review of Dewey 18," *South African Librarian*, v. 40, no. 2 (October 1972): 96.

[8]Melvil Dewey, *Dewey Decimal Classification and Relative Index.* Ed. 17 (Lake Placid Club, NY, Forest Press, 1965), pp. 43, 46.

[9]Benjamin A. Custer, "Dewey 17: A Preview and Report to the Profession," *Wilson Library Bulletin*, v. 39, no. 7 (March 1965): 557. Also published in *Library Association Record*, v. 67, no. 3 (March 1965): 81; and *Indian Librarian*, v. 19, no. 3 (March 1965): 193.

[10]Benjamin A. Custer, "Dewey Decimal Classification," *Encyclopedia of Library and Information Science* (New York, Marcel Dekker, 1972), v. 7, p. 135.

[11]Benjamin A. Custer, "Dewey Lives," *Library Resources & Technical Services*, v. 11, no. 1 (Winter 1967): 59.

[12]*Guide to Use of Dewey Decimal Classification, Based on the Practice of the Decimal Classification Office at the Library of Congress* (Lake Placid Club, NY, Forest Press, 1962).

[13]Custer, "Dewey Decimal Classification," v. 7, p. 140.

[14]An interesting British review of the committee and its work can be found in: Joel C. Downing, "The Role of the Editorial Policy Committee in the Development of the Dewey Decimal Classification," *Dewey International: Papers Given at the European Centenary Seminar on the Dewey Decimal Classification* (London, The Library Association, 1977), pp. 30-42.

[15]Comaromi, p. 552.

[16]Benjamin A. Custer, "The View from the Editor's Chair," *Library Resources & Technical Services*, v. 24, no. 2 (Spring 1980): 102.

[17]See, for instance: Thelma Eaton, "Epitaph to a Dead Classification," *Library Association Record*, v. 57, no. 11 (November 1955): 428-30.

[18]Two views of this episode are available in: Leo E. LaMontagne, *American Library Classification, with Special Reference to the Library of Congress* (Hamden, CT, Shoe String Press, 1961), p. 224; and John Phillip Comaromi, *The Eighteen Editions of the Dewey Decimal Classification* (Albany, NY, Forest Press Division, Lake Placid Education Foundation, 1976), p. 231.

[19]"D.C. Numbers on L.C. Cards," *Library Journal*, v. 50, no. 17 (October 1, 1930): 786.

[20]*Cataloging Service*, bulletin 51 (December 1958): 1.

[21]William J. Welsh, "The Processing Department of the Library of Congress in 1968," *Library Resources & Technical Services*, v. 13, no. 2 (Spring 1969): 189.

[22]*Library of Congress Information Bulletin*, v. 39, no. 28 (July 11, 1980): 243.

[23]*Cataloging Service*, bulletin 32 (February 1954): 1-10.

[24]Benjamin A. Custer, "The Responsiveness of Recent Editions of the Dewey Decimal Classification to the Needs of Its Users," *General Classification Systems in a Changing World: Proceedings of the FID Classification Symposium Held in Commemoration of the Dewey Centenary* (The Hague, Fédération Internationale de Documentation [FID], 1978), p. 84.

[25]Library of Congress, *Annual Report of the Librarian of Congress for the Fiscal Year Ending June 30, 1974* (Washington, Library of Congress, 1975), p. 23.

[26]For specific titles, see the bibliography at the end of this text.

[27]Melvil Dewey, *Dewey Decimal Classification and Relative Index*. Ed. 19 (Albany, NY, Forest Press, 1979), v. 1, p. xxiii.

2

The General Character of DDC 19

Introduction

The history of the Dewey Decimal Classification was summarized in chapter 1. Many dependable traits of early editions remain. Others underwent metamorphosis, particularly after Dewey's death in 1931, and again upon Benjamin Custer's appointment to the editorship in 1956. The present edition incorporates very little revolution, and only a sedate amount of evolution.

Hierarchical Structure and Force

Logical, more or less symmetrical progression from general to specific concepts makes the system basically hierarchical, although it is easy enough to find flaws in certain specific developments on the grounds of hierarchical failure.

HIERARCHICAL STRUCTURE

After the "classification by attraction" (slot-ification) crisis of *DDC 16*, editorial policy has stressed disciplinary integrity, largely through the use of hierarchical subordination.

> The DDC is a hierarchical classification, which means that it develops progressively from the general to the specific in disciplinary and subject relationships. Even so, the overall arrangement is not necessarily theoretical or logical. The DDC is built on the premise that no one class can cover all aspects of a given subject.[1]

The growing emphasis is a Custer legacy, according to his successor, John Comaromi.

> Custer's major contribution to the development of the DDC ... was as new as it was useful.... When Custer wrote " ... none is as fundamental as the *new or renewed emphasis* [italics mine] on subject integrity and subject relationships," either he did not know that the new emphasis was a divergence from old policy or he was keeping the conservatives happy by telling them that renewal was occurring, not change.[2]

Hierarchies are not fully reflected in the terminology, although an effort is made to keep the language of the headings as representative as possible. The editor's introduction explains:

> Each heading consists of a word or phrase so inclusive that it covers all subordinate topics and entries. The actual working may be incomplete, because, from the principle of hierarchy, the heading must be read as part of the larger group that includes it, e.g. at 469 "Portuguese" means the Portuguese language, but at 769 the same heading means Portuguese literature....
>
> A heading includes the total concept expressed by it, even if some parts of that total concept are explicitly provided for in numbers that are not subdivisions of the number assigned to the heading.[3]

The latter paragraph refers to such cross-disciplinary instructions as the following:

374 Adult education
    Class special education of adults in 371.9; educational role of libraries in 021.24; programs leading to a degree, diploma, certificate with the subject, e.g., high school equivalency programs 373.238

HIERARCHICAL NOTATION

DDC 19 reiterates the two preceding editions on hierarchy in the notation as well as in the structure.[4] Most classifiers complain that extension of the notation develops unwieldy class numbers for even moderately specific concepts.

> The hierarchical building of numbers in the Dewey scheme has been considered an asset, but I am forced to the conclusion that nowadays it frequently reaches the stage of the ridiculous when 12 to 17 or more numbers are added after the decimal point.[5]

More fundamental questions are now being raised:

> Looking at the relative merits of DDC and LCC in an automated environment, it would seem at first sight that the Dewey hierarchical notation gives it an edge over LCC. However, if DDC were to be examined from the point of view of perfect hierarchy, where perfect hierarchy is defined in terms of the mathematical properties associated with the inclusion relation (transitivity, antisymmetry, and reflexivity), it would soon be seen to be shot through with imperfection.[6]

Notation is not the sole means of showing hierarchy. Format features such as schedule indentions and typography alert the user to dizzying juxtapositions. As Bloomberg and Weber suggest, hierarchical structure in a linear classification is not self-evident, nor even routinely orthodox. It requires a stop-and-go mind set to shift abruptly from minutiae in one topical sequence to a general, sometimes only tenuously related, topic coming next. Consider, for instance, the detailed botanical subdivision of 589.9 (Schizomycetes), which causes works in the highly specific 589.99 (Spirochaetales) to shelve just ahead of broad general works in 590 (Zoological sciences). The editors claim that any specific class has two or three sets of relationships: coordinate, subordinate, and sometimes superordinate.[7] Nevertheless, some classifiers hold that DDC's use of linear subdivision is unduly simplistic.

All attempts to classify the multidimensional literary patchwork are restricted by the single dimension of a shelf arrangement, but most schemes fail to exploit the fact that one dimension has *two* directions, and that clusters of chapters should overlap both in the left and right…. This "chain" principle was a major contribution to the art of bibliographic classification. The term is suitably evocative, but in these days might lead to confusion with "chain indexing." In the SRL [the Science Reference Library of the British Library] we use "ribbon" to express the same idea of linking each class to both neighbours.[8]

HIERARCHICAL FORCE

DDC headings, and some kinds of notes, apply to all subdivisions of a topic. Only a few instructions, listed below, block carryover to subdivisions of their categories.[9]

1. Inclusion notes have no hierarchical force, because they enumerate topics that do not obviously fit under the heading, but have insufficient literary warrant for their own headings, e.g.:

613.94   Birth control (Contraception)
    Including artificial insemination
    Class here family planning
  .942   Surgical methods of birth control
    Including sterilization, vasectomy
  .943   Chemical, rhythm, mechanical methods of birth control
  .9432   Chemical
    Example: pills (oral contraceptives)
  .9434   Rhythm
  .9435   Mechanical
    Example: intrauterine devices

"Artificial insemination" is included under "birth control" but does not pertain to the subdivisions of that topic. The lingering enumerative tendencies in DDC that such examples illustrate will be further discussed in the next section.

2. Multiple zero standard subdivisions from Table 1 do not carry over their notation to subdivisions of the topic. They apply only at the level indicated, e.g.:

391   Costume and personal appearance
  .001-.007   Standard subdivisions
              Notations from Table 1
  .008   History and description of costumes of groups
              of persons
  .009   Historical and geographical treatment of costume
  .01-.05   Costumes of specific economic, social, occupa-
              tional classes
                Add to base number 391.0 the numbers follow-
                ing 390 in 390.1-390.5, e.g., costumes of
                lawyers 391.04344

Illustrations of lawyers' costumes would carry the class number 391.04344022 (not 391.043440022).

3.   Add notes carry no hierarchical force unless they use a table which refers specifically to "each subdivision's language, term, etc. identified by *." At some places, e.g., centered heading 222-224 (Specific parts of the Old Testament), all subdivisions, including optional numbers in brackets, are starred. More commonly, as under 617 (Surgery and related topics), only some subdivisions are starred to respond to the hierarchical force of the instruction.

DDC 19 carries suggestions for checking the hierarchical "ladder" to ensure classing a work at the optimal point in the correct discipline.[10]

ANALYZING HIERARCHIES IN DDC

A few examples will show how hierarchical structure is often demonstrable through step-by-step analysis of specific numbers, e.g.:

574   Biology
  .5   Ecology
  .52   Specific relationships and kinds of environment
  .526   Specific kinds of environments
  .5263   Aquatic environments
  .52632   Fresh-water
  .526325 Wetlands: Bogs, marshes, swamps

Centered headings may have been introduced, and must be included in the analysis to show the hierarchical progression, e.g.:

621   Applied physics
  .4   Heat engineering and prime movers
  .433-.436 Specific internal-combustion engines
  .433   Gas-turbine engines
  .434   Spark-ignition engines
  .435   Jet and rocket engines
  .436   High-compression-ignition engines

Systematic hierarchical development is usually less ambiguous in the pure and applied sciences than in generalities, the humanities, or even the social sciences. However, the general principles of disciplinary subdivision may be demonstrated in all classes, e.g.:

494	Ural-Altaic, Paleosiberian, Dravidian languages
.4-.5	Uralic languages
.4	Samoyedic languages
.5	Finno-Ugric languages
.51	Ugric languages
	Including Ostyak, Vogul
.511	Hungarian (Magyar)

Faceting and Pattern Sequencing

Custer succinctly described these techniques:

> Superimposed on the decimal arrangement is a mnemonic system of repeaters, the utilization of certain digits and combinations of digits bearing again and again the same meanings, so that groups can be combined into synthetic numbers without constant enumeration of all possible variations.[11]

FACET ANALYSIS AND SYNTHESIS

What *DDC 17* called "slot-ification," or "classification by attraction," reached its zenith in the enumerations of *DDC 14*.[12] Subsequent editions increased synthetic modular devices such as auxiliary and precedence tables. Partly because of the enormous growth of factual knowledge, simple enumeration could not satisfy the requirements of literary warrant.[13] However, as Langridge comments, "Schemes are referred to as enumerative or faceted but these are really relative terms.[14] The DDC Glossary defines faceting as 'the division of a subject by more than one characteristic.' "[15] Ramsden sets it in context as follows:

> An important reason for distinguishing clearly between different characteristics is to make possible clear and unambiguous specification of compound subjects by combining terms from the different categories (i.e. facets) thus established.[16]

While the early editions of DDC were predominantly enumerative, Custer claims that:

> ... as early as 1876 Melvil Dewey understood the principle [of faceting] when, in the first edition, he developed class 400 *Language* both by individual languages (420-490) and by problems (411-418), and each language by problems (e.g. 421-428). It is true, nevertheless, that earlier editions have not always recognized and made provision for division of a subject by more than one principle, and that when

they have made such provision they have not always clearly differentiated among the various principles.[17]

In reporting his survey of DDC use, John Comaromi called it "an intensively developed faceted classification."[18] We have seen that some theorists contrast faceting with enumerative classification "by attraction." British classifiers are more inclined to contrast it with classification "by discipline." They seem unimpressed with American quibbles over "subject integrity."

In spite of this emphasis on classification by discipline, the conflict between this concept and the opposing one of "facet analysis" which was present in previous editions is still present in Edition 18. The two processes work in opposite directions and the basic problem is to decide where classification by discipline should cease and facet analysis begin.... For example, in 630 Agriculture the method of facet analysis is clearly at work. We have the energy facet stated at 631-632 under operations and problems in agriculture. The crop facet follows at 633-635, with the ability to qualify certain crops by operation and problem. This is pure facet analysis. But, as Austin points out, at 658 Management we find classification by discipline in operation:

658   Management
658.3   Management of personnel (problem)
658.97721 Management in the cotton industry (industry)

However, personnel management in the cotton industry is not subordinated to the industry, but the reverse, and we have:

658.3   Management of personnel
658.3767721 Personnel management in the cotton industry.[19]

To the British, failure to apply the salutary controls of facet analysis can lead to inadvertent classification by attraction, under the guise of classification by discipline. Incidentally, *DDC 19* scatters 658 by use of *ss*-068.

PATTERN SEQUENCES

One way to get a handle on the various uncoordinated techniques of classification might be to range them on a scale from the most random (enumeration by attraction) to the most systematic (sweeping facet analysis, with responsibility for number synthesis transferred to the local user). No scheme has yet relied exclusively on either extreme. DDC was never simply enumerative. From the first, its schedules carried repetitive sequences, often linked to mnemonic notation. The device is now called "fixed faceting."[20] As the system expanded it grew more synthetic. That is, its pattern sequences were remanded to auxiliary tables and Add instructions (formerly called "Divide likes").

CITATION ORDER

Problems of precedence, sequence, and relationship among topics represented by the notation are inevitable in a linear classification. Custer's reemphasis on hierarchical development brought renewed concern for consistent handling of nuclear topics or their facets with respect to their disciplines or subjects. The editor's introduction in *DDC 17* carried a new Section 3.354 on "Priorities of Arrangement." Its corresponding Section 3.555 in *DDC 18* adopted the more current name "Citation order," and carried a whole sequence of hints on modes of choice. The generalized instructions carried over into Section 8.55 of *DDC 19* with only minor revisions and expansions. They start with a reminder to check specific schedule tables and notes. Custer has said of *DDC 18* that it:

> ... featured a great increase in the number of definitions, scope notes, and instructions, particularly instructions on what to do with situations of cross classification, that is on how to class works that deal with subdivisions of a subject based on more than one characteristic even when faceting is not directed, e.g., 362.1-362.4 Illness and disability: "Class illnesses and disabilities of specific groups (such as the elderly, young people, minority groups, unmarried mothers) in 362.6-362.8," or 794.12 Strategy and tactics (of chess): "Class strategy and tactics with individual chessmen in 794.14."[21]

DDC 17 took a long step toward solutions at specific schedule points by introducing Tables of Precedence. They were infrequent and experimental, but the operation proved successful, even though a few patients died. The following example disappeared entirely from *DDC 18*.

641.6-641.8   Special cookery   *(DDC 17)*
    Observe the following table of precedence, e.g., roast-
    ing meats 641.66
        Composite dishes
        Specific materials
        Specific processes and techniques

Others required remedial surgery. Witness the following transitions.

331.3-331.6   Special classes of workers   *(DDC 17)*
    Observe the following table of precedence, e.g., aged
    Negro women 331.398
        Specific age groups
        Women
        Substandard wage earners
        Other groups

* *

331.3-331.6   Labor force by personal characteristics   *(DDC 18)*
    Observe the following table of precedence, e.g., aged
    Chinese women 331.398
        Workers of specific age groups
        Women workers
        Special categories of workers
        Categories of workers by racial, ethnic, national origin

* *

> 331.3-331.6 Labor force by personal characteristics   (*DDC 19*)
> Unless other instructions are given, class complex
> subjects with aspects in two or more subdivisions
> of the schedule in the number coming first in the
> schedule, e.g., aged Chinese women 331.398 (*not*
> 331.4 or 331.6251)

DDC 19 converted some minor tables into "order of precedence" notes, as can be seen above.[22] The number of such instructions has steadily increased, with elaborate schema now appearing in both the schedules proper and in auxiliary tables. They are distinctively formatted with class numbers to the right of the headings. Illustrative precedence instructions occur at the following places, but this list is by no means exhaustive:

011.1-.7	General bibliographies
242	Devotional literature
351.84	Social welfare and corrections
362	Social welfare problems and services
362.79	Other [non-maladjusted] young people
363.1	Public safety programs
378.4-.9	Higher education and institutions by locality
610.736	Specialized nursing
809.8	Literature for and by specific kinds of persons

Introduction to Auxiliary Table 1

Generalized citation order instructions in the editor's introduction next broach the use of multiple zeros as a device to show specificity. In this text the technique is discussed in Example 5 of chapter 3, and again in greater detail in the chapter 5 discussion of Table 1. For situations outside the *ss* notation, two general citation sequences are prescribed as follows:

1. Sequences of major facets
   a. By most specific discipline and subject
   b. By geographic/chronological specification
      1) By place
      2) By time
   c. By form
2. Sequences of facets for things
   a. Kinds of things
   b. Parts of things
   c. Materials from which the things, kinds, or parts are made
   d. Properties of the things, kinds, parts, or materials
   e. Processes within the things, kinds, parts, or materials
   f. Operations upon the things, kinds, parts, or materials
   g. Agents performing such operations

Options

The provision of options in DDC is a long-standing tradition. Dewey's introduction to *DDC 12* (1927), which was reprinted in later editions through the

18th, carried "Sugjested variations" that might be "practicable in adjusting to special local requirements."

The current DDC definition of "optional provision" is:

> a variation from the preferred provision, offered to users in the printed schedules and tables of the DDC, but not used in centralized classification as supplied by the Library of Congress and rarely used by other centralized services of national libraries.[23]

Recent emphasis on the international appeal of DDC has increased the number of options offered, although some have been dropped.[24] For example, *DDC 18* options to use a final zero or a letter/number combination with a topical class number to indicate a bibliography are missing from *DDC 19*. Letters of the alphabet are still optional notation at other places, however, as can be seen in classes 400 and 800. Options affecting whole classes 200, 400, and 800 were introduced with *DDC 18*. Those for class 400 (Language) are quoted in chapter 10.

Still another option allows redistribution of geographic or political subdivisions to avoid congestion and long numbers for local use. It is especially helpful for works dealing with bilateral or multi-lateral relations, e.g.:

> 337.3-.9   Foreign economic policies and relations ...
> Give priority in notation to the jurisdic-
> tion or group of jurisdictions emphasized.
> If the emphasis is equal, give priority to
> the one coming first in the sequence of area
> notations.
> If preferred, give priority in notation to
> the jurisdiction or group of jurisdictions
> requiring local emphasis, e.g. libraries in
> the United States class foreign economic
> relations between United States and France
> in 337.73044.

A more complex option of this kind occurs at 346.3-.9 (Private law of specific jurisdictions). Options are not recommended unless the local classifier finds cogent reasons for using them. DDC preference is always clearly shown.[25]

Broad and Close Classification

One of the most notable features of DDC is its adaptability to libraries of every size. Its hierarchical structure and decimal notation permit generalization of specific concepts, with correspondingly shorter class numbers, if the collection is not large.

> Any notation may be cut by as many digits as are desired, down to a minimum of three, each successively shorter number being less specific but equally correct.[26]

Libraries may crop their notation selectively, using longer numbers where they have more materials. Some small public and school libraries arbitrarily truncate notation to two, or at most three, places beyond the decimal point. The practice may have merit as a guideline, but there are other, better ways to determine length of class numbers. Library of Congress segmentation is the accepted criterion. Prime marks on printed cards (slashes in the MARC records) break long numbers at points most appropriate. Regardless of the original length (LC has on occasion supplied DDC numbers of 28 digits), it claims to mark no more than three segments, but a few cases show a fourth segment. See, for example, 614.5'73'2'094551 on page 250, 895.6'1'008'0354 on page 299, and 959.5'2'004'951 on page 322. Some short numbers are not segmented at all.

Abr 11 offers a short form of the system for small and slowly growing libraries.[27] It will be examined in detail in chapter 16. It is a true abridgment, rather than the adaptation which *Abr 10* offered on grounds of greater practicality. One reason for returning to a true abridgment may have been the popularity of segmentation. With it, libraries could cut long numbers more easily, if not more intelligently, than they could follow *Abr 10* variants. There are inherent dangers, though, in using Dewey for broad classification.

> ... Where Dewey numbers are truncated, as is done in smaller special libraries, there may be a tendency for unrelated items to cluster on the shelves.[28]

Format and Notation

The appearance of *DDC 19* differs from that of immediately preceding editions chiefly in its smaller physical size. Increasing costs of paper and binding, together with a gradual but significant growth in the total number of entries, stimulated the search for a more compact product. The following table compares the two most recent editions in gross content and size.

Table 1
DDC Size and Content

Edition	Height in cm.	Width in cm.	Thickness in cm. (3 v.)	Total pages	Total entries
18	26	18	14	2,716	26,141
19	24	16.5	13.5	3,380	29,528

While the overall dimensions have shrunk, the total number of pages increased by slightly under 24.5%. Total entries also increased, by nearly 13%. Thinner paper, smaller margins, and slightly reduced type account for most of the physical reduction. Possibly the average amount of material at each entry is reduced, but a rough examination leaves one with the impression that, if anything, it increased. Fortunately, the type is legible, with satisfactory contrast and distribution of black-on-white. There are no visual problems, while the compactness of the new edition makes handling definitely easier.

Typefaces vary in size according to the degree of subdivision within each hierarchy. They consist of roman upper- and lower-case, with italics for cross-references. Left-hand indentions, like size of type, signal degrees of specificity and subordination. Notation stands left of its caption in the auxiliary tables and the schedules, except for tables of precedence, as noted above. In the double-columned index, notation stands right of the entries. Numbers in the seven auxiliary tables are preceded by dashes to remind the user that they cannot stand alone. Add tables in the schedules lack the dashes, although their numbers similarly cannot stand alone.

NOTATION

DDC notation remains traditionally pure. That is, it consists only of the Arabic digits 0 through 9, plus the decimal point. The shortest possible number is three digits long, since lead zeros are written out in class 000. We have already seen that letters of the alphabet are occasionally suggested as optional notation for special local emphasis. Instructions in the editor's introduction permit other symbols such as the asterisk (*) or the dagger (†) to be substituted for letter options.[29]

Schedule, index, and auxiliary table numbers are printed in groups of three, e.g., 629.133 340 422 (Private airplanes), and -777 655 (Johnson County, Iowa). The groupings merely facilitate reading. Brackets contain recently or permanently vacated locations; italics mean new assignments. Format symbols and abbreviations are explained in the introductory pages of each DDC volume. Phoenix schedules will be discussed under "Reused numbers" in chapter 3.

CENTERED HEADINGS

In the hierarchies, superordinate steps that are not obvious from the notation are printed with arrow heads in the left schedule margin, as the following example shows.

▶ 536.51-536.54   Measurement of temperature
Class comprehensive works in 536.5028

SUMMARY TABLES

Summary tables are likewise often centered on the page to give overviews of highly detailed sequences. One of these immediately precedes a centered heading under 731 (Processes and representations of sculpture).

SUMMARY

731.2	Materials
.3	Apparatus and equipment
.4	Techniques and procedures
.5	Forms
.7	Sculpture in the round
.8	Iconography

MNEMONIC ASSOCIATIONS

Memory aids, as DDC prefers to call them, are a traditional feature. Custer's description of the "mnemonic system of repeaters" was cited in our section on Faceting and Pattern Sequencing. We have time only for a word of caution that the limited character set of 10 digits necessitates multiple meanings to attach in various contexts to the same number. While the context often furnishes some clue, the increased use of faceting multiplies the dangers of false assumptions. Changes caused by ongoing revision may trip the unwary, although traditional associations such as -73 for the United States, and -03 for encyclopedic or dictionary works, are usually preserved.

MONOGRAPHIC SETS AND SERIES

DDC does not address the problem of classifying together, or independently, separate works collected into a set or series. It is, after all, a general classification question, whatever the scheme adopted. Merrill's *Code for Classifiers* recommends keeping most sets or series together, unless their use as a group is merely current or temporary.[30] The Library of Congress inclines to this approach but frequently suggests specific monographic numbers as well.

Decimal numbers within parentheses printed before 1959 indicate the classification assigned to a monographic series, as distinct from that assigned to the individual monograph. Since 1969 an "s" has been placed immediately following the number for a monographic series; this number may then be followed on the same or the next line by a second number, in square brackets, standing for the individual monograph.[31]

540'.8 s   Trace elements in fuel : a symposium sponsored
[662'.622]   by the Division of Fuel Chemistry at the 166th
      meeting of the American Chemical Society ...
      1975.   (Advances in Chemistry series ; v. 141)
          75-15522

620.1'1'08 s American Society for Testing and Materials.
[665'.5385]   Committee D-2 on Petroleum Products and
      Lubricants. Shear stability of multigrade
      crankcase oil ... 1973.   (ASTM data series
      publication ; v. DS49)   73-78863

Both the "s" and the bracketed alternative numbers appear in the above illustrations. The final digits -08 signify "Collections" in accordance with *DDC 18*. *DDC 19* changes the meaning to "History and description of the subject among groups of persons," as we shall see in chapter 5. Local libraries must decide whether to reclassify, or to continue using the obsolete designation. The forthcoming *DC&*, v. 4, no. 2 will announce expansion of the "subject among groups" meaning to include "subject with respect to groups."

We will now be able to assign to a work on women in U.S. history the number 973.088042. The number could also mean, of course, the subject history among women.[32]

NOTES

Several kinds of instruction and scope notes were discussed in the section on hierarchical force. Add instructions are explained below. Other notes will be examined in chapter 3. Cross-references are especially frequent in the index, but may be found in auxiliary tables and in the schedule as well.

ADD INSTRUCTIONS

Faceting is governed by notes in the schedule to "Add from" or "Add to." One sign of the trend away from enumeration is a steady increase of Add notes. *DDC 19* has 1,327 more than its predecessor. "Add to's" are descendants of the old "Divide likes," which referred to schedule transpositions rather than to auxiliary tables, and which were not always easy to interpret. A major innovation in *DDC 18* was the use of "base numbers" on which to build the added portion of a synthetic number. One completed example is always given to complement the verbal instruction, e.g.:

025.28   Selection and acquisition of materials in special forms
　　　　　Add to base number 025.28 the numbers following
　　　　　025.17 in 025.171-025.179, e.g., acquisition of maps
　　　　　025.286

"Add to" syntheses can be accomplished without leaving the schedule volume. For instance, if one wishes to classify a work on the selection and acquisition of motion pictures the procedure is:

Base number for acquisition of special materials	025.28
Reference number (treatment of special materials)	025.17
Reference number for treatment of motion pictures	025.1773
Segment of the reference number for motion pictures	xxx.xx73
Addition of the "motion pictures" segment to base	025.28 + 73
Fully synthesized number	025.2873

"Add from's" get their synthetic facets from one or more of the auxiliary tables. Class number synthesis requires reference from the base location in volume 2 to the auxiliary table in volume 1. Two illustrations follow.

025.29   Selection and acquisition of materials from various
　　　　　specific places
　　　　　　Add "Areas" notation 1-9 from Table 2 to base num-
　　　　　　ber 025.29

Base number for selecting materials from specific places	025.29
Reference notations from Table 2 (Areas)	-1-9
Reference number for Puerto Rico	-7295
Addition of Area segment to base number	025.29 + -7295
Class number for selecting materials from Puerto Rico	025.297295

* *

808.89   Collections from more than one literature for and
        by specific kinds of persons
           Add notations 8-9 from Table 3-A to base number
           808.89, e.g., collections of literature in more
           than one language by persons of African descent
           808.89896, by painters 808.899275, by residents
           of Canada 808.89971

Base number for literary collections	808.89
Reference notations from Table 3-A	-8-9
Reference number for literature of specific groups	-8
Add "Racial, Ethnic, National Groups" notation	
03-99 from Table 5 to 8, e.g., literature by Africans	
and persons of African descent 896	
Addition of reference portion to original base	808.89 + -8
New base number	808.898
Reference notations from Table 5	-03-99
Reference number for ancient Greeks	-81
Addition of Table 5 segment to new base	808.898 + -81
Class number for literary collections for and by	
ancient Greeks	808.89881

Conclusion

Numerous references have been made to the *DDC 19* editor's introduction. This feature was improved and given its own index in *DDC 18*. *DDC 19* continues and modernizes its function as a detailed guide to correct, efficient use of the system. Relevant passages have been quoted or cited in this chapter. They should be read carefully, for they give official explanations of current practice. A separately published guide is promised in the near future.

The checkered career of the Relative Index was briefly reviewed in chapter 1. It will be further discussed in chapter 4, since it furnishes a case study of the contemporaneous qualities of each new edition. Many class numbers in the index are not spelled out in the schedules because they have been synthesized from Add instructions. Almost none of them come from classes 400 and 900, and very few are from class 800.

Sample Synthetic Numbers from the DDC 19 Index

Zoological sciences--subject headings	025.4959
Olfactory perception--psychology--influences	155.91166
Life--medical ethics--religion--Hinduism	294.5486424
Digests of budgets--public administration	350.72253
Aerosols--colloid chemistry--organic	547.134515
Agaricaceae--medical aspects--veterinary	
pharmacy--toxicology	636.089595292223
Sky--art representation	704.94952
Idealism--literary quality--general works	
--collections	808.8013

There is a standing injunction against assigning class numbers straight from the index without examining their schedule context. It is usually impossible to determine without consulting the schedule which numbers are included there and which are synthetically faceted. Understanding the function of any given number within its context is a prerequisite for any satisfactory subject classification.

Exercises in DDC Number Analysis

Analyze the following class numbers assigned by the Library of Congress. If the subject is not sufficiently clear from the title, LC subject headings or other suggestions are given. LC card numbers are included to facilitate retrieval of the full records. LC prime marks are included to show broad classification possibilities.

A.   Numbers fully developed in the *DDC 19* schedules:

001.6'4'04	Leventhal, Lance A. Microcomputer experimentation with the Intel SDK-85 ... c1980.	79-22052
155.8'1	Lévy-Bruhl, Lucien. How natives think ... 1979, c1926.	79-7006
341.7'38	SALT II Treaty : background documents ... 1979.	80-600546
355'.02184	Stratégies de la guérilla ... c1979. [Guerilla warfare--Addresses, essays, lectures]	79-125539
370.19'31	Salisbury, Robert Holt. Citizen participation in the public schools ... c1980.	79-7710
662.6'25	Advances in coal utilization technology : symposium papers ... c1979.	80-105708
722'.5	Lewcock, Ronald B. Traditional architecture in Kuwait and the Northern Gulf ... 1979.	80-464829
785'.06'61	Orchestra / edited by André Previn ... 1979.	79-7944
909.82	Stiker, Henri Jacques. Culture Brisée, culture à naître ... c1979. [Civilization, Modern--1950-]	79-123875
943.8'03	Rautenberg, Hans-Werner. Der polnische Aufstand von 1863 ... 1979. [Poland--History--Revolution, 1863-1864]	80-454676

B.   Numbers using instructions to add from other schedules:

016.334	Sager, Tore. Bibliography of cooperative economics, 1920-1975 ... 1979.	79-126643
016.9469'044	Lomax, William. Revolution in Portugal, 1974-1976 : a bibliography ... 1978.	79-106711
338.4'7662662	Stone, Charles L. Synthetic fuels program : final report ... 1979.	79-625550

353.008'8 s [353.008'8'0141]	National Association of Attorneys General. Committee on the Office of Attorney General. Public information programs for attorneys general's offices ... 1976.	77-374751
690'.8'0286	Levitt Bernstein Associates. Supervisor's guide to rehabilitation and conversion ... 1978.	79-303957

C. Numbers using instructions to add from other schedules and auxiliary tables:

282'.6891	Linden, Ian. Church and state in Rhodesia : 1959-1979 ... 1979.	80-457442
328.73'07'8	Sagstetter, Karen. Lobbying ... 1978.	77-12302
557.74 s [551.7'009774]	Lilienthal, Richard T. Stratigraphic cross-sections of the Michigan basin ... 1978.	79-626201
616.1'205	Hogan, Christine. Preventing heart disease in public safety employees ... 1979.	79-125855
737.49364	Nash, Daphne. Settlement and coinage in Central Gaul c.200-50 B.C. ... 1978.	80-463786
779'.99758231	McGee, E. Alan. Atlanta at home : photographs ... 1979.	80-107677

NOTES

[1]Marty Bloomberg and Hans Weber, *An Introduction to Classification and Number Building in Dewey* (Littleton, CO, Libraries Unlimited, 1976), p. 17.

[2]John Phillip Comaromi, *The Eighteen Editions of the Dewey Decimal Classification* (Albany, NY, Forest Press Division, Lake Placid Education Foundation, 1976), p. 552.

[3]Melvil Dewey, *Dewey Decimal Classification and Relative Index.* Ed. 19 (Albany, NY, Forest Press, 1979), v. 1, p. xli.

[4]Ibid., v. 1, p. xxxi.

[5]Dorothy Comins, "The Library Case for Conversion," *Problems in Library Classification: Dewey 17 and Conversion* (New York, School of Library and Information Science, The University of Wisconsin — Milwaukee; published in cooperation with R. R. Bowker, 1968), p. 90.

[6]Elaine Svenonius, "Directions for Research in Indexing, Classification, and Cataloging," *Library Resources & Technical Services*, v. 25, no. 1 (January/March 1981): 95.

[7]Dewey, *Dewey Decimal Classification and Relative Index.* Ed. 19, v. 1, p. xxxii.

[8]A. Sandison, "The Special Needs of a Classification for Books and Journals," *General Classification Systems in a Changing World: Proceedings of the FID Classification Symposium Held in Commemoration of the Dewey*

Centenary (The Hague, Fédération Internationale de Documentation [FID], 1978), p. 24.

[9]For the official explanation of hierarchical force, see Melvil Dewey, *Dewey Decimal Classification and Relative Index*. Ed. 19 (Albany, NY, Forest Press, 1979), v. 1, pp. xlvii, lii, and lxxix. See also examples 19-20 in chapter 3 of this text.

[10]Ibid., v. 1, pp. xl, xlvii-l, lii, and lxv.

[11]Benjamin A. Custer, "Dewey Decimal Classification," *Encyclopedia of Library and Information Science* (New York, Marcel Dekker, 1972), v. 7, p. 126.

[12]Peter Butcher, "Dewey? We Sure Do!," *Catalogue & Index*, no. 55 (Winter 1979): 8.

[13]W. E. Matthews, "Dewey 18: A Preview and Report," *Wilson Library Bulletin*, v. 45, no. 6 (February 1971): 572-77; also in *Library Association Record*, v. 73, no. 2 (February 1971): 28-30.

[14]Derek Langridge, *Approach to Classification for Students of Librarianship* (Hamden, CT, Linnet Books & Clive Bingley, 1973), p. 87.

[15]Dewey, *Dewey Decimal Classification and Relative Index*. Ed. 19, v. 1, p. lxxix.

[16]M. J. Ramsden, "Dewey 18," *Australian Library Journal*, v. 21, no. 3 (April 1972): 117.

[17]Benjamin A. Custer, "Dewey 17: A Preview and Report," *Wilson Library Bulletin*, v. 39, no. 7 (March 1965): 556.

[18]John Phillip Comaromi, "Decimal Classification Editorial Policy Committee Report," *Library Resources & Technical Services*, v. 21, no. 1 (Winter 1977): 93.

[19]James A. Tait, "Dewey Decimal Classification: A Vigorous Nonagenarian," *Library Review*, v. 23, no. 6 (Summer 1972): 227.

[20]Sarah K. Vann, "Dewey Decimal Classification," *Classification in the 1970's: A Second Look* (London & Hamden, CT, Clive Bingley & Linnet Books, 1976), p. 228.

[21]Benjamin A. Custer, "The Responsiveness of Recent Editions of the Dewey Decimal Classification to the Needs of Its Users," *General Classification Systems in a Changing World....* (The Hague, Fédération Internationale de Documentation [FID], 1978), p. 83. The reader should note that the instructions are from *DDC 18*. Edition 19 says at 362.1-362.4: "Class here illnesses and disabilities of specific kinds of people [*formerly* 362.6-362.8], medical missions [*formerly* 266.025]."

[22]Dewey, *Dewey Decimal Classification and Relative Index*. Ed. 19, v. 1, pp. xlvii-l.

[23]Ibid., v. 1, p. lxxx.

[24]Ibid., v. 1, p. xxiii.

[25]Ibid., v. 1, pp. xliv, lxviii-lxix.

[26]Custer, "Dewey Decimal Classification," v. 7, p. 135.

[27]Melvil Dewey, *Abridged Dewey Decimal Classification and Relative Index.* Ed. 11 (Albany, NY, Forest Press, 1979), p. 1.

[28]Svenonius, p. 95.

[29]Dewey, *Dewey Decimal Classification and Relative Index.* Ed. 19, v. 1, p. lxix.

[30]William Stetson Merrill, *Code for Classifiers: Principles Governing the Consistent Placing of Books in a System of Classification*, 2nd ed. (Chicago, American Library Association, 1939), pp. 10-12.

[31]*Library of Congress Catalogs: Monographic Series, 1976* (Washington, Library of Congress, 1977), v. 1, p. vi.

[32]John Phillip Comaromi. Communication to the publisher dated April 29, 1981.

3

The Modernization of DDC: Schedules and Notation

Introduction

Any organism, natural or artificial, displays a historical dimension. The traditional stages of its life cycle may vary in length or significance, but under normal circumstances it has a genesis, development, florescence, decline, and demise. The Dewey Decimal Classification is no exception, although its effective life-span already exceeds that of most competitors. Its remarkable longevity comes in part from adaptability to change without sacrificing basic morphology. Sustained by fundamental virtues, it has been equally fortunate in its sponsors, who created good support systems for progressive revision without disrupting into chaos. In response to questions and suggestions from users, instructions are clarified and terminology revised. New tables, and types of tables, are supplied to facilitate number synthesis. Typography improves. A signal system (indentions, special symbols, etc.) is progressively standardized, or altered to serve new needs. This pragmatic approach not only incorporates the foresight of Melvil Dewey, but accepts changed attitudes as they prove useful. Revision techniques are many. Let us explore those most frequently encountered in *DDC 19*.

Expansions

A schedule expansion introduces one or more numbers not used previously, or at least not recently. It represents "the development of a concept or series of concepts in the schedules or tables to provide for more minute subdivision" (v. 1, p. lxxix; cf. pp. lxxiii-lxiv for further discussion). Most expansions in *DDC 19* are extended decimals, but there are nine new section numbers which had been vacant since *DDC 16* (1958):

002 The Book (used in *DDC 16* with this meaning; moved in *DDC 17* and *18*.to 001.552; now restored)

302 Social interaction (last used in *DDC 16* meaning Handbooks and outlines of the social sciences)

303 Social processes (last used in *DDC 16* meaning Dictionaries and encyclopedias of the social sciences)

304   Relation of natural and quasi-natural factors to social processes (last used in *DDC 16* meaning Essays and lectures on the social sciences)

305   Social stratification (Social structure) (last used in *DDC 16* meaning Periodicals of the social sciences)

306   Culture and institutions (last used in *DDC 16* meaning Organization and societies of the social sciences)

307   Communities (last used in *DDC 16* meaning Study and teaching of the social sciences)

337   International economics (last used in *DDC 16* meaning Tariff)

404   Special topics of general applicability to language (last used in *DDC 16* meaning General essays and lectures on language)

Six of the above sections, with their subdivisions, form the bulk of the major "phoenix schedule" in *DDC 19*. But phoenix schedules are not merely expansions. They make use of reduction and relocation, as well as other related devices for schedule change. Expansible entries total 3,565 in *DDC 18*, as compared to 4,892 in *DDC 19* (v. 1, p. xxii). However, those totals do not include routine applications of the auxiliary tables (v. 1, p. xxi). There is no reliable way to estimate the number of expansions they might produce. The following examples are typical of explicit expansion techniques in *DDC 19*.

Example 1
Subdivision of a class number

A specific topic may have been included under a broad heading. The growth of knowledge or the increase in materials written on the subject now warrants giving it a place of its own. For instance, a *DDC 19* index entry reads "Intellectual life 001.1." In *DDC 18* the entry reads "Intellectual life 001.2." At first it looks like a relocation, but the schedule clearly shows an expansion.

001   Knowledge and its extension   (*DDC 18*)
  .2   Scholarship and learning

* *

001   Knowledge   (*DDC 19*)
  .1   Intellectual life Nature and value
            Class intellectual situation and condition in 909
            For scholarship and learning, see 001.2
  .14   Intellectual cooperation
  .2   Scholarship and learning

Example 2
Extended meanings for standard subdivisions

Deviations from Table 1 usage are often accompanied in the schedule by cross classification notes. *DDC 19* editorial practice requires fuller schedule specification than that in *DDC 18*, as the following comparison shows:

674   Lumber, cork, wood-using technologies   *(DDC 18)*
            Use 674.001-674.009 for standard subdivisions
.01-.09   Standard subdivisions of lumber technology
            Class specifications in 674.5

* *

674   Lumber, cork, wood-using technologies   *(DDC 19)*
            Use 674.001-674.009 for standard subdivisions
.01   Philosophy and theory of lumber technology
.02   Miscellany of lumber technology
.021   Tabulated and related materials
.0212   Tables, formulas, statistics
              Class specifications in 674.5
.028   Techniques, procedures, apparatus, equipment,
            materials
.0287   Testing and measurement
              Class grading lumber in 674.5
.03-.09   Standard subdivisions of lumber technology
            Notations from Table 1

Under 674.0212 "Specifications" is omitted in *DDC 19* because of a Class elsewhere note. The same note can be found in *DDC 18*, but is less obvious. Moreover, there is no -0287 in *DDC 18*'s Table 1. It is spelled out in the *DDC 19* schedule, with a Class elsewhere note at 674.0287, which adds clarity. It also adds bulk.

Example 3
Standard subdivision scatter

Another type of expansion embodies efforts to improve subject integrity. It relocates materials formerly grouped together because of a common "facet" or aspect, using a standard subdivision to scatter them to various subject areas. An important example in *DDC 19* is use of the new *ss*-068 to scatter materials formerly grouped under 658 (General management).

Example 4
Tables of precedence

Precedence instructions are not new to the Dewey classification, nor do they normally expand the schedules. What is expansive is their proliferation in *DDC 19*. They help users choose among competing concepts in the course of synthesizing numbers. For instance, the new one for auxiliary Table 1 helps solve doubts about which standard subdivision is preferred when more than one applies. DDC practice generally limits them to one per class number. In the schedule, tables of precedence are distinguished by having their class numbers to the right of their captions, as in the following illustration.

362	Social welfare problems and services	
.7	Problems of and services to young people	
	Through age 17	
.79	Other classes of young people	
	Observe the following table of precedence,	
	e.g., adolescent male immigrants 362.799	
	(*not* 362.792 or 362.796)	
	Miscellaneous classes	362.799
	Children	362.795
	Females	362.793
	Males	362.792
	Adolescents	362.796
	Young people of various specific	
	racial, ethnic, national groups	362.797
	Class maladjusted young people regardless	
	of other characteristics in 362.74, speci-	
	fic services to specific classes of young	
	people in 362.71-362.73	
.792	Males	
.793	Females	
.795	Children Through age 11	
.796	Adolescents Ages 12 to 17	
.797	Young people of various specific racial,	
	ethnic, national groups	
.799	Miscellaneous classes	
	Immigrants, city youth, rural youth	

Example 5
Multiple 0's for subdivision

A generalized expansion device introduced as early as *DDC 15* (1951) was heavily used in *DDC 17* (1965). It takes more than one faceting zero at junctures where single zeros are preempted for other kinds of subdivision. In a few well-populated categories, standard subdivisions (which usually have low hierarchy in number building) may require as many as three zeros. See chapter 5 for fuller discussion. Specific instruction notes are always given. Example 2 above shows one under the 674 illustration.

Example 6
New concepts

Expansion may insert a completely new concept, because of the growth of knowledge, or because library materials are now available on a topic not previously found in the literature. For example, the term "solar wind" appears nowhere in *DDC 18*. It is used twice in *DDC 19*, once with its own number, and again in an Inclusion note.

521.5	Theory of planets, stars, galaxies	(*DDC 18*)
.54	Of planets Including solar system	

| 523.5 | Meteors and zodiacal light | |

* *

521.5	Theoretical astronomy	(*DDC 19*)
.54	Theory of solar system Including theory of solar wind, of zodiacal light	

523.5	Meteoroids, solar wind, zodiacal light	
.58	Solar wind	

The *DDC 19* index carries the following new entries, although it gives no permuted access under "wind."

Solar
  wind
    astronomy
      description   523.58
      theory   521.54

Reductions

"A schedule reduction is the result of shifting one or more topics to a new number shorter than the old but otherwise not differing from it" (v. 1, p. 453). As the glossary says, it is the dropping "of some or all of the previous subdivisions of a number with resultant classification of those concepts in a higher number" (v. 1, p. lxxx). Reductions take several forms.

Example 7
Discontinued numbers (total reductions)

If a new edition removes the old meaning from a given location "to a more general number," the original number is "discontinued" (v. 1, pp. lxxix, 453). *DDC 19* furnishes a table of *Relocations and Schedule Reductions* at the close of volume 1, followed by lists of phoenix schedule changes. The *Relocations and Schedule Reductions* list (but not the accompanying phoenix change lists) is now reproduced in the front matter of all three volumes of Bowker's *Subject Authorities: A Guide to Subject Cataloging.*[1] Parallel columns arrange *DDC 18* numbers on the left, with corresponding *DDC 19* numbers on the right. Total reductions are bracketed, followed by an asterisk. There are about 150, including a few number spans. Nearly one-third are in the 300 class (19 in the 350's, 14 in the 360's). Another one-third fall in the 600 class (13 in the 610's, 12 each in the 620's and 650's). The 000's, 100's, 200's, and 500's have between 10 and a dozen each. There are 4 in the 700's, and 1 each in the 800's and Tables 1 and 3. In the schedules, these numbers are also bracketed, with a note: "Number discontinued; class in.... " The superordinate number *may* name the old caption in an Inclusion note, or it may give no reference to it. Illustrations from the *Relocations and Schedule Reductions* list are:

DDC 18	**DDC 19**
[351.87107-.87108]*	351.871
[351.8715]	351.82325
[351.8716]	351.871

Schedule entries corresponding to the above list read as follows:

351	Central governments
.8	Administration of agencies controlling specific fields of activity
.87	Public utilities and transportation
.871	Water supply
[.87107-.87108]	Urban and rural Numbers discontinued; class in 351.871
[.8715]	Pollution Class in 351.82325
[.8716]	Purification Number discontinued; class in 351.871

Example 8
Meaningless content

Another reason for discontinuing a number is that the topical content no longer has any meaning within its context (v. 1, p. 453). A type of total reduction results. The numbers are bracketed and starred in the *Relocations and Schedule Reductions* list, with "meaningless" beside them. There are only four in *DDC 19*.[2] The schedule gives the full rationale of discontinuance. Since the numbers are no longer significant, the index does not mention them.

[217]	Worship and prayer in natural religion Provision discontinued because without meaning in natural religion

332	Financial economics
.6	Investment and investments
[.68]	Lotteries Number discontinued because without meaning in this context

574.191	Biophysics
.1913	Effects of mechanical forces
[.19133]	Velocity and speed Provision discontinued because without meaning in this context

623	Military and nautical engineering
.4	Ordnance
.41	Artillery
[.4193]	Airborne Provision discontinued because without meaning in artillery

---

Example 9
Partial reduction

Sometimes a number loses only part of its meaning. There are 22 such numbers in *DDC 19*, with exactly half falling in the 500 and 600 classes. Partially reduced numbers are not bracketed in the schedules, but carry a Class elsewhere note. In the *Relocations and Schedule Reductions* list they are starred. See, for instance:

> 021 Library relationships
> .6 Library cooperation and networks Including centralization of systems
> Use of this number for development of library services discontinued; class in 021

> 612 Human physiology
> .8 Nervous and sensory functions
> .84 Eyes and vision
> Class here physiological optics, eyeballs
> .844 Aqueous humors, crystalline lenses, vitreous bodies
> Use of this number for comprehensive works on eyeballs discontinued; class in 612.84

> 780 Music
> .8 Scores and parts, and treatment among groups of persons
> Use of this number for collections of writings about music discontinued; class in 780

Relocations

When a topic is shifted to a number differing "in respects other than length" (i.e., other than mere reduction to a superordinate number), the change is called a relocation.[3] The old number may or may not be bracketed (i.e., vacated), depending on whether its meaning is totally or only partially gone. DDC editors relocate materials only where there is strong evidence that the disciplinary integrity of the system will best be served. The shifts inevitably separate materials which were some way related. The effect on established collections has been frequently discussed. The following comments are typical.

> Relocations ... are made for various reasons in DDC, to keep pace with new knowledge or to rectify some of the structural irregularities which have developed in the system over the years. These changes create special problems for libraries in that new books and previously cataloged books on the same subject would appear with different numbers. More serious is the fact that in cases where vacated numbers have been used with new meanings, books on different subjects may share the same number.

If, in the areas where relocations have been made, books previously cataloged according to the old editions were not adjusted, so that several numbers may represent the same subject or one number may represent several different subjects, the readers would be baffled and the whole purpose of classification — grouping books together on the same subject and separating those on different subjects — would be defeated. The ideal solution to this problem is naturally the reclassification of all books on subjects which have been relocated. However in many libraries this is not practical. In such cases, every effort should be made to reclassify books with numbers which have been reused with new meanings.[4]

Custer reminds us that "contrary to popular belief, relocations did not begin with the 15th edition."[5] Table 2 shows that he was at least technically correct.

Always the system was fought over by the established libraries that had an economic interest in maintaining the "integrity of numbers," and the service-oriented personnel who believed that an obsolete system could not long survive, and that the Decimal Classification should "keep pace with knowledge."[6]

Table 2
Relocated DDC Categories

Editions	Relocations[7]
2	approx. 100
15 (Standard)	1,015
16 (For users of the 14th ed.)	985[8]
(For users of the 15th ed.)	752
17 (Excluding remodeled schedule 150)	746
18 (Excluding phoenix schedules 340 & 510)	396
19 (Excluding phoenix 301-307, 324, and *area*-41-41)	340[9]

Example 10
Total relocation

If a number used in the preceding edition loses all of its meaning through total relocation, it appears in the new schedule in brackets. "Formerly ... " notes usually trace the old number, which is also bracketed (no asterisk) in the *Relocations and Schedule Reductions* list. *DDC 19* has roughly 170 in the following proportions: classes 300 and 600 have about 40 each; classes 000 and 200 have around 20 each; classes 100, 500, and 700, and Table 2 show about 10 each; the 900's have 3, while the 400's, 800's, and Tables 4 and 6 get 1 each. Most involve decimal extensions, but 7 section numbers are totally relocated as follows:

[024] Regulations for use of libraries Class in 025.56

[029] Documentation Class in 025

[112] Classification of knowledge Class in 001.012

[125] Finite and infinite Class in 111.6

[309] Social situation and conditions Class in 900

[329] Political parties and related organizations and processes
Class in 326

[416] Prosody Class in 808.1 [Numbers 426, 436, 446, 456, 466,
476, and 486 were also captioned "Prosody" for their specific languages, but are designated "Unassigned" in
DDC 19]

Example 11
Relocated spans

Not merely a single number, but a span of numbers may be relocated.
Example 7 shows both the relocated number 351[.8716] and the span
351[.87107-.87108].

Example 12
Relocation of split meanings

Topics with single numbers or spans may be discontinued to have their
meanings distributed, e.g.:

016   Subject bibliographies and catalogs
   [.09]   Bibliographies and catalogs of manuscripts and
           book rarities
           Class bibliographies of manuscripts [*formerly* 016.091]
           in 011.31, of incunabula [*formerly* 016.093] in 011.42,
           of rare books [*formerly* 016.094-016.099] in 011.44

Example 13
Partial relocation

If the original number retains some of its meaning, losing only part to a
different class number, the relocation is partial (v. 1, pp. 1, 453). There are
slightly over 150 such in *DDC 19*, not counting the phoenix schedules. The 300
class has one-third, or approximately 50. The 600's have 30, and the 500's have
20. Classes 100, 700, and Table 2 have about 10 each. The 000's, as well as Tables
1, 3, 4, and 6, have 1 to 3 each. In the *Relocations and Schedule Reductions* list,
the numbers undergoing partial relocation are unmarked. A Formerly note
appears in the schedules under both old and new numbers, as the following
illustration shows.

949.12   Iceland
  .1204   Modern period, 1848-1940 Including independence
           under Danish crown, 1918-1944
           Class 1940-   [*formerly* 949.1204] in 949.1205
  .1205   1940-   [*formerly* 949.1204]

Example 14
Split relocation

Compound meanings may be carried over intact to a new location. Or the meanings may be split: one part left with the old number, other parts shifted to various other places, as shown below.

736   Carving and carvings
  .4   Wood Simple wood carving and whittling
        Example: butter prints and molds
        Class totem poles in 731.7, techniques
        of carving totem poles in 731.462,
        scrollwork in 745.51 [*all formerly* 736.4]

Example 15
Splitting out comprehensive works

At 612.844 in Example 9, comprehensive works were reduced to 612.84. In other cases they are relocated to other hierarchies, or other portions of their original hierarchy, as in the following excerpt.

616   Diseases
  .2   Diseases of respiratory system
  .21   Of nose, larynx, accessory organs
        Class otorhinolaryngology, comprehensive works
        on diseases of eyes, ears, nose, throat [*both*
        formerly 616.21] in 617.51

Example 16
Partial relocation with partial reduction

A number may be discontinued because its meaning is split between relocation and reduction. It carries brackets in the schedule, but the *Relocations and Schedule Reductions* list omits the star. One illustration is:

382   International commerce (Foreign trade)
  .7   Tariff policy
  [.74]   Drawbacks and subsidies
        Use of this number for drawbacks discontinued;
        class in 382.7
        Class subsidies in 382.63

Example 17
Scatter relocation

When the meaning of the discontinued heading is dissipated so widely that full enumeration of its relocations would be impracticable, a general scatter note or its equivalent is given (v. 1, pp. li, lxxxv, and 454). In Example 3 we cited a partial scatter out of section 658 (General management) by means of the new *ss*-068 (Management of enterprises engaged in specific fields of activity, etc.). Scatter relocations are designed to improve subject integrity, although their efficacy is sometimes, as in the following illustration, debatable.

[029]   Documentation   Class in 025
  [.4]   Abstracting   Class composition of abstracts in 808.062, abstracting techniques in 025.4028
  [.756]   Machine translation   Class comprehensive works in 418.02; machine translation of a specific language with the language, using "Subdivisions of Individual Languages" notation 802 from Table 4, e.g., translation of French into other languages 448.02

Example 18
Complex readjustments

An unusually complicated situation arises at 220.66. Part of its meaning is reduced, part relocated, while at the same time it takes over the meaning of a discontinued number.

220   Bible
  .6   Interpretation and criticism (Exegesis)
  .66   Literary criticism
      Examination of literary genres in order to reach conclusions about authorship [*formerly* 220.14], structure, date
      Class here higher criticism, internal criticism
      Use of this number for exegesis discontinued; class in 220.6
      Class language and style of specific texts in 220.4-220.5

Example 19
Hierarchical force of relocation notes

If a topic with subdivisions is relocated, the subdivisions are also relocated or discontinued (v. 1, p. l). Usually hierarchical force is retained, though not necessarily in the old form or order.[10] Parallel passages from *DDC 18* and *19* will illustrate:

621 Applied physics   *(DDC 18)*
 .3   Electrical, electronic, electromagnetic engineering
 .35   Applied electrochemistry
        Generation and storage of electrical energy by
        chemical methods
 .353   Primary batteries Voltaic and dry cells
 .354   Secondary batteries (Storage batteries)
 .355   Lead-acid batteries
 .356   Alkaline batteries
 .359   Fuel cells

* *

621 Applied physics   *(DDC 19)*
 .3   Electromagnetic and related branches of engineering
 .31   Generation, modification, storage, transmission
        of electric power
 .312   Generation, modification, storage
 .3124   Direct energy conversion
 .31242   Applied electrochemistry *[formerly* 621.35]
         Generation and storage of electrical
         energy by chemical methods
 .312423   Primary batteries Voltaic and dry cells
 .312424   Secondary batteries (Storage batteries)
         Lead-acid and alkaline
 .312429   Fuel cells
 [.35]   Applied electrochemistry Class in 621.31242

Example 20
Failure of hierarchical force

An Inclusion note covers a special topic for which there is not enough literary warrant to justify its own class number (v. 1, p. xliii). The topic is located for the time being in a more general category. If a subdivided topic is thus reduced or relocated, its subdivisions may not go with it as part of the hierarchy (v. 1, p. l-li). Consider, for instance, a recent relocation from 621.75 to inclusion under 670.42:

621.7 Factory operations engineering   *(DDC 18)*
 .75   Shop and assembly-line technology
 .756   Inspection technology Equipment and techniques
 .757   Packaging technology Materials, equipment, techniques
 .78   Mechanization and automation of factory operations

* *

621[.7]   Factory operations engineering Class in 670.42   (*DDC 19*)
  [.757]   Packaging technology   Class in 688.8

670   Manufactures
  .4   Special topics of general applicability
  .42   Factory operations engineering [*formerly* 621.7]
            Including shop and assembly-line technology
            Class management of production in 658.5
              For tools and fabricating equipment, see 621.9;
              packaging technology, 688.8
  .423   Machine-shop practice
  .425   Inspection technology   Equipment and techniques
  .427   Mechanization and automation of factory operations

Reused Numbers

When a total change of meaning occurs, the class number is said to be "reused" (v. 1, p. lxxxi). Relocation and reuse have negative as well as positive effects, since they not only separate related materials, but collocate unrelated materials, depending on the aspects emphasized or de-emphasized by the change. Yet their purpose is to strengthen subject integrity in the system as a whole. DDC practice left a vacated number (except for phoenix schedules) unassigned for at least 25 years, but for *DDC 19* the time is shortened to permit numbers without meaning in *DDC 16* (1958) to be reused (v. 1, p. xxiv). No typographical or other warning is given in the schedule.

Because of changes in knowledge or literary warrant, or because of justifiable demand, situations do arise which require quicker reuse of a few numbers. They are held to a minimum, according to the editors, and several warnings are given. For instance, the editor's introduction lists them (v. 1, p. xxv). They appear in the schedule in italics, and are:

025.49   Controlled subject vocabularies [*DDC 18*: Reclassification]

351.007 Fundamentals of public [central government] administration
            [*DDC 18*: Conflict of interest (a discontinued number from
            the synthetic 350[.007])]

351.4   Central government work force   [*DDC 18*: Government
            service (a synthetic number from the discontinued
            350[.4])]

567.9   Fossil Reptilia   [*DDC 18*: Fossil Urodela]

597.9   Reptilia   [*DDC 18*: Urodela (Salamanders, newts, mud
            puppies)]

614.1   Forensic medicine (Medical jurisprudence)   [*DDC 18*: Public
            health registration and certification]

879.9   Osco-Umbrian literatures   [*DDC 18*: Other (non-Latinian,
            non-Sabellian) Italic languages]

901.9   Psychological principles of general history   [*DDC 18*: Civilization]

910.8   Travel by specific kinds of persons   [*DDC 18*: Collections of original accounts of travel][11]

940.11   [optional] Ancient European history to ca. 499   [*DDC 18*: Collections of original accounts of travel]

941.081 British history during the reign of Victoria, 1837-1901
             [*DDC 18*: 20th century history of Scotland and Ireland, 1901-   ]

area-719 Canadian Northern territories   [*DDC 18*: Labrador]

All but five of these instantaneous replay numbers stand in the list of *Relocations and Schedule Reductions*. It lacks 351.007 and 351.4, probably because they were synthetic (not explicitly printed out) in *DDC 18*. Numbers 614.1 and 879.9 are also missing, but their subdivisions are on the list. Omission of 941.081 may have been an oversight. It is reused in a new time span for nineteenth- and twentieth-century materials. Reuse of *area*-719 was first announced in *DC&*, v. 3, no. 3 (April 1973): 3. The *DDC 19* version adds minor extensions and terminological changes. Similarly, *DC&*, v. 3, no. 7 (April 1975): 6 first announced the change for 901.9. Reuse of 567.9 and 597.9 will be discussed in chapter 11.

Reassignments in phoenix schedules 301-307, 324, and *area*-41-42 are not counted with the 12. Nor does the schedule italicize newly assigned numbers in 301-307, although it does so for major changes in 324 and *area*-41-42. Table 1 italicizes *ss*-08, and the *Relocations and Schedule Reductions* list brackets it with an asterisk, signifying schedule reduction, but it is reassigned as follows:

-08   Collections   (*DDC 18*)
             Not planned as composite works
             Class belletristic essays in 800

* *

-08   History and description of the subject among groups(*DDC 19*)
             of persons
             Use of this number for collections discontinued
             except for 808 and where specified by Table 3
             Subdivisions of Individual literatures; class in
             main number[12]

Its two *DDC 19* subdivisions -088-089 were last used in *DDC 14*.

Other Bracketed Numbers

We have seen that totally reduced numbers, totally relocated ones, and those without meaning in their present context are bracketed. There are at least three other uses of brackets in *DDC 19*: for unassigned meanings, for options, and for numbers with a Do not use note. A long-standing format feature includes all

1,000 section numbers in the schedules whether or not they possess content. *DDC 19* brackets 86 unused section numbers. Various reasons are supplied. A few were never assigned; 1 is now permanently unassigned; 9 others have optional meanings. Table 3 summarizes their current status. Seven total relocations, with their cross classification notes, are listed in Example 10.

Table 3
Unassigned DDC Section Numbers

Section Numbers	Last ed. assigned	Explanation
[004-005]	None	Vacant
[006-007]	16	Vacant
[008-009]	None	Vacant
[024]	18	Class in 025.56
[029]	18	Class in 025
[040-049]	16	Vacant
[104]	16	Vacant
[112]	18	Class in 001.012
[125]	18	Class in 111.6
[132]	16	Vacant
[134]	16	Vacant
[136]	16	Vacant
[151]	16	Vacant
[163]	16	Vacant
[164]	17	Vacant
[217]	18	Meaningless within the context
[237]	16	Vacant
[244]	15	Vacant
[256]	14	Vacant [optional in *DDC 15*]
[257]	14	Vacant
[258]	17	Vacant
[298]	11	Permanently unassigned
[308]	16	Vacant
[309]	18	Class in 900
[311]	17	Vacant
[313]	14	Vacant [not bracketed, but unassigned in *DDC 19*]
[329]	18	Class in 324
[396-397]	16	Vacant
[416]	18	Class in 808.1
[424, 434, 444, 454, 464, 474, 484]	16	Vacant
[426, 436, 446, 456, 466, 476, 486]	18	Vacant
[504]	16	Vacant
[517]	17	Vacant
[518]	15	Vacant

(Table 3 continues on page 60)

Table 3 (cont'd)

Section Numbers	Last ed. assigned	Explanation
[524]	14	Vacant [optional in *DDC 15*]
[571]	16	Vacant
[626]	14	Vacant [optional in *DDC 15*]
[654]	14	Vacant [optional in *DDC 15*]
[655]	17	Vacant
[656]	14	Vacant [optional in *DDC 15*]
[689]	14	Vacant
[699]	14	Vacant [optional in *DDC 15*]
[744]	17	Vacant
[762]	14	Vacant [optional in *DDC 15*]
[768]	14	Vacant
[775-777]	14	Vacant [optional in *DDC 15*]
[804]	16	Vacant
[819]	14	Optional since *DDC 16*; prefer 810-818.
[908]	18	Vacant
[921-928]	16	Optional since *DDC 17*; prefer specific discipline with *ss*-092 from Table 1.
[991-992]	17	Vacant

Example 21
Permanently unassigned numbers

Besides the permanently unassigned section number identified in Table 3, there are two others bracketed in *DDC 19* for optional application to a locally preferred religion. These are directed primarily to non-American libraries. Their schedule contexts are as follows:

289   Specific Christian denominations and sects
  [.2]   [Permanently unassigned][13]
        (If it is desired to give local emphasis and a shorter number to a specific denomination or sect not separately provided for, it is optional to class it in this number)

290   Other religions and comparative religion
[298]   [Permanently unassigned]
        (If it is desired to give local emphasis and a shorter number to a specific religion, it is optional to class it in this number. Other options are described under 200)

704.9   Iconography
    .94   Various specific subjects
    .948   Religion and religious symbolism
    [.9481]   [Permanently unassigned]
                  If it is desired to give local emphasis and a shorter
                  number to iconography of a specific religion, class
                  it in this number

Example 22
Optional numbers

Besides the three permanently unassigned numbers, there are something over 175 options or optional spans in *DDC 19*. All are bracketed and accompanied by Prefer notes. Nine optional section numbers have the following context:

810   American literature in English
[819]   Literatures not requiring local emphasis
             (It is optional to class here English-language liter-
             atures of specific American countries, e.g., libraries
             emphasizing United States literature may class here
             Canadian literature, and libraries emphasizing Cana-
             dian literature may class here United States litera-
             ture. Prefer 810-818 for literature of all American
             countries, especially for description, critical
             appraisal, biography, works of individual authors.
             Other options are described under 800)

[921-928]   Biography of specific classes of persons
                Use is optional; prefer treatment described under
                920.1-928.9

Options appear most frequently in literature and history (over 50 in the 800's, over 100 in the 900's). The 700's have 12, all located between 739.2209 and 760.9, mostly to curtail long numbers for various types of artists. The 200's have 6, all involving canonical placement of biblical texts. There are 5 in the 300's, 4 of them in the 370's, suggesting that elementary school texts be classed with their disciplines. The only options in the 600's occur under 658[.9] (Management of enterprises engaged in specific fields of activity). These are related to the *ss*-068 change in *DDC 19*. One option in the 000's permits scatter of subject bibliography by topic. There are none in the 100's, 400's, or 500's.

Example 23
Do-not-use numbers

Over 200 bracketed numbers in *DDC 19* explicitly warn against use of a standard subdivision from Table 1. They appear at locations with a considerable amount of literature, carrying notes to class elsewhere (usually in a shorter number), e.g.:

537   Electricity and electronics
  [.076]   Review and exercise Do not use; class in 537.9

Summary

Controlled expansion, reduction, and relocation constitute the primary modes of schedule change. DDC editors often combine them in varying formats to make the system more responsive to contemporary needs, or to implement the goal of subject integrity from a modern perspective. What seems to be a small readjustment may turn out to be nearly as far-reaching, or just as controversial, as a sudden large one.[14] Phoenix schedules appear to be most revolutionary, but they differ only in degree, not in kind.

Tinkering with the schedules is not the only way to modify a classification scheme. The semantic, and even the structural, peculiarities of the mediating language have their own laws and pose their own problems of change. We shall, in the next chapter, examine syntactic and syndetic adjustments in the *DDC 19* index, noting their effect on modernization of the entire system.

NOTES

[1]*Subject Authorities: A Guide to Subject Cataloging* (New York & London, R. R. Bowker, 1981). 3 volumes.

[2]The *Relocations and Schedule Reductions* list gives only three, omitting 332[.68].

[3]See the paragraph on "Relocations" in the editor's introduction of *DDC 19*, v. 1, p. lxxiv; also the glossary entry, p. lxxx, and the *Relocations and Schedule Reductions* list, pp. 453-60.

[4]Lois Mai Chan, "The Tenth Abridged DDC ... and Children's Room/School Library Collections," *School Library Journal*, v. 20, no. 1 (September 15, 1973): 38.

[5]Benjamin A. Custer, "Dewey Lives," *Library Resources & Technical Services*, v. 11, no. 1 (Winter 1967): 55.

[6]Benjamin A. Custer, "Dewey Decimal Classification," *Encyclopedia of Library and Information Science* (New York, Marcel Dekker, 1972), v. 7, p. 139.

[7]Custer cites these figures for the second through the seventeenth editions in "Dewey Lives," pp. 55-56. His implied total of 1,737 relocations in *DDC 16* differs from the 1,603 cited in *DDC 17*, p. 48. The numbers for *DDC 18* and *19* come respectively from *DDC 18*, p. 10, and *DDC 19*, v. 1, p. xxiv. The user should remember that with systematic faceting the exact total of discontinued numbers and relocations cannot be precisely stated.

[8]Although it practiced relocation, as can be seen from Table 1, *DDC 16* restored 528 of the 1,015 relocations that had been made in *DDC 15*. Limited restoration is still possible. One such case in *DDC 19* at class number 002 was cited in our section on expansions.

[9]A distribution table of *DDC 19* relocations can be found in the editor's introduction, v. 1, p. xxiv.

[10]See the general discussion of hierarchical force in chapter 2.

[11]The *DDC 19* schedule does not italicize 910.8, although it is identified as one of the 12 in the editor's introduction.

[12]*DC&*, v. 4, no. 1 (June 1980): 8.

[13]Last assigned in *DDC 11* (1922).

[14]DDC's new editor names three types of modification: Radical (root) change of extensive scope; Substantial change; and Minor change. He then warns that "not unexpectedly, it is types 2 and 3 that engender the highest level of frustration and anger in both patron and librarian." John Phillip Comaromi, "DDC 19: The Reclass Project," *HCL Cataloging Bulletin*, no. 35 (July/August 1978): 12.

4

The Modernization of DDC: Index and Terminology

Introduction

While both the schedules and the index of a classification system match linguistic with notational representations of the concepts (more accurately, of the library materials) being classified, they have reciprocal functions, offering different insights. Schedules graph or delineate the structure, using notation to accent symmetries, analogies, and hierarchies. The index offers random access through alphabetized primary and subordinated terms. In chapter 3 we surveyed the major techniques of schedule change, most of which were related to notational change. We now shift focus to index revisions, which have a closer affinity to terminological change.[1] Can (does) DDC terminology adjust with adequate grace and alacrity to the inevitable metamorphosis of the language? To what extent does it respond to social and attitudinal shifts, or to technological and scientific advance as reflected in the literature? Have its efforts to overcome an early parochialism resulted in a wider, deeper international and cosmological sweep? Not all observers think so. One says:

> I have always maintained that the index to DDC is superfluous and that "I wouldn't want to employ any classifier who regularly uses the index." I stand by that still. The only acceptable approach to classing is via the main class, and then down through the hierarchy to the correct placing. There are obstacles to this course, the lack of adequate summaries at strategic points, particularly at the beginning of classes, the shortage (still) of "class elsewhere" notes. But it remains the only possible means of correct classing. Which leaves the index without any function....
>
> There is some evidence of tidying-up: scatter references are reduced, but still annoying. There are, as always, more entries under "Albigensian ... " than under "Computer.... " The index is still produced as a last-minute job after the schedules have been finished. Forest Press continued to resist computerisation—though they have been "examining the problem" for 5 or 6 years. Next time, perhaps?[2]

To gain perspective on these and related questions, let us evaluate various kinds of conceptual and linguistic development.

Sample Comparisons of Index Terms

A truly exhaustive index is physically impossible. The test of an index, then, is not its fullness, but the nature and extent of its omissions, its consistency, and its structure.[3]

The *DDC 19* editor's introduction says that "while the index retains the same pattern as in Edition 18, it has been refined and made into a more efficient tool" (v. 1, p. xxii). It is larger by about one-fifth (1,217 to 1,033 pages). But mere bulk is no guarantee of excellence. In a contrast of three random sequences, let us consider specific divergencies. Full *DDC 19* index pages quantify the entries compared from *DDC 18*. Only entries appearing uniquely in one or the other index are copied. Where *see* references call for more evidence, the referred-to entry will also be given. *DDC 18* entries will be copied first. Abbreviations are reproduced as found, and dashes replace indented lines to show subordination. A list of DDC abbreviations appears in the front of each index. Table 3, at the close of the comparisons, will summarize our findings.

Comparison A
DDC 19, v. 3, p. 81 and *DDC 18*, p. 1704

A-1.   Auctions--distribution channels--marketing   *(DDC 18)*
      management   658.84

    *

      Auctions *see* Distribution channels   *(DDC 19)*
      Distribution channels--marketing management   658.84

The schedule entry reads the same in both editions at 658.84. This comparison counters the general assurance that "many cross references have been deleted and replaced by numbers" (v. 1, p. xxii).

A-2.   Audenshaw Greater Manchester Eng.   *area*-42735 *(DDC 19)*

Table 2 entries highlight this new index term:

-427	North central England	*(DDC 18)*
-4272	Lancashire Including Liverpool, Manchester	

    *

-427	Northwestern England and Isle of Man	*(DDC 19)*
-4273	Greater Manchester Metropolitan County	
-42735	Tameside Including Ashton-under-Lyne, Audenshaw, Denton, Droylsden, Dukinfield, Hyde, Longdendale, Mossley, Stalybridge	

The increase in local and regional names is of more interest here than the phoenix shift in areas 41-42. Tameside and all the local designations under it are now included in the index. It is part of the expansion of local entries, especially for places outside the United States.

A-3. Audiences--soc. psych.   301.181 (*DDC 18*)

* *

Audiences--soc. interaction   302.33   (*DDC 19*)

A phoenix schedule reduction and relocation is reflected here.

A-4. Audio-lingual study--appl. ling.   418   (*DDC 19*)
Audio-lingual study--appl. ling.--spec. langs.   *lang. sub.*-83

These new entries cover an emerging field of inquiry. In *DDC 18*, only the Table 4 entry -83 used the term "audio-lingual." It was not indexed. In *DDC 19*, section 418 still does not use it.

A-5. Audiologists--biog. & work   617.89092 (*DDC 18*)
Audiologists--lit. & stage trmt. *see* Persons
 Other aspects see Medical scientists
 s.a.   *pers.*-6178

* *

Audiologists *see* Medical scientists   (*DDC 19*)

The synthetic 617.89092 and the Table 7 number are consistent with *DDC 19* practice, but the *DDC 19* index is less explicit.

A-6. Audiology--med. sci.   617.89   (*DDC 18*)
Audiology--med. sci.--geriatrics   618.97789
Audiology--med. sci.--pediatrics   618.9209789

* *

Audiology--med. sci.--hearing correction   617.89   (*DDC 19*)
Audiology--med. sci.--hearing correction--
  geriatrics   618.97789
Audiology--med. sci.--hearing correction--
  pediatrics   618.9209789
Audiology--med. sci.--otology *see* Otology

Another *see* reference has been added, but this one suggests a new access point. It also prompts the intermediate "--hearing correction" step, which increases the bulk and complexity of the index.

A-7. Audiology--music *see* Musical sound   (*DDC 18*)
Musical sound--music theory   781.22

* *

Audiology--music   781.22   (*DDC 19*)
 s.a. spec. mediums

DDC 19 trades a direct entry for a *see* reference, and adds a general *see also*.

A-8.   Audiovisual materials--art appreciation use   701.184 *(DDC 18)*

* *

Audiovisual materials--art appreciation use   701.1   *(DDC 19)*

The change reflects schedule reduction of 701[.184].

A-9.   Audiovisual materials--ed. use   371.335 *(DDC 18)*
        s.a. spec. levels of ed.

* *

Audiovisual materials--ed. use   371.335 *(DDC 19)*
    s.a. spec. levels of ed.; *also* Special education

Nothing under "Special education" in either index or schedule mentions audiovisuals.

A-10.   Audiovisual materials--library trmt.--acquisitions   025.287 *(DDC 19)*

This synthetic class number reflects a schedule expansion.

A-11.   Audiovisual materials--management use   658.451 *(DDC 18)*

The index entry is scrubbed because of the scatter relocation from section 658, which was pointed out in Example 17 of chapter 3.

A-12.   Audiovisual materials--rel. communication--   *(DDC 19)*
        Christian local church   254.3
    Audiovisual materials--rel. communication--
        Christian local church--parochial activities   259.7
        other rel. see Ecclesiastical theology
    Audiovisual materials--rel. instruction--
        Christianity   268.635
        other rel. see Religious instruction

Schedule changes give rise to the new index entries.

    254   Parish government and administration   *(DDC 18)*
      .3   Radio and television work
  [259.7]   [Not in *DDC 18*]
    268   Christian religious training and instruction
      .6   Methods of instruction and study
      .63   Lecture and audiovisual methods
      .635   Audiovisual methods

* *

    254.3   Use of communications media   *(DDC 19)*
          Including use of audiovisual materials

    259   Parochial activities by parishes and religious orders
      .7   Methods Examples: group work, telephone work,
          use of radio and television
          Class methods for specific activities with specific
          classes of people in 259.2-259.6

    268.635   [Same as in *DDC 18*]

A-13. Audiovisual materials--reviews   028.137 *(DDC 19)*

The synthetic number 028.137 signals a schedule refinement and expansion.

A-14. Audiovisual technology   621.38044 *(DDC 19)*
    s.a. spec. kinds e.g. Cinematography

DC&, v. 3, no. 2 (September 1972): 11 added this entry, using the broader class number 621.38. Use of the general *see also* turns up such entries as:

Cameras--photography--gen. techn.	770.282
Cameras--television--engineering	621.38834
Filmstrips--photographic projection	778.2
Graphic materials--manufacture--technology	686
Recordings--engineering--tech. & mf.	621.38932
Recording-telephones--wire telephony--tech. & mf.	621.3867
Slides--photographic projection	778.2

A-15. Auditing--mil. admin. *see* Financial administration armed   *(DDC 18)*
    forces
    Financial administration--armed forces   355.622
    s.a. spec. mil. branches

* *

    Auditing--mil. admin.   355.622 *(DDC 19)*
    s.a. spec. mil. branches

DDC 19 shortens the index with a direct number in place of a *see* reference.

A-16. Auditing--pub. admin.--central govts.--spec. jur.   353-354 *(DDC 19)*

The pattern subdivision "--specific jurisdictions" is new in *DDC 19*. Pattern subdivisions "--public administration" and "--central governments" are frequent throughout both indexes. See further discussion of patterns under Comparison B-13.

Comparison B
DDC 19, v. 3, p. 609 and *DDC 18*, pp. 2150-2151

B-1. Little Tennessee River   *area*-768863 *(DDC 19)*

This entry corresponds to a new Class here note in Table 2.

B-2. Little   *(DDC 19)*
    s.a. other spec. subj.

It is difficult to understand the function of this new *see also* reference.

B-3.   Littleborough Greater Manchester Eng.   *area*-427392 (*DDC 19*)
       Littlehampton West Sussex Eng.   *area*-42267

More evidence of the increase in local area names and numbers.

B-4.   Littoral *see* Shore; *also* Shorelands   (*DDC 19*)

The technical word "Littoral" appears nowhere else in *DDC 19*.

B-5.   Liturgical music--recordings   789.913632 (*DDC 18*)
       *
       Liturgical music--recordings   789.91232 (*DDC 19*)

Both class numbers are synthetic. Schedule contexts show relocation of the Add note in *DDC 19*.

B-6.   Liverpool Eng.   *area*-4272   (*DDC 18*)
       *
       Liverpool England   *area*-42753 (*DDC 19*)
       Liverpool N.S.W.   *area*-9441

Both *DDC 19* entries reflect Table 2 expansion. The England entry also represents phoenix change.

B-7.   Living conditions--armed forces   355.12 (*DDC 18*)
        s.a. spec. mil. branches
       *
       Living conditions--armed forces   355.12 (*DDC 19*)
       Living conditions--armed forces--law *see* Armed ser-
          vices--law
        s.a. spec. mil. branches

The primary change is the new *see* reference. The *see also* shifts down to the subordinate entry.

B-8.   Living organisms *see spec. kinds, e.g.* Animals   (*DDC 19*)

Here is a new general *see* reference.

B-9.   Living standard--macroeconomics   339.47 (*DDC 19*)

Both indexes have entries under "Standard of living." Only *DDC 19* permutes it to provide access under "Living."

B-10. Livingston-Lothian Scot.   *area*-4133 (*DDC 19*)

Another added British place name from a Table 2 phoenix change.

B-11. Livonian War hist.   947.04   (*DDC 18*)

* *

Livonian War hist   947.043 (*DDC 19*)

The number change reflects a chronological expansion of 947.04.

B-12. Lizard--Cornwall England   *area*-42376 (*DDC 19*)

This new place name represents an expansion (not a change) in Table 2.

B-13. Llama wool textiles--home sewing   646.1132   (*DDC 18*)
       Llama wool textiles--manufacturing--prod. econ. 338.4767732
       s.a. spec. aspects e.g. Finance
       other aspects see Manufacturing firms
       Llama wool textiles--marketing *see* Marketing

* *

Llama wool textiles--manufacturing--soc. and econ. aspects   (*DDC 19*)
       see Secondary industries

Both *DDC 18* numbers are synthetic. Only 388.4767732 can now be built since Add instructions at 646.11 have been dropped. *DDC 19* drops the pattern subdivisions "--production economics," as Comparison C-1 also illustrates (Cf. Section 1.4 in v. 1, p. xxii). There are numerous other cases under, e.g., "Aerostream engines," "Bush clovers," and "Halogenated rubbers." A frequent substitution is "--social and economic aspects," which often gives a *see* reference to "Secondary industries," where subdivisions are considerably extended in *DDC 19*.

B-14. Llamas--animal husbandry   636.296 (*DDC 18*)
       other aspects see Ruminants

* *

Llamas--animal husbandry   636.296 (*DDC 19*)
       other aspects see Tylopoda

Although earlier editions used "Tylopoda," the change represents terminological refinement. *DDC 16* freed Tylopoda from subordination to Ruminantia. The *DDC 18* index entry first carried a *see* reference under Llamas, but still sent the user to "Ruminants."

B-15. Llandeilo Dyfed Wales   *area*-42968 (*DDC 19*)
       Llandovery Dyfed Wales   *area*-42968
       Llandrindod Wells Powys Wales   *area*-42954
       Llandudno Gwynedd Wales   *area*-42927
       Llanelli Dyfed Wales   *area*-42967
       Llanfairfechan Gwynedd Wales   *area*-42927

At this point, the *DDC 19* index begins to resemble a gazetteer of Wales.

Comparison C
DDC 19, v. 3, p. 1136 and *DDC 18*, pp. 2598-2599

C-1.   Tuber crops--foods   641.3349   (*DDC 18*)
     Tuber crops--foods--cookery   641.6349
     Tuber crops--marketing *see* Marketing
     Tuber crops--prod. econ.   338.17349
     Tuber crops--prod. econ.--finance   338.13349
       s.a. other spec. aspects
       other aspects see Field crops

* *

     Tuber crops--foods   641.352 (*DDC 19*)
     Tuber crops--foods--cookery   641.652
       other aspects see Field crops; *also* Vegetables

    DDC 18 number 641.3349 appears to be a gratuitous projection of the Add principle. There was no schedule instruction at 641.33. The *DDC 19* numbers are built from Add notes at 641.35 and 641.63-.69. Entries for production and economic aspects are missing from *DDC 19*. Cf. Comparison B-13.

C-2.   Tuberoses *see* Amaryllidales   (*DDC 19*)

    Index entries under "Amaryllidales" are nearly identical in the two editions. "Tuberoses" appears nowhere in either schedule. *DDC 19* indexes it to facilitate searching under the popular name.

C-3.   Tubers *s.a.* Edible tubers   (*DDC 18*)
* *
     Edible tubers *see* Tuber crops   (*DDC 19*)
     Tubers *s.a.* Tuber crops

    DDC consolidates all aspects of "tuber."

C-4.   Tubes--metal prod. *see* Primary metal products   (*DDC 18*)
* *
     Tubes--metal prod. *see* Forged metal prod.   (*DDC 19*)
       s.a. Vacuum tubes

    Entries under "Forged metal products" are identical in the two indexes, but those under "Primary metal products" and "Vacuum tubes" reflect *DDC 19* elimination of many "--production economics" subdivisions, and many "--marketing *see* Marketing" references. Cf. Comparison B-13.

C-5.   Tubes (electronics)--gamma-ray *see* Gamma-ray tubes   (*DDC 19*)
     Tubes (electronics)--x-ray *see* X-ray tubes

    It has been DDC practice after Edition 16 (1958) to spell the noun "X rays" without a hyphen, but to insert a hyphen in the adjective form. Filing arrangement is affected, as the following selected index entries show.

X-ray--analysis physics		537.5352 (DDC 16)
X-ray--tubes physics	[formerly *535.66]	537.535
X-rays--& heredity		575.131
X-rays--physics	[formerly *535.66]	537.535
Xanthe Greece history		949.57
Xiphosura--paleozoology		565.392
Xylem--plant anatomy		581.41

* *

X rays--astrophysics	523.0197222 (DDC 19)
X rays--physics	539.7222
Xanthe Greece	area-4957
Xiphosura--paleozoology	565.392
X-ray--analysis--anal. chem.--gen. wks.	543.08586
X-ray--tubes--physics	537.5355
s.a. X rays	
Xylem--plant--anatomy	581.41

C-6.   Receptables--chem apparatus   542.2 (DDC 18)
          s.a. spec. appls. e.g. Organic chemistry
          Tubing--chem. apparatus *see* Receptacles--chem. apparatus

* *

          Tubing--chem. apparatus   542.2 (DDC 19)
          s.a. spec. appls. e.g. Organic chemistry

The promise that "many cross references have been deleted and replaced by numbers" is illustrated. Cf. Comparison A-7.

C-7.   Tubular bridges--structural eng.   624.4 (DDC 19)
          other aspects see Bridges (structures)

The entry appears in *DDC 18*, but without the *see* reference. Both indexes enter "Bridges (structures)," but interesting alterations can be found in its *DDC 19* subdivisions.

C-8.   Tubulidentata (Edentata) *see* Edentata   (DDC 18)
          Tubulidentata (Protungulata)--paleozoology   569.75

* *

Tubulidentata--animal husbandry	636.975	(DDC 19)
Tubulidentata--hunting--commercial	639.1175	
Tubulidentata--hunting--sports	799.25975	
Tubulidentata--paleozoology	569.75	
Tubulidentata--zoology	599.75	

          other aspects see Mammalia

Since Aardvarks constitute the entire order of Tubulidentata, the index shift under "Aardvark" is also interesting.

          Aardvarks *see* Edentata   (DDC 18)

* *

Aardvarks *see* Tubulidentata   (*DDC 19*)

DDC 19 schedule entries under 599.31 (Edentata and Pholidota) and 599.75 (Tubulidentata) corroborate the terminological refinement.

C-9.   Tucumán Argentina   *area*-824   (*DDC 18*)

* *

        Tucumán Argentina   *area*-8243 (*DDC 19*)

DDC 19 offers an expansion of the Table 2 division -824 (Northwestern provinces of Argentine).

C-10.   Tudors--Eng. hist.   942.05   (*DDC 18*)

* *

        Tudors--Eng. hist.   942.05   (*DDC 19*)
        Tudors--Gt. Brit. hist.   941.05
        Tudors--Ireland hist.   941.505
          s.a. spec. events & subj. e.g. Commerce

DC&, v. 3, no. 6 (October 1974): 1 announced "beginning spring 1975 the history of Great Britain will be classed in 941, while that of England will remain in 942."

C-11.   Tufa *see* Volcanic rocks   (*DDC 18*)

* *

        Tufa *see* Sedimentary rocks   (*DDC 19*)

The reference shift shows a refinement in geological terminology, just as Comparison C-8 showed a refinement in zoological terminology.

C-12.   Tug services--inland ports--govt. control   350.876866 (*DDC 18*)
          s.a. spec. levels of govt.
        Tug services--law--international   341.448
        Tug services--law--municipal   343.0967
        Tug services--seaports--govt. control   350.877166
          s.a. spec. levels of govt.

* *

        Tug services--inland ports--govt. control   350.876866 (*DDC 19*)
          --central govts.   351.876866
          --central govts.--spec. jur.   353-354
          --local govts.   352.916866
        Tug services--law--international   341.75667
        Tug services--law--municipal   343.0967
        Tug services--law--municipal--spec. jur.   343.3-.9
        Tug services--seaports--govt. control   350.877166
          --central govts.   351.877166
          --central govts.--spec. jur.   353-354
          --local govts.   352.917166

Two kinds of change can be seen here. The synthetic number for international law of tugboat services now puts it under international maritime law (341.7566) rather than the jurisdictional relations of states in territorial waters (341.448). The second change is part of a general increase in index subdivisions "--government control," e.g.:

> Consumer protection--government control
> Labor--government control
> Minority groups--social welfare--general works--government
>   control

There is also more emphasis on building numbers to differentiate international, central, local, and municipal governments, specific jurisdictions, etc.

C-13.   Tughluk dynasty--India hist.   954.023   (*DDC 18*)

* *

   Tughluk dynasty--India hist.   954.0236 (*DDC 19*)
      s.a. spec. events & subj. e.g. Arts

The longer number comes from a chronological expansion. The new general *see also* reminds classifiers of related aspects in other disciplines. The value of such random instructions has been debated by indexers.

C-14.   Tuition.   371.22   (*DDC 18*)
      s.a. spec. levels of ed.

* *

   Tuition--private   371.206 (*DDC 19*)
   Tuition--public   379.13
      s.a. spec. levels of ed.

This entry alerts us to an unobtrusive, but fairly significant schedule change reflecting social change by providing more recognition of private schools, and separation of their literature from that on public schools. It might be well to have the numbers italicized in the schedule, since they constitute immediate reuse involving a considerable shift of library materials. "Class here" and "Formerly" notes are given.

C-15.   Tulip trees *see* Magnoliales   (*DDC 19*)
      Tulips *see* Liliaceae

Two popular botanical names are introduced for ready reference.

SUMMARY OF DDC 18 AND 19 INDEX COMPARISONS

Tables 4 and 5 give a summary of the changes from our three-page sample. The "total case" count in Table 5 often exceeds the number of comparisons cited because different examples frequently appear in one comparison. Only a few general comments need be made. Nineteen primary headings (entries and cross-references in the main alphabet) were added; four were dropped. The increase is 15 (from 58 to 73), or slightly under 26%. When secondary entries (main alphabet subdivisions) are included, the net increase is 47 (240 over 193, or between 24 and 25%). Class and auxiliary table numbers and number spans increased from 125 to 157 (25.6%). Seventy-six cross-references in the *DDC 19* sample means an increase of 11.76% over the 68 in *DDC 18*. No doubt the claim that "many cross references have been deleted and replaced by numbers" (v. 1, p. xxii) is true, but it does not tell the whole story, as both tables show. New terminology is rare. Even so, there is more terminological than class number change. New-term entries, permutations, refinements, and subdivision changes total 33, nearly 18% more than the 28 number expansions, discontinuances, and relocations.

The general impression is one of moderate growth. Yet the *DDC 19* samples take less gross page space than their *DDC 18* counterparts. Moreover, page size (but apparently not type size) is reduced, and the proliferation of extended subdivisions, each with its own indention and page line, would indicate that the increase is not the full 19% which the page count suggests. Changes seem to owe more to formatting and to schedule and index refinements than to new words, which are largely gazetteer-type, with a few popular scientific names added for reference. Some updating of scientific and technical nomenclature can be seen. Pattern subdivisions in economics, manufacturing, and political science have been revised and somewhat expanded.

Table 4
Comparative Index Spans

	Comparison A		Comparison B		Comparison C		Totals	
	Ed. 18	Ed. 19	Ed. 18	Ed. 19	Ed. 18	Ed. 19	Ed. 18	Ed. 19
Primary Headings	13	16	19	28	26	29	58	73
Total Entries	59	73	64	79	70	88	193	240
Schedule Numbers	23	25	17	19	15	18	55	62
Aux. Table Numbers	3	4	11	23	10	10	24	37
Number Spans	1	6			1	3	2	9
Synthetic Numbers	11	11	13	11	20	27	44	49
See References	17	16	16	18	12	14	45	48
See also References	5	8	7	8	11	12	23	28

Table 5
Indexing Differences

Type of Difference	Comparison Numbers	Total Cases
New place-name entries: A-2, B-1, B-3, B-6, B-10, B-12, B-15		13
New entry terms (Non place-name): A-4, B-4, C-2, C-15		5
New permuted entries: B-9		1
Terminology refined: B-14, C-3, C-4, C-8, C-11, C-15		7
Entries with numbers replaced by *see* references: A-1, A-5, C-3		3
See references replaced by entries with numbers: A-7, A-15, C-6, C-8		4
Pattern subdivisions added: A-6, A-12, A-16, B-7, B-13, C-8, C-12		11
Pattern subdivisions deleted: B-13, C-1, C-3		8
New subdivisions based on schedule relocations: A-3, B-6, C-10, C-14		4
DDC number expansions: A-2, A-10, A-12, A-13, B-3, B-6, B-11, B-12, B-15, C-9, C-13		16
DDC number reductions: A-8, A-11, B-5		3
DDC number discontinuations: A-8, A-11		2
DDC number relocations: A-2, A-3, B-5, B-6, B-10, C-1		7

Terminological Changes in DC& and DDC 19

Within a year of *DDC 18* publication (1971), the first issue of *DC&* volume 3 went to all purchasers who had put their names on the mailing list. It was largely preoccupied with typographical and other technical slips, but much substantive material was included. Seven issues (March 1972-April 1975) preceded *DDC 19*. They introduced 64 new index terms as follows, not counting the phoenix shifts for the British Isles.

Abominable snowman	001.944
Afars territory	*area*-6771
Alpes-de-Haute-Provence	*area*-4495
Alpine gardens--floriculture	635.9672
Anthropogeography *see* Anthropology	
Bangladesh	*area*-5492
Biological clocks *see* Control mechanisms	
Biological periodicity *see* Control mechanisms	
Biological rhythms *see* Control mechanisms	
Biological timing *see* Control mechanisms	
Bonsai	[multiple entry]
Brain-damaged students *see* Crippled students	
Busing school students	[multiple entry]
Cerigo *see* Kythera	
Chesapeake Bay	[multiple entry]
Choice of vocation	[multiple entry]
Commencements--customs	394.2
Comparative literature	809
Copra *see* Coconut oil; *also* Coconuts	

Cossacks	*r.e.n.*-91714
Cythera *see* Kythera	
Ecologists	[4 *see* references]
Erotica	[multiple entry]
Ethnogeography	572.9
Federation of Arab Republics	*area*-62
Ford, Gerald Rudolph--admin. — U.S. hist.	973.925
Four Corners region--southwest U.S.	*area*-78827
Glasses *see* Eyeglasses	
Graduation	[multiple entry]
Hijacking *see* Criminal offenses	
Historiographers *see* Historians	
International cookery	641.59
Interviews *see* Anthologies	
Issas territory	*area*-6771
Karnataka	*area*-5487
Least-squares math.	[multiple entry]
Loch Ness, Scot.--monster	001.944
Lost-found Nation of Islam in the West *see* Black Muslims	
Macramé *see* Needlework	
Monsters--controversial knowledge	001.944
Neuston	[multiple entry]
North Frigid zone	*area*-113
North Temperate zone	*area*-123
Pawpaws *see* Papayas	
Performance contracting--education	371.15
Phytoneuston	[multiple entry]
Postal Service--U.S. govt.	353.08873
Prisoners of war *see* War prisoners	
Pyrénées-Atlantiques France	*area*-4479
Rubbings--graphic arts	760
Snowmobiles	[multiple entry]
Social ecologists *see* Sociologists	
South Frigid zone	*area*-116
South Temperate zone	*area*-126
Sri Lanka	*area*-5493
Street-lighting *see* Public lighting	
Terrariums--floriculture	635.9824
Tertiary treatment--sewage--technology	628.357
United-Arab Emirates	*area*-5357
Urban renewal	[multiple entry]
Value-added tax .*see* Excise taxes	
Variant sexual relations *see* Sexual aberrations	
Viticulture	634.8
Zaire	[multiple entry]

The 24 proper names are nearly all personal or geographic. Other terms come largely from psychology, sociology, education, literature, arts and crafts, science and technology, economics, or agriculture. Twenty-one (33%) are *see* references to *DDC 18* terms. All are in the *DDC 19* index, but with the following revisions:

Bangladesh	[multiple entry]
Biological clocks *see* Biological rhythms	
Biological periodicity *see* Biological rhythms	
Biological rhythms	[multiple entry]
Biological timing *see* Biological rhythms	
Copra	[multiple entry]
Ecologists	[multiple entry]
Glasses	[multiple entry]
Hijacking *see* Larceny [*DDC 19*]	
Hijacking *see* Robbery [*DC&*, v. 4, no. 1]	
Macramé--textile arts	760
North Frigid zone	[multiple entry]
North Temperate zone	[multiple entry]
Performance contracting--education	[multiple entry]
Rubbings--brasses--graphic arts	760
Snowmobiles--sports	796.94
South Frigid zone	[multiple entry]
South Temperate zone	[multiple entry]
Tertiary treatment--sewage--technology	[multiple entry]
Value-added tax *see* Added-value taxes	
Variant sexual relations *see* Sexual deviations	
Viticulture	[multiple entry]

"Added-value taxes" was a primary entry in the *DDC 18* Relative Index. Perhaps the *DC&* reference to "Excise taxes" was an oversight. In another interesting *DC&* adjustment, the cross-reference under "Negroes" changed in 1973 from "*other aspects see* Minority groups" to "*other aspects see* Ethnic groups." Both *DDC 18* and *19* carry entries under both reference terms. A similar juggling took place in the replacement of "Pornography--arts" by "Pornography--arts *see* Erotica--arts," as a corollary of the new entry "Erotica."

In addition to the systematic comparisons of this chapter, a random list of new or changed terms is given below. Unless otherwise noted, they represent *DDC 19* Relative Index entries. They prove nothing, but give some insight into the nature and extent of terminological change.

ADC--soc. services	362.713
Activity therapies	615.8515
Aerosols--meteorology--artificial modification	551.68
Afro-American ...	[multiple entry]
Aid to dependent children ...	
DDC 18: ... --law *see* Welfare services--law	
DDC 19: ... --soc. services	362.713
Aid to education--law	[multiple entry]
Aids to perfection ...	
DDC 18: ... *see* Self-discipline	
DDC 19: ... --rel. self-discipline *see* Asceticism	
Altered states of consciousness--depth psychology	154.4
Alternative education	371.04

American quarter horse--animal husbandry	636.133
Antigens immunology--physiology	
DDC 18: ... *see* Immunology	
DDC 19: ... --med. sci.	612.118222
Appliqué--textile arts	
DDC 18: ... *see* Embroidery	
DDC 19:	746.445
Arabian horses	
DDC 18: ... *see* Oriental horses	
DDC 19: ... --animal husbandry	636.112
Art deco	[multiple entry]
Art nouveau	[multiple entry]
Artificial insemination--hygiene	613.94
Auction catalogs--articles ...	
DDC 18:	*ss*-0216
DDC 19:	*ss*-0294
Bagpipe music	
DDC 18:	788.9
DDC 19:	788.925
Beads ...	[multiple entry]
Beagles	
DDC 18: ... *see* Hounds	
DDC 19: ... --animal husbandry	636.753
Benin ...	
DDC 18: ... Nigeria	*area*-6693
DDC 19:	[multiple entry]
Bicycle paths ...	[multiple entry]
Bicycles--safety aspects *see* Vehicular transport	
Black-letter alphabets--lettering dec. arts	745.61975
Blackouts--mil. eng.	623.77
Blackwater ...	[multiple entry]
Bliss's Bibliographic Classification ...	[multiple entry]
Blowpipes ...	
DDC 18: ... --hunting & shooting sports	799.2028
DDC 19: ... (weapons)--hunting & shooting sports	799.20282
Bobbin laces--textile arts	
DDC 18:	746.22
DDC 19:	746.222
Boomerangs--customs	399
Boomerangs--mil. eng.	623.441
Bottles ...	
DDC 18: ... *see materials, e.g.* Glass	
DDC 19: ... --glass	[multiple entry]
CAT--air transp. hazard	363.12412
CATV *see* Community antenna television	
Cable television *see* Community antenna television	
Calcium soaps ...	
DDC 18: ... *see* Insoluble soaps	
DDC 19: ... --chem. tech.	668.125
Calles Mexico--hist.	972.0823
Calories ...	[multiple entry]

Disorderly conduct ...
    DDC 18:   [multiple entry]
    DDC 19: ... *see* Public order crimes against
Displaced persons ...
    DDC 18: ... --soc. welfare   361.53
    DDC 19: ... --soc. services *see* Victims of
                             political oppression
Djibouti   *area*-6771
Drinking-glasses--dec. arts   748.83
Drug abuse   [multiple entry]
Duplex houses
    DDC 18: ... *see* Multiple dwelling buildings
    DDC 19:   [multiple entry]
Eggs--biology *see* Embryology
Eggs--decorating   745.5944
Electric slow cookery   641.5884
Emergency services--telephony *see* Telephone calls
Emission control devices   [multiple entry]
Energy engineering--technology   621.042
Extended care facilities ...   [multiple entry]
Forenames   929.44
Found objects   [multiple entry]
GATT *see* General Agreement on Tariffs and Trade
GAW *see* Guaranteed-wage plans
Game birds--culture   636.63
Gandhi Indira admin.--India hist.   [multiple entry]
Gas-solid chromatography *see* Gas chromatography
General Agreement on Tariffs and Trade   [multiple entry]
Gourmet cookery   641.514
Greeting cards--handicrafts   745.594
Guaranteed minimum income--soc. welfare   362.582
Guests--seating table service   642.6
H--I & II regions *see* Interstellar matter--
    astronomy--Milky Way
HMOs *see* Health maintenance organizations
Haile Selassie Ethiopia--hist.   963.055
Hatcheries--fish   639.311
Hatha yoga   613.7046
Health foods ...   [multiple entry]
Health maintenance organizations ...   [multiple entry]
Health resorts--soc. aspects *see* Extended care facilities
Hippies
    DDC 18:   [multiple entry]
    DDC 19: ... *see* Lower classes
Immune reactions--physiology
    DDC 18: ... *see* Immunology
    DDC 19: ... --med. sci.   612.118225
Immunity of witnesses--law *see* Witnesses--law
Industrial parks--civic art   711.5524
Intensive care   [multiple entry]
Intraocular lenses--optometry   617.7524

Jabots *see* Neckware
KWIC indexing--library operations   025.486
KWOC indexing--library operations   025.486
Katsu *see* First aid
Kitsch   [multiple entry]
Lancelets--zoology   596.4
Lances
     DDC 18: ... *see* Side arms
     DDC 19: ... *see* Edged weapons
Leopard games   [multiple entry]
Leprechauns--lit. & stage trmt. *see* Supernatural beings
Library of Congress ...   [multiple entry]
MP--mil. sci   355.13323
Madrigals
     DDC 18: ... *see* Choral music
     DDC 19:   [multiple entry]
Minibikes *see* Motorcycles
Minicomputers   [multiple entry]
Mizoram India   *area*-54166
Mopeds *see* Bicycles
Moving households--home econ.   648.9
Myocardial infarction   [multiple entry]
Nabberu Lake W. Aust.   *area*-9415
Nablus Jordan   *area*-56953
Nonlinguistic *see* Nonverbal
Normative ethics--philosophy   170.44
Off-road vehicles   [multiple entry]
Op art *see* Optical art
Operators--calculus   515.724
Optical art   [multiple entry]
Optical character recognition--cybernetics   001.534
Orangutans
     DDC 18: ... *see* Ponginae
     DDC 19: ... *see* Pongo
Organic farming   [multiple entry]
Organically grown foods--agriculture *see* Organic
     farming
Organisms (biology) *see spec. kinds e.g.* Animals
Organs (anatomy) transplants--legal aspects   [multiple entry]
Osaka Japan
     DDC 18:   *area*-5218
     DDC 19:   *area*-52183
PPB *see* Program-performance budgeting
PRECIS *see* Precoordinate indexing
PT boats *see* Destroyer escorts
Paleolithic Age--arts   [multiple entry]
Paramagnetic resonance   [multiple entry]
Particle astronomy   522.686
Pastries
     DDC 18: ... *see* Bakery goods
     DDC 19:   [multiple entry]

Pastry mixes
    DDC 18: ... *see* Mixes (pastry)
    DDC 19: ... --comm. proc.   664.753
Personal improvement   [multiple entry]
Plasma (ionized gas)--engineering--technology   621.044
Plate tectonics--geophysics   551.136
Pot gardening--floriculture   635.986
Prescriptive linguistics *see* Applied linguistics
Quabe kingdom--hist.   968
Quadraphonic systems--tech. & mf.   621.389336
RTTY *see* Radiotelegraphy
Race (competition)--tracks   [multiple entry]
Remodeling--buildings   [multiple entry]
Restrictive practices   [multiple entry]
Revegetation ...   [multiple entry
Ricinuclei--zoology   595.41
Rock and roll *see* Rock (music)
Rock arts   [multiple entry]
Rock-'n'-roll
    DDC 18: ... *see* Jazz
    DDC 19: ... *see* Rock (music)
SIDS   618.920078
SLR cameras *see* Single-lens reflex cameras
Saccharomycetaceae--agric. pathogens   632.433
Scientology--religion   299.936
Seljuks Turkey--hist.   956.101
Sexism--ed. soc.   370.19345
Shopping guides *see* Consumer education
Sickle cell anemia   [multiple entry]
Silver processes--photography   772.4
Snooker   [multiple entry]
Snuffboxes--handicrafts   745.5934
Solar wind   [multiple entry]
Soul--cookery   641.59213
Soul--music   [multiple entry]
Soul--transmigration *see* Reincarnation
Space shuttle astronautics   [multiple entry]
Sports complexes bldgs.   [multiple entry]
Strategic missiles
    DDC 18: ... *see* Guided missiles
    DDC 19:   [multiple entry]
Strategic weapons--control internat. law   341.738
Stratford-on-Avon Warwickshire Eng.   *area*-42489
Sung dynasty China hist.   951.024
Surgical gauzes   [multiple entry]
Surnames   929.42
Sutures--surgical use   617.9178
Syncarida   [multiple entry]
T'ai chi ch'uan [*DD&*, v. 4, no. 1 (June 1980): 33]   [multiple entry]
Terrorism--sociology   303.62
Third World--regional subj. trmt.   *area*-1716

Thoroughbred ...
    DDC 18: ... horses *see* Saddle horses
    DDC 19: ... horse--animal husbandry   636.132
Townhouses   [multiple entry]
Trade cards--illustrations   741.685
UMT--mil. sci.   355.225
UNESCO   [multiple entry]
United Nations--philatelic issues--prints   769.561
Unmarried parenthood *see spec. kinds of parents,*
    e.g. Unmarried mothers; *also* Sexual relations
Unwed *see* Unmarried
VAT *see* Added-value taxes
Vasectomy--birth control meas.   613.942
Vegetarianism--hygiene
    DDC 18:   613.26
    DDC 19:   613.262
Venesection--therapeutics   615.899
Waadt Switzerland   *area*-4943
War correspondence   [multiple entry]
Wars--disaster relief   363.3498
Weapons--illegal carrying *see* Public order--crimes
    against
Womanpower ...
    DDC 18:   [multiple entry]
    DDC 19: ... *see* Manpower
Women & state--pol. sci.   323.34
Women's suffrage--pol. sci.   324.623
Xerography
    DDC 18: ... *see* Electrostatic photoduplication
    DDC 19:   [multiple entry]
Yard sales--commerce   381.19
ZBB *see* Zero-base budgeting
Zero-base budgeting   [multiple entry]
Zimbabwe   *area*-6891
Zip codes--postal commun.   383.145
Zodiacal light--astronomy--theory   521.54

Prejudice and Antipathy: The Berman View

Sanford Berman, head cataloger of the Hennepin County Library, Edina, Minnesota, has been the Socratic gadfly of subject cataloging for at least a decade. The close, but never placid, association between his library and the classification scheme it somewhat plaintively "uses" sparked an exchange in the *Hennepin County Library Cataloging Bulletin* just prior to *DDC 19* publication.[4] But the problem of terminological change was not addressed. Berman later turned to *Library Journal* with his complaints.[5] He mourned the disappearance of Teenagers from the Sociology schedule, as the following comparison shows:

DDC 18		DDC 19	
301.43	Specific age levels	305.2	Age levels
.431	Minors	.23	Young people Through age 20
.4314	Children Thru age eleven	.24	Adults Class adults of spe-
.4315	Adolescents		cific sexes in 305.3-.4
	Ages twelve to twenty	.26	Adults aged 65 and over
.434	Mature and middle-aged persons	.3	Men Class here comprehensive
.435	Aged persons		works on specific sexes
	Including retirement	.4	Women

He looked in vain for a *DDC 19* counterpart to the former 301.41 (The sexes and their relations). Also, *DDC 19* lumped together in its 301[.414] to 306.7 shift previously distinguished and separately numbered topics on sexuality, e.g.:

DDC 18		DDC 19	
301.414	Courtship	306.7	Institutions pertaining to
.4142	Dating		relations of the sexes
.4143	Choice of mate		Including courtship, pre-
.415	Extramarital and variant sex-		marital relations, unwed
	ual relations [DC& v. 3, no. 1		parenthood, incest, sadism,
	(March 15, 1972): 7]		masochism
.4152	Premarital relations		*For marriage, see 306.8*
	Including illegitimacy	.73	Extramarital relations
.4153	Adultery		Class here group sex
.4154	Prostitution		Class prostitution in
.4157	Homosexuality		306.74
.4158	Other abnormal sexual relations	.74	Prostitution
	Incest, bestiality, sadism,	.76	Homosexuality
	masochism		Including bisexuality

The editors claim literary warrant for reducing previously numbered divisions to an Inclusion note under 306.7. And there is some new terminology in the *DDC 19* sequence. "Unwed parenthood" is indexed as "Unmarried parenthood," but neither term was in *DDC 18.* "Group sex" and "Bisexuality" (in this context) are new.

LOCAL "DDC" NUMBERS AT THE HENNEPIN COUNTY LIBRARY

Berman offers a list of 62 concepts he finds neglected by DDC. He suggests class numbers, with their HCL adoption dates, for clues to the *HCL Cataloging Bulletin* recording the decision. Most of the work pre-dated *DDC 19*, but Berman urges that

> ... expansions of many fields and subjects that should have been effected years ago by means of semi-annual *Dewey Decimal Classification additions, notes, and decisions* (*DC&*) have not yet been instituted.[6]

His evidence is designed to reveal either classificatory or terminological inadequacies, although he does not always make clear which he means. Let us examine the list, first in the light of the HCL decision. Then we shall interpolate the HCL numbers into *DDC 19* schedule contexts. Finally, we shall compare HCL and *DDC 19* terminology, as well as that used in *Library of Congress Subject Headings*, 9th edition. In these comparisons, LC means the Library of Congress; LCSH refers to its subject list. *HCL Cataloging Bulletin* citations take the form "HCLCB 37:5" for, e.g., "issue #37 (November/December 1978): 5." HCL references to actual titles are copied, and LC assignments of DDC numbers for the same titles are given when available.

Alternative medicine. HCL no.: 610.42   Date: Nov. 1978

HCLCB 37:5 cites Bloomfield and Kory's *Holistic way to health and happiness* (LCCN 78-5683). LC gave it the number 613 (General and personal hygiene). See also the entry under "Holistic health" below.

Appropriate technology. HCL no.: 604.3   Date: Sept. 1977

HCLCB 30:1 cites two works for this topic: 1) The Center for Science in the Public Interest's *99 ways to a simple lifestyle* (LCCN 77-76831). LC assigned it DDC number 640 (Home economics and family living). 2) *Rainbook: resources for appropriate technology* (LCCN 76-49721). LC assigned it *DDC 18* number 301.3107 (Study and teaching of ecology). The *DDC 19* relocation for the topic would be 304.207.

Backpacking. HCL no.: 796.53   Date: July 1977

HCLCB 29:28. The *DDC 19* number 796.53 signifies "Beach activities." See pp. 103 and 105 for *DDC 19* and LC handling of backpacking.

Ballooning. HCL no.: 797.57   Date: July 1977

HCLCB 29:29. See pp. 104 and 105 for *DDC 19* and LC handling of this topic.

Barbershop quartets. HCL no.: 784.72   Date: Sept. 1978

HCLCB 36:13. One of Mr. Berman's strongest criticisms of *DDC 19* is its inaction on any proposed phoenix schedule for the 780 (Music) class. He is particularly concerned about its inhospitality to popular music. Six (10%) of the terms on this sample list fall into this category.

Battered women. HCL no.: 362.882   Date: July 1977

HCLCB 29:27 distinguished between this topic and "Wife battering," for which it used the *DDC 18* number 301.4275, its own subdivision of the *DDC 18* number 301.427 (Intrafamily relationships). *DDC 19* relocates "Intrafamily relationships" to 306.87, with no subdivisions. But does the distinction make subject integrity sense? See p. 98 for the *DDC 19* context of 362.882.

Belly dancing. HCL no.: 793.325   Date: April 1974

HCLCB 6/7:18. The Library of Congress has given the more general DDC number 793.3 (Dancing) to at least two books on this topic. They are: 1) Adela Vergara's *The new art of belly dancing* (LCCN 74-9756) and 2) Ozel's *The belly dancer in you* (LCCN 77-411).

Bermuda Triangle. HCL no.: 001.946   Date: Nov. 1977

HCLCB 31:17. The *DDC 18* number 001.94 (Mysteries; Reported phenomena not explained, not fully verified, e.g., unidentified flying objects, Loch Ness monster) was subdivided in *DC&*, v. 3, no. 4/5 (April 1974). See p. 95 for the *DDC 19* subdivisions.

Biorhythm theory. HCL no.: 133.34   Date: Nov. 1978

HCLCB 37:5 cited P. C. Bartel's *Biorhythm: discovering your ups and downs* (LCCN 77-17588) as evidence of the need for this class number. LC classed the book in 001.9 (Controversial knowledge). See p. 106 for further discussion.

Cinematic poetry. HCL no.: 791.4354   Date: Sept. 1974

HCLCB 8/10:47. *Poetry and film*, by Dylan Thomas and others (LCCN 72-87891) appears to have been the occasion for this local assignment. LC gave it the DDC number 791.4301 (Philosophy, theory, and aesthetics of motion pictures). However, LC has frequently used 791.435 (Kinds of motion pictures) to class works on experimental films.

Computer art. HCL no.: 744   Date: Sept. 1978

HCLCB 36:13. LC uses the synthetic DDC number 702.854, built from 702.8 (Techniques, etc. of fine and decorative arts) and *ss*-02854 (Electronic date processing).

Copy art. HCL no.: 778.1   Date: Nov. 1979

HCLCB 43:8. LC uses the broad DDC 760 (Graphic arts; Printmaking and prints) for *Electroworks* (LCCN 79-67569), to which it assigns the single subject heading "Copy art--Exhibitions." HCL makes use of an old "Photoduplication (Photocopying)" assignment, which was dropped in *DDC 18* in favor of 686.4.

Dance drill teams, chorus lines. HCL no.: 793.326   Date: Sept. 1977

HCLCB 30:2 cites F. J. Myers' *Guidelines for the formation and administration of dance drill teams* (National Cheerleaders Association). There is no LC cataloging available. See pp. 102 and 106 for *DDC 19* and LC handling of related topics.

Ethnic publishers. HCL no.: 070.596[?]   Date: March 1975

HCLCB 11/13:13 says the local number is 070.597. It was apparently mis-copied on the Berman list. See pp. 95 and 107 for *DDC 19* and LC handling of this topic.

Frisbee. HCL no.: 796.23   Date: July 1977

HCLCB 29:28. M. Poynter's *Frisbee fun* (LCCN 77-23328) and similar works are classed by LC in the broader 796.2. However, the number of "Frisbee" titles continues to grow. Perhaps literary warrant justifies an official DDC subdivision by now.

GI Movement. (Including coffeehouses, underground press, American Servicemen's Union, anti-war activities). HCL no.: 355.227 Date: Aug. 1975

HCLCB 16:3. LC is more likely to use 355.10973 (U.S. military life and postmilitary benefits) for works dealing with one or more of this cluster of topics. HCL's enthusiastic support of individual rights and alternative lifestyles may have influenced its classification decision here.

Genetic engineering. HCL no.: 575.3   Date: July 1977

HCLCB 29:27 cites LC's choice of the *DDC 18* number 301.423 (Family and social change) as a poor assignment for L. C. Karp's *Genetic engineering, threat or promise*? (LCCN 76-3497). In any case, the *DDC 19* phoenix schedule retires that number, giving its contents no specific relocation. Probably 303.4 (Social change) corresponds best. See p. 99 for further comment under the HCL number 575.3.

Governesses/wet-nurses/nannies. HCL no.: 649.2   Date: Jan. 1974

HCLCB 5:6 cites J. Gathorne-Hardy's *Unnatural history of the nanny* (LCCN 73-255). LC assigned 649.1 (Home care of children [Child rearing]) to that work. See p. 100 for further comment.

Government grants. HCL no.: 336.395   Date: May 1978

HCLCB 34:18 cites H. Hillman's *Art of winning government grants* (LCCN 77-155964) as the occasion for this local DDC assignment. LC's choice for the work was 658.1522 (Procurement of capital). See p. 97 for further discussion.

Greenhouses. HCL no.: 728.93   Date: May 1978

HCLCB 34:19 cites Fisher and Vanda's *Food and heat producing solar greenhouse: design, construction, operation* (LCCN 76-47993). LC classed it in 690.89 (Accessory domestic buildings: planning, analysis, engineering, design, etc.). The LC number was built from an "Add to" instruction based on the 725-728 span. The nice distinction which DDC tries to maintain between the two disciplines "architecture" and "construction" (at least on the level of "accessory domestic structures") is difficult for a common garden-variety classifier to grasp. Both *DDC 18* and *DDC 19* provide 728.69 for the architecture, and 690.69 for the design and construction, of solar houses. But there is no specific number provided for other types of solar building.

Hang gliding. HCL no.: 797.553   Date: June 1975

HCLCB 14/15:17 refers to R. Carrier's *Fly: the complete book of sky sailing* (LCCN 74-4221), for which LC used the broader DDC number 797.55 (Gliding and soaring).

High-fiber cooking. HCL no.: 641.5637   Date: Sept. 1977

HCLCB 30:2. *DDC 19* poses a conflict with this HCL assignment by introducing another, more general meaning for the same number, namely "Health food cookery." There is an inherent inconsistency in this DDC span, which tries to mix apples with oranges (see it on p. 100). LC has used the broader 641.563 for works on a high-fiber diet.

Holistic health. HCL no.: 610.42   Date: Nov. 1978

HCLCB 37:5 cites Bloomfield and Kory once again (Cf. "Alternative medicine").

Homesteading. HCL no.: 630.43   Date: Aug. 1975

HCLCB 16:14. The mid-1970s saw a revival of interest in "homesteading," but LC, fearing terminological confusion, still uses the term chiefly as a *see* reference, although it now does recognize "urban homesteading" (Cf. p. 99).

Hospices. HCL no.: 362.19604   Date: July 1978

HCLCB 36:13. See pp. 98 and 108 for a review of present classifying and terminological possibilities.

Ice skate dancing. HCL no.: 793.336   Date: April 1977

HCLCB 27:9. Dancing must be a preoccupation of the Hennepin County natives (Cf. "Belly dancing," "Dance drill teams, chorus lines," and "Roller skate dancing" in this list of 62 terms).

Jury reform. HCL no.: 347.0753   Date: Oct. 1975

HCLCB 17:13. HCL's example of the need for this assignment is M. Timothy's *Jury woman: the story of the trial of Angela Y. Davis-- written by a member of the jury* (LCCN 75-301731). LC classed this title in 345.73 (Criminal law in the United States). A hint of local editorializing seems implicit in the HCL treatment.

Kirlian photography. HCL no.: 778.38   Date: Sept. 1976

HCLCB 23/24:5 uses H. S. Dakin's *High-voltage photography* (LCCN 74-77233) as the occasion for adding this subdivision to the *DDC 18* schedule. *DDC 19* adds an "Inclusion" note to 778.3 (Special kinds of photography). See p. 101.

Mainstreaming (Education). HCL no.: 371.9046   Date: Sept. 1978

HCLCB 36:13. While *DDC 19* does not yet use the now-current term "mainstreaming," it supplies its own 371.9046 (Special education in special schools versus special education in general schools). See pp. 98 and 109 for context.

"New Age". HCL no.: 132   Date: May 1979

HCLCB 40:23 says to "Class here comprehensive or multifaceted works on such 'Aquarian' topics as consciousness, meditation, spiritual growth, holistic life-styles." Since there is nothing uniquely "Aquarian" about consciousness, meditation, or spiritual growth, we seem to be left with "holistic lifestyles," which HCL addresses in part under "Holistic health" above. In preempting the unassigned DDC number 132 for comprehensive works, HCL evidently hopes to consolidate such materials as are not strictly medicine- or health-related.

Oral history. HCL no.: 907.204   Date: Mar. 1978

HCLCB 33:28-29. LC classes the HCL example, C. Davis' *Oral history: from tape to type* (LCCN 77-4403), in 907 (Study and teaching of general history). In view of current interest, DDC might well consider a more specific class number, or at least an "Inclusion" note.

Orienteering. HCL no.: 796.55   Date: Apr. 1977

HCLCB 27:9. LC assigns 796.42 (Track and field athletics) to most publications with "orienteering" in their titles. DDC should consider a more specific class number or an "Inclusion" note.

Packhorse camping. HCL no.: 796.546   Date: Sept. 1977

HCLCB 30:3. Again, DDC should consider a more specific class number or an "Inclusion" note.

Paddle tennis. HCL no.: 796.344   Date: Mar. 1979

HCLCB 39:33. HCL was evidently not satisfied with the long-standing DDC (since edition 17) index *see* reference to "Racket games" and the "Inclusion" note at 796.34.

Paddleball. HCL no.: 796.348   Date: Mar. 1979

HCLCB 30:3. DDC is less explicit for this game. One must assume that it belongs in 796.34. No index entry or "Inclusion" note is given.

Parent education. HCL no.: 649.107   Date: July 1977

HCLCB 29:27. The HCL number for this topic is synthetic, and built in a quite straightforward manner by the adding of a standard subdivision from Table 1.

Planned unit development. HCL no.: 333.382   Date: Nov. 1977

HCLCB 31:17 says to "Class here comprehensive works on community associations and condominiums." See pp. 97 and 109 for further comment on this assignment.

Police malpractice. HCL no.: 363.25   Date: Jan. 1974

HCLCB 5:6 cites M. J. Arlen's *American verdict* (LCCN 73-79640) as its example of the need for this class concept. Unfortunately, as in the "Jury reform" treatment above, the example looks dangerously like a case of labeling. Arlen's book is "about" a particular lawyer and a particular social group. It may contain a charge against police practices, but it is not a study of police malpractice in general. LC gave the same title the DDC number 345.7302523 (Law of murder in the United States).

Popular culture. HCL no.: 301.17   Date: Jan. 1978

HCLCB 32:13. The proper relationship of socioeconomic and cultural history to political history has never been solved to any classifier's satisfaction. There is no lighthouse. The good ship Subject Integrity, whichever way it turns, hits a hard rock of practical inconsistency. *DDC 19* is still tinkering with its hierarchies. The new phoenix schedules transfer "Culture" and "Cultural anthropology" from 301.2 to 306. At the same time, "Philosophy and theory of history" moves from 901.9 to 909 (General world history). See also the new instruction under 910 to "Class works, other than accounts of travel, limited to civilization in general in 909."

Protest songs. HCL no.: 784.67   Date: May 1976

HCLCB 21:10. The general unhappiness of classifiers over the unrevised 780 (Music) schedule was mentioned under "Barbershop quartets" above. See further review of HCL's problems with the 780's on pp. 101-102.

Psychic archaeology. HCL no.: 133.87   Date: Sept. 1978

HCLCB 45:25. At least two books have been published on this topic. LC gave both the subject heading "Parapsychology and archaeology," but it was less consistent with its DDC assignments. The earlier title, J. Goodman's *Psychic archaeology: time machine to the past* (LCCN 76-51638), is classed in 001.9 (Controversial knowledge). The second, S. A. Schwartz's *The secret vaults of time: psychic archaeology and the quest for man's beginnings* (LCCN 77-71742) went to 133.80926 (Case histories in psychic phenomena). A DDC index *see* reference or an "Inclusion" note might help.

Pyramid energy. HCL no.: 118.2   Date: Apr. 1977

HCLCB 27:7. LC classes G. P. Flanagan's *Pyramid power* (LCCN 73-86022) and *Beyond pyramid power* (LCCN 75-32705) in 133 (Parapsychology and occultism). In choosing to start from 118 (Force and energy), HCL blurs the traditional distinction between 110 (Metaphysics; Speculative philosophy) and 130 (Paranormal phenomena and arts). DDC and LC may be old-fashioned, but they still have plenty of literary warrant.

Race walking. HCL no.: 796.427   Date: Mar. 1975

HCLCB 11/12/13:18. Who but a professional classifier — or a footsore library patron — could guess that the aspects of walking are distributed among so many disciplines? LC distinguishes walking for physical fitness in 613.71 (Exercise and sports activities), from walking as a pastime in 796.51, under 796.5 (Outdoor life). Guidebooks for walking tours generally fall somewhere in the 910's (Travel), depending on the region. "Race walking" is classed in 796.42 (Track and field athletics), of which the above HCL number is a proposed subdivision.

Rape victims. HCL no.: 362.883   Date: Sept. 1977

HCLCB 30:1 follows the frequent HCL characteristic of classing more specifically than the DDC schedules warrant. LC puts E. Hilberman's *Rape victim* (LCCN 76-5627) in the more general 362.88 (Victims of crimes). See also pp. 98 and 110 for further context.

Rock opera. HCL no.: 782.2   Date: Apr. 1974

HCLCB 6/7:18. Until more literature and discography are devoted exclusively to rock opera, there is little need for a special subdivision of DDC's 782.1 (Opera). This observation has nothing to do with basic criticisms of the 780 class. See p. 110 for more insight on present provisions for rock music.

Roller skate dancing. HCL no.: 793.336   Date: April 1977

HCLCB 27:9. See the discussion of "Ice skate dancing" above.

Rope skipping. HCL no.: 796.45   Date: Dec. 1976

HCLCB 25:16. LC has in the past decade classified some half-dozen books on rope skipping for physical fitness. All but one went to 796.2 (Active games requiring equipment). The exception was Curtis Mitchell's *The perfect exercise: the hop, skip, and jump way to health* (LCCN 75-38844), which it placed in 613.71.

Runaway services. HCL no.: 362.75   Date: Apr. 1977

HCLCB 27:8. Mr. Berman says that DDC "subsumes this topic under 'Maladjusted young people,' 362.74." In fact, *DDC 18* made no provision for runaways in either index or schedule. Only in *DDC 19* does an index entry and an "inclusion" note appear. See pp. 98 and 111.

Senior power. HCL no.: 301.43532   Date: Oct. 1975

HCLCB 17:13. HCL cites P. Kleyman's *Senior power: growing old rebelliously* (LCCN 74-7286), which LC assigned to 301.435097. Both the LC and the HCL assignments are relocated in *DDC 19* to 305.26. See pp. 96 and 111 for context.

Singing commercials. HCL no.: 784.69   Date: July 1977

HCLCB 29:28. Once again, dissatisfaction with the 780 (Music) schedule surfaces. The work HCL cited is a score: P. and C. Norback's *Great songs of Madison Avenue* (LCCN 75-37374). LC does not suggest DDC numbers for music and sound recordings. See pp. 102 and 111 for further context.

Skateboarding. HCL no.: 796.22   Date: Sept. 1976

HCLCB 23/24:6. Reference to pp. 103 and 111 will show a rare case of DDC's indexing a term which does not appear in the schedule even as an "Inclusion" note (at 796.21).

Small presses. HCL no.: 070.598   Date: June 1975

HCLCB 14/15:16. HCL makes several expansion assignments under DDC's 070.59 (Kinds of publishers). See pp. 95 and 111 for context.

Space colonies. HCL no.: 629.447   Date: Sept. 1977

HCLCB 30:2. LC makes do with DDC's 629.445 (Space laboratories) for such works as D. C. Knight's *Colonies in orbit* (LCCN 76-56086). Whether every space exploration term needs its own subdivision is questionable, but an "Inclusion" note would help.

Sports betting. HCL no.: 796.04   Date: Oct. 1975

HCLCB 17:14. Sports betting is not necessarily, nor even invariably, either an "athletic" or an "outdoor" event, as the disciplinary 796 location implies. But there is a DDC precedent under "Horse racing," where the subdivision "betting" has been a DDC feature since Edition 16 (it was relocated from 798.48 to 798.401 in Edition 17). At any rate, DDC should make some twentieth-century accommodation to this complex topic.

Style manuals (Journalism/publishing). HCL no.: 070.0202   Date: July 1978

HCLCB 35:16 cites the *Washington post deskbook on style* (LCCN 77-22958), to which LC assigned the DDC number 651.7402 (Style manuals in communication; Creation and transmission of records). Two similar works for which LC used the same number are Ross Turner's *U.S. news & world report stylebook for writers and editors* (LCCN 77-21337), and *The Associated Press stylebook and libel manual* (LCCN 77-7007).

Volunteer workers/volunteerism. HCL no.: 331.53   Date: Sept. 1976

HCLCB 23/24:5. Both DDC and LC tend to scatter works on this topic to the various disciplines or activities where the voluntary work is done. There is no doubt good literary warrant for this approach, although the new *DDC 19* number 361.37 might serve as a gathering point for more general works on voluntarism.

War games. HCL no.: 794.4   Date: April 1974

HCLCB 6/7:10, 18. The *DDC 19* index introduces a new entry: "War games--recreation 793.9," although nothing at that location in the schedule says so. Both the DDC and HCL assignments obviously cover only sophisticated board games on the market today. Subject integrity would require professional military gaming to fall under 355.4 (Military tactics). LCSH makes it look as if the term "war games" covers *only* this latter meaning (Cf. p. 112).

Women and labor unions. HCL no.: 331.882   Date: Mar. 1975

HCLCB 11/12/13:17. There is now a sizeable literature in this field, enough to warrant a dedicated official DDC number, but neither DDC nor LC has yet directly recognized it. See pp. 96 and 112 for context.

Women's music. HCL no.: 780.46   Date: Sept. 1976

HCLCB 23/24:5 says to "class songs for women in 784.65" (Cf. "Women's songs" below). The local assignment 780.46 locates the topic under 780.4 (Special topics of general applicability).

Women's publishers. HCL no.: 070.596   Date: March 1975

HCLCB 11/12/13:13. This is the third local subdivision under 070.59 (Kinds of publishers) on the HCL sample list. See p. 95 for context.

Women's songs. HCL no.: 784.65   Date: May 1976

HCLCB 21:10. This is the last of the six local adjustments to the 780 (Music) schedule included on the Berman list. See discussions of the others above.

Wood heating. HCL no.: 697.041   Date: Aug. 1975

HCLCB 16:3. LC still uses the broader 697.04 (Heating with specific sources of energy) for the half-dozen or so recent books on this topic. Since DDC subdivides that broad number into special groupings for coal, gas, oil, and electric heating, it is probably time to consider making the same provision for wood, solar, and even possibly nuclear heat sources. See the discussion under "Greenhouses" above, as well as p. 100 for context.

Of the 62 unauthorized DDC numbers on Berman's sample list, the 6 in music clearly point to a need for schedule updating. Many users of the classification agree, but hesitate to patch in local numbers. The next most frequent causes for Berman criticism are recent social and cultural preoccupations. For instance, seven terms on his list directly reflect current interest in women's liberation. Four name popular types of dancing. Two suggest modern scepticism of established institutions for law and order.

Other HCL terms, e.g., Oral history, Popular culture, and Senior Power, indicate that DDC is deliberate in providing for cultural change, in spite of its phoenix sociology schedule and its "civilization" revisions at 909-910.[7] Lag is still greater for fringe topics such as Biorhythm theory, GI Movement, Holistic health, New Age, Psychic archaeology, Pyramid energy, and the like, although it may be more terminological than classificatory. *DDC 19* index entries for Skateboarding and War games suggest that new concepts are sometimes indexed before they appear in the schedule. The index thus is a first, experimental threshold for novel terminology. Inclusion notes, with corresponding index entries or *see* references, form the second line of defense against a rash of new numbers, many of which may have but passing literary warrant.

Other topics such as Computer art, Hang gliding, Mainstreaming, Orienteering, Rope skipping, and Sports betting may be ready for their own class numbers. Let us next examine the suggested HCL numbers in their *DDC 19* context, remembering that they were originally used with *DDC 18*. Schedule passages are selectively copied, omitting extraneous material.

SAMPLE HCL NUMBERS IN DDC 19 CONTEXT

001.9	Controversial knowledge
.93	Curiosities: Well established phenomena not scientifically explained, e.g. frozen mammals in Siberia, fire walking
.94	Mysteries: Reported phenomena not explained, not fully verified
.942	Unidentified flying objects (UFO's, Flying saucers)
.944	Monsters and related phenomena; Examples: Loch Ness monster, Abominable snowman
.946	*Bermuda Triangle* (HCL) [LC uses the broader 001.94]
.95	Deceptions and hoaxes; Example: Piltdown man
.96	Errors, delusions, superstitions

070	Journalism, publishing, newspapers
.01-.08	Standard subdivisions of newspapers and journalism
.0202	*Style manuals (Journalism/publishing)* (HCL) [This number can be synthetically constructed with Table 1. LC uses 651.7402 (Style manuals for written communication).]
.41	Editing
.412	Editorial policy
.415	Editorial mechanics; Copyreading, headlines, style
.5	Publishing
.59	Kinds of publishers
.592	Commercial
.593	Private
.594	Institutional; Examples: university, academic, society, church
.595	Governmental and intergovernmental
.596	*Women's publishers* (HCL) [DDC 18-19 show 070.48347 (Journalism for the special group Women).]
.597	*Ethnic publishers* (HCL) [*DDC 18-19* show 070.484 (Journalism for foreign-language and nondominant racial, ethnic, national groups).]
.598	*Small presses* (HCL) [DDC has no unique number for this topic]

---

110   Metaphysics (Speculative philosophy)
118   Force and energy
  .2   *Pyramid energy* (HCL) [LC assigned 133 (Parapsychology and occultism) to this topic]

130   Paranormal phenomena and arts
131   Parapsychological and occult techniques for achievement of well-being, happiness, success; Class New Thought in 289.98
[132]   [Unassigned; Most recently used in *DDC 16*]
132   *"New Age"* (HCL) [Cf. the Class note under 131 above]
133   Parapsychology and occultism Including frauds in occultism
  .3   Divinatory arts
  .32   Fortunetelling and radiesthesia
  .33   Symbolic divination
  .34   *Biorhythm theory* (HCL) [LC uses 001.9 or 574.1, depending on the "personal" or the scientific application of the term]
  .8   Psychic phenomena
  .82   Telepathy
  .84   Clairvoyance
  .85   Clairaudience
  .86   Precognition
  .87   *Psychic archaeology* (HCL)
  .88   Psychokinesis

301   Sociology
  .17   *Popular culture* (HCL)
  [.21]   Folkways Class in 390
  [.418]   Manuals of sexual technique Class in 613.96
  [.4272]   Guides to harmonious family relationships Class in 646.78
  .43532   *Senior Power* (HCL)
  .7   Kinds of societies

331   Labor economics
  .5   Special categories of workers
  .51   Prisoners and ex-offenders Including political and war prisoners
  .52   Veterans
  .53   *Volunteer workers/volunteerism* (HCL)
  .54   Economically disadvantaged workers
  .55   Apprentices Class training of apprentices in 331.25922
  .59   Workers suffering physical and mental handicaps
  .8   Labor unions (Trade unions) and collective bargaining
  .88   Labor unions (Trade unions)
  .881   In specific industries and occupations
  .882   *Women and labor unions* (HCL) [LC uses 331.88 for this topic]
  .883   Kinds of unions
  .886   Revolutionary unions
  .889   Union security arrangements

333   Land economics
  .3   Individual (Private) ownership
  .33   Transfer of possession and right to use
  .338   Buildings and other fixtures; Including apartments, condominiums, mobile homes
  .38   Subdivision and development
  .382   *Planned unit development* (HCL) [Neither 333.338 nor 643.2 (Special kinds of housing: Mobile homes, vacation homes, modular and prefabricated houses, condominiums, apartments) was available until *DDC 19*]

---

336   Public finance
  .3   Public securities, debt, expenditure
  .31   Public securities
  .32   Short term securities
  .34   Public borrowing and public debt
  .36   Debt management
  .39   Expenditure: Character, principles, classification, justification
  .395   *Government grants* (HCL) [*DDC 19* adds "Grants" under 001.44 (Support of and incentives for research) but indexes only 336.185 and 338.922 (Subsidies and grants under Government programs and policies for economic development and growth).]

---

347   Civil procedure and courts
  .07   Trials
  .075   Trial (Courtroom procedure)
  .0752   Juries and their selection
  .0753   *Jury reform* (HCL)
  .0758   Instructions to juries

---

355   Military art and science
  .1   Military life and postmilitary benefits
  .2   Military resources
  .22   Human resources
  .223   Procurement
  .224   Conscientious objectors
  .225   Universal training and service
  .227   *GI Movement (Including coffeehouses, underground press, American Servicemen's Union, anti-war activities)* (HCL)
  [.229]   Womanpower Number discontinued; class in 355.22

---

362   Social welfare problems and services
  .1   Physical illness
  .19   Services to specific classes of patients; Including dying and terminal patients, indigent patients
  .196-.198   To those suffering from specific illnesses or requiring specific kinds of care; Add to base number 362.19 the numbers following 61 in 616-618 ...
  .19604   *Hospices* (HCL) [This number is routinely synthetic. LC formerly used 362.616, but it is not available in *DDC 19*.]
  .7   Problems of and services to young people
  .74   Maladjusted young people; Including predelinquents [*formerly* 364.35] runaways
  .75   *Runaway services* (HCL) [*DDC 19* introduced the Includes note to 362.74]
  .8   Problems of and services to other groups
  .82   Families Class here families with specific problems [*formerly* with the specific subject], e.g. those with chronically ill members, those with one parent
  .83   Women
  .88   Victims of crimes
  .882   *Battered women* (HCL) [HCL used the now-vacant 301.427 for Wife battering; LC uses 362.82 for Abused wives.]
  .883   *Rape victims* (HCL) [*DDC 19* classes Rape in 364.1532]

363   Other social problems and services
  .1   Public safety programs
  .2   Police services
  .22   Personnel
  .23   Police functions
  .24   Auxiliary services
  .25   Detection of crime (Criminal investigation)
  .25   *Police malpractice* (HCL)
  .28   Services of special kinds of security and law enforcement agencies

---

371   Generalities of education
  .9   Special education
  .904   Special topics of general applicability
  .9042   Administration
  .9043   Teaching methods; Including use of behavior modification
  .9044   Special subjects
  .9045   Facilities
  .9046   Special education in special schools versus special education in general schools
  .9046   *Mainstreaming (Education)* (HCL) [LC has used 371.9 for works on this topic; the official meaning of 371.9046 is new in *DDC 19*]

---

575   Organic evolution and genetics
  .1   Genetics; Heredity and variation
  .11   Laws of genetics; Examples: Laws of Weismann, Mendel, Galton
  .12   Genetic makeup; Including genotypes, phenotypes
  .13   Factors affecting heredity and variation
  .15   Population genetics
  .2   Variation
  [.21]   Physiological genetics Class in 574.87322
  .22   Environmental factors in heredity and variation
  .28   Variations; Including hybrids
  .29   Abrupt deviations
  .3   *Genetic engineering (Including cloning and sex-selection)* (HCL)
        [Under 174.2 (Ethics of the medical profession) *DDC 19* offers
        174.25 (Innovative procedures; Examples: organ transplants,
        genetic engineering).]

---

604   General technologies
  .2   Technical drawing
  .3   *Appropriate technology* (HCL)
  .6   Waste technology
  .7   Hazardous materials technology

---

610   Medical sciences; Medicine
  .28   Techniques, procedures, apparatus, equipment, materials
  .42   *Alternative medicine; Holistic health* (HCL)
  .6   Organizations, management, professions

629.4   Astronautics
  .41   Space flight: Principles and problems
  .43   Unmanned flight
  .44   Auxiliary spacecraft: Operations and engineering
  .441   Space shuttles
  .442   Space stations
  .445   Space laboratories
  .447   *Space colonies* (HCL) [LC has used 629.442, 629.445, and
        629.477 for this topic.]
  .45   Manned flight
  .46   Engineering of unmanned spacecraft
  .47   Astronautical engineering

630   Agriculture and related technologies
  .2   Miscellany and scientific principles
  .43   *Homesteading* (HCL) [The best *DDC 19* location seems to be 306.3
        (Economic institutions; Examples: systems of labor, e.g. slavery;
        serfdom; systems of land tenure; property systems).]
  .7   Study and teaching

---

641   Food and drink
    .5   Cookery
    .56   For special situations
    .561   For one or two persons
    .562   For persons of specific ages
    .563   For health, appearance, personal reasons
    .5631   For sick persons
    .5632   Cookery with specified vitamin and mineral content
    .5634   High-calorie cookery
    .5635   Low-calorie cookery
    .5636   Vegetarian cookery
    .5637   Health-food cookery
    .5637   *High-fiber cooking* (HCL) [LC has used 641.563]
    .5638   Protein, fat, carbohydrate cookery

---

649   Child rearing and home care of sick and infirm
    .1   Home care of children (Child rearing)
    .102   Miscellany
    .1024   Works for specific types of users
    .10242   Works for expectant parents
    .10243   Works for single parents
    .10245   Works for older children in family
    .10248   Works for baby-sitters
    .107   *Parent education* (HCL) [LC has used 649.1. Table 1 permits
               the synthetic 649.107]
    .2   *Governesses/wet-nurses/nannies* (HCL) [DDC has provided
               649.10248 since Edition 17. LC classes Governesses in 371.1 (Teach-
               ing and teaching personnel).]

---

697   Heating, ventilating, air-conditioning engineering
    .04   Heating with specific sources of energy; Class here specific fuels
    .041   *Wood heating* (HCL) [LC uses 697.04]
    .042   Coal and coke heating
    .043   Gas heating
    .044   Oil heating
    .045   Electric heating

---

728   Residential buildings (Domestic architecture)
    .9   Accessory domestic structures; Including gatehouses, garages, con-
            servatories, saunas, swimming pools, bathhouses, patios
    .92   Farm buildings other than human residences
    .922   Barns
    .93   *Greenhouses* (HCL)

741	Drawing and drawings
742	Perspective
743	Drawing and drawings by subject
[744]	[Unassigned]
744	*Computer art* (HCL) [The *DDC 19* number 702.872 (Reproductions and copies) might be used.]
745	Decorative and minor arts
746	Textile arts and handicrafts
747	Interior decoration
748	Glass
749	Furniture and accessories

778	Specific fields and kinds of photography
.1	*Copy art* (HCL) [The *DDC 19* number 702.872 might serve; Cf. Computer art.]
.2	Photographic projection; Including filmstrips, filmslides
.3	Special kinds of photography; Including high-frequency photopsychography, high-voltage photography
.31	Photomicrography
.32	Photography in terms of focus
.34	Infrared photography
.35	Aerial and space photography
.36	Panoramic photography
.37	High-speed photography
.38	*Kirlian photography* (HCL) [LC uses 778.3]
.4	Stereoscopic photography and projection
.5	Motion-picture and television photography
.6	Color photography and photography of colors
.7	Photography under specific conditions
.8	Special effects and trick photography
.9	Photography of specific subjects

780	Music
.4	Special topics of general applicability
.42	Popular music
.43	Art ("Classical") music
.46	*Women's music* (HCL) [The only *DDC 19* possibility seems to be 780.4.]

782	Dramatic music and production of musical drama
.1	Opera
.2	*Rock opera* (HCL) [The only *DDC 19* choice seems to be 782.1]
.8	Theater music
.9	Music for ballets, masques, pageants, pantomimes

784   Voice and vocal music
.6   Songs for specific groups and on specific subjects
.61   For home and community
.62   For students and children
.65   *Women's songs* (HCL) [The only *DDC 19* choice seems to be 784.6]
.66   For societies and service clubs
.67   *Protest songs* (HCL) [Add instructions could produce synthetic 784.6832244 or 784.6836123]
.68   On specific subjects (Topical songs) Add 001-999 to base number.
.69   *Singing commercials* (HCL)
.7   Other kinds of songs
.71   National airs, songs, hymns
.72   *Barbershop quartets* (HCL)
.75   Songs of ethnic and cultural groups in the U.S. and Canada
.76   Songs of ethnic and cultural groups other than the U.S. and Canada
.8   Collections of vocal music
.84   Quartets
.9   The voice
.96   Vocal ensemble; Class here community singing, singing in the home

---

791.4   Motion pictures, radio, television
.43   Motion pictures; Class films themselves on a specific subject with the subject, e.g. flower gardening 635.9; photography aspects in 778.53
.433   Types of presentation; Examples: Home and amateur films, cartoon films
.435   Kinds of motion pictures
.4352   Dramatic films (Photoplays); Class texts of plays in 800
.4353   Educational and documentary films; Including newsreels
.4354   *Cinematic poetry* (HCL)
.44   Radio
.45   Television

---

793   Indoor games and amusements
.3   Dancing
.31   Folk and national dances
.32   Theatrical dancing; Including artistic, classical, interpretive
.324   Tap and clog dancing
.325   *Belly dancing* (HCL) [LC uses 793.3]
.326   *Dance drill teams, chorus lines* (HCL) [LC puts Baton twirling in 785.0671 (Marching band: Wind, brass, military, school; drum and bugle corps).]
.33   Ballroom dancing (Round dances)
.336   *Ice skate dancing; Roller skate dancing* (HCL) [LC uses 796.91 (Ice skating) for works on figure skating.]
.34   Square dancing
.35   Dances with accessory features; Examples: sword-dance, cotillions....
.38   Balls; Class Ballroom dancing in 793.33

---

794   Indoor games of skill
.1   Chess
.2   Other board games
.3   Darts
.4   *War games* (HCL)
.6   Bowling
.7   Ball games

---

796   Athletic and outdoor sports and games
.01   Philosophy and theory
.019   Activities and programs for specific classes of people
.04   *Sports betting* (HCL)
.06   Organizations and management
.2   Active games requiring equipment
.22   *Skateboarding* (HCL) [*DDC 19* assigns Skateboarding to 796.21]
.23   *Frisbee* (HCL) [LC uses 796.2]
.24   Pitching games; Examples: quoits, horseshoes
.3   Ball games
.34   Racket games Including court tennis, paddle tennis
.342   Tennis (Lawn tennis)
.343   Rackets and squash
.344   *Paddle tennis* (HCL) [LC uses 796.346]
.345   Badminton
.346   Table tennis
.347   Lacrosse
.348   *Paddleball* (HCL) [LC uses 796.34]
.35   Ball driven by club, mallet, bat
.4   Athletic exercises and gymnastics
.41   Calisthenics
.42   Track and field athletics
.426   Running, sprinting, hurdling
.427   *Race walking* (HCL) [LC uses 796.426]
.43   Jumping, vaulting, throwing
.44   Horizontal and parallel bars
.45   *Rope skipping* (HCL) [LC uses 796.2]
.46   Trapeze work, rope climbing, wire walking
.47   Acrobatics, tumbling, trampolining, contortion
.48   Olympic games
.5   Outdoor life
.51   Walking; Class here Backpacking
.52   Walking and exploring in various specific kinds of terrain
.53   Beach activities. For aquatic sports, see 797.1-797.2
.53   *Backpacking* (HCL) [*DDC 19* uses 796.51; LC has used 796.5]
.54   Camping
.542   Kinds of camps
.545   Activities; Examples: woodcraft, campfires, games
.546   *Packhorse camping* (HCL) [LC uses 796.51]
.55   *Orienteering* (HCL) [LC uses 796.42; *DDC 19* has 152.1882 (Orientational perceptions).]
.56   Dude ranching and farming

---

797 Aquatic and air sports
 .5 Air sports
 .52 Racing
 .53 Flying for pleasure
 .54 Stunt flying
 .55 Gliding and soaring
 .553 *Hang gliding* (HCL) [LC uses 797.55]
 .56 Parachuting (Skydiving)
 .57 *Ballooning* (HCL) [LC uses 629.1309 for Balloon ascensions]

---

907 Study and teaching of general history
 .2 Historiography; Class writing of history in 808.0669
 .202 Historians and historiographers
 .204 *Oral history* (HCL) [LC uses 907.2]

For the 62 "new" topics which Berman cites, there are duplicate unauthorized DDC assignments in two cases (610.42 for both Alternative medicine and Holistic health, and 793.336 for both Ice skate dancing and Roller skate dancing). There are, then, 60 HCL versions of DDC numbers in the sample. They are distributed in the DDC main classes as follows:

DDC class	Sample HCL numbers
000	5
100	4
300	14
500	1
600	8
700	27
	6 in the 780's
	17 in the 790's
900	1

Examined from another point of view we find that:

One number (301.43532) no longer has subject integrity, because of a *DDC 19* phoenix change.

Two numbers (132 and 744) preempt unassigned DDC section numbers.

Three numbers (070.0202, 362,19604, and 649.107) coincide with *DDC 18-19* number-building instructions.

Three numbers (362.75 and 796.53 explicitly; 778.38 implicitly) are covered by Inclusion or Class here notes at nearby DDC locations.

Four numbers (363.25, 371.9046, 641.5637, and 796.53) conflict with, or partially duplicate, authentic *DDC 19* assignments.

Seven numbers (070.0202, 301.43532, 347.0753, 362.19604, 371.9046, 641.5637, and 791.4354) require four or five places beyond the decimal point.

Ten numbers (118.2, 301.17, 333.382, 336.395, 362.882-362.883, 610.42, 630.43, 793.336, and 797.553) extend the notation to new decimal subdivisions.

Thirty-eight numbers introduce non-DDC assignments (usually with one or two decimals) into existing, but only partially filled subdivisions spans. One of these (784.67) short-circuits two possibilities for lengthy number synthesis using an Add instruction under 784.68.

The sample, while representative of only one large public library system's classification priorities, seems to reflect limited current literary warrant (i.e., topics with which material has recently become somewhat more identified) rather than new developments in intellectual activity and knowledge. Most of these topics can be reasonably well accommodated in the *DDC 19* schedules. However, terminological hurdles are more troublesome. Let us next compare HCL access terms with those used in *DDC 19* and the *Library of Congress Subject Headings* (LCSH), 9th edition. When LCSH adds a unique LC class number to its entry, it will be included in parentheses.

HCL, DDC 19, AND LCSH TERMINOLOGY COMPARED

Alternative medicine. HCL no.: 610.42   Date: Nov. 1978

> *DDC 19*: [Not found]
> LCSH: [Not found]

Appropriate technology. HCL no.: 604.3   Date: Sept. 1977

> *DDC 19*: [Not found]
> LCSH: [Not found]

Backpacking. HCL no.: 796.53   Date: July 1977

> *DDC 19*: Backpacking *see* Walking (sports)
> LCSH: Backpacking (GV199.6)

Ballooning. HCL no.: 797.57   Date: July 1977

> *DDC 19*: Balloons--aircraft *see* Lighter-than-air aircraft
>   [But this entry does not lead to 797.5
>   (Air sports).]
> LCSH: Balloon ascensions (TL620)
>   Balloon racing (GV763)

Barbershop quartets. HCL no.: 784.72   Date: Sept. 1978

> *DDC 19*: Quartets--songs ...
>   Vocal ensemble--music   784.96
> LCSH: Barbershop quartets (M1580.4; M1581.4;
>   M1594; M1604)

Battered women. HCL no.: 362.882   Date: July 1977

> *DDC 19*: Assault & battery ...
> > Protection *see spec. subj. e.g.* Young people--
> > soc. services
> > Women ...
> LCSH: Battered wives *see* Abused wives
> > Women--Crimes against (HV6250.4.W65)

Belly dancing. HCL no.: 793.325   Date: Apr. 1974

> *DDC 19*: [Not found]
> LCSH: Belly dance
> > Belly dance music

Bermuda Triangle. HCL no. 001.946   Date: Nov. 1977

> *DDC 19*: [Not found]
> LCSH: [Proper name, not included]

Biorhythm theory. HCL no.: 133.34   Date: Nov. 1978

> *DDC 19*: Biological rhythms ...
> LCSH: Biorhythms *see* Biological rhythms

Cinematic poetry. HCL no.: 791.4354   Date: Sept. 1974

> *DDC 19*: [Not found]
> LCSH: Cinema *see* Moving-pictures
> > Moving-pictures and poetry *see* Moving-pictures
> > and literature

Computer art. HCL no.: 744   Date: Sept. 1978

> *DDC 19*: [Not found; but see "Computer games"]
> LCSH: Computer art (N7433.8)

Copy art. HCL no.: 778.1   Date: Nov. 1979

> *DDC 19*: [Not found]
> LCSH: Copy art (NE3000)

Dance drill teams, chorus lines. HCL no.: 793.326   Date: Sept. 1977

> *DDC 19*: Cheerleading [*DC&*, v. 4, no. 1 (June 1980): 26]
> LCSH: Baton twirling   (MT733.6)
> > Cheerleading   (LB3635)
> > Drill (not military)   (GV1797)
> > Drum majorettes   (GV1797)
> > Drum majors   (MT733.5)
> > Flag-waving (Exercise) (GV488)
> > Marching bands   (MT733.4)
> > Musico-callisthenics   (Callisthenics,
> > > GV463-4;
> > > Music, M1993)

Ethnic publishers. HCL no.: 070.597   Date: Mar. 1975

> *DDC 19*: Ethnic groups ...
> LCSH: Ethnic press

Frisbee. HCL no.: 796.23   Date: July 1977

> *DDC 19*: [Not found; "Flying disks" has a different
>   meaning]
> LCSH: Frisbee (Registered trademark) *see* Flying discs
>   (Game)

GI Movement. (Including coffeehouses, ...) HCL no.: 355.227
Date: Aug. 1975

> *DDC 19*: Military life ...
>   Social customs--armed forces   355.12
> LCSH: Coffee-houses (NA7855; TX901-910)
>   Military life *see* Soldiers
>   Peace ... *subdivision* Peace *and* Protest move-
>   ments under *names of wars*

Genetic engineering. (Including cloning ...) HCL no.: 575.3
Date: July 1977

> *DDC 19*: Genetic engineering *see* Eugenics
> LCSH: Cloning (QH442.2)
>   Genetic engineering
>   Sex predetermination *see* Sex--Cause and
>   determination

Governesses/wet-nurses/nannies. HCL no.: 649.2   Date: Jan. 1974

> *DDC 19*: Baby sitters' handbooks--home econ. 649.10248
>   Tutoring *see* Individualized instruction
> LCSH: Governesses (LC41)

Government grants. HCL no.: 336.395   Date: May 1978

> *DDC 19*: Grants ...
> LCSH: Federal aid to ...
>   Grants-in-aid

Greenhouses. HCL no.: 728.93   Date: May 1978

> *DDC 19*: Agricultural structures ...
>   Greenhouses ...
>   Solar houses ...
> LCSH: Greenhouses (SB415-416)
>   Solar greenhouses (SB415-416.3)

Hang gliding. HCL no.: 797.553   Date: June 1975

> *DDC 19*: Gliding ...
> LCSH: Hang gliding

High-fiber cooking. HCL no.: 641.5637   Date: Sept. 1977

    DDC 19: Fiber--crops--agriculture   633.5
            Health foods--cookery   641.5637
    LCSH: Food--Fiber content
            High-fiber diet--Recipes

Holistic health. HCL no.: 610.42   Date: Nov. 1978

    DDC 19: Holistic psychologies   150.19332
    LCSH: Holism (B818)

Homesteading. HCL no.: 630.43   Date: Aug. 1975

    DDC 19: [Not found]
    LCSH: Homesteading *see* Agriculture--Handbooks,
                      manuals, etc.
                 Frontier and pioneer life
                 Homestead law
          Homesteading, Urban *see* Urban homesteading

Hospices. HCL no.: 362.19604   Date: July 1978

    DDC 19: Dying patients--health services   362.19
            Medical services--organizations ...
            Terminal care--diseases   616.029
            Terminal patients--health services   362.19
    LCSH: Hospices (Terminal care) *see* Terminal care
               facilities

Ice skate dancing. HCL no.: 793.336   Date: Apr. 1977

    DDC 19: Dancing ...
            Ice skating--sports--recreation   796.9
    LCSH: Dancing (GV1580-1799)
            Figure skating *see* Skating
            Ice skating *see* Skating

Jury reform. HCL no.: 347.0753   Date: Oct. 1975

    DDC 19: Juries--law ...
            Reform movements--spec. problems &
               groups   362-363
    LCSH: Juries see Jury

Kirlian photography. HCL no.: 778.38   Date: Sept. 1976

    DDC 19: High-frequency photopsychography--
              technique   778.3
            High-voltage photography--technique   778.3
    LCSH: Kirlian photography (TR760)

Mainstreaming (Education). HCL no.: 371.9046   Date: Sept. 1978

    DDC 19: Education--spec. subj.--elementary   372.3-.8
                Exceptional children--education   371.9
                Special education   371.9
    LCSH: Mainstreaming in education

"New Age." HCL no.: 132   Date: May 1979

    DDC 19: [Not found]
    LCSH: [Not found]

Oral history. HCL no.: 907.204   Date: Mar. 1978

    DDC 19: History ...
    LCSH: Oral history

Orienteering. HCL no.: 796.55   Date: Apr. 1977

    DDC 19: Orientational perceptions--psych.   152.1882
    LCSH: Orienteering *see* Orientation

Packhorse camping. HCL no.: 796.546   Date: Sept. 1977

    DDC 19: Camping-sports   796.54
    LCSH: Packhorse camping (GV199.7)

Paddle tennis. HCL no.: 796.344   Date: Mar. 1979

    DDC 19: Paddle tennis *see* Racket games
    LCSH: Paddle tennis (GV1003)

Paddleball. HCL no.: 796.348   Date: Mar. 1979

    DDC 19: Racket games--sports   796.34
    LCSH: Paddleball (GV1017.P17)

Parent education. HCL no.: 649.107   Date: July 1977

    DDC 19: Family relationships--appl. psych.   158.24
                Parenthood--customs   392.3
                Parents--psychology   155.646
    LCSH: Parent education *see* Parenting--Study and
                    teaching

Planned unit development. HCL no.: 333.382   Date: Nov. 1977

    DDC 19: Condominiums--law *see* Horizontal property
                 law
    LCSH: Real estate development

Police malpractice. HCL no.: 363.25   Date: Jan. 1974

    DDC 19: Malpractice ...
                Police--powers ...
                Police--services ...
    LCSH: Police corruption
                Police ethics (HV7924)

Popular culture. HCL no.: 301.17   Date: Jan. 1978

DDC 19:	Cultural processes--sociology	306
LCSH:	Popular culture	

Protest songs. HCL no.: 784.67   Date: May 1976

DDC 19:	Protest groups--soc. action	361.23
	Topical songs	784.68
LCSH:	Protest songs (M1977.P75; M1978.P75)	

Psychic archaeology. HCL no.: 133.87   Date: Sept. 1978

DDC 19:	Archaeology	930.1
	Parapsychology	133
LCSH:	Parapsychology and archaeology (BF1045.A74)	

Pyramid energy. HCL no.: 118.2   Date: Apr. 1977

DDC 19:	Bioenergetics--biophysics	574.19121
	Energy--metaphysics	118
LCSH:	Energy *see* Force and energy	
	Energy, Biological *see* Bioenergetics	
	Energy, Vital *see* Vital force	
	Hylomorphism (BD648)	

Race walking. HCL no.: 796.427   Date: Mar. 1975

DDC 19:	Racing--sports--men	796.426
	Walking (sports) ...	
LCSH:	Racewalking *see* Walking (Sports)	

Rape victims. HCL no.: 362.883   Date: Sept. 1977

DDC 19:	Rape--criminology	364.1532
	Victims of crime--welfare services	362.88
LCSH:	Rape victim services (HV6558-6569)	

Rock opera. HCL no.: 782.2   Date: Apr. 1974

DDC 19:	Opera--music	782.1
	Rock (music)	780.42
	Rock (music)--songs	784.54
LCSH:	Opera (Aesthetics, ML3858; Hist. and crit., ML1700-2110)	
	Operas (ML1500-1508)	
	Rock music	

Roller skate dancing. HCL no.: 793.336   Date: Apr. 1977

DDC 19:	Dancing ...	
	Roller skating--sports	796.21
LCSH:	Dancing (GV1580-1799)	
	Figure skating *see* Skating	
	Roller skating (GV851)	

Rope skipping. HCL no.: 796.45   Date: Dec. 1976

    DDC 19: [Not found]
    LCSH: Rope skipping (GV498)

Runaway services. HCL no.: 362.75   Date: Apr. 1977

    DDC 19: Runaway young people--soc. services to 362.74
    LCSH: Runaway children
             Runaway youth

Senior power. HCL no.: 301.43532   Date: Oct. 1975

    DDC 19: Aged people--sociology   305.26
    LCSH: Aged--political activity (HQ1061)
             Senior power

Singing commercials. HCL no.: 784.69   Date: July 1977

    DDC 19: Commercials--broadcast advertising   659.14
             Radio advertising   659.142
             Television advertising   659.143
    LCSH: Singing commercials (M1977.S5; M1978.S5)

Skateboarding. HCL no.: 796.22   Date: Sept. 1976

    DDC 19: Skateboarding--sports   796.21
    LCSH: Skateboarding (GV859.8)

Small presses. HCL no.: 070.598   Date: June 1975

    DDC 19: Printing ...
             Publishing operations   070.5
    LCSH: Small presses *see* Little presses

Space colonies. HCL no.: 629.447   Date: Sept. 1977

    DDC 19: Colonies--states *see* Dependent states
             Space stations astronautics--technology 629.442
    LCSH: Space colonies (TL795.7)

Sports betting. HCL no.: 796.04   Date: Oct. 1975

    DDC 19: Betting ...
    LCSH: Sports betting (GV117)

Style manuals (Journalism/publishing). HCL no.: 070.0202
    Date: July 1978

    DDC 19: Style--journalism   070.415
             Style manuals ...
    LCSH: Newspaper style *see* Journalism--Handbooks,
                manuals, etc.
             Style manuals ...

Volunteer workers/voluntarism. HCL no.: 331.53 Date: Sept. 1976

> *DDC 19*: Volunteers *see spec. occupations e.g.* Volunteer
> nurses   610.730698
> LCSH: Volunteer workers in ...
> Volunteering *see* Voluntarism
> Volunteerism *see* Voluntarism
> Volunteers *see* Voluntarism

War games. HCL no.: 794.4   Date: Apr. 1974

> *DDC 19*: War games--recreation   793.9
> LCSH: War games (U310)

Women and labor unions. HCL no.: 331.882   Date: Mar. 1975

> *DDC 19*: Labor unions ...
> Women--labor ...
> LCSH: Women in trade-unions (HD6079)

Women's music. HCL no.: 780.46   Date: Sept. 1976

> *DDC 19*: Music ...
> LCSH: Women as musicians *see* Women musicians

Women's publishers. HCL no.: 070.596   Date: Mar. 1975

> *DDC 19*: Publishing operations ...
> Women--journalism for   070.48347
> LCSH: Women in journalism
> Women in the book industries and trade
> Women in the mass media industry
> Women publishers

Women's songs. HCL no.: 784.65   Date: May 1976

> *DDC 19*: Women's songs *see* Women's vocal music
> LCSH: Women--Songs and music (M1977.W64;
> M1978.W64)

Wood heating. HCL no.: 697.041   Date: Aug. 1975

> *DDC 19*: Fuels--bldg. heating   697.04
> Heating--buildings   697
> LCSH: Wood as fuel (TP324)

For the 62 "homeless" Berman concepts, 86 entries from the *DDC 19* index and 97 from LCSH are represented above as being sufficiently equivalent to furnish at least partial access and coverage. Admittedly, they reflect only this author's judgment of pertinence. Incidentally, 42 of the 97 LCSH terms appeared in supplements after the ninth edition was published in 1980. Thirty-five (most of them recent) are identical, or nearly so, to HCL usage. They do not include "Balloon ascensions," "Battered wives," "Grants-in-aid," "Homesteading," "Moving-pictures and poetry," "Parapsychology and archaeology," and similar near-misses. HCL is not always the first agency to offer a precise new term, viz., "Solar greenhouses."

A systematic link between 184,000 unique LC subject headings and their corresponding DDC numbers, as assigned by the Library of Congress from 1973 to 1981, has recently been published. Bowker's three-volume *Subject Authorities* devotes volume 2 to a classified arrangement of the DDC numbers, each followed by the appropriate subject heading and LC class number.[8] Volume 1 alphabetizes the same subject entries, appending the DDC and LC class numbers. Volume 3 gives the information in LC classification order. All three volumes warn the user that the class numbers assigned in the early 1970s from *DDC 18* have not been revised. The *Relocations and Schedule Reductions* list from *DDC 19*, volume 1, is reproduced in each *Subject Authorities* volume, but without the associated lists of phoenix changes.

The *DDC 19* Relative Index has numbered entries identical to HCL language in only two instances of the above Berman list, but one of these (War games) is closer to the HCL meaning than its LCSH equivalent. Four DDC *see* references use language equivalent to that of HCL. The remaining DDC and LCSH terms are either broader or more specific than HCL usage. The Dewey schedule tends to be more hospitable to "new" topics than its Relative Index shows, but its hospitality is oftenest achieved by including the concept at broader, more traditionally phrased locations. Berman demands greater explicitness.

The Berman critique, then, is more terminological than classificatory. The *HCL Cataloging Bulletin* has since mid-1979 carried only subject heading data, omitting classification decisions. Publication of *DDC 19* may have allayed some classing problems, although the Berman and Freedman critiques do not sound like it. A few new topics, e.g., "Skateboarding" and "War games," are in the Relative Index, though not in the schedule. Others, such as "Backpacking" and "Runaways," are in both. DDC indexing is sometimes obscure, e.g., for "Genetic engineering" and "Government grants."

Our findings only reiterate what most of us already suspected: that a well-tended subject list reflects terminological change quicker than does a classification system. Approximately two-thirds of Berman's topics have no really satisfactory counterpart in *DDC 19*. Not all are equally significant, but the more glaring omissions, such as those relating to institutional reform, music, and women, confirm the impression that the system modernizes itself with very deliberate speed. Let us not forget, on the other hand, that self-appointed critics tend to overstate their complaints. For at least a few HCL suggestions, even indexing might be supererogatory. Such are the highly experimental "Cinematic poetry," the amorphous "GI movement," the quaint "Governesses," and the occult "Pyramid energy."

Conclusion

This long chapter was chiefly directed to an examination of DDC terminology. There is much consonance between the wording of the schedule and that of the index, although the "relative" construction of the index makes it frequently less specific than corresponding schedule entries. There are exceptions. Geographic terms, synthetic numbers, and new usages are indexed more specifically than corresponding representations in the schedule. The continued vigor of DDC confirms its conservatism in avoiding concepts which may be too specific or too tentative, or at most, by testing them in Inclusion notes, or by indexing only. *DC&* has in the past concerned itself as much or more with announcements of DDC policy and typographic corrections as with new material that cannot wait for a fully revised edition. Still, if classifiers would take the time to transfer its information to the pages of their DDC volumes, recording their own decisions and interpretations, they would find that it communicates significant new topics and terminology. The transition to a new edition could be partly anticipated over the interim, and would thus be smoother and less disruptive to existing practice.

NOTES

[1]The variable fortunes of pre-*DDC 19* indexing are discussed in: John Phillip Comaromi, *The Eighteen Editions of the Dewey Decimal Classification* (Albany, NY, Forest Press Division, Lake Placid Foundation, 1976), pp. 560-74 and 601-606.

[2]Peter Butcher, "Dewey? We Sure Do!," *Catalogue & Index*, no. 55 (Winter 1979): 8.

[3]Lois Mai Chan, "Dewey 18: Another Step in an Evolutionary Process," *Library Resources & Technical Services*, v. 16, no. 3 (Summer 1972): 395.

[4]Benjamin A. Custer, "DDC 19: Characteristics," *HCL Cataloging Bulletin*, no. 35 (July/August 1978): 9-11.
John Phillip Comaromi, "DDC 19: The Reclass Project," *HCL Cataloging Bulletin*, no. 35 (July/August 1978): 12-15.
Maurice J. Freedman, "Better Latent Than Never--A Few Short Comments on the Proposed DDC 19, and the Custer/Comaromi Statements in HCLCB #35," *HCL Cataloging Bulletin*, no. 37 (November/December 1978): 6-10.

[5]Sanford Berman, "DDC 19: An Indictment," *Library Journal*, v. 105, no. 5 (March 1, 1980): 585-89.

[6]Ibid., p. 587.

[7]Even phoenix 301-307, the only sweeping revision in *DDC 19*, is still unfinished. The Decimal Classification Editorial Policy Committee, at its April 10, 1980 meeting, agreed that work on the span should continue to be a top priority at the Decimal Classification Office in the coming year. Presumably the clarifications, refinements, and expansions will be published in successive issues of *DC&*, volume 4.

[8]*Subject Authorities: A Guide to Subject Cataloging* (New York & London, R. R. Bowker, 1981). 3 volumes.

5

Auxiliary Tables

Introduction

The seven sisters of DDC faceting debuted in their present full dress in *DDC 18*. To be sure, a maternal ancestor of Table 1 was chaperoned, though not yet christened, by the very first edition. Its nickname, "Form Divisions," served until someone remarked that several features were in no way expressive of physical format. Other precursors of the modern auxiliary tables appeared and disappeared abruptly. Already in *DDC 2* (1885) three new ones were appended. One was called "Geographical divisions," but it merely listed topics which could be subdivided by region. The user was supposed to strike the initial 9 from history numbers in schedule 930-999, attaching what remained to the table numbers. Two more tables gave pattern lists of class numbers and subject divisions for the various languages identified in the 400 class. In *DDC 13* (1932), a fifth was added to subdivide literatures in the 800 class. All of these auxiliary aids lasted until the so-called "Standard" edition 15 dropped everything except a brief introductory reference to a method of subdividing "where consideration of the form or style in which the book is written, as well as the subject, is important."[1]

DDC 16 restored the form divisions in a separate list similar to today's Table 1. The old "Geographic Table" reappeared as a sequence of numbers "accompanied by instructions in the schedules to 'divide like 930-999,' or 'like 940-999.' "[2] *DDC 17* renamed the "Form divisions" and restructured the Geographic Table into an "Area Table" with all the characteristics of the present Table 2. *DDC 18* reactivated the discontinued tables for language and literature (Tables 3, 4, and 6). It also added two more: one for racial, ethnic, and national groupings (Table 5), the other for differentiating persons (Table 7).

Table 2 is by far the longest, occupying 373 pages, as contrasted with 13 pages for Table 1, 17 for Table 3, 4 for Table 4, 10 for Table 5, 14 for Table 6, and 21 for Table 7. *DDC 19* retains the basic format and most of the content of the *DDC 18* tables, making some additions and other changes which will be examined in due course.

Table 1. Standard Subdivisions

From the first, Mr. Dewey applied a rudimentary pattern for "mode of treatment" subdivisions. *DDC 2* gave it a fixed form, reflecting to some extent notable features built into the schedule proper. The morphology of Table 1 has changed little over the intervening years, although extensive expansions and a few significant alterations took place. Comparison of *DDC 18* and *19* summaries shows two important changes at -06 and -08.

Summary (*DDC 18*)		Summary (*DDC 19*)	
-01	Philosophy and theory	-01	Philosophy and theory
-02	Miscellany	-02	Miscellany
-03	Dictionaries, encyclopedias, concordances	-03	Dictionaries, encyclopedias, concordances
-04	General special	-04	Special topics of general applicability
-05	Serial publications	-05	Serial publications
-06	Organizations	-06	Organizations and management
-07	Study and teaching	-07	Study and teaching
-08	Collections	-08	History and description of the subject among groups of persons
-09	Historical and geographical treatment	-09	Historical and geographical treatment

Before we discuss the -06 and -08 revisions, let us list the notational differences introduced by *DDC 19*. Parallel passages from *DDC 18* are copied, but explanatory notes and some subdivisions of discontinued facets are omitted. The reader should consult the respective Table 1 editions for the full story.

Table 1 (*DDC 18*)		Table 1 (*DDC 19*)	
-0147	Nonverbal language	-0147	Nonlinguistic communication
-0149	Techniques of writing [optional]		
-017	Professional and occupational ethics [optional]		
-0182	Statistical method	-[0182]	Statistical method
-0183	Data processing	-[0183]	Data processing
-0184	Operations research	-[0184]	Operations research
-[0185]	Empirical tests and testing		
-[0186]	Case studies		
		-0218	Standards
		-0221	Drafting illustrations
		-[026]	Law
		-0287	Testing and measurement
		-0288	Maintenance and repair
		-0289	Safety measures
-061	Permanent govt. organizations		
-0611	International		
-0613-9	National, state, provincial, local		
-062	Permanent nongovernment organizations	-[062]	Permanent organizations
-063	Temporary organizations	-[063]	Temporary organizations

Table 1. Standard Subdivisions / 117

	Table 1 (*DDC 18*) (cont'd)		**Table 1 (*DDC 19*)** (cont'd)
-065	Business organizations	-[065]	Business organizations
		-068	Management of enterprises ...
		-0701-9	Geographical treatment of study and teaching
		-07509	Historical and geographical treatment of collecting objects
-08	Collections	*-08*	History and description of the subject among groups of persons
		-088	Among groups of specific kinds of persons
		-089	Among specific racial, ethnic, national groups

The changes from the above comparison may be grouped by type:

1. *Terminological change.* At -0147 the *DDC 19* caption reflects current usage, but the *DDC 19* index still says "Nonlinguistic *see* Nonverbal."

2. *Dicontinued facets.* Seven *DDC 18* numbers or spans are vacated in *DDC 19*. Five of the seven had no warning brackets in *DDC 18*, but -[0149] and -[017] were optional, with schedule numbers preferred. The -[0185-6] pair move to -076 (Review and exercise) and -0722 (Historical research). The -[061] group died on the vine.

3. *Bracketed facets.* *DDC 19* brackets seven numbers. The -[0182-4] trio are on their way to -072. The law facet -[026] is scattered by topic throughout class 340. The -[062-5] sequence is following its withered -[061] partner into oblivion.

4. *Additions.* Seventeen new facets, including extended subdivisions not copied above, are in the *DDC 19* table. Most respond to growing literary warrant, although some are aimed at closer disciplinary arrangement. The 7 under -068 (Management of enterprises) and the 2 under a reconstituted -08 (Subject among groups of persons) deserve some examination.

DEVELOPMENT OF ss-068

This change scatters works on management of specific enterprises to their disciplinary affiliations, as the following example shows:

687'.068'7   Advanced inventory and distribution systems :
conference proceedings ... c1979.

       1. Clothing trade--United States--Inventory
control--Congresses.   79-125864

---

680   Manufacture of products for specific uses   *(DDC 19)*
687   Clothing
   .06   Organizations and management   [Table 1]
   .068   Enterprises engaged in specific fields of activity
   .0687   Management of materials

Butcher calls the move "a welcome relocation from 658.9," where an option is still retained in *DDC 19.* But he is not fully satisfied:

> Unfortunately, specification has been sacrificed to enumeration in another failure to sanction synthesis; -0681/-0688 are spelt out, exactly mirroring 658.1/658.9, without further subdivision: a simple "add note" ("add to -068 the numbers following 658 in 658.1/658.8") would have been easier and more effective. (Better yet, of course, should have been the use of -01658 ... it's those long numbers, though).[3]

The relocation not only strengthens disciplinary integrity but gives more equitable schedule development, and distinguishes general management from particularized accounts. Until the change is fully digested, chiefly through use at the Library of Congress, there may be some ambiguity about it. Although they are now optional, 658[.91] and 658[.92-.99] still carry Add notes, the first of which suggests "Management of libraries 658.9102." Under 020 (Library and information sciences), use of the new *ss*-068 is forbidden, but the cross classification instruction leads on to a still different solution:

020[.68]   Management of library and information sciences
           Do not use; class in 025.1

It is not unusual to find applications of standard subdivisions countermanded by local schedule instructons (Cf. Example 23 in chapter 3). Nonetheless, it would be comforting not to have optional examples complicated by disciplinary exceptions.

CONVERSION OF ss-08

DC& has already revised the first note under *ss*-08, as we saw under "Reused numbers" in chapter 3. Application of -08 to signify collections or anthologies is not universally discontinued. For literature, where ana are a frequent and valuable form of publication, it retains the older meaning. See the discussion of Table 3 in this chapter. In other contexts *ss*-088-089 (Treatment with respect to various groups of persons) relieve a tendency to overuse *ss*-092 (Persons associated with a subject). If LC has classed Loften Mitchell's *Voices of the Black*

Table 1.   Standard Subdivisions / 119

Theatre (LCCN 74-30081) using *DDC 19*, its 792.0280922 might have been 792.02808996073, as shown below.

792	Theater (Stage presentations)	*(DDC 19)*
.02	Handbooks, techniques ... materials, miscellany	
.022-.028	Handbooks, techniques ... materials	
	Use "Standard Subdivisions" notation 01-09	
	(except 028) from Table 1 under each subdivision identified by *, e.g., periodicals	
	on amateur theater 792.022205	
.28	*Acting and performance	
.02808	History and description of the subject among groups of persons	[Table 1]
.028089	Among specific racial, ethnic ... groups	
	Add ... notation 01-99 from Table 5 to base number -089 ...	
.0280899	Other racial, ethnic, national groups	[Table 5]
.02808996	Africans and people of African descent	
.02808996073	United States blacks (Afro-Americans)	

SCHEDULE MANIPULATION OF TABLE 1 MEANINGS

Table 1 facets may attach to class numbers of any length, e.g.:

403   Language dictionaries, encyclopedias, concordances
150.1   Philosophy and theory of psychology
581.072   Botanical research
614.43205   A serial publication on insects as disease carriers

It is the only fully generalized faceting device offered in *DDC*, the only auxiliary table by which class numbers may be subdivided without specific schedule instructions. Conversely, it is subject to special instructions. Sometimes it is flatly forbidden, as we saw in Example 23 of chapter 3. Elsewhere it is conceptually or notationally distorted, e.g.:

401   Philosophy and theory of language Including Value
.3   Universal languages Class Value in 401

* *

372.9   Historical and geographical treatment of elementary education
.901-.905   Historical periods
Add to base number 372.90 the numbers following 090 in "Standard Subdivisions" notation 0901-0905 from Table 1, e.g., elementary schools in modern period 372.903

Sometimes part of the Table 1 meanings and notation are repeated in the schedule under a particular class number. Prima facie this practice seems redundant, but closer examination shows that in every case certain *ss* meanings are expanded, negated, or superseded, as was shown in Example 2 of chapter 3.

Standard subdivision -04 (Special topics of general applicability) is designed for local schedule manipulation. In Table 1 it carries a note to use only when specifically "set forth in the schedules." Not all classifiers approve of this technique, as the following remark shows:

-04 remains, subtly renamed but still as objectionable as ever, nestling between the last remaining "outer form divisions," -03, -05 and bits of -02.[4]

MULTIPLE ZEROS TO REGULATE CITATION ORDER

We observed in chapter 2 that faceting often poses citation order problems. Dewey's interposition of the 0 in front of his "form divisions" was to ensure their precedence over all other subdivisions of general class numbers. By *DDC 14* (1942), a variety of other subdivision categories were often needed to section a broad topic adequately. Variation in the number of intervening zeros was the solution. All auxiliary tables except Tables 2 and 6 start their notation with -01 (Table 1 alone confines it to the -01-09 span). Standard subdivision notation, which normally carries minimal hierarchical force because it is designed to be most universally applicable, must be adjusted to provide normal citation order. The double zero is the commonest way to do the job.[5] More complicated situations require a third zero when the second one is, or may be, preempted, as in the sequence below, where 025.49000148 (Abbreviations and symbols for controlled subject vocabularies) would precede 025.49001422 (Controlled subject vocabularies for statistical methodology).

025.49	Controlled subject vocabularies
	Subject headings, descriptors, thesauruses, indexing terms
	Use 025.490001-025.490009 for standard subdivisions
.49001-.49999	Vocabularies of specific disciplines and subjects
	Add 001-999 to base number 025.49, e.g., subject headings in science 025.495

The classifier is instructed to use "three or even four 0's."[6] If there is any place where a note of the pattern "Use xxx.x00001-xxx.x00009 for standard subdivisions" can be found, it is extremely well hidden. However, at least one case shows triple zero standard subdivisions added to a broad class number ending in zero:

350	Public administration Executive branch of government Military art and science
.0001-.996	Standard subdivisions and specific aspects of public administration, of executive branch of government

It means, of course, that a directory of schools and courses for public administration would have the class number 350.00071.

Table 1.   Standard Subdivisions / 121

A TABLE OF PRECEDENCE FOR TABLE 1

DDC places a virtual taboo on adding one standard subdivision to another in the same number unless there are specific instructions to do so.[7] Classifiers may find themselves in a quandary when more than one applies to the same work, e.g., a programmed text (-077) on the maintenance and repair (-0288) of photographic equipment (771). *DDC 19* introduces a citation order for Table 1. In its revised *DC&* format it reads:[8]

Unless other instructions are given, class works to which two or more standard subdivisions are applicable according to the following table of precedence, e.g., illustrations of the technique of the subject -028 (*not* -022).

Special topics of general applicability	-04
Persons associated with the subject	-092
Techniques, procedures, apparatus, equipment, etc.	-028
Study and teaching (*except* -074, -075, -076, -077)	-07
Management	-068
Philosophy and theory (*except* -014, -016)	-01
The subject as a profession, occupation, hobby	-023
Patents and identification marks	-027
Commercial miscellany	-029
Treatment by specific continents, countries, etc.	-093-099
Treatment by areas, regions, places in general	-091
Treatment among groups of persons	-08
Historical periods	-0901-0905
Works for specific types of users	-024
Collecting objects	-075
Museums, collections, exhibits	-074
Review and exercise	-076
Programmed texts	-077
Miscellany (*except* -023, -024, -027, -028, -029)	-02
Organizations	-06
Languages (Terminology) and communication	-014
Dictionaries, encyclopedias, concordances	-03
Serial publications	-05
Indexes	-016

According to the table, our programmed text on the maintenance and repair of photographic equipment should be classed in 771.0288 (*not* 771.077 or 771.0288077). The programmed text aspect should drop out of the classification because the maintenance and repair facet takes precedence. Although the preferred -0288 does not appear as such in the table, its citation order is governed by its superordinate -028 (Techniques, procedures, etc.).

There is one type of situation where the Library of Congress uses more than one standard subdivision to build numbers, but such cases involve the use of Table 2 (Areas). They will be reviewed later in this chapter.

STANDARD SUBDIVISION FOR NONSPECIFIC NUMBERS

DDC editors place a second general restriction on the use of Table 1, but the serious student soon discovers that the taboo, like that on double use, has exceptions. The basic problem lies in the practical need to develop numbers for some concepts with abnormally fuzzy edges. In the chapter 2 section on hierarchical force, Inclusion notes were seen to shelter topics of minor literary warrant. Classifiers all know of library materials which defy easy pigeon-holing. There is a pragmatic tendency in the Library of Congress system to construct a new class number for the maverick when it appears. DDC is more cautious, not being representative of any one collection. Its attempts to provide a flexible spectrum of broad-to-close classifying possibilities often result in its not fitting exactly the materials being classified. General principles of classification formulated by William Merrill, W. C. Berwick Sayers, and others were largely designed to help solve such dilemmas.[9] Yet the subject integrity of class concepts remains a problem, as was shown in the sections on reduction and relocation in chapter 3.

This second DDC restriction on free use of standard subdivisions affects works on topics that are merely "included" in their nonspecific numbers. Confusion could arise from adding Table 1 facets for such topics. There is an esoteric attempt at "adjustment" through listing a number of exceptional situations:

1. The *ss*-0924 (Individual persons associated with the subject) may be added regardless of the failure of that "subject" to coincide with the primary extension of its class concept.

2. A standard subdivision may be used if the class concept is unlikely to receive further subdivision at some future time.

3. A standard subdivision may be applied if the subject of the work "approximates the whole," that is, constitutes not quite all, but the greater part of the class concept at which it is located.

The subtle burden of interpretation is likely to discourage any but the most experienced classifiers. The reader should consult the official explanation offered in the editor's introduction (v. 1, pp. lii-liii). Most Inclusion notes appear under extended decimal numbers, e.g.:

020.711	Schools and departments of library and information sciences and their curriculums Including programs for library technicians
179.7	Respect and disrespect for human life Including genocide, homicide, suicide, capital punishment, dueling
252.55	Texts of sermons for young adults Including academic, chapel, convocation, commencement sermons

Table 1.   Standard Subdivisions / 123

327.101   Philosophy and theory of international relations
             Including nature of power in international rela-
             tions, role and position of small states, econo-
             mic bases of international relations

491.487   Nonstandard Sinhalese
             Including Mahl dialect

539.2   Radiations (Radiant energy)
             Including electromagnetic spectrum and radiations

616.964   Diseases due to tapeworms (Cestoda)
             Including hydatid diseases (echinococcosis)

738.4   Enameling and enamels
             Including basse-taille, champlevé, ronde bosse

801.92   The psychology of literature
             Including literature as a product of creative
             imagination

929.97   Names as forms of insignia and identification
             Including names of ships, houses, pets

Such numbers are not likely to be further subdivided for shelf use because excessive precision is unnecessary. DDC numbers tend to lengthen in inverse proportion to the amount of materials they include. However, the fullest possible extension may prove useful for indexing projects.

The Decimal Classification Editorial Policy Committee still tries to clarify the characteristics of schedule concepts as they affect hospitality to Table 1 notation.[10] The criterion is "whole" versus "partial" content. When a number covers two or more concepts, the Decimal Classification Division of the Library of Congress is charged to determine, on the basis of literary warrant, if they are hierarchically equal. If not, only the primary concept is to be named in the caption, and is eligible for standard subdivision. Everything else should go to an Inclusion note, a function of which is to prevent its topics from being subdivided.

CHRONOLOGICAL SUBDIVISION

While there is no general auxiliary table for time divisions, Tables 1, 2, and 3 are frequently associated with temporal concepts. *Ss*-0901-0905 (Historical periods) is a comprehensive span of time period numbers. Unless the schedule gives a specific chronology, these numbers may be applied, like any Table 1 aspect, without instructions, as in the following example.

646.309022   Clothing in the thirteenth century

Clothing	646.3
Historical ... treatment of clothing [Schedule number]	646.309
Table 1 notation for the 13th century	-09022
Table 1 segment minus the redundant -09	-022
Schedule number plus Table 1 segment	646.309 + -022
Synthetic number for clothing in the 13th century	646.309022

The two classes 800 and 900 contain many local chronologies. Internal period tables are frequently used with auxiliary tables to build class numbers where time is a significant, but not the only, facet. *DDC 18* ran into homonym trouble, however, with its instructions for adding historical periods at *ss*-093-099 (p. 122) and at *area*-3-9 (p. 134). Contradictory instructions at some schedule locations led to identical synthetic class numbers with two possible meanings.[11] *DDC 19* dropped the homonymic instructions in Tables 1 and 2, but usually retained the specific schedule instructions. The following examples include recent area relocations for the United Kingdom (see the discussion of Table 2 in this chapter).

332.67342081	British foreign investments during the [Table 2 instr.] reign of Victoria	(*DDC 18*)
332.67342081	British foreign investments in Brazil [Sched. instr.]	(*DDC 18*)
332.67341081	British foreign investments in Brazil [Sched. instr.]	(*DDC 19*)

* *

328.4205	U.K. Parliament in the Tudor period [Table 2 instr.]	(*DDC 18*)
328.4205	U.K. Parliament Rules and Regulations [Schedule table]	(*DDC 18*)
328.4105	U.K. Parliament Rules and Regulations [Schedule table]	(*DDC 19*)

It is perhaps of minor consequence, but both DDC and LC classifications take such dates as 1800 and 1980 to be initial years of a new century or decade. The *New York Times* for January 1, 1901 carried a front-page headline: "Twentieth Century's Triumphant Entry," but since that bold affirmation, terminology has grown more ambivalent, and much recent usage flaunts the arithmetic significance of the notation. Current reference books tend to sidestep the issue, although the *Encyclopedia Americana* article "Twentieth century" still uses the phrase "after 1900" twice in its first four paragraphs.[12] The *World Book* is explicit:

> Century ordinarily means 100 years.... The years 1 through 100 after the birth of Christ are called the first century; from 101 through 200 was the second century.... [13]

The *Anglo-American Cataloguing Rules* in both editions carry uniform title rules for "Works written after 1500," and "Works written before 1501."[14] But the oracular *Webster's New International Dictionary* retrenched between its second (prescriptive) and third (descriptive) editions:

Table 2. Areas / 125

CENTURY ... specifically, one of the hundred-year divisions of the Christian Era, as, the *first century* (A.D. 1-100 inclusive); the *nineteenth century* (A.D. 1801-1900).[15]

* *

CENTURY ... specifically one of the 100-year divisions of the Christian era, or of the preceding period (the 19th ~) (the fourth ~ B.C.).[16]

There has come to be more consensus on numbering decades. Webster's *Third*, for instance, is explicit in identifying their coverage, as it is not for centuries:

DECADE ... especially : a 10-year period beginning with a year ending in 0 (as 1900-1909) (the ~ of the twenties runs from Jan. 1, 1920 to Dec. 31, 1929.[17]

Sanford Berman could not complain of outdated DDC usage on this point, although things were not ever thus. Example 20 of chapter 3 illustrates the *DDC 18* caption at 941.081: "20th century history of Scotland and Ireland, 1901-   ."

Table 2.   Areas

Geographic or political subdivision was long dependent on the history divisions 930-990. Not only were subdivisions of 910 (Geography and travel) drawn from that span, but regional division in any discipline was based on Divide-like instructions referring to those numbers for patterns. As time went on, two problems emerged. First, the WASP bias from which DDC struggled to escape still dominated the history schedule, stressing political units, especially in Europe and the United States, over physical and other regional areas, that had to be spelled out as they were needed. Second, the Divide-like instructions were hard to follow. *DDC 17* initiated the now-familiar Area Table, with a section for regions and places in general. Other parts of the table expanded jurisdictional sequences, expanding those for Asia, Africa, and Oceanica particularly. Although it retained its Divide-like's to cite other schedule spans, that edition referred to its auxiliary tables by means of Add notes. Divide-like's gave way entirely in *DDC 18* to "Add to's" (from schedule spans) and "Add from's" (for tables). See the discussion in chapter 2.

The demarcation between areas -3 and -4-9 is not always so clear as could be wished, especially in view of the note under -3 to "class a specific part of ancient world not provided for here in -4-9" (v. 1, p. 27). A British classifier recently offered some advice:

Under -3 "The Ancient world" are gathered those parts of the world more or less known *to* classical antiquity, and considered only during the period of "ancient history." The same areas in later times, as well as other areas such as America in both ancient and later times, are classed in -4-9.... [18]

The phoenix changes in *area*-41-42 are not really new, having been partially introduced by *DC&* in 1974.[19] They include not only political units, but physiographic regions or major features, e.g., "Great Glen" under *area*-41175 (Inverness district). A list of British places with changed numbers is appended to volume 1, pages 467-70, of *DDC 19*. Table 2 carries 994 new entries, an increase of nearly 17%, from 5,939 to 6,933. Many new or changed names in South America can be found. *DC&*, v. 4, no. 1 (June 1980): 9-10 adds 25 Pinyin name forms to established Chinese place names. Butcher's implication that the European Economic Community must be faceted with *area*-177 (Nations belonging to specific international organizations), since it is not mentioned in the Relative Index, is puzzling.[20] There are a number of index and schedule entries for it under various disciplines, which no doubt account for its absence from Table 2. *Area*-719 (Canadian Northern Territories) is "reused."

Many class numbers can be geographically divided without specific instructions by going first to Table 1. The *ss*-093-099 span (Treatment by specific continents, etc.) is most frequently used, but nine other Table 1 entries say to add "Areas" notation from Table 2. The Table 1 "stile" applies as follows:

380.1094   *Commerce in Europe*

Commerce (Trade)	380.1
Standard subdivisions of commerce [Schedule entry]	380.103-.109
Subdivisions for geographic treatment [Table 1]	*ss*-093-099
Segment for Europe [Table 2]	*area*-4
Addition of facets to base	380.1 + -09 + -4
Completed number for commerce in Europe	380.1094

Exponents of the Universal Decimal Classification, or other highly faceted systems, find such manipulations worthwhile, but primitive.

> ... Notational signaling allowed what had been done in limited areas in Dewey's scheme to be done in UDC universally without specific instruction. Whereas Dewey sometimes divided a subject by place without his usual indicator 09, but otherwise left it to the classifier to add 09, etc., on his own initiative, UDC created a general auxiliary for place by using Dewey's detail for 940-999 (now the *Area Tables*) and enclosing the number in parentheses to be used anywhere. Whereas Dewey almost always limited chronological subdivision to places specified in *history*, UDC created a general auxiliary for time, and enclosed dates, periods and notation for other chronological phenomena like periodicity in quotation marks, and allowed them to be used with any number in the scheme.[21]

In our discussion of standard subdivisions we noted that two are not used in the same number except for special purposes. The most frequent exceptions are for catalogs of exhibits with geographical facets, housed in museums also characterized by geographical facets. The following example makes double use of both Tables 1 and 2, plus an Add step from another schedule sequence.

Table 3. Subdivisions of Individual Literatures / 127

730'.0966'074017427   Kresge Art Center. Gallery.
Ceremonial art of West Africa ... an
exhibition.   79-67209

---

730   Plastic arts; Sculpture
Use 730.01-.09 for standard subdivisions ...
.09   Historical and geographical treatment   [Table 1]
.093-.099   Treatment by specific continents, etc.
Add "Areas" notation 3-9 from Table 2 ...
-6   Africa   [Table 2]
-66   West Africa
-07   Study and teaching   [Table 1]
-074   Museums, collections, exhibits
-0   Add to base -0740 the numbers following 708 in 708.1-.9
-1   In North America   [708.1 ...]
-13-19   United States
Add to base 780.1 the numbers following 7 in "Areas" notation 73-79
from Table 2 ...
-7   North Central U.S.   [Table 2]
-74   Michigan
-742   South central counties ...
-7427   Lansing and East Lansing

Table 3.   Subdivisions of Individual Literatures

DDC 19, Table 3 supplies new seven-step instructions for building numbers.
They are duplicated in volume 2 under centered heading 810-890 (Literatures of
specific languages), and are used exclusively with that span. *DDC 19* also
introduces sub-table 3-A (Notations to be added where instructed throughout
Table 3). It consolidates much complex, reduplicated information scattered
through the *DDC 18* version. There may now be more page flipping (the price of
faceting devices), but comprehension and accuracy should improve. The list of
Relocations and Schedule Reductions cites only four notational shifts. Limericks
and clerihews move from -108 (Light and ephemeral verse) next door to -107
(Satirical and humorous poetry). Subdivisions -[302-303] (Novelets and novels)
are reduced to -3 (Fiction). In Table 3-A, "Crime as a literary theme" goes from
facet 353 (Human qualities and activities) to facet 355 (Social themes), while facet
[376] (Supernatural, mythological and legendary things) reduces to facet 37.
Three illustrations from LC records show, in order, Table 3 use of -08 in its
"Collections" sense, use of a literary period table from class 800, and application
of Table 3-A. Another example of the latter is given on page 40.

821'.008   Gaige, Grace.
                    Recitations : old and new, for boys and girls
                    ... 1979.   78-73486

_____

82   Base for English. Add as instructed under 810-890   [Schedule]
 -1   Poetry   [Table 3]
 -1008   Collections by more than one author from more
              than one period
82 + -1008 = Collections of English poetry by more.... ,
              with decimal point after third digit.[22]

* *

843'.9'14   Lefèvre, Françoise.
                        Le bout du compte : roman ... 1977.   79-350223

_____

84   Base for French literature   [Schedule]
 -3   Fiction   [Table 3]
 -914   Later 20th century, 1945-   [Schedule]
84 + -3 + -914 = A modern French novel

* *

808.8'9973   MELUS; Society for the Study of the Multi-
                        Ethnic Literature of the United States ...
                        1979?   79-642925

_____

808.89   Literary collections for and by specific kinds   [Schedule]
              of persons
              Add notations 8-9 from Table 3-A to base 808.89 ...
      -93-99   For and by persons resident in ...   [Table 3-A]
                    Add "Areas" notation 3-9 from Table 2 to 9 ...
         -7   North America   [Table 2]
         -73   United States
808.89 + -9 + -73 = A literary collection by and for U.S. residents

Table 4. Subdivisions of Individual Languages

Just as Table 3 is designed for use with class 800, so Table 4 is designed for
class 400. Its format is virtually identical with that of *DDC 18*. There is a new
scope note for -03, a *DC&* interpolation, and a discontinued -[06]:

-03   Dictionaries, encyclopedias, concordances
              Class dictionaries of the standard form of the lang-
              guage in -3, of nonstandard forms in -7
-042   Bilingualism
              Add "Languages" notation 2-9 from Table 6 to -042
              for the nondominant language ...
-[6]   [Prosody of the standard form of the language] Class in 808.1

Table 5. Racial, Ethnic, National Groups / 129

General instructions for use of Table 4 are given under centered heading 420-490 (Specific languages). We are told that *lang. sub.*-01-86 may be added to base numbers for individual languages, or, after adding 04, to the notation for any group of languages. An apparent homonymic conflict may have minor practical importance. For 430 (Germanic languages), use of the 04 facet would give, e.g., 430.04244 (Romance language elements in Germanic languages). But a schedule note at 430 says "Use 430.01-.09 for standard subdivisions of Germanic languages." *DC&*, v. 4, no. 1 (June 1980): 11 inserts *ss*-04 (Special topics of general applicability) and -042 (Bilingualism) into Table 4, as noted above. Using this second interpretation, the meaning of 430.04244 would be "Franco-Germanic bilingualism."

Table 5. Racial, Ethnic, National Groups

Changes in this table are minimal, designed either to facilitate use or to reflect social change:

1. New concepts:

   -42   Walloons
   -9167   Cornishmen
   -9911   Negritos
   -9915   Australian native races

2. New terminology:

   -96073   U.S. blacks (Afro-Americans) [*DDC 18*: U.S. Negroes]
   -961   Hottentots (Khoi-Khoin) and Bushmen (San)
           [*DDC 19* adds vernacular names "Khoi-Khoin" and "San"]
   -97   North American native races [*DDC 18*: American aborigines]
   -98   South American native races [*DDC 18*: South American
           aborigines]

3. New instructions

   DDC 19 inserts "Arrange alphabetically" and Inclusion notes or *see* references in the -9 (Other racial ... groups) span of Table 5. *DC&* adds a "For Afro-Americans, see -96073" to -13 (Americans).

Table 5 is frequently used to extend other facets. See, for instance, the synthetic 792.02808996073 (page 119), where *ss*-08 is the switching device. Analogous use of the digit 8 from Table 3-A occurs in building 808.89881 on page 40. Some prescriptions in *DDC 18* led to peculiar hierarchical interpretations, if not "incorrect number synthesis," as Harris and Clack charged.[23] They argued that classing Chicanos under 301.4512-.4519 (Aggregates of "other" [i.e., non-North American] origins) made the classification incorrect. The problem was inherent in the schedule separation of 301.4511 from 301.4512-.4519, and has been corrected in the *DDC 19* phoenix schedule as follows:

301.4516872073   Chicanos [i.e. Mexicans] in the United States   (DDC 18)

301   Sociology
  .4   Social structure
  .45   Nondominant aggregates
  .451   Aggregates of specific national, racial, ethnic origins
  .4511   Aggregates of general, mixt, North American origins
  .4512-.4519   Aggregates of other origins
            Add "Racial, etc." notation 2-9 from Table 5 to base number 301.451 ... ; then, unless it is redundant, add 0 and to the result add "Areas" notation 1-9 from Table 2

  .4516   Spanish and Portuguese   [-6 from Table 5]
  .45168   Spanish Americans
  .451687-.451688   National groups
            Add "Areas" notation 7-8 from Table 2 to base number -68
  .451687   North America   [-7 from Table 2]
  .4516872   Middle America
  .451687207   In North America   [2nd use of Table 2]
  .4516872073   In the United States

* *

305.86872073   Chicanos [i.e. Mexicans] in the United States   (DDC 19)

305   Social stratification (Social structure)
  .8   Racial, ethnic national groups
            Add "Racial, etc." notation 01-99 from Table 5 to base number 305.8 ... ; then, unless it is redundant, add 0 and to the result add "Areas" notation 1-9 from Table 2
  .86   Spanish and Portuguese   [-6 from Table 5]
  .868   Spanish Americans
  .8687-.8688   National groups
            Add "Areas" notation 7-8 from Table 2 to base number -68
  .8687   North America   [-7 from Table 2]
  .86872   Middle America
  .8687207   In North America   [2nd use of Table 2]
  .86872073   In the United States

Table 6.   Languages

While most libraries using DDC seldom need to subdivide by language, it is a facet which should be recognized in any fully developed classification scheme. For instance, certain classic works are held in a variety of translations by special libraries, or in comprehensive collections. A few other situations can profit from applying linguistic categories. The *ss*-03 (Dictionaries) and *area*-175 (Regions where specific languages predominate) both carry instructions to add "Languages" notation from Table 6 to a base number. Table 6 stems from class 400, although it warns that its notation does not necessarily correspond to the

Table 7. Persons / 131

schedule spans 420-490 and 810-890 (v. 1, p. 418). The *Relocations and Schedule Reductions* list cites three shifts (v. 1, p. 460). Dano-Norwegian [*formerly* -3981 (Danish)] moves to -3982 (Norwegian). Entry -[9911] carries a note to class Negrito languages in -9593 (Mon-Khmer languages). Jakun [*formerly* -9593] is now included at -9928 with Malay (Bahasa Malaysia). Uses of Table 6 are illustrated by the following examples:

297.122521   *An English translation of the Koran*

297	Islam and religions derived from it
.1	Sources, relationships, attitudes of Islam
.12	Sacred books and scriptures
.122	Koran
.1225	Translations
	Add "Languages" notation 1-9 from Table 6 to base number 297.1225
.12252	English and Anglo-Saxon languages [-2 from Table 6]
.122521	English

* *

896.397208   *A post-1960 collection of satire and humor in Zulu*

896	African literatures
	Add to 896 the numbers following 96 in "Languages" notation 961-965 from Table 6
.3	Niger-Congo languages [-963 from Table 6 minus the -96]
.39	Bantu languages Including Zulu
.397	Satire and humor [-7 from Table 3; see instruction 2]
.3972	Later 20th century, 1960- [2 from Period Table for specific African literatures; see instruction 4]
.397208	Collections by more than one author [-08 from Table 3; see instruction 5]

Table 7.   Persons

Table 7 may be used according to instructions at specific schedule locations, or in other tables, as the following examples illustrate. Note that the Table 1 precedence list prefers *ss*-024 (Works for specific types of users) to its superordinate *ss*-02 (Miscellany), which makes the hierarchical representation at 743.4602 somewhat ambiguous. *Ss*-088 (Treatment among specific kinds of persons) makes use of Table 7, but warns against redundancy, e.g., as "treatment of medicine among physicians."

390.43661   *Customs of Freemasons*

390	Customs, etiquette, folklore
.4	Customs of people of various specific occupations
	Add "Persons" notation 09-99 from Table 7 to base number 390.4 ...
.43	Persons occupied with the social sciences [-3 from Table 7]
.436	Persons occupied with welfare and public protection
.4366	Belonging to esoteric associations and societies
.43661	With Freemasonry

* *

741.9088616   A collection of drawings made by physicians

741   Drawing and drawings
 .9   Collections of drawings
 .908   History and description among groups of persons   [-08 from Table 1]
 .9088   Treatment among groups other than racial, ethnic, etc.
            Add "Persons" notation 04-99 from Table 7 to base number -088
 .09886   Persons occupied with applied sciences   [-6 from Table 7]
 .908861   Persons occupied with medical sciences
 .9088616   With general medicine

* *

743.46024616   Anatomical drawings for physicians

743   Drawing and drawings by subject
 .4   Drawing human figures
 .46   Bones (Skeletal system)
 .4602   Miscellany   [-02 from Table 1]
 .46024   Works for specific types of users
            Add "Persons" notation 03-99 from Table 7 to base number -024
 .460246   Persons occupied with applied sciences [-6 from Table 7]
 .4602461   Persons occupied with medical sciences
 .46024616   With general medicine

Conclusion

Faceting has become commonplace in *DDC 19*. Professional reaction is nearly unanimously favorable.[24] Some writers urge that "the principle of separate tables for certain subjects ought to be extended in future editions."[25] They may have in mind classes 500 and 600, which use numerous Add instructions for transferring spans from other schedule locations, making almost no use of the auxiliary tables except for a rare reference to Table 2, or, even more rare, to Table 1. DDC editors seem more concerned to refine and expand the existing auxiliaries. They are also aware that faceting inevitably tempts classifiers to push close classification to the limits of its practicability. Witness the excessively long DDC numbers often found on Library of Congress records. They may be justifiable for indexing uses, such as the UDC was designed for, but they are usually more bother than help at the shelves. To illustrate their infinite variety, see the exercises in number analysis and synthesis which follow this and each of the succeeding chapters.

Exercises in the Use of Auxiliary Tables

I.   Table 1

   A.   Analyze the DDC numbers assigned by the Library of Congress to the following works.

285'.9'022	Alexander, G.M. Changes for the better ... 1976-1978. [Puritans--England]	80-461441
300'.7'2	Knowledge (Beverly Hills) v. 1- Sept. 1979- [Social science research--Periodicals]	79-644770
669'.003	American Society for Metals. Committee on Definitions of Metallurgical Terms. Glossary of metallurgical terms and engineering tables ... c1979.	79-25837
791.43'01	Issari, Mohammad Ali. What is cinéma vérité? ... 1979. [Moving-pictures--Philosophy]	79-20110
982'.06'0924	Bankoff, George Alexis. Mourning becomes Argentina ... 1978. [A book about Eva Peron]	80-458969

B. Synthesize DDC numbers for the following class concepts. Examples from Library of Congress assignments are given on pages 138-39.

1. A work titled *The Reception of unconventional science* sponsored by the American Associaton for the Advancement of Science. Its sole LC subject heading is "Science--History," but it deals with science in the twentieth century.

2. A work issued by the Nursing Theories Conference Group entitled *Nursing theories : the base for professional nursing practice.*

3. A work on dynamic agricultural systems, subtitled "economic prediction and control." The LC subject heading is "Agriculture--Economic aspects--Mathematical models."

4. A work by the National Association of College and University Business Officers entitled *Management of student aid.*

5. The autobiography of the movie actor Oliver Reed.

6. A book on automated library circulation systems and data processing.

II. Table 2

A. Analysis

741.5'973	Animals, animals, animals : a collection of great animal cartoons ... c1979. [American wit and humor, Pictorial]	79-1653
507'.1044	Choisnard, Jacques. Organisation de l'enseignement supérieur et de la recherche scientifique et technique ... 1979. [Science--Study and teaching (Higher)--France]	79-124644
323.4'9'0963	Amnesty International. Human rights violations in Ethiopia ... 1978.	80-461176
331.2'81388324'0973	American Trucking Association. ATA trucking salaried employees compensation study ... c1979.	79-129414

271'.53'024	Ligthart, C. J. The return of the Jesuits ... 1978. [The story of the Dutch Jesuit Johannes Philippus Roothaan, 1785-1853]	80-457441
418'.007'042	Salmon, Vivian. The study of language in 17th century England ... 1979.	80-459677
914.4'72	Sadouillet-Perrin, Alberte. Périgueux de A à Z ... 1978. [Périgueux, France--Streets]	80-458901
808.5'1'02573	American Society of Association Executives. Finding the right speaker ... c1979.	80-100360
709'.94'0740994	Australia Council. Visual Arts Board. Regional Development Program. Works on paper ... 1978.	80-462470

B. Synthesis

1. A study of the economic aspects of agriculture in Asia.

2. Pictures and descriptive notes on the social life and customs in St. Ives, Cornwall, England.

3. A book of teaching secondary school art in the United States.

4. A history of the Roman Catholic Church in Southern Rhodesia.

5. Standards and rules of procedures for accrediting law schools in the United States.

6. Annotated 1850 census reports for Carroll County, Virginia.

7. A study of agricultural cropping systems in the tropics.

8. A look at the use of marijuana in the United States.

9. A news letter on abortion legislation in the United States.

10. Sixteenth-century origins of Spanish lyric vocal music.

III. Tables 3 and 3-A

A. Analysis

811'.008 s [811.54]	Amprimoz, Alexandre L. Against the cold ... 1978. (Fiddlehead poetry books : 237)	79-303197
808.8'038	Anthologie de l'au-delà ... c1978. [Future life--Literary collections]	80-459193
823'.0876'08	Aries I / edited by John Grant ... c1979. [Science fiction, English]	80-464040
891.6'611'09	Astudiaethau ar yr hengerdd = Studies in old Welsh poetry ... 1978	79-342602
848'.91407	Bailly, Jean Christophe. L'étoilement ... c1979. ["Five hundred copies printed."]	80-462603

| 840'.8'09715 | Anthologie de textes littéraires acadiens ... c1979. [French-Canadian literature] | 79-115909 |

| 840'.9'38 | Bady, René. Littérature et spiritualité ... 1978. [French literature--History and criticism] | 80-455535 |

| 791.43'09'0916 | American nightmare : essays on the horror film ... c1979. | 80-464090 |

B. Synthesis

1. An examination of the appearance of nature in Greek literature.

2. An anthology of contemporary mathematical poetry.

3. A critical study of seventeenth-century French drama about Don Juan.

4. An anthology of Australian science fiction.

IV. Table 4

A. Analysis

| 428'.4'3 | Rubin, Dorothy. Reading and learning power ... c1980. | 79-11663 |

| 495.1'5'02854 | Suen, Ching Y. Computational analysis of Mandarin. | 80-461537 |

| 449'.7 | Lescale, Paul. Recherches et observations sur le patois du Quercy : dialecte de Cahors et environs ... 1978. [Provençal language, Modern--Dialects] | 80-463587 |

| 491'.47321 | Bhatt, Narhari K. Mānavavidyāo ane samājavidyāonā pāribhāshika śabdono Aṅgreji-Gujarāti vinayana śabdakośa = English-Gujarati dictionary of technical terms in humanities and social sciences ... 1979. [English language--Dictionaries--Gujarati] | 79-906255 |

| 440'.7'10713 | Ontario. Ministerial Committee on the Teaching of French. Report ... 1974. | 75-310443 |

B. Synthesis

1. A guide to English usage.

2. A guide to becoming an effective diagnostic-remedial teacher of reading and language skills.

3. A textbook and reader for foreign students of English.

4. An analysis of intonation in modern Russian.

5. A Dutch-English dictionary.

V. Table 5

A. Analysis

| 970.004'97 | Alford, Thomas Wildcat. Civilization, and the story of the Absentee Shawnees ... c1979. | 79-129832 |

745'.089945	Rácz, István. Finno-ugric folk art ... 1979.	80-459144
946'.55004924	Régné, Jean. History of the Jews in Aragon ... 1978.	79-116614
700'.917'4927	Aziza, Mohamed. L'Image et l'Islam : l'image dans la société arabe contemporaine ... 1978 [Art--Arab countries]	80-467237
811'.008'0897	El Nahuatzen. 1- 1978- ["A magazine with emphasis on poetry by Chicano and native American writers."]	79-644841

B. Synthesis

1. A study of native Indian tribes of South America.

2. An elementary genealogy guide for Australians.

3. A history of Armenians in Turkey.

4. A history of the Acadians in Canada.

5. A bibliography of works on Afro-Brazilians.

VI. Table 6

A. Analysis

033'.1	Bilder-Conversations-Lexikon für das deutsche Volk : e. Handbuch zur Verbreitung gemeinnütziger Kenntnisse u. zur Unterhaltung ... 1977.	79-363849
220.5'3'1	Volz, Hans. Martin Luthers deutsche Bibel : Entstehung u. Geschichte d. Lutherbibel ... 1978.	79-361728
893'.1	Les Livres de sagesses des pharaons / [textes choisis, traduits de l'égyptien et présentés par] Élisabeth Laffont ... 1979.	79-114748
686.2'1'924	Strasbourg. Bibliothèque nationale et universitaire. Le livre hébraïque : incunables et chefs d'oeuvre de l'imprimerie strasbourgeoise du XVIe siècle ... 1963.	75-511189
808'.066'6021	Pickett, Nell Ann. Technical English : writing, reading, and speaking ... 2d ed. ... c1975.	75-23422

B. Synthesis

1. A dictionary in English of the real estate business.

2. A bibliography of Arabic typography.

3. A handbook of scientific writing: how to do it.

4. A study of Englishisms in modern Spanish.

5. Effective rhetoric and writing in French.

VII.   Table 7

    A.   Analysis

704'.7 [B]	Hyams, Barry. Hirshhorn, Medici from Brooklyn : a biography ... c1979. [Art--Collectors and collecting--Biography]	78-10120
174'.9'301	Diener, Edward. Ethics in social and behav- ioral research ... 1978.	78-8881
362.4'088054	Allée, Robert. Rôle des équipes techniques des centres régionaux pour l'enfance et l'adolescence inadaptées ... 1978.	80-457165
940.53'1503'924	Syrkin, Marie. Blessed is the match : the story of Jewish resistance ... 1976.	76-22216
973.7'1503'96073	Berry, Mary Frances. Military necessity and civil rights policy : Black citizenship and the constitution, 1861-1868 ... 1977.	76-53822

    B.   Synthesis

        1.   An investigation of journalistic ethics.

        2.   A survey of folklore of the sea.

        3.   A guide to federal income tax law for teachers.

        4.   The role of the British navy in American waters during the Civil War.

        5.   A study of American blacks in World War II.

VIII.   Chronological sequences

    A.   Analysis

909.07	Artz, Frederick Binkerd. The mind of the Middle Ages, A.D. 200-1500 : an historical survey ... 3d ed. rev. ... c1980. [See *DC&*, v. 4, no. 1 (June 1980): 22 for entry change]	79-16259
974.9'27'043	Amato, Matthew F. Jersey City, a city in socio- economic and political change ... c1980.	79-55721
871'.01	Alpers, Paul J. The singer of Eclogues : a study of Virgilian pastoral, with a new translation of the Eclogues ... c1979.	77-93465
915.19'5'0443	Adams, Edward Ben. Kyongju guide : cultural spirit of Silla in Korea ... 1979. [A descriptive guidebook for travellers in post-war South Korea]	79-670108

324.954'84'052	Acharya, K. R. The critical elections ... 1979. [Post-1977 elections in Andhra Pradesh, India; see *DC&*, v. 4, no. 1 (June 1980): 24 for schedule change]	79-905233
779'.99440836'0924	Argencé, Philippe d'. Le général de Gaulle en France : les Français regardent de Gaulle / [photographies de] Philippe d'Argencé ... c1979.	80-455467
891.7'8'307	Rozanov, V. V. (Vasiliĭ Vasilévich) Solitaria / V. V. Rozanov ; with an abridged account of the author's life by E. Gollerbach ; other biographical material, and matter from The apocalypse of our times ... 1979.	79-13120

B. Synthesis

1. A serial devoted to the twentieth-century art movement known "Art brut."

2. A recent book of children's poetry about food by an American.

3. A tourist's guide to present-day New York City.

4. A selection of plays by the ancient Greek dramatist Aristophanes.

5. History and criticism of Arabic poetry during the Abbasid period.

6. A French translation of *Juha*, a nineteenth-century Finnish novel.

DDC Class Numbers Assigned by the Library of Congress Which Illustrate the Exercises in Number Synthesis

Table 1

B. 1. 509'.04	The Reception of unconventional science ... 1979.	78-19735
2. 610.73'01	Nursing Theories Conference Group. Nursing theories : the base for professional nursing practice ... c1980.	79-15063
3. 338.1'01'51	Rausser, Gordon C. Dynamic agricultural systems : economic prediction and control ... c1979.	78-31859
4. 378'.3'068	National Association of College and University Business Officers. Management of student aid ... c1979.	79-66149
5. 791.43'028'0924	Reed, Oliver. Reed all about me : the autobiography of Oliver Reed ... 1979.	80-460127

6. 025.6'028'54 Bahr, Alice Harrison. Automated library circulation systems, 1979-80 ... c1979.   79-16189

Table 2

1. 338.1'095   Agricultural situation, Asia; review and outlook.
1978/79-   79-644508

2. 942.3'75   A St. Ives album / [compiled by] Andrew Lanyon ...
1979.   80-459690

3. 707'.1273   Linderman, Earl W. Teaching secondary school art :
discovering art objectives, art skills, art history,
art ideas ... c1980.   79-52779

4. 282'.6891   Linden, Ian. Church and state in Rhodesia : 1959-1979
... 1979.   80-457442

5. 340'.07'1173 American Bar Association. Approval of law schools :
American Bar Association standards and rules of
procedure, as amended, 1979 ... c1979.   79-128499

6. 929'.3755714 Alderman, John P. 1850 census, annotated, Carroll
County, Virginia ... c1979.   80-106779

7. 631.5'0913   Norman, M.J.T. (Michael John Thornley). Annual
cropping systems in the tropics : an introduction
... c1979.   79-10625

8. 613.8'3'0973 Novak, William. High culture : marijuana in
the lives of Americans ... 1980.   79-2229

9. 344'.73'048 Abortion law reporter / National Abortion Rights
Action League, Antioch School of Law ... c1976-   76-366339

10. 784'.0946   Aguirre, Mirta. La lírica castellana hasta los
siglos de oro : de sus orígenes al siglo XVI
... 1977-   79-120225

Tables 3 and 3-A

B. 1. 880'.8'036   Préaux, Claire. Le paysage grec ... 1979.   80-462738

2. 808.81'9356   Against infinity : an anthology of contemporary
mathematical poetry ... 1979.   79-90106

3. 842'.4'080351 Balmas, Enea Henri. Il mito di don Giovanni
nel Seicento francese ... 1977-1978.   80-465553

4. 823'.0876'08994   Alien worlds / edited by Paul Collins ...
1979.   80-456044

Table 4

B. 1. 428.1   Bailie, J.M. The Hamlyn guide to English usage
... 1979.   80-457457

2. 428'.4'207   Bader, Lois A. Reading diagnosis and remediation
in classroom and clinic : a guide to becoming an
effective diagnostic-remedial teacher of reading
and language skills ... c1980.   79-10042

3. 428'.6'4   Live, Anna Harris. American mosaic : intermediate-advanced ESL reader ... c1980.   79-16352

4. 491.71'6   Baldwin, John R. A formal analysis of the intonation of modern colloquial Russian ... 1979.   80-456955

5. 439.3'1'321   Jaeger, A. A new pocket-dictionary of the English and Dutch, and Dutch and English languages ... 2d ed. ... 186-?   78-311648

Table 5

B. 1. 980'.004'98   Alegre G., Florencio P. Tashorintsi, tradi-ción oral matsiguenka ... 1979.   79-126312

2. 929'.1'08924   Ancestors for Australians : a guidebook for beginners which points the way to wider horizons of genealogy ... 1978.   80-458714

3. 956.1'00491992 [B]   Aved, Thomas G. Toomas, the little Armenian boy : childhood reminiscence of Turkish-Armenia ... c1979.   79-90192

4. 971'.004114   Arsenault, Bona. History of the Acadians ... c1978.   80-460092

5. 016.981'00496   Alves, Henrique L. Bibliografia afro-brasileira : estudos sobre o negro ... 1979.   79-124090

Table 6

B. 1. 333.33'03'21   Abraham, Samuel V. Real estate dictionary and reference guide ... c1979.   79-90761

2. 016.6862'19'27   Krek, Miroslav. A bibliography of Arabic typography ... 1976.   77-352780

3. 808'.066'5021   Monroe, Judson. The science of scientific writing ... c1977.   76-46822

4. 468'.2'421   Altabé, David F. Temas y diálogos ... 3rd ed. ... c1980.   79-21992

5. 808'.0441   Richaudeau, François. L'Écriture efficace ... 1978.   80-460375

Table 7

B. 1. 174'.9'097   Questioning media ethics / editor, Bernard Rubin ... c1978.   78-16561

2. 390'.4'6238   Baker, Margaret. Folklore of the sea ... c1979.   80-455982

3. 343.7305'2'024372   Arch, John C. NEA Federal income tax guide for teachers : 1980 handbook ... c1980.   80-105435

4. 973.7'15'3590941   Courtemanche, Regis A. No need of glory : the British navy in American waters, 1860-1864 ... c1977.   76-56069

5. 940.53'15'0396073   Wynn, Neil. The Afro-American and the Second World War ... 1976.   76-375980

Chronological sequences

B. 1.	709'.04	L'Art brut. fasc. 10- ... 1977-	79-648526
2.	811'.5'4	Adoff, Arnold. Eats : poems ... c1979.	79-11300
3.	917.47'1'044	Appleberg, Marilyn J. The I love New York guide : the ultimate source book for New Yorkers and visitors ... c1979.	79-15990
4.	882'.01	Aristophanes. Clouds; Women in power; Knights ... 1979.	78-51680
5.	892'.7134	Abū Dīb, Kamāl. Al-Jurjānī's theory of poetic imagery ... 1979.	80-457981
6.	894'.54132	Aho, Juhani. L'Écume des rapides : roman ... 1978.	79-114319

Exercises in DDC 19 Table 2 Changes

DDC 18 area-41-42 numbers included in the following Library of Congress records have been changed. See the *DDC 19 List of Changed Numbers: British Isles* (v. 1, pp. 467-70). Give the full class number you would assign if you were cataloging these works today.

016.378422'7	Southampton, Eng. University. Research report and publications ... 197-?	71-244932
016.9428'5	Hodgson, Henry Wigston. A bibliography of the history and typography of Cumberland & Westmoreland ... 1968.	70-458113
312'.09411'2	Barclay, Robert Steven. The population of Orkney, 1755-1961 ... 1965.	70-465806
796.5'1'0942746	Wainwright, Alfred. Walks on the Howgill fells and adjoining fells ... 1972.	73-151641
914.14'7	Roxburgh : the official guide to the county ... 1970.	75-565048
914.24'3'03	Severn & Wye review. v. 1- 1970- [The final 03 in this number has been discontinued. See *DC&*, v. 3, no. 7 (April 1975): 9.]	71-27549
914.27'2	The Official guide to West Lancashire Rural District ... 1971.	72-183892
914.27'4'03	Andrews, William. Bygone Yorkshire ... 1970.	79-875925

DDC 19 numbers for the exercises in Table 2 changes:

016.37842276	Southampton, Eng. ...
016.94278	Hodgson ...
312.0941132	Barclay ...
796.51094281	Wainwright ...
914.1392	Roxburgh ...
914.299	Severn ...
914.276	The Official guide ...
914.281	Andrews ...

NOTES

[1]Melvil Dewey, *Decimal Classification*. Standard (15th) ed. (Lake Placid Club, NY, Forest Press, 1951), p. xiii.

[2]Melvil Dewey, *Dewey Decimal Classification and Relative Index*. Ed. 16 (Lake Placid Club, NY, Forest Press, 1958), v. 2, p. 2421.

[3]Peter Butcher, "Dewey? We Sure Do!," *Catalogue & Index*, no. 55 (Winter 1979): 1, 7.

[4]Ibid., p. 7.

[5]Cf. Example 2 in chapter 3.

[6]Melvil Dewey, *Dewey Decimal Classification and Relative Index*. Ed. 19 (Albany, NY, Forest Press, 1979), v. 1, p. xliv.

[7]Ibid., v. 1, p. liii.

[8]*DC&*, v. 4, no. 1 (June 1980): 8.

[9]See, for instance, William Stetson Merrill, *Code for Classifiers, Principles Governing the Consistent Placing of Books in a System of Classification*, 2nd ed. (Chicago, American Library Association, 1939); and W. C. Berwick Sayers, *Sayers' Manual of Classification for Librarians*, 5th ed. [rev. by] Arthur Maltby (London, André Deutsch, 1975), Section one: Principles of Library Classification.

[10]Margaret E. Cockshutt, "Annual Report of the Decimal Classification Editorial Policy Committee, July 1, 1979-June 30, 1980," *Library Resources & Technical Services*, v. 25, no. 1 (January/March 1981): 123.

[11]P. Gangadhara Rao, "Homonyms in Dewey Decimal Classification Edition 18: Case Studies," *Library Science with a Slant to Documentation*, v. 14, nos. 3-4 (September-December 1977): 120-23.

[12]*Encyclopedia Americana*, 1980 International ed. (Danbury, CT, Americana Corporation, 1980), v. 27, p. 297.

[13]*The World Book Encyclopedia* (Chicago, World Book-Childcraft International, 1981), v. 3, p. 271.

[14]*Anglo-American Cataloging Rules*, North American Text (Chicago, American Library Association, 1967), pp. 147-51: Rules 101 and 102.
Anglo-American Cataloguing Rules, 2nd ed. (Chicago, American Library Association, 1978), pp. 443-47: Rules 25.3-.4.

[15]*Webster's New International Dictionary of the English Language*, 2nd ed., unabr. (Springfield, MA, G. & C. Merriam, 1958), p. 437.

[16]*Webster's Third New International Dictionary of the English Language*, unabr. (Springfield, MA, G. & C. Merriam, 1969), p. 364.

[17]Ibid., p. 582.

[18]Ross Trotter, "Dewey 19—A Subjective Assessment," *Catalogue & Index*, no. 59 (Winter 1980): 4.

[19]See *DC&*, v. 3, nos. 4-7 (April 1974-April 1975) for announcements and summaries. Concise reviews of this change are available in Ann Hobart, "The Work of the Dewey Decimal Classification Sub-Committee, 1968-1979," *Catalogue & Index*, no. 58 (Autumn 1980); 6; and Trotter, "Dewey 19—A Subjective Assessment," pp. 1-2.

[20]Peter Butcher, "Dewey? We Sure Do!," *Catalogue & Index*, no. 55 (Winter 1979): 7.

[21]Charles D. Batty, "Library Classification: One Hundred Years after Dewey," *Major Classification Systems: The Dewey Centennial* (Urbana-Champaign, IL, University of Illinois Graduate School of Library Science, 1976), pp. 4-5.

[22]Use of Table 3-A could have extended this number to 821.00809282 (An anthology of poetry for children including several poets from several periods).

[23]Jessica L. Milstead Harris and Doris H. Clack, "Treatment of People and Peoples in Subject Analysis," *Library Resources & Technical Services*, v. 23, no. 4 (Fall 1979): 385.

[24]P. Dhyani, "DDC 18: Critical Appraisal of Some Auxiliary Tables," *International Library Review*, v. 9, no. 2 (April 1977): 175-81.

[25]Antony Croghan, "The Dewey Decimal Classification and Its Eighteenth Edition," *Library Association Record*, v. 74, no. 7 (July 1972): 120-21.

6

Class 000   Generalities

Introduction

This class carried no name in Dewey's first edition (1876), but it has long been called the "General works" or "Generalia" class. Comaromi observes that including Bibliography [and Library Science] here at the very beginning of the schedules was a sound way to make the tools of librarianship immediately accessible.[1] The Library of Congress had a similar purpose in view when it copied the Cutter Expansive System in developing its class Z first, but it placed it at the close, rather than the beginning, of its schedules. Bloomberg and Weber remark that division 070 (General journalism, publishing, newspapers) might better be located with the disciplinary material in sections 383-384 (Specific kinds of communication).[2] Be that as it may, few changes appear in the broad outline of the class, as may be seen from the following comparison:

Summary (*DDC 18*)		Summary (*DDC 19*)	
000	GENERALITIES	000	GENERALITIES
010	Bibliographies & catalogs	010	Bibliography
020	Library & information sciences	020	Library & information sciences
030	General encyclopedic works	030	General encyclopedic works
040		040	
050	General serial publications	050	General serial publications
060	General organizations and museology	060	General organizations & museology
070	Journalism, publishing, newspapers	070	Journalism, publishing, newspapers
080	General collections	080	General collections
090	Manuscripts & book rarities	090	Manuscripts & book rarities

Notable changes in each division will be considered briefly, followed by exercises in the use of the class.

Division 000   Knowledge, the Book, and Systems

In this division, the updates are chiefly expansive and terminological, all modest.

Section 001 (Knowledge), which was first introduced in *DDC 12* (1927), has many new scope and cross-classification notes, attesting to the problems of disciplinary integrity that still pop up. "Classification of knowledge" is shifted to 001.012 from its former subordination to Metaphysics. A new section 001.1 (Intellectual life) has been added (see Example 1 in chapter 3). At 001.4, the *DDC 18* "Methodology and research" caption is reduced to simply "Research," but the subdivisions emphasizing methodology remain. The language of communication is somewhat modernized.

Section 002 (The Book) reactivates a number unassigned since *DDC 16*. It receives much material formerly classed in 001.552 (Printed and written mediums). "Book collecting," which was formerly classed as a standard subdivision of library science, is now housed here. Literary warrant and disciplinary integrity appear to have inspired these changes.

Section 003 (Systems) remains unpartitioned, but a new Inclusion note covers "forecasting." General systems analysis in data processing still classes in 001.61, while *ss*-02851 provides a facet for systems analysis in specific subject areas. Not all the literature on systems will be found in 003.

Sections [004] through [009] are unassigned.

Division 010   Bibliography

There is considerable expansion throughout. An Inclusion note under 010 brings in bibliographies, etc., for children and young adults from 028 (Reading).

Section 011 (General bibliographies) adds nearly three pages of subdivision:

> ... to provide for numerous kinds of bibliography that are not confined to specific subjects, specific places of publication, or various types of authorship. There will be, among others, provisions for bibliographies of government documents, or rare books, or university and college presses.[3]

Sections 012 through 016 (Special bibliographies and catalogs) now have a centered heading and a table of precedence, but expansion is minimal. The options in section 016 (Subject bibliographies ...) are curtailed, but new subdivisions with Add instructions are now available.

Sections 017-019 (General catalogs) are grouped under a centered heading, but there is little other change. *DC&*, v. 4, no. 1 (June 1980): 11 adds "Register number" to the 018 caption.

Division 020   Library and Information Sciences

Schedule development at 020.6 looks more like the *ss*-06 in *DDC 18* than like its counterpart in *DDC 19*. For disciplinary integrity, "Book collecting" moves from 020[.75] to new section 002 (The book) plus *ss*-075 (Collecting objects).

Section 021 is now called "Library relationships." Its former name was "The library and society." Three numbers and a number span are discontinued [bracketed]. All four are reduced—three to Inclusion notes. *Cf.* Example 9 in chapter 3.

Section 022 (Physical plant of libraries and information centers) likewise shows consolidation. Subdivisions 022[.5-.6] (Reading rooms and other special rooms) go to an Inclusion note under 022.

Section 023 (Personnel and positions) introduces a centered heading 023.2-023.4 (Types of positions). Three new numbers distinguish professional, technician, and in-service training personnel. The old 023[.5] (Staff) is reduced, while 023.9 (Elements of personnel administration) is expanded.

Section [024] (Regulations for use of libraries) and its subdivision [024.6] (Interlibrary loan regulations) transfer to subsections of 025.

Section 025 (Library operations) is extensively expanded, particularly for collection analysis and control, but also for selection and acquisition of types of materials, and for services to users. Its 025.49 experiences instant metamorphosis from "Reclassification" to "Controlled subject vocabularies." A few other shifts occur, mostly internal.

Sections 026-027 (Specific kinds of institutions) change very little. A few notes are added or reworded, and a couple of specifications dropped, e.g., centered heading [027.1-.5] (By forms of ownership), and 027[.42] (Specific kinds of public libraries). *DC&*, v. 4, no. 1 (June 1980): 11 deletes "for area served" in the Add note under 027.53-.54 (Specific government libraries).

Section 028 (Reading and use of other information media) seems to anticipate future expansion with its "and use of ... " added to the caption, but for the time being the change is more terminological than classificatory. Subtopics 028.1 (Reviews) and 028.5 (Reading ... by children and young adults) are moderately expanded. The relocation of 028[.52] was cited under division 010.

Section [029] (Documentation) is gone to 025 (Library operations), where its modest set of subdivisions are regrouped and extended. Two discontinued subtopics remain to guide the user. At [029.4] a disconcerting split scatters abstracting techniques to 025.4028, while the composition of abstracts goes to 808.062. We are not told where to class collections of abstracts. Presumably they belong with their subject matter if the following LC records are typical. Note that *ss*-05 (Serial publications) is added to one class number, and the now-obsolete *ss*-08 (Collections) to two others.

330.9'439'05	Abstracts of Hungarian economic literature. v. 1- 1971-	71-617384
338.2'7'282	Abstracts of transportation and storage literature and patents. New York, American Petroleum Institute.	75-23106
370'.78	Abstracts of research projects. Dayton, Ohio, School of Education, University of Dayton.	72-622165
581.1	Abstracts of papers presented at the first Egyptian Congress of Botany, Cairo, 25-17 March, 1972.	72-189279
589'.2'08	Abstracts of mycology. v. 1- 1967-	68-3752
665'.53'08	Abstracts of refining literature. v. L8- Jan. 1961-	73-643589

929.3'773'6   Abstracts of the records of the Society of
Friends of Vermillion Quarterly Meeting
in Vermillion Grove, Illinois. Danville,
Ill., 1970.   75-24907

We shall find other technique/product splits. Compare, for example:

242 (Devotional literature)/248.3 (Worship)
328 (Legislation)/340 (Law)
526.8 (Map drawing and projection)/912 (Graphic representations)

Division 030   General Encyclopedic Works
Division [040]   Unassigned
Division 050   General Serial Publications and Their Indexes

No significant changes can be found in any of these divisions.

Division 060   General Organizations and Museology

Very few changes occur. A series of instructions clarifies relationships between 069 (Museology) and *ss*-068 (Management of enterprises engaged in specific fields of activity). There are two minor adjustments under 069.5 (Collections and exhibits of museum objects).

Division 070   Journalism, Publishing, Newspapers
Division 080   General Collections
Division 090   Manuscripts and Book Rarities

The span 070[.53-.54] (Design and manufacture of publications) goes to 686 (Printing and related activities) for better disciplinary integrity. A new 070.5795 includes microforms with other special kinds of publications. A note under 090 now says to class a manuscript or rare book, or their art aspects, with the specific subject. "Early printed books to 1700" enters at 094.2.

Conclusion

The major alterations in class 000 are designed to mirror the changing world of knowledge, publication formats, libraries, and the information sciences. It is on the one hand easier, but on the other riskier, to evaluate developments in one's own field. Here in their professional territory, DDC classifiers try to be progressive, yet unswayed by what may turn out to be only passing fads. Further adjustments will surely be made for, e.g., systems approaches and the electronic revolution. *DDC 19* does little more than weed out obsolete concepts or shift their disciplinary focus to make way for the growth that undoubtedly will occur.

Exercises in the Use of Class 000

One of the difficulties a neophyte classifier faces is to determine the optimum amount of faceting, with its number-length corollaries, for a given topic. Experience is the best teacher. The relation of the work at hand to the entire collection should be a determining factor. Always consult the shelf list to see what else has been classed in alternative locations, and how populous the assignments are. Observing Library of Congress practice is another useful technique. It may at first seem curious how close the classing is done at certain points, contrasted with how broad it remains at others. Undoubtedly some control is exercised to maintain consistency and propriety, although there is evidence of personal and subject difference in the assignments being made. The following exercises, like all those used in this study, not only give practice in interpreting and assigning DDC numbers, but are selected from recent LC cataloging output to demonstrate the nature and relative quantity of its DDC classifications. All records have been checked against both the print *National Union Catalog* and the MARC tapes. When there is variance, the MARC record is preferred.

A.   Analysis

001'.01'2	Classifications in their social context ... 1979. [Primitive classification processes]	79-50312
001.6'4	Donaldson, Hamish. Designing a distributed processing system ... 1979. [Electronic data processing--Distributed processing]	79-22523
001.64'04	Association for Computing Machinery. German Chapter. Microcomputing ... 1979. [Microcomputers and microprocessors]	79-397400
001.6'424	The BYTE book of Pascal / Blaise W. Liffick, editor ... c1979. [PASCAL (Computer program language)]	79-22958
001.9'4	Dankenbring, William F. Beyond Star wars ... c1978. [Civilization, Ancient--Extraterrestrial influences]	78-60520
016.3805'068	Gatto, Dominick J. Planning principles for transpor- tation systems ... 1979.	79-110653
027.5794	Directory of archival and manuscript repositories in California. 1975-	79-643347
028.1	Greenfield, Jeff. Jeff Greenfield's book of books ... c1979. [Witty anecdotes of publishing and the book trade]	79-126485
070.5'025'73	Brewer, Annie M. Book publishers directory : a guide ... c1979.	77-74820
081 s	Rand Corporation. Rand report ... Rand Corporation. Research memoranda ... [See records for individual monographs in these two series as they appear in the *Library of Congress Catalogs : Mono- graphic series*, 1974-]	

B. Synthesis: Examples from LC records are given on pp. 150-53.

1. A collection of papers from an international conference on information storage and retrieval.

2. A bibliography of a core media collection for secondary schools.

3. An English-Portuguese dictionary of electronic data processing.

4. The biography of an American journalist.

5. A dictionary catalog of Gabriella Mistral's personal library, now housed in the Barnard College Library, New York City.

6. An introduction to systems analysis and design for electronic digital computer work.

7. A bibliography of music therapy.

8. The proceedings of a conference on construction and use of mathematical models.

9. A manual on cataloging serials publications.

10. A bibliography of Oklahoma folk music.

11. A guide to Manhattan booksellers and book marketing.

12. An American almanac, handbook, or book of days.

13. A work on engineering microcomputers.

14. A bibliography of published statistical sources of U.S. commodity movements.

15. A collection of stories about strange mysteries of the sea.

16. A book on semiotics and discourse analysis.

17. A bibliography on the United Nations.

18. An index to book reviews in scholarly journals.

19. A listing of literary manuscripts in the Huntington Library, San Marino, California.

20. Conference proceedings on oral communication and applied linguistics.

21. A set of standards for compiling newspaper and periodical publication statistics.

22. A guide to information sources on remote sensing of the earth's resources.

23. A work on community college instruction in use of the library.

24. An introduction to the state archives located in the province of Namur, Belgium.

25. An index of Jewish bibliographical periodicals and book reviews.

26. An investigation of reputed Aztec and Mayan contacts with extraterrestrial phenomena.

27. A list of readings on municipal government and politics.

28. Statistics on British abstracting and indexing services.

29. A catalog of Arabic and Persian medical manuscripts in the library of the Institute of History of Medicine and Medical Research.

30. A list of source materials on Brittany at the time of the French Revolution and the Empire.

31. A how-to-do-it book on community-based library fund raising.

32. A thesaurus of subject headings for studies on women.

33. A reprint of a general periodical originally issued in 1792 in Mainz, Germany.

34. Conference papers on post-secondary and vocational education in electronic data processing.

35. Use of mathematical models in management, and in the social and biological sciences.

36. An index to Canadian newspapers.

37. The proceedings of a workshop on micro-climates for museums.

38. The series known as "Publications" of the Early English Text Society.

39. A chart book for computer graphics.

40. A selection of readings on East-West commercial relations.

41. A history of the School of Library Science at Case Western Reserve University.

42. A book of miscellaneous curiosities and wonders.

43. A list of electronic music recordings.

44. Programming and debugging in the TRS-80 machine language.

45. A book on the psychology of librarians. [The DDC number originally used by the Library of Congress for a work on this topic has been reduced in *DDC 19*]

46. A 15-volume set of miscellaneous materials for children.

47. A list of bibliographies about Arab women.

Examples of LC Cataloging to Illustrate the Above Exercises in DDC Number Synthesis

1. 001.64   ACM-Sigir International Conference on Information Storage and Retrieval (1978 : Rochester, N.Y.) ... 1978.   79-128809

2. 016.3731'33   Brown, Lucy Gregor. Core media collection for secondary schools ... 2d ed. ... 1979.   79-6969

3. 001.64'03   Camarão, Paulo César Bhering. Great technical dictionary : English-Portuguese Dicionário técnico : inglês-português : processamento de dados, câmbio, banco, importação, exportação ... c1979.   79-122945

4. 070'.92'4   Faber, Doris. The life of Lorena Hickok : E. R.'s friend ... 1980.   79-91302

5. 019'.2'097471   Barnard College, New York. Library. Catalog of the Gabriela Mistral collection ... 1978.   78-105468

6. 001.6'1   Introducing systems analysis and design / edited by Barry Lee ... 1978-1978.   79-301329

7. 016.6158'5154   Hôpital Rivière-des-Prairies. Bibliothèque du personnel. Thémathèque. La musicothérapie ... 1978.   79-115822

8. 001.4'24   Constructive approaches to mathematical models : proceedings of a conference ... 1979.   79-51673

9. 025.3'4'3   Cannan, Judith Proctor. Special problems in serials cataloging ... 1979.   79-13774

10. 016.7817766   Carney, George O. Oklahoma's folk music traditions : a resource guide ... 1979.   79-129285

11. 070.5'7'0688   Egan, Robert. The book store book : a guide to Manhattan booksellers ... c1979.   79-51897

12. 051   The Illuminated book of days / edited by Kay & Marshall Lee ... c1979.   79-87621

13. 001.64'04   Doty, Keith L. Fundamental principles of microcomputer architecture ... c1979.   78-71524

14. 016.3805'24'0973   Carter, Elizabeth R. Guide to published statistical sources of U.S. commodity movements ... 1979.   79-110676

15. 001.9'4'09162   50 strange mysteries of the sea / edited by John Canning ... c1979.   80-461470

16. 001.51   Hénault, Anne. Les enjeux de la sémiotique : introduction à la sémiotique générale ... c1979.   79-123472

17. 016.34123   Hüfner, Klaus. The United Nations system, international bibliography = Das System der Vereinten Nationen, internationale Bibliographie ... 1976-1979.   77-566745

18. 028.1   Combined retrospective index to book reviews in scholarly journals, 1886-1974 ... 1979-   79-89137

19. 011'.31   Henry E. Huntington Library and Art Gallery. Guide to literary manuscripts in the Huntington Library ... 1979.   79-84369

20. 001.54'2   International Congress of Applied Linguistics (4th : 1975 : Stuttgart) Speech education ... 1978.   80-451953

21. 071'.3   American National Standards Institute. American national standard for compiling newspaper and periodical publishing statistics ... c1979.   79-123017

22. 016.62136'7   Bryan, M. Leonard. Remote sensing of earth resources : a guide to information sources ... c1979.   79-22792

23. 027.7   Cammack, Floyd M. Community college library instruction : training for self-reliance in basic library use ... 1979.   79-17531

24. 027.5493'4   Belgium. Archives de l'État, Namur. Musée. Une visite au Musée des Archives de l'État à Namur / par Jean Bovesse ... 1978.   79-114858

25. 016.909'04924   Dán, Róbert. Accumulated index of Jewish bibliographical periodicals ... 1979.   80-461498

26. 001.9'4   Casgha, Jean Yves. Mayas, Aztèques et extraterrestres ... c1979.   79-121991

27. 016.352'008'0973   Coppa, Frank J. Urban government and politics : a bibliographical overview ... 1979.   79-109484

28. 025.3'0941   East, Harry. Some statistical indicators of UK abstracting and indexing services ... 1979.   80-450728

29. 016.61   Institute of History of Medicine and Medical Research. Library. A catalogue of Arabic and Persian medical manuscripts in the library ... 1970-   75-902196

30. 016.944'104   Conan, Jules. L'histoire de la Révolution et l'Empire en Bretagne, 1940-1974 ... 1978.   79-121740

31. 021.8'3   Baker & Taylor Co. Winning the money game : a guide to community based library fundraising ... 1979.   79-90713

32. 025.4'63054   Burgess, K. Glenda. A special collection thesaurus : women studies ... 1979.   79-115518

33. 053.1   Der Fränkische Republikaner. Nr. 1-   1792-   79-649470

34. 001.6'4'0711   IFIP TC-3 Working Conference on Post-Secondary and Vocational Education in Data Processing (1979 : Amsterdam, Netherlands) ... 1979.   79-20798

35. 001.4'24   Burghes, David N. Mathematical models in the social, management, and life sciences ... 1979.   79-40989

36. 071'.1   The Canadian newspaper index. v. 1-   1977-   78-643000

37. 069'.29   In search of the black box : a report on the proceedings of a workshop on micro-climates held at the Royal Ontario Museum ... 1979-   80-451962

38. 082 s   Early English Text Society. Publications ... [See records for individual monographs in this series as they appear in the *Library of Congress Catalogs : Monographic series*, 1974-   ]

39. 001.55   Data Resources, Inc. EPS chart book ... 1979.   80-100481

40. 016.382'091713'01717   Ervin, Linda. Selected bibliography
                            on East-West commercial relations
                            ... 1978, c 1979.   80-454433

41. 027.7771'32   Cramer, C.H. (Clarence Henley). The School of
                           Library Science at Case Western Reserve
                           University : seventy-five years, 1904-
                           1979 ... c1979.   79-4453

42. 031'.02   Harris, Sydney J. Would you believe? ... c1979.   79-55055

43. 016.7899'12   Fletcher, David Jeffrey. David Robert Jones
                          Bowie, the discography of a generalist, 1962-
                          1979 ... 1979.   79-122495

44. 001.64'2   Imman, Don. Introduction to T-BUG : the TRS-80
                          machine language monitor ... c1979.   79-67471

45. 027.5794   Directory of archival and manuscript repositories
                          in California.   1975-   79-643347

46. 081   Childcraft : the how and why library ... c1980.   79-88042

47. 016.0163054'2'09174927   Barbar, Aghil M. The study of Arab
                             women : a bibliography of bibliographies
                             ... 1980.   80-113012

NOTES

[1]John Phillip Comaromi, *The Eighteen Editions of the Dewey Decimal Classification* (Albany, NY, Forest Press Division, Lake Placid Education Foundation, 1976), p. 33.

[2]Marty Bloomberg and Hans Weber, *An Introduction to Classification and Number Building in Dewey*, edited by John Phillip Immroth (Littleton, CO, Libraries Unlimited, 1976), p. 43.

[3]*Cataloging Service Bulletin*, no. 4 (Spring 1979): 15.

7

Class 100
Philosophy and Related Disciplines

Introduction

DDC 19 changes in the broad outlines of class 100, as for class 000, are not substantive, and only minimally terminological. Major criticisms have long centered around the meager development of many topics, and the physical intrusion of psychology. The historical accident which left the latter umbilically tied to philosophy is too well documented to need further comment.[1] The confusion was further componded because psychology was itself long split between divisions 130 and 150. Renovation, begun in *DDC 17* (1965), is still in progress, and will be reviewed briefly in the course of this chapter. Enumerative and exemplary scope notes, Inclusion notes, and cross-classification hints are designed to keep concepts and terminology clear. A comparison of *DDC 18* and *19* divisional summaries shows moderate updating.

Summary (*DDC 18*)		Summary (*DDC 19*)	
100	PHILOSOPHY AND RELATED DISCIPLINES	100	PHILOSOPHY AND RELATED DISCIPLINES
110	Metaphysics	110	Metaphysics
120	Knowledge, cause, purpose, man	120	Epistemology, causation, humankind
130	Popular & parapsychology, occultism	130	Paranormal phenomena & arts
140	Specific philosophical viewpoints	140	Specific philosophical viewpoints
150	Psychology	150	Psychology
160	Logic	160	Logic
170	Ethics (Moral philosophy)	170	Ethics (Moral philosophy)
180	Ancient, medieval, Oriental	180	Ancient, medieval, Oriental
190	Modern Western philosophy	190	Modern Western philosophy

Division 100   Standard Subdivisions of Philosophy

The user is reminded that this division is reserved for "philosophy," leaving "related disciplines" for later development. Its section (three-digit) numbers embody the major facets of Table 1, but are spelled out anyway because *all* section numbers are given in the DDC schedule, as we learned in chapter 3.[2] One or two are worthy of comment.

Section [104] has been vacant since *DDC 16* (1958). *Ss*-04 (Special topics of general applicability) is restricted to explicit schedule instructions.

Section 106 (Organizations of philosophy) lacks the management aspect which *ss*-06 now includes.

Division 110   Metaphysics (Speculative Philosophy)

While this division is not extensively developed, several conceptual and terminological changes adumbrate developments in cosmology and the philosophy of science.

Section 111 (Ontology) adds three divisions, one of which (Finite and infinite) comes from [125]. Other changes add "Substance" and "Accidents" to 111.1, and substitute "Classical" for "Transcendental" at 111.8 (Classical properties of being).

Section [112] loses "Classification of knowledge" to 001.012.

Section 113 (Cosmology ...) adds "Philosophy of nature" to its *DDC 18* caption. In this short section, two subtopics reduce to an Inclusion note. The remaining 113.8 (Philosophy of life) gets scope and cross-classification notes.

Sections 114 (Space) and 115 (Time) are no longer partitioned. Discontinued 115[.4] (Space-time) reduces to an Inclusion note.

Section 116 (Evolution) reduces the concepts of "Motion" and "Change" to an Inclusion note.

Section 117 (Structure) rewords the *DDC 18* caption "Matter and form."

Sections 118 (Force and energy) and 119 (Number and quantity) are unaltered. Both concepts are more often discussed in their scientific and technological than in their metaphysical sense in today's literature.

Division 120   Epistemology, Causation, Humankind

One critic calls this a catch-all division, apparently because it covers the fall-out from section 153 (Intelligence) and from those parts of division 230 which she terms "mental processes and theology."[3] Traditional use of 370 (Education) and the 1927 (*DDC 12*) appearance of section 001 (Knowledge and learning) aggravate the problem in disciplinary integrity. Shifts still occur in a never-ending search for the best hierarchy.

Section 121 (Epistemology ...) now has the parenthetical caption "Theory of knowledge," plus three new numbers. Each has scope notes, examples, Inclusions, or cross-classification suggestions. Number 121.6 converts from "Belief and certitude" to the more methodological "Nature of inquiry," and is given three new subdivisions.

Section 122 (Causation) updates its caption from the older "Cause and effect."

Section 123 (Determinism ...) is also renamed "Determinism and indeterminism." It was "Freedom and necessity" before. The ousted terms are split into numbered subdivisions alongside "Chance."

Section 124 (Teleology) is unchanged and unpartitioned.

Section [125] (Finite and infinite) shifts to 111.6.

Section 126 (The self) subordinates former caption "Consciousness and personality" to a scope note for reasons known only to the DDC editors.

Section 127 (The unconscious and the subconscious) is unchanged and unpartitioned.

Section 128 (Humankind) is but one of several captions in *DDC 19* which substitute this painfully non-vernacular word for the discredited generic "Man." A Class here note recognizes recent interest in philosophical anthropology and the philosophy of human life. A number of examples such as "reason," "memory," and "appetite" illustrate 128.3 (Attributes and faculties). It used to be captioned "Man's nature."

Section 129 (Origin and destiny of individual souls) reduces 129[.4] (Incarnation and reincarnation) and 126[.6] (Immortality) to an Inclusion note. They are now investigated more frequently in religious or quasi-religious than in philosophical contexts.

Division 130   Paranormal Phenomena and Arts

It is more than an idle pun to say that skeletons from the DDC closet emerge in this division. The 130's traditionally covered works on mind/body interactions up to and including hypnotism, spirits, etc.[4] Well-nigh universal dissatisfaction with the whole class 100 arrangement brought major changes, some of which proved in the long run to be equally unsatisfactory. For example, *DDC 7* introduced 136.7 (Child study and paidology), relocating it from its former "nursery" associations in 649. Comaromi says:

> The expansion here was indicative of the concern with education that was prominent in this edition, probably because of Miss Seymour's specialty in this field.[5]

The shift was crass slotification. It severed child study from division 150 (Mind and body) on the one hand, and from division 370 (Education) on the other. Later editions, particularly *DDC 13* (1932), augmented the problem until the long-awaited revision of *DDC 17* (1965) moved section 136 (Differential and genetic psychology) to section 155. It took two more editions to expunge all phantasms of psychology as a scientific discipline from the 130's, whose *DDC 18* caption still read "Popular psychology, parapsychology, occultism." A scope note sends the user to class 200 for the phenomena of religious experience.

Section 131 (Parapsychological and occult techniques for achievement of well-being, happiness, success) sports a new name and total discontinuance of its former subdivisions. "Nonoccult means for achievement of personal well-being, happiness, success" are shipped off to section 158.

Section [132] remains unassigned.

Section 133 (Parapsychology and occultism), for which literary warrent has long demanded extensive subdivision, has a few new notes to clarify interrelationships and contrasts. Minor terminological changes serve the same purpose. At 133.122 (Specific types of haunted places), refinements on the *DDC 19* captions can be found in *DC&*, v. 4, no. 1 (June 1980): 12. "Voodooism" (133[.47]) shifts to 299.67 (Various specific cults of Black African and Negro origin). "Frauds in occultism" (133[.7]) is reduced. Cf. the excerpt from this section reproduced on page 96.

Section [134] is unassigned.

Section 135 (Dreams and mysteries) is little changed, except that all aspects of Rosicrucianism are grouped here, its fraternal elements being no longer located at 366.4.

Section [136] has been vacant since *DDC 17* moved its content to section 155.

Section 137 (Divinatory graphology), like section 131, sheds all the psychological overtones lingering in its *DDC 18* caption "Personality analysis and improvement." Its new name is borrowed from its discontinued subdivision. *DC&*, v. 4, no. 1 (June 1980): 12 strikes the word "Analytic" from the *DDC 19* "analytic and divinatory graphology."

Sections 138 (Physiognomy) and 139 (Phrenology) are unchanged and unpartitioned.

Division 140   Specific Philosophical Viewpoints

This division had a short-lived "relocation" in *DDC 15* (1951). It slunk home again in the general retreat sounded by *DDC 16* (1958), but classifiers who deplore that surrender to alleged slotification can still be found.[6] It is the division of "isms," and can claim some literary warrant, perhaps, from the peculiarities of its literature. Midway between *DDC 18* and *19* the editor promised a "clarification of relationship between 140 and 180-190," but more pressing needs must have intervened.[7] Only minuscule (though certainly warranted) expansions can be found.

Section 141 (Idealism and related systems and doctrines) elevates modern Platonism and Neoplatonism from an Inclusion note to full subdivision status.

Section 142 (Critical philosophy) does the same for Existentialism.

Sections 143 (Intuitionism and Bergsonism), 144 (Humanism and related systems and doctrines), and 145 (Sensationalism and ideology) are unchanged.

Section 146 (Naturalism, etc.) has three timely additions: 146.32 (Dialectical materialism), 146.42 (Logical positivism), and 146.44 (Empiricism).

Sections 147 (Pantheism, etc.) and 148 (Liberalism, eclecticism, syncretism, traditionalism, dogmatism) are barely changed. Only a note under 147 transfers "Theosophy" to 299.934.

Section 149 (Other philosophical systems and doctrines) relocates Anthroposophy from 149.3 (Mysticism) to its own 299.935. Occult mysticism moves back to division 130; Religious mysticism moves forward to class 200. "Linguistic analysis" is now subordinate to a recaptioned 149.94 (Linguistic philosophies), while Semantics gets its own 149.946, and Structuralism comes in at 149.96.

Division 150   Psychology

There has been ferment here for several decades. The phoenix revision of *DDC 17* was to be

...a wholly new schedule for the entire subject, including psychological topics formerly in 130 (which retains only pseudo- and parapsychology and occultism), and relocating topics that belong in 614 and 616 to those numbers. New meanings will be assigned to numbers as freely as is required to make a schedule that will classify modern literature.[8]

There were 65 "reused" numbers and 27 relocated topics in that revision.[9] Yet by early 1976, divisions 130 and 150 had once again taken high priority (fifth place) on a list of needed revisions.[10]

Thanks to relocations, the scattering in the seventeenth and currently used eighteenth editions of the DDC is lower than in previous editions. Yet it is difficult to understand why the schedule of 150: Psychology does not include such a typically psychological field as Social Psychology, which is under Sociology: 301.1. One can also wonder why Mental Deficiency is under Medical Science (616.8588) and Performance Rating under Management (658.3125). But in comparison to the Library of Congress Classification, it is true progress that Physiological, Clinical, and Educational psychology are in the 150: Psychology section.[11]

As a matter of fact, Educational psychology has not budged from its 370.15 location since it first appeared as "Psychology applied to education" in *DDC 8* (1913). In *DDC 19*, Social psychology is still classed as a subdiscipline of sociology (in phoenix 302) with a cross-classification note under 150. The other examples cited above remain in their *DDC 18* locations, i.e., subsumed under other disciplines. Nor is there much other substantive change, as the following sectional review shows. A table of precedence is added, to which *DC&*, v. 4, no. 1 (June 1980): 12 adds 153.94 (Aptitude tests) at the top.

Section [151] has been unassigned since Edition 16.

Section 152 (Physiological psychology) removes "Experimental" from its caption to a Class here note. Butcher predicts hopefully that "one day it will reach its proper home, in 152.8."[12] The caption at 152.5 substitutes "Physiological drives" for "Motivation (Drives)." Its subdivisions drop out because Motivation shifts to an Inclusion note under 153.8 (Volition).

Section 153 (Intelligence, intellectual and conscious mental processes) is only slightly changed. Number 153.32 (Eidetic imagery) seems to have been inadvertently dropped, for it is already restored by *DC&* under the rewording "Imagery, including visualization." Number 153.6 (Communication) will complicate disciplinary classification. For example, Psychic communication belongs in 133.93, Communication in child psychology uses 155.413, and the psychology of animal communication is at 156.36 (a synthetic number found only in the Relative Index under "Communication--psychology--animals," but see also "Communication--animal ecology 591.59"). These subtle shades of application, if rigidly observed, will scatter materials frequently used together.

Section 154 (Subconscious and altered states and processes) adds "and altered" to the *DDC 18* caption because of 154.4 (Altered states of consciousness, including alterations due to use of drugs). Under 154.7 (Hypnotism), an unused subdivision "Special developments" is reduced.

Section 155 (Differential and genetic psychology) has a table of precedence already revised in *DC&*, where specific reference to 155.28 (Appraisals and tests) is eliminated. It moves from second rank to last, subordinate to 155.2 (Individual psychology). "Developmental psychology" (formerly 155.4-.7) gives way to a Class here note at 155.4-.6 (Psychology of specific ages). "Creativity" is relocated to 153.35, where "Intellectual and conscious mental processes" has for several editions recognized it.

Section 156 (Comparative psychology) starts with a reworded definition and a cross-classification note, sending material on the behavior of nonhuman organisms to 574.5 (Ecology). Works on the habits and behavior of animals go to 591.51; those on plant behavior, to 581.5 (Ecology of plants). This section is one of the few in class 100 where Add notes offer expansion from sequences at other schedule locations.

Section 157 (Abnormal and clinical psychologies) moves Organic psychoses to 616.892-.898. Examples replace Add notes under divisions of the centered heading 157.3-.7 (Psychoneuroses).

Section 158 (Applied psychology) houses the popular materials on personal well-being, happiness, and success which *DDC 18* classed in 131[.3]. At 158.1 the caption is converted from "Successful living" to "Personal improvement and analysis." An Inclusion note absorbs those aspects which were deleted from section 137 (Divinatory graphology). The new 158.9 (Systems and schools) takes over 131[.35] (Dianetics). Scientology (a new topic in *DDC 19*) is listed as a religion at 299.936.

Section 159 (Other aspects) is undeveloped and unchanged.

Division 160   Logic

There isn't much going on in this division nowadays. Symbolic logic has gone off to do its thing at 511.3, without even a cross-classification note. None of the sections are subdivided; two are vacated. Is this backwater area being held in anticipation of the future expansion of psychology?

Division 170   Ethics (Moral Philosophy)

In contrast to the preceding division, modest changes here reflect the sizeable body of literature available on contemporary ethical topics. Two standard subdivisions receive special development. Number 170.202 (Normative ethics for special groups) used to be called "Practical ethics (Conduct of life)." Two "Special topics of general applicability" distinguish "Normative" from "Critical" ethics. Both are included without distinction under 171 (Systems and doctrines) and 172-179 (Applied ethics).

Section 171 (Systems and doctrines) changes little except for deletion of a cross-classification note at 171.1 (Based on authority). Its reference to 241 (Moral theology) becomes a cross-classification note under 170.

Section 172 (Political ethics) incorporates minor vocabulary changes expressing revised concepts of state/individual interaction. A new 172.42 (Warfare) hosts the wealth of post-nuclear and Viet Nam material on the ethics of weapons testing, strategic arms limitations, etc.

Section 173 (Ethics of family relationships) is unexpanded. Most of its potential content is in various sociology locations (301-307) or in 640 (Home economics and family living). A note transfers the ethics of sex and reproduction to section 176.

Section 174 (Economic, professional, occupational ethics) drops an option to scatter these materials, now that the optional *ss*-017 facet is gone from Table 1. A few concepts widen, e.g., the expanded caption for 174.25 (Innovative procedures in the medical professions) replacing "Organ transplants." The added 174.28 (Experimentation) distinguishes the use of human subjects from the long-standing 179.4 (Experimentation on animals), formerly called "Vivisection."

Section 175 (Ethics of recreation and leisure) shows minor patchwork. "Athletics" is added to "Games of skill" at 175.4, but "Including chess, checkers" affirms that skill can also be sedentary. Perhaps the antics of certain international chess and tennis stars occasioned its negligible literary warrant. A note under 175.5 (Games of chance) seems to say that "Gambling business" is different from church bingo or a Saturday night poker game among friends. A discontinued 175[.83] (Reading comics) must have fallen victim to a more permissive social climate.

Section 176 (Ethics of sex and reproduction) shows little more than window dressing. An Inclusion note covers premarital and extramarital relations. There is now a direction to transfer Abortion to the new 179.76. Number 176.7 is no longer limited to obscenity in art, although obscenity in literature (176.8) and obscenity in speech (179.5) are carefully distinguished. Most other aspects fall into class 200, or with specific social problems in the 360's.

Section 177 (Ethics of social relations) converts the 177.7 caption "Philanthropy, benevolence, kindness" to a simple, charismatic "Love."

Section 178 (Ethics of consumption) replaces the more emotionally charged "Temperance and intemperance."

Section 179 (Other ethical norms) avoids *DDC 18*'s "Cruelty." "Respect for life" shows up at 179.1, to cause cross-classification problems with 174.24 (Questions of life and death, including euthanasia), 179.3 (Treatment of animals), and 179.7 (Respect and disrespect for human life, including genocide, etc.). The new Abortion number was cited under section 176.

Division 180   Ancient, Medieval, Oriental Philosophy
Division 190   Modern Western Philosophy

All sections are essentially the same as in *DDC 18*. There is much implicit and explicit reliance on Table 2 (Areas). A few options permit collections to be placed in shorter numbers. One Add note at 181.04-.09 (Oriental philosophies based on specific religions) sends the user to division 290. "Jewish philosophy" sidles from 181.3 to 181.06, according to an Add example. Jurisdictional terminology is modernized, e.g., "Iraq" for "Mesopotamia" at 181.6. The seldom-used 181[.49] (Other Indian philosophies) is dropped.

Conclusion

Class 100 suffers from a split personality, but since it is a relatively small class its problems are not totally dysfunctional. Current literature tends to merge its disciplinary aspects with religion, linguistics, and the social, biological, or even the physical sciences. Classification problems lurk not so much in the technical hazards of number synthesis as in standardizing interpretations of subject integrity. There are many scope notes but few Add instructions. Most of the class numbers assigned to Library of Congress records in the following exercises are available in schedule or index. These exercises will give a background insight into disciplinary placement rather than provide useless drill in synthesizing numbers.

Exercises in the Use of Class 100

A. Analysis

111.1	Hélal, Georges. L'homme, l'inconscient, le réel vital ... c1977.	78-367433
121'.09'034	Habermas, Jürgen. Knowledge and human history ... 2nd [English] ed. ... 1978.	78-324845
133.3'2424	Balin, Peter. The flight of Feathered Serpent ... c1978.	78-64357
133.4'09714	Séguin, Robert Lionel. La sorcellerie au Québec du XVIIe au XIX siècle ... c1978.	79-341752
133.5'01'5	Gauquelin, Michel. Dreams and illusions of astrology ... c1979.	78-68134
133.8'028	Watkins, William Jon. The psychic experiment book ... 1980.	80-10895
141'.3'0922	Bedell, Madelon. The Alcotts ... 1980.	79-26741
149'.94	Ferré, Frederick. Language, logic, and God ... 1977, c1961. [A study of logical positivism]	77-9060
150'.19'50924	Raditsa, Leo. Some sense about Wilhelm Reich ... 1978.	77-9222
153.9'4'355	Bayroff, Abram G. The armed services vocational aptitude battery ... 1970.	71-608825
155.2'8	Andréani, Ghislaine. Testez-vous vous-même ... 1978.	80-457226
155.4'02'4649	Frijling-Schreuder, E. C. M. Children, what are they? ... 1975. [Child psychology]	74-19889
155.4'22	Tronick, Edward. Babies as people : new findings on our infants' social beginnings ... 1980.	80-14355
155.4'5'11	Edna Adelson, Paul Bach-y-Rita, Gershon Berkson, Joan Chase, Stella Chess, Paulina Fernandez, William Fowler, Selma Freiberg, Bernard Z. Friedlander, Agnes H. Ling, James W. Prescott, Charles E. Rice, Manly Spigelman on the effects of blindness and other impairments on early development ... 1976.	77-151181
155.4'5'5	Hollingworth, Leta Stetter. Children above 180 IQ : Standford-Binet origin and development ... 1975, c1942.	74-21417
155.4'5'67	Armen, Jean Claude. Gazelle-boy : a child brought up by gazelles in the Sahara Desert ... 1976.	77-365004

155.8'4'6872079177 Paschal, Franklin Cressey. Racial influences in the mental and physical devel-
opment of Mexican children ... 1925, 1971.   74-147289

155.9'114   Gibson, James Jerome. The ecological approach
to visual perception ... c1979.   78-69585

158'.24   Lilly, John Cunningham. The dyadic cyclone : the
autobiography of a couple ... 1976.   75-45307

162'.076   Pospesel, Howard. Arguments : deductive logic
exercises ... c1978.   77-16006

170'.0938   Boer, William den. Private morality in Greece
and Rome ... 1979.   80-461489

174'.3'0973   American Bar Foundation. Annotated code of
professional responsibility ... 1979.   79-55893

174'.9'301   Diener, Edward. Ethics in social and behavioral
research ... 1978.   78-8881

181'.043   Mookerjee, Satkari. The Buddhist philosophy of universal flux : an exposition of the philosophy of
critical realism as expounded by the school of
Dignāga ... 1975.   75-907666

181'.09'512   Hsün-tzu, 340-245 B.C. The works of Hsüntze
... 1977.   [Philosophy, Chinese]   75-41145

190'.2'02   Kreyche, Gerald F. Thirteen thinkers : a sampler
of great philosophers ... c1976.   76-25405

193   Hayman, Ronald. Nietzsche : a critical life ...
[B]   1980.   80-14218

199'.438   Ajdukiewicz, Kazimierz. The scientific world-
perspective and other essays, 1931-1963 ... c1978.   77-21887

B. Synthesis: Examples from LC records are given on pp. 165-68.

1. The development of family ties and personal attachment in small
    children.

2. The life and work of Harry Stack Sullivan.

3. A modern edition of the letters between Abélard, the twelfth-century
    scholastic monk, and the nun Héloîse.

4. A guide to conditions, problems, and therapies in psychology.

5. An introduction to cognitive development in children.

6. A doctor's case for euthanasia and suicide.

7. A plea for animal rights and human responsibilities for animals.

8. A study of male attitudes toward the sexual liberation of women.

9. A selection from the works of the behaviorist B. F. Skinner.

10. A psychohistory of research into consciousness-raising and improving
    group relations.

11. A presentation of the psychoanalytic ideas and concepts of Melanie Klein.

12. A study of relationships among women as presented in literature, conversations, diaries, and the like.

13. An inspirational treatise on cultivating friends in middle age.

14. A book on the causes and effects of loneliness in childhood and adolescence, with some suggestions for solutions.

15. Advice on coping with grief over the death of a loved one.

16. Time as we experience it, contrasted with time as implied by the structure of the atom and of the universe.

17. A work on the psychology of successful competition.

18. Texts of the Hindu philosophy known as Advaita.

19. A study of motor learning.

20. A key to sacred symbolic books and their use in divination.

21. A bibliography with abstracts on the behavioral development of non-human primates.

22. A philosophy of the self as expressed in the consciousness and personality of man.

23. A work on theosophy and the relation between reality and consciousness as expressed in a theory of knowledge.

24. A book of witchcraft.

25. A book on human relations in business and industry.

26. Collective biography of famous mediums, fortune-tellers, witches, and astrologists.

27. An examination of French movements in psychoanalysis.

28. A biographical and critical study of Sören Kierkegaard.

29. A study of the thirteenth-century English thinker, Roger Bacon.

30. The revival of Kantianism in German social and historical thought.

31. A picture book of the Athenian Agora and the Socratic presence there.

32. A look at education and survival from the nihilist point of view.

33. A light-hearted look at the 100 "greatest thinkers of all time."

34. An examination of dialectic in the logic of science.

35. A Wittgensteinian review of belief and doubt in the language of experience.

36. A book of essays on a variety of general philosophical topics.

37. A series of papers on Edmund Husserl's *Logische Untersuchungen.*

38. A series of investigations on the development of cognitive knowledge in children.

39. An investigation into heritable intelligence levels and racism.

40. The Rasch model for evaluating objective mental measurement.

41. An early eighteenth-century metaphysical theory of the ideal or intelligible world.

42. A handbook on the therapeutic use of one's fantasies.

43. An astrological approach to child rearing.

44. A work on the moral life.

45. A book on the uses of silence in developing consciously controlled thought processes.

46. Three essays applying the doctrine of materialism to consciousness, language, and cognition.

47. The development of personality in chidlren.

48. An introduction to Hindu cosmological views of man and his universe.

49. A historical outline of Jain philosophy.

50. Comparative analysis and interpretation of dreams.

51. A reader to accompany a newspaper study course on modern attitudes toward death and dying.

52. Professional concepts and methods in clinical psychology.

53. A study of Carl Rogers' humanistic psychology as it affects his client-centered psychotherapy.

54. A historical review of Polish logical methodology.

55. A study of the correlation between aptitude tests and shorthand achievement.

C. Reclassification

1. The following records carry pre-*DDC 19* number assignments by the Library of Congress. What adjustments should be made?

128'.3	Agassi, Joseph. Towards a rational philosophical anthropology ... 1977.	78-300043
131'.32	Kinney, Jean Brown. 57 tests that reveal your hidden talents ... 1972. [Ability testing; Success]	71-792435
142'.7	Gorz, André. Le Traître / André Gorz ; avant-propos de Jean-Paul Sartre ... 1978. [Existential philosophy]	78-399706
149'.9	Structuralism and since : from Lévi-Strauss to Derrida ... 1980.	79-40746
171	Barnes, Hazel Estella. Existential ethics ... 1978.	78-55038

2. Things (including books) are not always what they seem. Why do you suppose LC classed the following work as it did, and where else might you think of classing it?

121   Hardy, William C. Language, thought, and experience : a tapestry of the dimensions of meaning ... c1978. [Meaning (Philosophy); Semantics (Philosophy); Semiotics; Languages--Philosophy]   77-28163

3. At least two versions of the following record are available. Which classification do you prefer, and why?

    a. *Booklist*, v. 77, no. 6 (November 15, 1980): 424.

133   Randi, James. Flim flam! The truth about unicorns, parapsychology, and other delusions ... 1980. [Occult sciences--Controversial literature; Psychical research--Controversial literature]   80-7852

    b. MARC tapes.

001.9   Amazing Randi. Flim flam! ... 1980.   80-7852

Examples of LC Cataloging to Illustrate the Above Exercises in DDC Number Synthesis

1. 155.4'22   Brazelton, T. Berry. On becoming a family: the growth of attachment ... 1981.   80-25399

2. 150.1957 [B]   Chapman, A. H. (Arthur Harry). Harry Stack Sullivan : his life and his work ... 1976.   75-42926

3. 189'.4   Abelard, Peter. 1079-1142. Correspondence / Abélard et Héloïse ... 1979.   80-462599

4. 150   Bugelski, B. R. (Bergen Richard). Handbook of practical psychology ... 1980.   80-17677

5. 155.4'13'0924   Pulaski, Mary Ann Spencer. Understanding Piaget : an introduction to children's cognition development ... 1980.   80-7595

6. 174'.24   Barnard, Christiaan Neethling. Good life/good death : a doctor's case for euthanasia and suicide ... 1980.   80-18839

7. 179'.3   Fox, Michael W. Returning to Eden : animal rights and human responsibilities ... 1980.   79-56281

8. 155.3'4   Rubin, Jerry. The war between the sheets ... 1980.   80-16541

9. 150.19'434   Skinner, B. F. (Burrhus Frederic). Notebooks ... 1980.   80-20094

10. 158'.2   Houston, Jean. Lifeforce : the psycho-historical recovery of the self ... 1980.   80-23726

11. 150.19'5'0924   Segal, Hanna. Melanie Klein ... 1980.   80-14056
    [B]

12. 155.6'33   Bernikow, Louise. Among women ... 1980.   79-24733

13. 155.6   Sparks, James Allen. Friendship after forty ...
                   1980.   80-10629

14. 152.44   Killinger, John. The loneliness of children ...
                   1980.   79-56378

15. 155.9'37   Tatelbaum, Judy. The courage to grieve ... 1980.   80-7868

16. 115   Park, David Allen. The image of eternity : roots
                   of time in the physical world ... 1980.   79-22984

17. 158'.1   Walker, Stuart H. Winning : the psychology of compe-
                   tition ... 1980.   79-27032

18. 181'.482   Advaitāksaramālikā : Advaitasabhāsuvarṇamahotsave
                   samarpitā ... 1978.   79-901040

19. 155.4'12   Anton, Montserrat. La psicomotricitat al parvulari
                   ... 1979.   79-125808

20. 133.3   Áryádeva, 1917-1970. La clef : Vajrakuñcikāvidyā :
                   Saṅketavidyā = : le livre sacré des livres sacrés
                   : ou, la symbolique universelle restituée ... 1979-   80-459033

21. 156   Behavioral development of nonhuman primates : an
                   abstracted bibliography ... c1980.   79-26700

22. 126   Bennett, John Dogolphin. Deeper man ... 1978.   80-458731

23. 121   Bruteau, Beatrice. The psychic grid : how we create
                   the world we know ... c1979.   79-64096

24. 133.4'3   Carrer, Danièle. La désencraudeuse ... c1978.   80-455231

25. 158.7   Carvell, Fred J. Human relations in business ...
                   c1980.   79-11639

26. 133'.092'2   Chaleil, André. Les Grands initiés de notre
                   temps ... 1978.   79-127596

27. 150'.19'50944 Psychoanalysis, creativity, and literature
                   : a French-American inquiry ... 1978.   77-26613

28. 198'.9   Hohlenberg, Johannes Edouard. Sören Kierkegaard
    [B]   ... 1978, c1954.   78-946

29. 189   Westacott, Evalyn. Roger Bacon in life and legend
                   ... 1978, c1953.   78-532

30. 142'.3   Willey, Thomas E. Back to Kant : the revival of
                   Kantianism in German social and historical
                   thought, 1860-1914 ... 1978.   77-29215

31. 183'.2   Lang, Mabel L. Socrates in the Agora ... 1978.
    [B]   (Excavations of the Athenian Agora ...)   78-103576

32. 149'.8   Holbrook, David. Education, nihilism, and
                   survival ... 1977.   78-313687

33.	109	Schlossberg, Edwin. The philosopher's game : match your wits against the 100 greatest thinkers of all time ... 1978, c1977.	78-315995
34.	160	Hubig, Christoph. Dialektik und Wissenschaftslogik : e. sprachphilos.-handlungstheoret. Analyse ... 1978.	78-375181
35.	121'.6	Needham, Rodney. Belief, language, and experience ... 1972.	72-87712
36.	100	Lindley, Richard. What philosophy does ... 1978.	78-314811
37.	193	Readings on Edmund Husserl's Logical investigations / edited by J. N. Mohanty ... 1977.	78-300932
38.	153.4 s [370.15'2]	Piaget and education / edited by Jeanette McCarthy Gallagher and J. A. Easley, Jr. ... c1978. (Knowledge and development ; v. 2)	79-103886
39.	155.7	Lawler, James M. IQ, heritability, and racism ... 1978.	78-14264
40.	153.9'3	Hashway, Robert M. Objective mental measurement : individual and program evaluation using the Rasch model ... c1978.	78-19739
41.	110	Norris, John, 1657-1711. An essay towards the theory of the ideal or intelligible world, 1701-1704 ... 1978.	75-11243
42.	154.3	Collins, David. Daydreams : making your fantasies work for you ... 1979.	78-31733
43.	133.5'8'6491	Edmands, Dodie. The children's astrologer ... c1978.	78-53406
44.	170	Beehler, Rodger. Moral life ... 1978.	78-13113
45.	153	Wallach, Wendell. The undistracted mind ... c1978.	78-59732
46.	146'.3	Colman, Morris. On consciousness, language, and cognition : three studies in materialism ... c1978.	79-100449
47.	155.4'18	Mussen, Paul Henry. Child development and personality ... c1979.	78-9840
48.	113	Bhallacharjee, Siva Sadhan. The Hindu theory of cosmology : an introduction to the Hindu view of man and his universe ... 1978.	78-907130
49.	181'.04'4	Bhattacharyya, Narendra Nath. Jain philosophy : historical outline ... 1976.	76-902152
50.	154.6'34	Dream interpretation : a comparative study ... c1978.	78-5874
51.	128'.5	Death and dying : challenge and change / edited by Robert Fulton ... c1978.	78-59488
52.	157'.9	Phares, E. Jerry. Clinical psychology : concepts, methods, and profession ... 1979.	78-62632

53. 150'.19'2	Kirschenbaum, Howard. On becoming Carl Rogers ... c1979.	78-13308
54. 160'.9438	Twenty-five years of logical methodology in Poland ... c1977.	76-7064
55. 153.9'4'653	Osborne, Agnes Elizabeth. The relationship between certain psychological tests and short-hand achievement ... 1943, 1972.	78-177137

NOTES

[1]See, for example, Marty Bloomberg and Hans Weber, *An Introduction to Classification and Number Building in Dewey* (Littleton, CO, Libraries Unlimited, 1976), p. 58.

[2]Some enthusiastic faceters argue that section entries which duplicate, or nearly duplicate, auxiliary table sequences are inefficient and make the schedule bulky. See, for instance: P. Dhyani, "DDC 18: Critical Appraisal of Some Auxiliary Tables," *International Library Review*, v. 9, no. 2 (April 1977): 177.

[3]Doralyn J. Hickey, "Problems Associated with Presenting and Teaching the Schedules: Philosophy (100); Religion (200); and the Fine Arts (700)," *The Dewey Decimal Classification: Outlines and Papers Presented at a Workshop on the Teaching of Classification* (New York, School of Library Service, Columbia University, 1968), p. 32.

[4]The present DDC editor says that "Fire walking" (001.93) is wrongly classed and should also be in the 130's.

[5]John Phillip Comaromi, *The Eighteen Editions of the Dewey Decimal Classification* (Albany, NY, Forest Press Division, Lake Placid Education Foundation, 1976), p. 250.

[6]Hickey, p. 32.

[7]Benjamin A. Custer, "Dewey Decimal Classification One Hundred Years After," *Catalogue & Index*, no. 39 (Winter 1975): 3.

[8]Benjamin A. Custer, "Dewey 17: A Preview and Report," *Wilson Library Bulletin*, v. 39, no. 7 (March 1965): 557.

[9]Melvil Dewey, *Dewey Decimal Classification and Relative Index*. Ed. 17 (Lake Placid Club, NY, Forest Press, 1965): v. 1, p. 49.

[10]John P. Comaromi, "Decimal Classification Editorial Policy Committee Report," *Library Resources & Technical Services*, v. 21, no. 1 (Winter 1977): 94.

[11]Miluse Soudek, "On the Classification of Psychology in General Library Classification Schemes," *Library Resources & Technical Services*, v. 24, no. 2 (Spring 1980): 122.

[12]Peter Butcher, "Dewey? We Sure Do!," *Catalogue & Index*, no. 55 (Winter 1979): 8.

8

Class 200 Religion

Introduction

Criticisms of Dewey's personal religious biases and of the shortcomings of class 200 are not wanting. They arose early on, from most types of libraries and most faiths, e.g., Roman Catholicism, Christian Science, Mormonism, Judaism, and the Oriental religions. Doctrinal, textual, philosophic, psychological, and social aspects were interminably shuffled and rebalanced in successive DDC editions. According to one voice of reason:

> There surely have been inadequacies and religious biases in Dewey's Decimal Classification. Some of these faults are attributable to the personal peculiarities of Dewey himself; some to the kinds of libraries for which early editions of the system were designed; and some to the later editors of the scheme. Most of these biases are forgivable because they were inevitable—or at least human.
>
> Probably any general library classification is more likely to be—or seem—biased in religion than in any other discipline. Several factors account for this warpage: the large number of materials to be classified; the parochial and controversial vein of many books in the field; the fact that, traditionally, people are likely to be narrow-minded in religion—not considering beliefs other than their own to be particularly important. Any hierarchical classification is, as we have been reminded so often, always unsatisfactory to most users, but its faults are likely to be magnified when it is examined by religionists. On the whole then, it seems fair to conclude that the Decimal Classification's sections devoted to religion have stood up reasonably well against charges of opponents.[1]

A battery of techniques was supplied in *DDC 18* to allow preferred treatment, with shorter numbers, for any belief. The options are summarized in Bloomberg and Weber.[2] They include two permanently unassigned numbers for local use (see Example 21 in chapter 3).

The divisional summaries of the two most recent DDC editions have such minor wording differences that they are hardly worth repeating:

Summary (*DDC 18*)		**Summary** (*DDC 19*)	
200	RELIGION	200	RELIGION
210	Natural religion	210	Natural religion
220	Bible	220	Bible
230	Christian doctrinal theology (Christian dogma)	230	Christian theology; Christian doctrinal theology
240	Christian moral and devotional theology	240	Christian moral and devotional theology
250	Local Christian church and Christian religious orders	250	Local Christian church and Christian religious orders
260	Christian social and ecclesiastical theology	260	Christian social and ecclesiastical theology
270	Historical and geographical treatment of organized Christian church (Church history)	270	Historical and geographical treatment of organized Christian church (Church history)
280	Denominations and sects of Christian church	280	Denominations and sects of Christian church
290	Other religions and comparative religion	290	Other religions and comparative religion

Other terminology changes show up regularly throughout the class, sometimes signifying conceptual shifts, but at other times merely conforming to modern usage. Representative ones are:

1. The *DDC 19* substitution of "Humankind" for "Man" at 218, 233, 291.22, and 297.22. This effort at non-sexism was noted in division 120 and its subsection 128.

2. The substitution of "secular disciplines" for "intellectual development" in the captions at 261.5 (Christianity and ...) and 291.175 (Other religions and ...).

3. A similar preference for "political affairs" over "civil government" at 261.7 (Christianity and ...) and 291.177 (Other religions and ...).

4. A subtle psychological shift in rewording the captions for "guides" to various types of religious life and practice. See, for instance:

248.4	Christian life and practice	(*DDC 19*)
	[Guides to conduct of Christian life]	(*DDC 18*)
248[.42]	General guides [Reduced to 248.4]	
248.48	Guides to Christian life for specific denominations and sects [*formerly also* 248.9]	
248.8	Guides to Christian life for specific classes ...	(*DDC 19*)
	[Personal Christianity for specific classes ...]	(*DDC 18*)

248[.9]	Guides to Christian life for specific denominations and sects Class in 248.8	(*DDC 19*)
291.44	Comparative religions: religious life and practice	(*DDC 19*)
	[Personal religion: guides to conduct of life]	(*DDC 18*)
296.74	Jewish religious life and practice	(*DDC 19*)
	[Jewish guides to conduct of life]	(*DDC 18*)

Division 200   Religion in General

Section 200, like sections 100, 300-400, and 700-800, starts with a definition. All except the 000 and 600 sections give initial cross-classification notes. The 200, 400, and 800 sections also give options for manipulating a local preference throughout the class. Modern linguistic interests receive disciplinary affiliation at 200.14 (Religious language ...), just as they do in 149.94 (Linguistic philosophies), 401.9 (Psycho- and sociolinguistics), etc. Similarly, 200.19 (Psychological aspects Including religious experience based on psychedelic drugs) competes with 154.4 (Altered states of consciousness, including alterations due to use of drugs). "Mythology ... " moves out for disciplinary consolidation at 291.13. A Class elsewhere note at 200.71 sends the user to 377.1 for religious instruction and exercises in nonsectarian schools. See further comment at section 268 on the disciplinary scattering of "religious education." History subdivision 200.901 is now specifically pre-499 A.D., but prehistoric religions and those of nonliterate peoples go to 291.042.

Sections 201-209 (Standard subdivisions of Christianity) follow closely upon the 200.1-.9 span for religion in general. Christian theology is relocated to division 230, while the geographic span 207[.104-.109] moves to shorter notation at 207.4-.9 (Schools and courses in specific continents, etc.).

Division 210   Natural Religion

The option note is slightly expanded. There is a disciplinary preference note, and another which relocates sub-topics, e.g., "Concepts of God" for any given religion with the religion. But not all disciplinary dilemmas are solved. The topics recapitulate many of those in 110 (Metaphysics) and 120 (Epistemology, etc.). Heavy traffic in topical affiliation occurs at some cross-roads or other in every hierarchical classification scheme. The trick is to supply adequate signals to keep it moving and prevent snarls.

Sections 211-212 (Concepts and nature of God) have considerably revised subdivisions, as Custer predicted.[3] Anthropomorphism is reduced to an Inclusion note. Pantheism moves next door. Both relocations expand 211 at the expense of 212. So does the Theism shift, with its new divisions for Polytheism, Dualism, and Monotheism. Still other discontinuances send materials on Theosophy and Anthroposophy into the 299's.

Section 213 (Creation) drops its single subdivision for an Inclusion note which covers both "evolution as a method of creation" and "evolution versus creation." Apparently *DDC 19* thinks the Scopes trial is over, but what will it do about Creationism?

Sections 214 (Theodicy), 215 (Science and religion), and 216 (Good and evil) are unchanged except for a note under 215.7 (Life sciences) to put evolution vis-à-vis creation in 213.

Section [217] (Worship and prayer) has vacated the premises more or less gracefully "because without meaning in natural religion" (CF. Example 8 in chapter 3).

Sections 218 (Humankind) and 219 (Analogy) are little changed except for the new word "Humankind."

Division 220   Bible

Besides 822.33 (Shakespeare) and 829, where two Anglo-Saxon poets and an anonymous epic are cited, the only literary materials specifically identified in DDC are sacred scriptures. In keeping with a general Christian emphasis, one whole division is dedicated to the Bible, with its apochryphal works, versions, and commentaries. Other religious works are all crowded into division 290. Rearrangement and expansion of Bible materials were greater in immediately preceding editions. The separation of 221 (Old Testament) from 296.1 (Sources of Judaism) is regrettable, but will probably continue to make do. There is a one-way reference from the latter to the former.

Section 220 (Bible in general) does a bit of juggling. "Biblical authorship" moves to a redefined 220.66 (Cf. Example 18 in chapter 3). Concordances and indexes lose their general 220[.2] for more specific distribution under 220.4-.5 (Texts, versions, translations). Hermeneutics (220[.63]) falls into longer notation at 220.601. A few Inclusion and Class elsewhere notes come and go. Captions are refined. There is a new table under 220.5201-.5209 (English versions and translations), with numbers for standard or special editions, paraphrases, explanations, etc.

Sections 221-229 (Specific parts of the Bible) have minor adjustments. The Hagiographa and the Megillot (Five Rolls) get their own numbers under 221.04 (Special groupings of Old Testament books). The few other changes are instructional or editorial except for a reduction under 229.9 (Other pseudepigrapha).

Division 230   Christian Theology

Section 230, heretofore reserved for strictly doctrinal works, now hosts the more general literature from 201[.1]. Centered heading 230.042-.044 (Specific types of Christian theology) has places for "Catholic" and "Protestant," but sends all theologies which trace their origins directly to the Apostolic church to 230.1-.9 (Doctrines of specific denominations and sects).

Section 231 (God) shows desultory tinkering, but the only substantive changes are some extensions and a new caption. At 231.7 "Sovereignty" becomes "Relation to human experience," gaining four new subdivisions. Christ the Redeemer takes leave of the Holy Trinity for a new home in Christology (232.1-.8).

Section 232 (Jesus Christ and his family) likewise shows meager change, including the one just mentioned. A variety of notes now accompany 232.8 (Divinity and humanity of Christ). Number 232.9 (Family and life of Jesus) explicitly covers non-Trinitarian concepts. "Jesus as teacher and exemplar" replaces "Influence of Jesus" at 232.904, carrying a note to "Class teachings in 232.954." New "miracles" numbers are 232.917 (under Mary) and 232.955 (under Public life of Jesus).

Section 233 (Humankind) treats its topic from a Christian perspective, as 218 does for natural religion, but is more long-winded about it in deference to literary warrant. Sins are relocated to 241.3, where they become merely a matter of moral theology. The "soul" expands (or contracts) into the "Nature of humankind" at 233.5, with some Class elsewhere suggestions.

Section 234 adds "Grace" to "Salvation," with a luminous separation of "gifts of the Holy Spirit" from "spiritual gifts" and longish lists of specific gifts for the edification of the ungrateful. A couple of Inclusion notes yoke "confession" with "penance," and "reconciliation" with "repentance and forgiveness." *DC&* added "hope" to "faith." If anyone wonders what happened to "charity," it is a social, ethical, and nominal (but not religious) concept according to the Relative Index. A bit of religious schedule searching finds it identified with the Christian virtues at 241.4.

Section 235 (Spiritual beings) is unchanged and unmindful of its sinister (literally, left-handed) cousin 133.4 (Demonology and witchcraft).

Section 236 (Eschatology) is barely touched. The world stubbornly refuses to come to an end, and medical science, in spite of its new burst of "research," cannot tell us precisely what to expect when we die, which we all continue to do.

Section [237] continues unassigned.

Section 238 (Creeds, confessions of faith, etc.) remains orthodox.

Section 239 (Apologetics and polemics) may be the focus of plenty of disputation, but its *DDC 18* arrangement is unaltered.

Division 240   Christian Moral and Devotional Theology

There are several heavily populated, minutely subdivided sections here.

Section 241 (Moral theology) adds Inclusion and cross-classification notes. Number 241.3, with its fresh burden of sin from 233[.2], now distinguishes mortal and venial sins from those against the Holy Spirit. The Sermon on the Mount gets its own number under "Biblical precepts."

Section 242 (Devotional literature) has a precedence table for various kinds of prayers. A bit of reduction and a bit of expansion, take place.

Section 243 (Evangelistic writings) is unexpanded and unchanged except for a "Class evangelistic sermons in 242.3."

Section [244] continues unassigned.

Section 245 (Hymns without music) now makes an Add reference to Table 6.

Sections 246 (Art in Christianity) and 247 (Church furnishings and related articles) remain virtually in their *DDC 18* format, a long way from the 700's. See further comment at section 254.

Section 248 (Christian experience, practice, life) was heralded prior to publication as "much revised."[4] Literary warrant is abundant in this field, but there is not much change. The 248.3 (Worship) caption is shortened and its contents subdivided. An instruction to class texts (literature) of prayers (meditations) in 242 might help us remember the action/product split. Pilgrimages are reduced to an Inclusion note at 248.46.

Section 249 changes "Christian worship" to "Christian observances" in family life, and adds a list of specifics.

Division 250   Local Christian Church and Religious Orders

A centered heading warns us that the next four divisions, nearly half of the religion class, cover various specifics of the Christian church. But comprehensive works on the church class in section 260. The order of divisions leaves something to be desired, both from a classificatory and from a mnemonic perspective. A better arrangement might be:

250   Christian social and ecclesiastical theology
260   Local Christian church and Christian religious orders
270   Denominations and sects of the Christian church
280   Historical and geographical treatment of the organized church

Works on the church as a social witness to the Word, immediately after Christian theology (240), could be followed by the two divisions on specific practices and organizations. Church history would come last, where DDC traditionally puts historical and regional aspects of a topic. But such sweeping revision, with all the reclassification it would entail, is unlikely.

Section 250 is one of those places (like 020.68) where *ss*-068 is expressly forbidden. Works on management of local churches are presumably numerous enough to merit their own section 254. Organization and administration of religious orders belongs in 255.

Sections 251 (Preaching) and 252 (Sermon texts) show the familiar separation of "how-to" and "what" materials (Cf. section [029] in chapter 6). At least the two aspects are kept side by side in this discipline. The "evangelistic sermons" location was cited under section 243.

Sections 253 (Pastoral duties) and 254 (Parish government) have only a few additions. Three subtopics differentiate urban, suburban, and rural parishes under 254.2. The 254.3 caption is now "Use of communications media" instead of "Radio and television work." Christian church buildings" at 254.7 still overlap with "Christian architecture" at 246.9 and "Christian church buildings" at 726.5. There may be disciplinary justification, but closely related materials are scattered without cross-references.

Section 255 (Religious congregations and orders) supplies an internal Add table for commonly shared concepts, e.g., 02 (Constitutions). New orders are enumerated, while the redundant 255[.979] under 255.97 (Other Roman Catholic orders of women) has withered.

Sections [256], [257], and [258] are unassigned.

Section 259 (Parochial activities) is considerably expanded.

Division 260   Christian Social and Ecclesiastical Theology

Section 261 (Social theology and interreligious relations and attitudes) shows ecumenical expansion. *DC&*, v. 4, no. 1 (June 1980): 13 corrects the example number at 261.835. It should be 261.83576 (Christian attitude toward homosexuality). Ubiquitous questions of disciplinary affiliation bob up once more. What materials should class here, as distinct from those which go to 306.6 (Religious institutions) and/or to 306.7 (Institutions pertaining to the regulations of the sexes)? And does the scattering impair efficient use?

Section 262 (Ecclesiology) opens new subdivisions for ecumenical works and for church renewal. We shall find the former treated again in historical context at 270.82. A second expansion comes from *DC&* in the form of an Add note for denominations under 262.14 (Local clergy).

Section 263 (Days, times, places of religious observance) is unaltered.

Section 264 (Public worship) displays a few liturgical expansions.

Section 265 (Other rites, ceremonies, etc.) loses the Eucharist to 264.36, and gains 265.94 (Exorcism). The addition no doubt has recent literary warrant, but lands us back in a disciplinary standoff with 134.427 (Exorcism of demons).

Section 266 (Missions) reduces and relocates two general subtopics. Changing social, and even religious, attitudes toward mission work are implicit in the shift.

Section 267 (Associations for religious work) has minor changes. Moral rearmament as an organized movement comes in from 248.25. History periods for the YMCA include cheery anticipation of the twenty-first century.

Section 268 (Religious training) forbids *ss*-068 in favor of the shorter 268.1. A few notes are lost, a few gained. One mentions 377.1 (Nonsectarian schools) and 649.7 (Children's moral ... training), but does not suggest 200.7 (Study and teaching of religion) or 207 (... of Christianity).

Section 269 (Spiritual renewal) is very brief. Social change causes demotion of "Revivals and camp meetings" to subtopic status under "Evangelism." Pentecostalism is provided a place, with a reference to 270.82 (20th century church) for its historical aspects.

Division 270   Christian Church History

This division is so little touched by the passage of DDC time that there is little new to say about it. Minuscule terminology changes and note expansions appeared in the first volume 4 issue of *DC&.*

Division 280   Denominations and Sects of the Christian Church

The changes are likewise minimal in this division. New extensions identify hitherto unestablished or unrecognized denominations, e.g., the United Reformed Church in the United Kingdom, and the Jehovah's Witnesses. One of the permanently unassigned numbers of local option falls here (Cf. Example 21 in chapter 3).

Division 290   Other Religions and Comparative Religion

Most of the changes in this important and overburdened division are reprisals of those we have noted for natural religion and Christianity. Some expansions cover texts or doctrines with increasing literary warrant, e.g., 297.86

(Ahmadiyya movement). Related are a short series of replacements such as that of the pantheistic Subud out of 212[.5] into 299.933, and comprehensive works on Judaic worship from 296.4 to 296.72. A second permanently unassigned (optional) number is included at [298].

Conclusion

Because the varieties of organized religion tend to be more analogical in structure and regional in character than the branches of philosophy and psychology, class 200 has more faceting than class 100. Two new supplementary tables, one with footnote references to starred digits, encourage synthetic number building. There are over 60 other Add directions. Most referrals are internal, but spans from classes 100, 300, 700, and the auxiliary tables are employed. Two tables of precedence are available. Still, most Library of Congress bibliographic records carry DDC numbers taken directly from the schedule. Extensive optional possibilities for local preferences are summarized at the head of the class, but of course do not affect LC assignments.

Exercises in the Use of Class 200

The following exercises follow the same pattern, and are subject to the same conditions, as the earlier ones in this text. The student should read the prefatory remarks to the exercises in chapters 2 and 6 before attempting to do the ones given here.

A.   Analysis

220.8'1521'66	Amerding, George D. The fragrance of the Lord : toward a deeper appreciation of the Bible ... c1979.	79-1774
221.6	Schultz, Samuel J. The gospel of Moses ... 1979. [Bible--History of biblical events]	78-11662
226'.05'91817	Zhivkova, Liudmila. Das Tetraevangeliar des Zaren Ivan Alexander ... 1977.	77-558805
227'.91'06	Wiersbe, Warren W. Be mature : an expository study of the Epistle of James ... c1978.	78-52558
262'.03'0681	Young, Frances Merle. Thankfulness unites : the history of the United Thank Offering, 1889-1979 ... c1979.	79-124170
266'.39467	Brownrigg, Marcus. Mission to the islands : the missionary voyages in Bass Strait of Canon Marcus Brownrigg, 1872-1885 ... 1979.	80-458003
272'.2'09466	Henningsen, Gustav. The witches' advocate : Basque witchcraft and the Spanish Inquisition, 1609-1614 ... 1980.	79-20340
274.23'78	Hull, P. L. A thousand years : Kenstec to Benson ... 1977.	78-325346

294.3'4'2	Asaṅga. On knowing reality : the Tattvārtha chapter of Asaṅga's Bodhisattvabhūmi ... 1979. [Yogācāra (Buddhism)]	79-16047
294.5'178358	Apte, Usha Mukund. The sacrament of marriage in Hindu society, from Vedic period to dharma-śāstras ... 1978.	78-904032
296.3'877	Lévy, Bernard Henri. Testament of God ... c1980 [Religion and politics; Covenants (Theology)]	80-7589
299'.21	Dougherty, Raymond Philip. The shirkûtu of Babylonian deities ... 1980.	78-63548

B. Synthesis: Examples from LC records are given on pp. 179-82.

1. An administrative and program manual on church family camps and conferences.

2. A personal encounter with death and its impact on concepts of immortality.

3. A book on the Hutterite Brethren and the Bruderhof communities.

4. A presentation of contemporary Catholic existentialism.

5. A study of hallucinogenic drugs and religious experience among the Yaqui Indians of Mexico.

6. A book of biblical archaeology and antiquities.

7. A concordance of the Revised Standard Version of the New Testament.

8. Mission work by the Church of Jesus Christ of Latter-day Saints.

9. A topical Bible index and collections of sermon outlines.

10. A record of life at the Reverend Jim Jones' Peoples Temple.

11. A Jewish interpretation of the life of Jesus Christ.

12. An eschatological study of death and the future life.

13. The Chaitanya movement in Visnuism.

14. Religion in ancient Rome.

15. A memoir of Protestantism in the Deep South a generation ago.

16. Marriage and the Catholic Church.

17. The history of the National Baptist Convention.

18. A study of the sacred scripture known as the Rig Veda.

19. Use of hallucinatory drugs in the religious rites of the Tucano Indians of Colombia.

20. A book of the Free Communion Church, the Laughing Man Institute, and the religious leader Da Free John.

21. A biographical dictionary of the Bible.

22. A study of religious education in the Philippine Islands.

23. A history of the Christian Church in the seventeenth and eighteenth centuries.

24. A history of old Korean religions.

25. A handbook of parish work.

26. A book on prayer.

27. A Christian "theology of education."

28. An anthology of Kirby Page's writings on theology, the church, and social problems.

29. A Brazilian bishop's views of Christianity and justice.

30. A collection of papal documents on the historical stance of Catholicism toward social problems.

31. A study of Origen and his influence on church/state relations.

32. Evangelistic work in Asian Indian missions.

33. A commentary on the book of Genesis.

34. A philosophical study of religion.

35. Relations of church and state in Alsace.

36. The religious life of the Arapesh tribe of New Guinea.

37. Papal attitudes toward medieval heresies.

38. Trade-union movements among the Mormons in territorial Utah.

39. The application of Christian principles to family living.

40. Christianity, politics, and business in South Africa.

41. A "new" approach to creationism.

42. A book on living a Christian life through meditation.

43. A collection of Roman Catholic sermons.

44. A guide for home study of the Psalms.

45. An exposition of the Roman Catholic sacraments.

46. A guide for personal development toward Christian maturity.

47. A biography of a Morman who lived in Utah from 1884 to 1965.

48. Studies of women's religious experience, life, and practice.

49. Fresh interpretation and criticism of the Old Testament.

50. Astrological elements in the religion of North American Indians.

51. A commentary on marriage as represented in the Code of canon law.

52. An anthology of one man's writings on Judaic theology.

53. The use of gaming in religious family life instruction.

54. Mary as a womanly ideal for Christian living.

55. The influence of the Apostle Paul's writings on the development of Christianity.

56. A theosophist's guide to death and dying.

C. Reclassification

    1. The following DDC numbers were assigned prior to publication of *DDC 19*. Moreover, one of them seems to contain a typo. If you were classing these works today, how would you change the numbers? Suggested numbers are given on page 182.

220.6'3	Structuralism and Biblical hermeneutics : a collection of essays / edited and translated by Alfred M. Johnson, Jr. ... 1979.	79-9411
261.8'34'510420977311	Ziegenhals, Walter E. Urban churches in transition : reflections on selected problems and approaches to churches and communities in racial transition based on the Chicago experience ... c1978.	78-16422
261.8'34'510968	Ecumenical Consultation of Christian Practice and Desirable Action in Social Change and Race Relations in Southern Africa (1964 : Kitwe, Zambia). Some addresses ... 1964.	79-373092
261.8'54'51960730763	Labbé, Dolores Egger. Jim Crow comes to church : the establishment of segregated Catholic parishes in South Louisiana ... 1978, c1971.	77-11295

    2. Since the following DDC number assignment was made, *DC&*, v. 4, no. 1 (June 1980): 13 has expanded possibilities for specific classification. What longer number could you assign to it today?

262'.14	Dicken, Hélène. Women and the apostolic ministry ... 1979. [Ordination of women--Church of England]	79-300127

Examples of LC Cataloging to Illustrate the Exercises in DDC Number Synthesis

1. 259	Genné, Elizabeth. Church family camps and conferences : an administrative and program manual ... c1979.	78-24395
2. 248'.86	Hall, Pearl Crist. Long road to freedom : one person's discovery of death ... c1978.	78-60562
3. 289.7'3	Arnold, Eberhard. Foundation and orders of Sannerz and The Rhön Bruderhof ... c1976-	76-5856
4. 230'.2	Hamer, Colin. Voice in the darkness : (an essay in contemporary Catholic existentialism) ... 1978.	78-326233

5. 299'.7   Castaneda, Carlos. The second ring of power ... c1977. 78-26557

6. 220.9'3   Schoville, Keith N. Biblical archaeology in focus ...
                   c1978.   78-62914

7. 225.5'204   Morrison, Clinton. An analytical concordance to the
                   Revised Standard Version of the New Testament ...
                   c1979.   77-26210

8. 266'.9'33   Palmer, Spencer J. The expanding church ... 1978.   78-26082

9. 251'.02   Marsh, F. E. (Frederick Edward). 500 Bible study out-
                   lines ... c1980.   79-2549

10. 289.9   Mills, Jeannie. Six years with God : life inside Reverend
                   Jim Jones's Peoples Temple ... c1979.   79-50356

11. 232.9'01   Maccoby, Hyam. Revolution in Judaea : Jesus and the
                   Jewish resistance ... 1980.   80-16752

12. 236   Ratzinger, Joseph. Eschatologie, Tod und ewiges Leben
                   ... 1977.   78-397134

13. 294.5'512   Kennedy, Melville T. The Chaitanya movement ...
                   1980.   78-74267

14. 292'.07   Liebeschuetz, John Hugo Wolfgang Gideon. Continuity
                   and change in Roman religion ... 1979.   78-40499

15. 280'.4'0975   Caldwell, Erskine. Deep South : memory and observa-
                   tion ... 1980.   80-16013

16. 248.4'82   Gallagher, Chuck. Love takes greatness ... 1980,
                   c1977.   79-6884

17. 286'.133   Jackson, Joseph Harrison. A story of Christian
                   activism : the history of the National Baptist
                   Convention, U.S.A., inc. ... 1980.   80-17408

18. 294.5'9212   Johnson, Willard L. Poetry and speculation of
                   the Rig Veda ... c1980.   80-14040

19. 299'.8   Reichel-Dolmatoff, Gerardo. Beyond the Milky Way :
                   hallucinatory imagery of the Tukano Indians ...
                   c1978.   78-620014

20. 299'.93   Bubba Free John. Bodily worship of the Living God :
                   the esoteric practice of prayer taught by Da Free
                   John : the devotional way of life practiced by
                   members of the Free Communion Church, and students
                   of the Laughing Man Institute ... 2nd ed. ... 1980. 80-52893

21. 220.9'2   Wright, John Stafford. Revell's Dictionary of Bible
                   people ... c1978.   78-20810

22. 201   Panlasigui, Isidoro. Religion and education on trial
                   ... 1956.   78-325160

23. 282'.09'03   Clouse, Robert G. The church in the age of Ortho-
                   doxy and Enlightenment : consolidation and chal-
                   lenge from 1600 to 1800 ... c1980.   79-17381

24. 299'.5   Clark, Charles Allen. Religions of old Korea ... 1980. 78-74297

25. 254	Mueller, Charles S. God's people at work in the parish ... c1979.	79-11541
26. 248.3'2	Bewes, Richard. Talking about prayer ... 1980.	80-7781
27. 261.1	Towards a Christian theology of education / [by] M. Calvert ... [et al.] ... 1977.	78-320319
28. 230	Page, Kirby. Kirby Page and the social gospel : an anthology ... 1976.	70-147695
29. 282'.092'4	Casaldáliga, Pedro. I believe in justice and hope ... c1978.	78-21694
30. 262.9'1	Catholic Church. Pope. La doctrine sociale de l'Église à travers les siècles : documents pontificaux du XVième siècle : textes originaux et traducions / publiés et introduits par Arthur F. Utz ... 1970.	78-375507
31. 230'.1'3	Caspary, Gerard E. Politics and exegesis : Origen and the two swords ... c1979.	77-71058
32. 269'.2'0954	Karokaran, Anto. Evangelization and diakonia ... 1978.	78-905126
33. 222'.1107	Willis, John T. Genesis ... c1979.	78-52455
34. 200'.1	Tiele, C. P. (Cornelis Petrus). Elements of the science of religion ... 1979.	79-9495
35. 261.7'0944'383	Églises et État en Alsace et en Moselle : changement ou fixité? / Études publiées sous la direction de Jean Schlick ... 1979.	79-376035
36. 299'.92	Tuzin, Donald F. The voice of the Tambaran : truth and illusion in Ilahita Arapesh religion ... c1980.	79-64661
37. 272	Shannon, Albert Clement. The popes and heresy in the thirteenth century ... 1949.	78-63192
38. 261.8'5	Davies, Joseph Kenneth. Deseret's sons of toil : a history of the worker movements of Territorial Utah, 1852-1896 ... c1977.	76-26459
39. 248'.4	Reed, Bobbie. Stepfamilies living in Christian harmony ... c1980.	79-20168
40. 261.1'0968	Desmond, Cosmas. Christians or capitalists? : Christianity and politics in South Africa ... 1978.	78-325747
41. 213	Clark, Harold Willard. New creationism ... c1980.	79-22250
42. 248'.3	Moffatt, Doris. Christian meditation the better way ... c1979.	78-64842
43. 252'.02	Burghardt, Walter J. Tell the next generation : homilies and near homilies ... c1980.	79-91895
44. 223'.2'0076	Burnham, David. Psalms : songs of life : a discussion guide for home Bible study ... c1980.	79-26115

45.	234'.16	Chauvet, Louis Marie. Du symbolique au symbole : essai sur les sacrements ... 1979.	79-121530
46.	248'.4	Oglesby, William B. With wings as eagles : toward personal Christian maturity ... 2d ed. ... 1980.	79-18717
47.	289.3'3 [B]	Child, Leo Wright. Ancestry and history of Leo Wright Child, 1884-1965 ... c1979.	80-105366
48.	291.4	Christ, Carol P. Diving deep and surfacing : women writers on spiritual quest ... c1980.	79-51153
49.	221.6	Clements, R. E. (Ronald Ernest) Old Testament theology : a fresh approach ... 1979, c1978.	79-16704
50.	299'.7	Sun Bear (Chippewa Indian) The medicine wheel : earth astrology ... c1980.	79-26146
51.	262.9'33	Siegle, Bernard Andrew. Marriage today : a commentary on the Code of canon law ... 3rd rev. ed. ... c1979.	79-18786
52.	296.3	Kook, Abraham Isaac. Abraham Isaac Kook : The lights of penitence, The moral principles, Lights of holiness, essays, letters, and poems ... c1978.	78-70465
53.	268'.6	Benson, Jeanette. Becoming family ... c1978.	78-62677
54.	248'.843	Hertz, Geraldine. Following Mary today ... c1979.	78-74624
55.	225.9'24	Pfleiderer, Otto. Lectures on the influence of the Apostle Paul on the development of Christianity ... 1979.	77-27166
56.	299'.934	White, John Warren. A practical guide to death and dying ... c1980.	80-19350

Reclassification: Suggested DDC 19 numbers for pre-DDC 19 number assignments

1. 220.601   Structuralism ...
    261.83480977311   Ziegenhals ...
    261.83480968   Ecumenical Consultation ...
    261.8348960730763   Labbé ...

2. 262.143   Dicken ...

NOTES

[1]Robert N. Broadus, "Dewey and Religion," *Library Resources & Technical Services*, v. 14, no. 4 (Fall 1970): 574-78.

[2]Marty Bloomberg and Hans Weber, *An Introduction to Classification and Number Building in Dewey* (Littleton, CO, Libraries Unlimited, 1976), p. 59.

[3]Benjamin A. Custer, "DDC 19: Characteristics," *HCL Cataloging Bulletin*, no. 35 (July/August 1978): 11.

[4]Ibid.

9

Class 300   Social Sciences

Introduction

Although the 300's sustained considerable change in *DDC 18* (1971), its pace accelerated with *DDC 19*.[1] One characteristic of both editions is the increase of scope notes and references in all classes. Catalogers complained when *DDC 17* (1965) reduced the number and content of such aids. The outcry stimulated a restoration process in *DDC 18*.[2] The schedule page that opens class 300 in *DDC 19* consists almost entirely of notes.

Let us first make our comparison of divisional summaries in the last two editions. At this level, no major shifts occur. Even terminology is barely altered.

Summary (*DDC 18*)		Summary (*DDC 19*)	
300	THE SOCIAL SCIENCES	300	SOCIAL SCIENCES
310	Statistics	310	Statistics
320	Political science	320	Political science (Politics and government)
330	Economics	330	Economics
340	Law	340	Law
350	Public administration, Executive branch; Military art and science	350	Public administration; Executive branch of government; Military art and science
360	Social pathology, social services, association	360	Social problems and services; association
370	Education	370	Education
380	Commerce, communications, transportation	380	Commerce, communications, transportation
390	Customs and folklore	390	Customs, etiquette, folklore

At its March 1976 meeting, the Decimal Classification Editorial Committee heard a survey report pinpointing 11 areas "needing extensive revision most urgently."[3] Of these, 6 were class 300 sequences. In the order of urgency (minus the 5 from other classes), they were:

301   Sociology
330   Economics
360   Social problems and services; association
370   Education

320   Political science (Politics and government)
350   Public administration; Executive branch of government;
        Military art and science.

There was little or no time to react to these recommendations before the 1979 appearance of the present edition. On the other hand, the survey results were not altogether unexpected. Actual changes will be examined below.

DDC 19's major phoenix revision occurs at the very beginning of class 300. Farther into the class, section 324 changes its caption from "Electoral process" to "The political process" and absorbs the entire content of former section [329].[4] Two instant metamorphoses occur in section 351, as the editor's introduction (v. 1, pp. xxiv-xxv) warns.

There are 4,321 total entries in this class, second only to the 6,089 in class 600. Nearly 26% (891) represent a net increase above the 3,430 in *DDC 18*'s class 300. Relocations and new entries are designed in large part to internationalize the coverage, as can be inferred from the nearly triple 1,080 expandable entries over 398 in *DDC 18*. Three tables of changed numbers are given at the close of volume 1. Over 90 relocations, apart from the phoenix switches, are cited in numerical order in *Relocations and Schedule Reductions*. Two alphabetical *Lists of Changed Numbers* cover "Sociology" (the phoenix 301-307 span) and "The Political Process" (phoenix 324). Their entry words largely duplicate Relative Index entries. A numerical ordering like that in *Relocations and Schedule Reductions* would have been more useful.

Division 300   Sociology

According to a centered heading, only phoenix sections 301-307 are officially reserved for Sociology. Sections 308-309 have no content in *DDC 19*. Section 301 has barely any. In *DDC 18* it comprised the whole Sociology schedule, and was highly extended, with 190 subdivisions, 24 already bracketed for discontinuance. It now stands stripped, in deference to a long-standing taboo on reuse of numbers for approximately a quarter of a century. Phoenix schedules are often excepted from this limitation, but sections 302-308 had been vacant since *DDC 17* (1965), so there was plenty of room without infringing on former 301 assignments.

The switch was much discussed prior to its inauguration.[5] Its *DDC 19* format was noticeably streamlined. The number of subdivisions, now spread from 302 to 308, has dwindled to 102, 5 of which are bracketed. A precedence note under centered heading 301-307 says to class complex subjects with the number coming last in the span unless specifically countermanded. One analyst broadly interprets the changes as follows:

> It might have been thought that the revisions would have allowed a significant reduction in the length of class numbers. But this is not the case, new numbers tending to be one or two digits shorter, rarely more....

> The focus of the sociology section as a whole appears more circumscribed than in DDC 18. Applied sociology materials have been specifically relocated (see 301[.418-.516]) as have materials on folkways (see 301[.21]). Moreover, materials on the general historical

and geographical treatment of culture and institutions have been removed from cultural and institutional studies at 306 and relocated in the 900s. What remains, therefore, appears to be sociological and anthropological materials more narrowly oriented to a synchronic approach to social phenomena. Materials written from a historical (that is, diachronic) point of view (including historical treatments of the specific topics in 306, although this is not at all clear) appear destined for the 900s (history). Regardless of what was ultimately intended, it is unfortunate that an explanation was not provided of the general tone of the new sociology schedule. That the movement of much, if not all, social and cultural history materials to the 900s is intended seems strongly confirmed by changes in the 900s themselves, however.[6]

British comments are largely concerned with the same shifts out of the 300's into the 900's, and with the meager explanations provided:

> 308-309 are left vacant. This obviously has an effect upon area studies — in other words the present split between 301.29 (social change and cultural processes), 309.1 (social conditions) and 930-999 disappears — they will all class in the 900s.... When you first look at the new schedule it may seem a little sparse. This is done on purpose — a phoenix schedule is always kept to a minimum on its first appearance, until usage shows how heavily worked some parts of it are. It is then expanded for subsequent editions in the light of this experience.[7]

> There are some obvious improvements in collocation and subordination — e.g. "Co-ordination and control" moves out of "Social interaction" and into "Social processes." Men and women are no longer considered solely as sex-objects, sex having moved from "social structure" to "culture and institutions." This move, though, looks like a piece of classification by attraction — why isn't sex "Social interaction"? — as does the placing of "movement of populations" next to "population" in 304 (Relation of natural and quasi-natural factors to social processes). There is doubtless a good reason for the apparent cross-classification here between 304.8 (Movement of populations) and 307.2 (Population "[Including] ... movement ... ") within 307 (Communities): it is a pity that the Sociology schedules, so badly in need of explanation to the non-specialist, have inadequate notes.[8]

As Trotter says, previous experience with phoenix schedules foreshadows a number of refinements yet to come. Continued editorial work is already mandated:

> At the April 10, 1980 meeting of the Decimal Classification Editorial Policy Committee, it was determined that further refinement, expansion, and classification of the 302-307 schedule would have top priority at the Library of Congress Decimal Classification Office, for the next year.[9]

Professional concern is directed primarily to eliminate all lingering prejudicial terminology. A Subcommittee on Racism and Sexism, operating within the structure of the American Library Association, makes two official recommendations to the DCEPC:

> 1. Use of recommended changes to 305/306 for creation of an alternative schedule.
>
> 2. Breakup of indiscriminate groupings of women, slaves, and ethnic groups.[10]

Section 300 (The social sciences in general) houses all works devoted to three or more of the social sciences.

Section 301 (Sociology), as has been said, is nearly vacated. Only a few discontinued numbers from which important materials shifted to other divisions, or even other classes, remain in brackets to guide the user.

Section 302 (Social interaction) includes 34 topics, according to the *List of Changed Numbers: Sociology* (v. 1, pp. 461-65). Its schedule has only four major divisions, two briefly subdivided. The seeming discrepancy arises from the large number of terms indexed from scope notes. Its themes are general and theoretical. No Add instructions appear, which means that numbers can be expanded only by means of standard subdivisions.

Section 303 (Social processes) has three subtopics, one less than 302, but these are more minutely subdivided, and carry a greater number of cross-classification notes. Butcher says:

> There are many more notes and explanations in the schedules; particularly useful are the expanded and much improved "class elsewhere" notes. A good example is at 303.66 (DDC 18: 301.6334). DDC 18 had no notes here, and a misleading heading, "Wars"; DDC 19 has the heading "War" and five lines of "class elsewhere" notes.[11]

Section 304 (Relation of natural and quasi-natural factors to social processes) covers such topics as the sociological impact of human ecology, genetic influences, demography, etc. All but one of its four primary subtopics are further subdivided. The span 304.83-.89 (Movement to specific areas) encourages direct expansion with Table 2. Nineteen relocations are on the *List of Changed Numbers: Sociology*.

Section 305 (Social stratification and structure) groups people by age, sex, occupation, religion, language, and racial, ethnic, and national background. According to its 50 entries in the *List of Changed Numbers: Sociology*, materials on group conflict related to these themes class here, as distinct from those on broader civil disorders, revolution, and war, which belong in 303.6. Modern terms like "Sexism" can be found in both the *List* and the Relative Index, but for this particular term the *List* suggests 305.3-.4 ("Men" *and* "Women"), while the only specific Index reference is to 370.19345 (Sex of students Including sexism in education).

A precedence instruction says to class complex topics with the aspect numbered first in 305, disregarding general instructions for 301-307 to class with the topic numbered last. The final three of its main subtopics make use of Tables

7, 6, and 5, in that order, for expansion of religious, linguistic, and racial, etc., groups. This section and the next are not yet fully accepted by the profession.

Section 306 (Culture and institutions) also has seven main subtopics, but most of them are unextended, and none carry Add references. A quick survey of its 42 entries in the *List of Changed Numbers: Sociology* confirms an impression from the schedule that this section deals chiefly with sexual relations and the family. See, for instance, the 306.7 portion reproduced on page 85. Comment on assigning historical treatments of these topics can be found in the division 300 introduction above.

Section 307 (Communities) has only three major subtopics, and only the last is subdivided. "Population" at 307.2 may split some cognate materials from 304.6 (Demography) and 304.8 (Movement of populations), as Butcher warns. No Add instructions are given. There are 15 concepts relocated from *DDC 18*, according to the *List of Changed Numbers: Sociology*.

Section [308] continues to be unassigned.

Section [309] (Social situation and conditions) is on its way out to class 900. We have already reviewed considerable comment on the 300/900 relocations. Butcher is more specific:

> 900 has—wrongly, I think—subsumed 309, but with no instructions on what to do with the sort of material we used to class at 309.[12]

Division 310   Statistics

This division is so little changed from its *DDC 18* composition that there is no point in reviewing it. The "Add Areas ... " instructions are generalized into a centered heading at 314-319, with specific numbers starred and footnoted. The shortcut saves schedule space, but does not materially alter results.

Division 320   Political Science (Politics and Government)

The second major phoenix change in class 300 occurs in this division by total reduction of [329] (Practical politics; Political parties) to absorption in phoenix 324 (The political process). Comment such as the following was not unexpected.

> The 324/329 eliminates 329 completely, placing "the political process" (organisations, processes, elections) entirely in 324. We are still unfortunately left with 328 hanging out on its own after 325/327; but this phoneix goes some way towards rationalisation. It loses, too, some of the US bias that it had, and the whole thing looks less messy.[13]

Section 320 (Political science in general) extends *ss*-01 to distinguish general theory from psychological aspects. Along with section 302, it splits a sizeable body of social psychology materials away from the 150's. We must also separate biography of political thinkers (320.092) from description and critical appraisal of their work in 320.5 (Political theories and ideologies). The five major subtopics of this section transfer from *DDC 18* nearly intact, with one number added: 320.8 (Theories, forms, and relations of local governments). Part of the exodus to class 900 occurs at 320.9.

Section 321 (Kinds of governments and states) covers factual, as distinct from theoretical, works. Its former caption was "Forms of states," but there isn't much except terminological change in any of its subdivisions. One is new: 321.023 (Intergovernmental relations within federal states). A couple of scope notes are added.

Sections 322-323 deal with the internal relations of any state. Section 322 (Relation of state to organized social groups snd their members) shows no change in its five subtopics. Section 323 (Relation of state to its residents), which was already well expanded under five subtopics, receives extension dealing chiefly with the contemporary topics "Women as a social aggregate" and "Right to privacy."

Section 324 (The political process) is, as previously noted, a phoenix replacement for the old "Electoral process." The British understandably hail it as "a great improvement," because it "removes the U.S. bias and rationalizes the whole."[14] Subtopic 324.1 (International organizations and activities), not yet subdivided, replaces *DDC 18*'s triply subdivided "Qualifications for voting." The latter content, along with the old 324.2 material, is moved to 324.6 (Elections). In the move, arrangement and relationships were partially revised. The new 324.2 (Political parties) absorbs most of [329], although a few topics are transferred to 324.7 (Practical politics). Other realignments include specifically named political parties of the United Kingdom, South Africa, Canada, and Australia. An internal table at 324.24-.29 (Regional treatment) helps the user assign party numbers for other countries. "Add Areas ... " notation appears at six points. Five of the remaining seven Add notes refer us to the internal table cited above. The *List of Changed Numbers: Political process* (v. 1, pp. 465-67) tabulates 92 *DDC 18* terms against phoenix 324 assignments.

Section 325 (International migration) has only one significant change. Under the hitherto pragmatically descriptive 325.3 (Colonization), an editorial 325.32 (The practice and policy of imperialism in gaining control of political and economic life of other areas) is inserted.

Section 326 (Slavery and emancipation) seems to retain its status more for symbolic and historical reasons than for its literary warrant. In other words, its literary warrant does not ensure it the normal complement of subtopics. Claims of disciplinary integrity scatter its many facets to ethics (177.5), Christianity (241.675), other religions (e.g., 291.5675), sociology (306.3), labor economics (331.11734), law (e.g., 343.0854), and commerce (380.144). This is one of the areas which the Subcommittee on Racism and Sexism finds "indiscriminate." The user should consult the Relative Index before attempting to assign class numbers.

Section 327 (International relations) has a few wording changes, number extensions, and standard subdivision warnings. Two extensions may take their literary warrant from the apparent increase in acts of terrorism and violence throughout the world. They are 327.117 (Use of force and threats of force) and 327.16 (International conflict).

Section 328 (Legislation) covers the nature and activities of law-making assemblies. It would make good classification sense to follow this section with law (i.e., official enactments produced by such bodies), but history and inertia combine to hold the latter to division 340, with the 330's (Economics) coming in between. Changes in 328 are minimal, offering a few standard subdivision specifics, plus extra categories for members, auxiliary organizations, and committees. The internal table under 328.4-.9 (Legislatures of specific jurisdictions) has its 07 section newly extended.

Section *[329] (Political parties and related organizations and processes)* has its contents transferred to section 324, as we saw.

Division 330 Economics

In discussing section 328, we regretted the placement of Economics between Legislative bodies (328) and Law (340). Considering their disciplinary relationships, Economics and Commerce (380) should be closer to each other. Theoretically and practically, some arrangement such as the following would make better sense, but every order has its drawbacks.

300 SOCIAL SCIENCES
310   Statistics
320   Political science
330   Law
340   Public administration; Executive branch, etc.
350   Social pathology, social services, etc.
360   Education
370   Customs and folklore
380   Commerce, communications, transportation
390   Economics

The 330's were second only to section 301 on Comaromi's list of class 300 schedules urgently needing revision, but so much time went into developing 302-307 and 324 that the changes here are mostly confined to expansion of some overcrowded topics.

Section *330 (Economics in general)* has no changes.

Section *331 (Labor economics)* is by far the longest yet encountered. It occupies 20 pages of schedule, and is still growing. Three 3- to 5-place numbers are bracketed for discontinuance. The losses are offset by nearly 50 new numbers and spans, 27 of which are under 331.1 (Labor force and market). Add notes render many of these further expandable. Spans under centered heading 331.3-.6 (Labor force by personal characteristics) use Add notes for aspects of employment as well as kinds of employees. "Persons at specific educational levels" and "White-collar workers" get their niches. Under 331.8, labor union topics have some half-dozen extensions. Forty-three Add notes (36 referring to other schedule spans) increase the potential for densely populated spans with extremely long numbers. It seems odd that this much-discussed topic has not been extended into vacant 331[.9].

Section *332 (Financial economics)* takes 14 pages, and shows propensities for continued expansion. Thirty-two extensions are offset by three discontinuances. Two numbers are reduced; one is vacated because "without meaning in this context" (Cf. Example 8 in chapter 3). Of the eight Add notes, five send the classifier to Area Table 2.

Section *333 (Land economics)* takes up about 10 pages. There are 33 new numbers with no discontinuances. Besides the rare uses of Table 2, and two references to other schedules, a new internal table at 333.7 (Natural resources) serves one specific, and repeated distributive Add situations throughout the second half of the section. Asterisked or daggered captions are controlled by footnotes telling the classifier either to apply the 333.7 table across the board, or to use it with stipulated reservations. There is "a whole new development at 333.79 for energy and energy resources."[15] The abridged *DDC 11* alerts us, with both a centered heading at 333.7-.9 (Utilization of specific natural resources) and an entry in its *Relocations and Schedule Reductions* list, that pollution and its control, which formerly classed here, now belongs in 363.7.

Section 334 (Cooperatives) is comparatively short, with five primary numbers, few extensions, and only two Add references to other spans.

Section 335 (Socialism and related systems) is not intensively subdivided. Five of its seven new extensions show DDC's increasing provision of numbers for proper name concepts. The Library of Congress classification has long assigned unique class numbers to individual entities, e.g., literary works, persons, etc. DDC after edition 14 (1942) kept its categories more general. But numbers such as 335.22 (Saint-Simonism) and 335.4347 (Cuban communism [Castroism, including ideas of Che Guevara]) can now be found. A *DC&* volume 4 discontinuance reduces 335[.436] (Critical works on Marxist-Leninist communism) to its superordinate number. An effort to improve disciplinary integrity scatters works formerly classed in 335[.438] (Marxist-Leninist attitude toward and influence on other subjects) to the respective subject areas.

Section 336 (Public finance) is predictably more detailed than the previous two sections, and grows rapidly. There are 16 new locations under 336.2 (Taxes). Also, a precedence table for complex topics is provided. The "local," "state," and "national" subdivisions of 336.343 (Public debt) are furnished with shiny new "Add Areas ... ," evidence of the pervasive spread of Keynesian economics, with its recent "balanced budget" and "supply side" rivals.

Section 337 (International economics) is reactivated to hold what it says was formerly the content of 382.1, but neither the terminology nor the subdivision pattern looks hereditary. Butcher remarks that "trade and commerce are still lurking in the 380s."[16] The one topical span under 337.1 (Spheres of economic cooperation) shows increasing use of proper names. Geographic arrangement under 337.3-.9 can be adjusted to local preferences, as we saw in the Options section of chapter 2.

Section 338 (Production) has 13 pages of subdivisions. Twenty-six numbers or spans are new, e.g., 338.48 (Government policies with respect to goods and services) and 338.6422 (Minority enterprises). Terminology changes occasionally, e.g., "Restrictive practices" replaces "Monopoly and monopolies." Scope notes are plentiful. So are Add notes. Other schedule spans are invoked 15 times; Table 2, 7 times.

Section 339 (Macroeconomics and related topics) is moderately subdivided under four main parts. The last of these changes its caption from "Economic stabilization and growth" to "Macroeconomic policy." Use of fiscal policy is extended to cover "Government spending," "Budget surpluses and deficits," and "Taxation." There is no guidance for distinguishing much of this material from that in section 336, but the assumption seems to be that 336 is practical, 339 theoretical.

Division 340 Law

It was remarked in discussing division 300 that most phoenix schedules are refined in subsequent editions. The 340's were overhauled in *DDC 18*

(1971) with qualified success. The story is of sufficient interest to be repeated here.

> When work on the 340's began, it was thought that there were three ways to arrange the materials in it. Using traditional Dewey practice, jurisdiction could be attached to type of law by means of -09. Thus, 345.0973 would be used for a work on criminal law in the United States. A second method was to add jurisdiction directly to 34-, thus gathering law books together first by jurisdiction and then by type of law, as law was generally studied. A third way was to add jurisdiction directly to type of law. This would be followed by standard subdivisions or special subdivisions peculiar to that type of law. Of the three ways, the third was the second choice of librarians in the United States, who preferred arrangement by jurisdiction first. British law librarians in particular called for a citation order that reflected the way law was actually studied — first by jurisdiction, then by type of law. The opinion of American law librarians — who usually do not use the DDC — and of American librarians of general collections — in which law is usually of secondary importance — weighed equally, however, in the scales of judgment. Hoping to alienate no one, the Decimal Classification Division opted for everyone's second choice, namely, method number three. The editors reasoned that in this way no one would be offended by having someone else's first choice named. It appears, however, that two second choices do not make a first, for many British librarians have called for reversal of the decision in favor of the second method. The Americans have said little on the matter.[17]

In consequence, *DDC 19* suggests three options, following general instructions for building numbers. Option A subdivides types of law by jurisdiction. Option B allows primary arrangement by jurisdiction or area. Option C classes law of a specific discipline or subject with that discipline or subject, as the LC system did prior to development of its K schedules. Two DDC choices now appear on LC records for law materials.

> On December 15, 1980, the Decimal Classification Division began assigning two numbers to works classed in 340 Law. The first number is the preferred number that is built from the base number 34, followed by the notation for the branch of law, then by the area number for the jurisdiction, and last by the notation for a subdivision of the branch of law, e.g., 345.9405 stands for law (34), criminal (5), Australia (94), general procedure (05).

> The second number reflects Option B set forth at 340 in Edition 19. It is built from the following parts: base number 34, followed by the area number for the jurisdiction, by the notation for the branch of law, and by the notation for the subdivision of the branch, e.g., 349.4055 stands for law (34), Australia (94), criminal (05), general procedure.

> Option B brings the law of a jurisdiction to one place; the preferred practice brings a branch of the law to one place. The British Library is using Option B for the *British National Bibliography.*[18]

This appeal to the international crowd brought the following response:

> Law: This is heavily expanded, especially in 341 International law. The Editors have begun to realise that if you class the law of everything in law there must be a place in law for everything. There are some things I do not like. I've been arguing with DCD for years that the law of double taxation should class in International economic law at 341.75, as it does in the Moyes Classification, but DC19 has a place for this subject in 341.484, under Jurisdiction over aliens, which I consider wrong. There are, however, improvements throughout. For example, following pleas from me, there is a new number in Private law at 346.004 for Equity. And there are special expansions at 345 and 347 for the English and Scottish court systems ... which were impossible to class by DC18. The most important thing is that alternative facet orders are fully worked out.[19]

Section 340 (Law in general) changes very little except for its page and a half of instructions and a centered heading whose chief function seems to be providing an address for a note on classing comprehensive works.

Section 341 (International law) is the one exception to the jurisdictional options. it is also the section most refined and expanded in *DDC 19.* Forty-four extensions are new in its 13 pages. United Nations subdivisions increase under 341.23, and there is now a place for the European Economic Community. "Hijacking of aircraft" and "Drug traffic" get numbers under International criminal law (341.77), although neither is yet directly indexed in volume 3. Starred entries revive locally the otherwise defunct *ss*-[026] for treaties and cases in a particular legal field. Six numbers have Add notes leading to other schedule spans. Four references to Table 2 include a new one at 341.0268 (General treaty cases, decisions, and reports).

Sections 342-348 (Law of individual states and nations ...) reiterate Option B. The extended subdivision table under 026 is unchanged.

Section 342 (Constitutional and administrative law) begins with special instructions for both Options A and B. Optional local emphasis with shorter numbers is possible under 342.3-.9. Since the span occupies most of the section, the eight topical divisions have notation -02 through -09. Twenty-eight new extensions are distributed among all but 342.09 (Local government). The starred distributive use of -026 is frequent, and could lead to very long numbers.

Section 343 (Miscellaneous public law) shows similar characteristics in format and development. There are 63 expansions of its subtopics. The distributive use of -026 is familiar, as are the jurisdictional options.

Section 344 (Social law) continues the pattern. Its nine subtopics get 44 additional extensions.

Section 345 (Criminal law) is considerably shorter. There are only nine extensions of its eight subtopics, but 345.41-.42 receives its own development for the United Kingdom.

Section 346 (Private law) has 23 expansions, one of which relocates Equity from its former subordination under 340.57. Mr. Trotter's complacency over this achievement has already been recorded. *DC&*, v. 4, no. 1 (June 1980): 14 revises 346.07 (Commercial law). There are optional provisions under 346.3-.9, similar to those at 342.3-.9.

Section 347 (Civil procedure and courts) resembles section 345 in size, format, and the amount of updating, except that it develops a schedule not only for the United Kingdom, but also for the United States.

Section 348 (Statutes, regulations, cases) is even briefer, with two pages of topical development, and three of jurisdictional development.

Section 349 (Municipal law) is unexpanded and unchanged, being reserved largely for local development. There is a note to class here comprehensive works on law of specific jurisdictions and areas in the modern world. They were formerly under 340.09.

Division 350   Public Administration; Executive Branch of Government; Military Art and Science

The Comaromi survey uncovered enough dissatisfaction with the schedule formatting and long numbers in this division to rank it among the six in class 300 which needed early reprocessing.[20] A major content shift from 350 to 351, largely for the sake of easier faceting and cleaner disciplinary hierarchy, does not appease those critics who find the division "as much a mess as before."[21]

Section 350 (Standard subdivisions and specific aspects ...) appears at first to have been robbed of all its former content. The loss is specious, however. A schedule note tells use:

> In the interest of making the schedules easier to use, the subdivisions of 350 that were given in detail in Edition 18 are now given under 351. The "add" note just above makes available under both 350 and 351 all the provisions of Edition 18, as well as many new ones. There are no relocations from 350 to 351 or the reverse.[22]

Only comprehensive treatments of central and local government now belong under 350. All specifics are moved into the 351-354 span, which not only absorbs much of the former content of section 350, but splits the civil from the military portions of the division.

Section 351 (Central governments) covers the executive branches of both national and state governments. It expands to nearly three times its old 12 pages in spite of 26 discontinuances, all but 4 of which are reductions. They are heavily outweighed by nearly 200 extensions. One (351.007) is listed among the 11 reused numbers in the editor's introduction (v. 1, p. xxv). In *DDC 18* it meant "Conflict of interest" at the old 350[.007]. It now signifies "Fundamentals of public administration." Add notes use Table 1 facets to scatter materials on civil service exams (351.3), and on safety measures for accident prevention (351.783). Terminology changes at 351.4, from "Government service" (350[.4]) to "Government work force." Medical screening by public agencies is now at 351.774, and includes pre-marital examinations and certification (formerly 614[.17]). Registration and certification of births and deaths is also relocated, from 614[.11-.12] to 351.816. We shall see more disciplinary shifts out of 614 when we come to division 360. Nearly every entry has scope notes, usually with cross-classification instructions. A distributive Add instruction footnotes several starred entries under 351.724 (Tax administration). An internal table at 351.8 (Administration of agencies controlling specific fields of activity) expands *ss*-04. "Programs for racial, ethnic, national groups" (351.814) are referred to Table 5. Twelve other numbers may be extended from schedule spans.

Section 352 (Local governments), while not so long (10 pages), has some 40 new assignments, balanced by five discontinuances (all but one, reductions of intra-section transfers). Twelve Add instructions send the user to some portion of section 351. A thirteenth uses Table 2.

Section 353 (U.S. federal and state governments) can be preempted for local emphasis. Spans 353.01-.09 and 353.911-.919, formerly faceted, are now spelled out for more precise terminology. Scope notes and Add instructions are sometimes inserted. The Department of Energy is recognized at 353.87. The span for States is shortened from 353.94-.99 to 353.97-.99, to forestall the kind of hierarchical failure which Harris and Clack found in the *DDC 18* Sociology schedule (Cf. discussion on page 129). Span 353[.94-.96] must have been included there for possible local option. It of course had no meaning in a United States setting.

Section 354 (Public international organizations and specific non-U.S. central governments) elaborates the *DDC 18* caption "Other central governments." This section is short, but almost indefinitely expansible, with geographic reference in 354.3-.9 and an internal table for topical aspects, with Add references to section 351. Three new extensions under 354.1 provide for the United Nations, etc. This section would be reciprocally involved in any optional use of section 353 for local emphasis.

Section 355 (Military art and science) and the remaining sections in this division have been criticized as not belonging in the social sciences. Section 623 covers military and nautical engineering, but there is some disciplinary justification for keeping military organization under the executive branch of government, at least in democratic countries. Another cross-classification problem has been raised with regard to 355.48 (Technical analyses of military events). Detailed schedules are provided at 940.4 and 940.54 (Military history of World Wars I and II), including "Campaigns." Certain other wars (particularly those involving the United States) receive similar, though less detailed development of their military history, e.g., 959.70434 (Military operations in the Vietnamese War). Questions of disciplinary integrity arise, particularly for the use of DDC abroad. Military libraries might want to use the 355.48 number for all historical, as well as technical, campaign and battle literature. But if so, no Add instruction leads directly to Table 2. Historical/geographic aspects must use the needlessly long *ss*-09 notation.[23] This 12-page section has eight discontinued numbers or spans. *DC&*, v. 4, no. 1 (June 1980): 15 has two relocations, and warns against use of *ss*-068 for military management. Nine new extensions and six Add notes show up in *DDC 19*.

Sections 356-357 (Land forces and warfare) are both short, with no new material.

Sections 358-359 (Armored and technical land forces and warfare, air, space, and naval forces and warfare) are also short and barely changed. Two new divisions of "Air forces and warfare" are added. A few instructions are available in the first issue of volume 4 of *DC&*.

Division 360   Social Problems and Services; Association

The Comaromi survey placed this division fourth among those in class 300 which needed revision. The word "Association" in the caption seems to puzzle users, rather than adding the specification it must be intended to do.[24] Most applied sociology (social work) is now gathered in this division by reason of modern literary warrant for social welfare problems and services. Considerable reorganization of, and relocation into, the early sections have occurred.

> ... 361-363, though not given phoenix treatment, have been very heavily revised. Not only that, but it was also realised that 614 Public health should be limited to concrete *measures* and techniques, and that any service aspects contained in 614 were in the wrong discipline. These also move to 361-363, which makes it quite a new package. 361 is expanded, as well as taking from 301 such topics as social reform.[25]

Section 361 (Social problems and social welfare) was formerly called "Social welfare work." Nineteen new numbers contrast with 12 disappearances. Miksa summarizes the changes briefly:

> This section has been recast by the use of 361.1-.2 for "Social problems" and "Social action" in general. The social work profession is now formally placed in 361.3. However, the two general numbers above include "History ... of problems endemic to human society," "Protest and dissent," and "Reform movements," topics also listed generally at 303.4 (Social change) with no explicit demarcation between the two locations.[26]

Sections 362-363 (Specific social problems and services) occupy 9 and 11 pages of schedule, respectively. An internal table under the centered heading is available

> ... where there are 20 special topics listed which may be applied to certain subdivisions in the class — e.g. control, prevention, counselling and guidance. Even here, though, the provision is patchy: it is, for instance, possible to say employment services for alcoholics (362.29284) but not for the mentally ill. Incidentally, "employment services" in this special topics table is not indexed, although some other topics here are.[27]

Section 362, devoted to personal handicaps and poverty, starts with a precedence table for various kinds of problems. A second precedence table is at 362.79 (Classes of young people other than the maladjusted). Not all changes are universally welcomed:

> 362 is much expanded, but keeps the same basic plan as before — with one momentous exception. Illnesses and disabilities of specific classes of persons now class in 362.1-.4 rather than in 362.6-.8. Thus old persons with heart disease and children with heart disease both class at 362.19612 rather than at 362.6119612 and

362.7819612 respectively as at present. I myself do not like this change.[28]

Nearly 40 new numbers or spans are traded for 12 discontinuances (most for disciplinary integrity, not reduction). Add notes refer to another schedule, and to Tables 1, 2, and 5.

Section 363 is essentially more of the same, except that its contemporary problems (civil safety, mores, and living conditions) are extensively developed. There is a precedence table under the three-page 363.1 (Public safety programs), freshly transferred and reorganized from 614[.8]. "Police services" at 363.2 gets a page and a half of new subtopics and updated terminology, for recent literary warrant. Primary subdivisions 363.3-.6 are all expanded. Number 363.7 (Environmental problems and services) takes over and rearranges the content of former 614[.7]. Trotter predicts that 363.73 will become the main number for pollution.[29] It is not quite clear whether the 614-to-363 shifts were inspired by a compelling urge to disciplinary integrity (as he says), or in anticipation of free space for future expansion of 614 (Public health and related topics). The new 363.8 (Food supply) is undeveloped, except for its starred Add instructions. New topic 363.9 (Population problems) has five subdivisions. Beyond references to the 362-363 table, there is but one Add note, at 363.119 (Occupational and industrial hazards in specific industries and occupations).

Section 364 (Criminology) is only moderately extended with 21 subtopics, as against 10 transfers out. The precedence table is new, and there is slight rearrangement. "Illegal sale, possession, use of drugs" moves from 364.157 under "Offenses against persons" to 364.177, under "Offenses against public morals." More changes, particularly in notes, were appended in the first issue of DC& volume 4. Expansion through Add instructons is rare. At 364.34 (Offenders), the user is referred to Table 5. The only other auxiliary table use is chronological and geographical at the close of the section.

Section 365 (Penal institutions) loses three and gains six extensions. It starts with a precedence instructon to class subjects with complex aspects in the number coming last in its short sequence. The only new faceting is chronological at the close of the section.

Sections 366-369 are devoted to "organizations formed for common purposes of a fraternal nature or for mutual assistance," as the definition at the head of section 366 states. Their voluntary nature is chiefly what distinguishes this last half of the 360's from the largely public and official nature of the topics covered in sections 361-365.

Section 366 (Association) relocates the fraternal aspects of Rosicrucianism, as already noted, to section 135. No other changes appear.

Section 367 (General clubs) got no change at all in DDC 18, and extends only historically and geographically here.

Section 368 (Insurance) is revised by DC& at 368.364 (Life insurance for members of the armed services), which only shows how difficult disciplinary integrity is, since that kind of insurance is legally determined and provided.

Section 369 (Miscellaneous kinds of associations) is innocent of any tampering in DDC 19.

Division 370   Education

Like most other class 300 divisions, the 370's take their share of criticism. The Comaromi survey ranked them ahead of Political science and Public administration, and behind only Sociology, Economics, and Social problems, in their need for revision. Superficial refinements appear in each new DDC edition, but recently there has been little basic change. Purists complain that the different aspects are not cleanly grouped.[30] Sections dealing with characteristics of the persons acted upon scatter into 371.9 (Special education for exceptional students), 372 (Elementary education), 373 (Secondary education), 374 (Adult education), 376 (Education of women), and 378 (Higher education). A "problems" facet bobs up at 371 (Generalities), 377 (Schools and religion), and 379 (Education and the state). Curricula, which relate to 371.3 (Methods of instruction and study) and 372.3-.8 (Specific subjects), are isolated at 375, interrupting the natural flow of other sequences.

Section 370 is essentially an elaboration of *ss*-01 and *ss*-07. But there is enough expansion and juggling of meanings to require nearly five pages of schedule. Of the nine new subtopics, six fall under 370.15 (Educational psychology). One is 370.151 (Differential psychology), but neither here nor anywhere else are these materials demarked from what belongs in 155 (Differential and genetic psychology). The presupposition that everything there is "educational" will be difficult to interpret consistently. The single schedule use of "Sexism" is in an Inclusion note at 370.19345, although, as we saw in section 305, there is obscure coverage of the concept elsewhere. A warning at 370[.68] exchanges the normal *ss* facet for 371.2 (Educational administration). Another Table 1 variation puts teachers' conferences in 370.72, transferring educational research to 370.78.

Section 371 (Generalities of education) used to be captioned "The School." It is a potentially confusing change, since "Generalities" are routinely associated with Table 1 and class 000. The content undergoes a bit of elaboration. *DC&*, v. 4, no. 1 (June 1980): 16 withdraws 371[.1028] almost before it can be recognized, probably because of duplication with 371.256 (Open plan). There are 31 new topics; an Add note at 371.9122-.9126 has been revised.

Section 372 (Elementary education) has one important change. In the distributive table under centered heading 372.3-.8 (Specific ... subjects) 045 is now bracketed. It was the *DDC 18* place for elementary textbooks, with an option to class with the subject. *DDC 19* reverses the option, preferring scatter to the various subject locations. Five bracketed schedule entries give further detail. A corresponding note under *ss*-07 in Table 1 says to "Class textbooks on a subject as treatises." Besides this change there are four new topics, including "Experimental schools" and "Sex education."

Section 373 (Secondary education) has even less revision. A new 373.011 (For specific objectives) is borrowed from the analogous 372.011. Each has a double Add reference to nearby schedules. "Experimental schools" echoes the 372.10424 caption, but uses shorter notation. "Work-study plans" is a third addition to this section.

Section 374 (Adult education) receives several extensions under 374.013 (Vocational and occupational education) and 374.014 (Liberal and recreational education). Except for a euphemistic change from "Remedial" to "Adult basic" at 374.012, and a shift of "Educational techniques," there are no alterations.

Section 375 (Curriculums) has been cited for its awkward placement. Only 375.008 (Curriculums ... directed toward specific objectives) is introduced, with expansions for "International studies," "Environmental studies," "Ethnic studies," "Consumer education," and the like.

Section 376 (Education of women) is practically untouched.

Section 377 (Schools and religion) is unaltered. It poses some disciplinary questions vis-à-vis 200.71 (Religious schools and courses), and perhaps even more with 268 (Religious traiing and instruction) and 649.7 (Moral, religious, character training in the home). However, the lines are fairly clear. Consistency could be improved with scope notes, now given only at 200.71 and 268.

Section 378 (Higher education) is very little changed. There are new entries at 378.03 (Alternative, nontraditional higher education) and 378.125 (Teaching in colleges and universities). The optional table of letters for kinds of publications of specific institutions has disappeared.

Section 379 (Education and the state) is slightly expanded under 379.11 (Financial administration in public education), and by 379.1215 (Assistance by national governments to adult education). Among other small changes, 379.1552 now means "Vocational education programs."

Division 380   Commerce, Communications, Transportation

Our introductory discussion for division 330 (Economics) intimated that all was not well with the placement of these two related disciplines. Although the 380's were not on the Comaromi list for urgent revision, one critic calls them a mishmash, citing the separation of transport in general (380.5) from specific kinds of transportation (385-388).[31] Disciplinary integrity often depends on whose integrity is being gored, so a general classification scheme will never please everybody. A distributive Add note recaptions *ss*-0294 (Price lists and trade catalogs) to "Offers for sale," available to all starred entries.

Section 380 provides facets vaguely resembling standard subdivisions for the three broad areas in this division. Only under 380.5 (Transportation) are new subtopics given (four, to be exact).

Sections 381-382 are devoted to commerce, trade, and marketing. Section 381 (Internal commerce) nearly doubles its one page. The established 381.4 (Specific commodities and services) encourages expansion out of classes 500 and 600. Section 382 (International commerce) is longer by some three pages, but has less new material. Two numbers are reduced, one of them partially relocated. There are various Add notes for specific commodities and services, as well as for historical/geographical treatment.

Sections 383-384 (Specific kinds of communications) comprise the second broad grouping. Its disciplinary relationship to division 070 (Journalism, etc.) was mentioned in the introduction to chapter 6. There is also potential involvement with 651.7 (Communication; Creation and transmission of records) and with 652 (Processes of written communication). Section 383 (Postal communication) has two internal transfers from bracketed numbers. The other changes are minor, from *DC&*, v. 4. Section 384 (Other systems ... Telecommunication) is understandably longer, and growing. New developments of *ss*-04 and *ss*-06 appear. Three new numbers introduce Satellite communication, Cable television, and Computer communications.

Sections 385-388 (Specific kinds of transportation) undergo about the same amount and kind of change as their neighbors. Section 385 (Railroad transportation) gets six new numbers, including two extensions of *ss*-06. Section 386 (Inland waterway and ferry transportation) has only one new subtopic and some minor changes in captions and notes. Section 387 (Water, air, space transportation) is more developed. Besides standard subdivision specifications, eight added numbers cover entries analogous to those in sections 385-386. Section 388 (Ground transportation) gets standard subdivision extensions from *DC&*, v. 4. Eighteen new subtopics include "Operation of vehicles," an expansion also apparent in sections 385-387.

Section 389 (Metrology and standardization) is short and growing shorter. Does the waning literary warrant reflect the waning American resistance to the metric system? Skirmishes still appear in journals and newspapers, but the war is over. Besides, there is 530.8 (Physical units, dimensions, constants).

Division 390   Customs, Etiquette, Folklore

This division encountered moderate reduction, as well as expansion, in *DDC 18*, but the present changes are mostly cosmetic.

Section 390 uses multiple zeros for Table 1 reference on materials covering more than one of the three division topics, freeing 390.01-.07 for standard subdivisions of customs alone. Number 390.088 looks innocuous, but poses disciplinary dilemmas. "Customs" are surely an aspect or facet of the group in which they are practiced, not a true discipline or topic. Shouldn't the customs of, say, Boy Scouts be classed in 369.43? The scope notes at 390.088 are negative, leaving the classifier uncertain about correct use of the number.

Sections 391-394 (Customs) continue the theme introduced by 390.01. The 391.1-.4 span generalizes to include more than "Outer garments," and takes over the meaning of former 391[.07]. There is also an elaborated standard subdivision schedule under 392.36 (Customs of dwelling places).

Section 395 (Etiquette and Manners) shows a certain change at 395.3 from "Hospitality and entertainment" to "For social occasions," reflecting, perhaps, the lessening use of the home for social entertaining.

Sections [396-397] remain unassigned.

Section 398 (Folklore) presents no particular problems except that inexperienced classifiers might try to put here collections of children's literature which belong in 808.068. There is one internal transfer for the sociology of folklore. Folk literature can now be subdivided by language, using Table 6. And there are two additions, for "Artistic and literary themes" and "Historical and political themes" under 398.35 (Humanity and human existence as subjects of folklore).

Section 399 (Customs of war and diplomacy) is unchanged and unpartitioned, with the same scope notes used in *DDC 18*. The failure of literary warrant to stimulate expansion of this section makes grim testimony to the savagery of civilized warfare. Another explanation may be the disciplinary impasse mentioned in our discussion of section 355.

Conclusion

Class 300 is unquestionably the most reworked of any in *DDC 19*, but our survey reveals what many fault as its tentative, rather than decisive, phoenixing. It may have been wiser on both the short and the long views to proceed cautiously. While changes are being digested, and reclassification snags put to rest, users can comment, editors can experiment, and new interpretations can be made for this broad field of human study which daily widens, deepens, and refines its procedures.

Exercises in the Use of Class 300

A. Analysis

305.8'2'0714	Clift, Dominique. Le fait anglais au Québec ... c1979.	79-127988
312'.39'09794	Claifornia. Dept. of Health Services. Infectious Disease Section. Communicable diseases, 1975-1977 ... 1979.	79-625568
324.2595'1075	Cheah, Boon Kheng. The masked comrades : a study of the communist united front in Malaya, 1945-48 ... 1979.	79-940892
327.5694017'4927	Said, Edward W. The question of Palestine ... 1980, c1979.	80-12146
330.9'73'0926	Cluster, Dick. Shrinking dollars, vanishing jobs : why the economy isn't working for you ... c1980.	79-53756
338.4'76644	Choudhury, Sadananda. Economic history of colonialism : a study of British salt policy in Orissa ... 1979.	79-903779
343.549'1056	Choudhry, Najib A. Customs tariff and trade controls ... 1979.	79-930843
345'.758'075	Ridley, John Hood. Requests to charge in criminal cases : the law in Georgia ... 1980, c1978.	78-103987
347.68'02	Buckle, Harry Osborne. The civil practice of the Magistrates' Courts in South Africa ... 7th ed. ... 1979-	80-463605
353.97980083	Burch, Rebecca. Alaska prime sponsor profiles ... 1978.	79-625179
363.3'763'09794	California. Fire Incident Reporting System. Annual report ...	80-640464
375'.3034	Allain, Violet Anselmini. Futuristics and education ... c1979.	79-89541
378.1'98'0973	National Institute for Campus Ministries. The NICM journal for Jews and Christians in higher education. v. 1- winter 1978-	79-642695

380.1'45'00097471	The Underground shopper. New York City. 1st- ed. c1979-	79-644665
387.2'23	Simper, Robert. Gaff sail ... 1980.	79-670388
398.2'1'0944	Brown, Kay. Beauty and the beast / retold by Kay Brown ... c1978.	79-51394

B.   Synthesis: Examples from LC records are given on pp. 205-208.

1.   A review of the currency question in foreign exchange.

2.   Women in politics in India.

3.   A study of rural development and federal aid to education in the South.

4.   A handbook for staff and directors of small community-based social-service agencies.

5.   A book about being a modern father.

6.   The story of the development and demise of the Edsel automobile.

7.   Legends of the Cree Indians of Manitoba.

8.   The study and teaching of political science in West Germany.

9.   Economic conditions in Chile from the third decade of the twentieth century.

10.   A follow-up study on financing community mental health centers in the United States.

11.   A railroad passenger time-table for inter-city, local, and suburban services in Great Britain.

12.   Joint occupancy of housing in Manchester, England.

13.   Economic relations between Mexico and the United States.

14.   A periodical on government paperwork in the U.S. Executive Office.

15.   Industrial relations in Great Britain.

16.   A book on classroom management and discipline.

17.   A guide to personal finance and money management.

18.   A Canadian insurance directory and statistical handbook.

19.   An introduction to social work administration.

20.   A history of abortion in the Netherlands.

21.   Social stratification among adolescents.

22.   Foreign relations between East and West Germany.

23.   A personal narrative of a political prisoner and refugee.

24.   A congressional committee report on recent legislation for community mental health centers and biomedical research extension.

25. The history of Clara Barton and the American National Red Cross.

26. The bicameral organization of the Italian parliament.

27. Social services to battered women.

28. Contract law in New Zealand.

29. Urban local transit in Boston, New York, and Philadelphia.

30. Agricultural water supply and water resources development in the state of California.

31. Methodology in political science research.

32. A collection of essays on the regulation of marketing and other United States commercial policies.

33. Official plans for the conservation and restoration of historic buildings in Nevada.

34. A history of social democracy in Sweden.

35. Legislative development of housing policies in California.

36. The handling of terrorist disorder and violence.

37. American social security law and legislation.

38. The coordination and cooperation of community organizations in France.

39. A periodical issued by and about Rice University in Houston, Texas.

40. Attendance statistics in California's private elementary schools and high schools.

41. A GAO report to Congress on conflict of interest and federal employment policies.

42. Financing fraternity houses on American campuses.

43. The revitalization of small urban seaports and waterfronts.

44. Court procedures in American commercial law.

45. Water resources development in the western United States.

46. The use of high school entrance exams for prognosis and placement.

47. A case history of social welfare services to a woman with breast cancer.

48. A collection of biographies of anthropology teachers.

49. The economic roles of professional women in the United States.

50. An anthology of inaugural speeches given by college presidents in Great Britain.

51. The legal aspects of nonprofit corporations in Austria.

52. Evaluating administrative proposals for mass transportation in the United States.

53. Instructions on what to do if you receive notice from the IRS that your income tax report will be audited.

54. Tools and techniques for teaching language arts in the elementary schools.

55. A report on the McClellan Committee hearings on improper activities in the labor or management field.

56. The economic feasibility of solar energy production systems.

57. The use of real objects and models as instructional and study aids.

58. A history of arms and armor used in India.

59. A selected list of science and mathematics films for all ages and educational levels.

60. A Cuban's story of 10 years of political exile in Quebec.

61. The organization and administration of elementary instruction in how to make the best use of television.

62. Social and political violence and conflict in Colombia.

63. The proceedings of a workshop on car pooling.

C. Reclassification: What *DDC 19* numbers would you assign to the following records? Suggestions are offered on pp. 208-209.

1. 301.11   Charmaz, Kathy. The social reality of death ... 1980.   79-21838

2. 301.11'3   Schelling, Thomas C. Micromotives and macrobehavior ... c1978.   78-17119

3. 301.15'72'0967827   Varkevisser, Corlien M. Socialization in a changing society : Sukuma childhood in rural and urban Mwanza, Tanzania ... 1973.   74-196672

4. 301.2'1   Gal, Susan. Language shift : social determinants of linguistic change in bilingual Austria ... c1979.   78-23330

5. 301.24'1   Acculturation, theory, models, and some new findings / edited by Amado M. Padilla ... 1980.   79-21617

6. 301.31   Roberts, Walter Orr. The climate mandate ... c1979.   78-25677

7. 301.32'1'095195   Coale, Ansley J. Estimation of recent trends in fertility and mortality in the Republic of Korea ... 1980.   79-22705

8. 301.34   Sussman, Marvin B. Community structure and analysis ... 1978, c1959.   78-5894

9. 301.36'3   Abrahamson, Mark. Urban sociology ... 2nd ed. ... c1980.   79-18712

10. 301.41'1'0973   Avedon, Burt. Ah, men! : What do men want? : a panorama of the male in crisis, his past problems, present uncertainties, future goals ... c1980.   78-74675

11. 301.41'2'095332   Makhlouf, Carla. Changing veils : women
                       and modernization in North Yemen ...
                       c1979.   79-307921

12. 301.42'1'0942   Wachter, Kenneth W. Statistical studies
                       of historical social structure ... 1978.   78-51232

13. 301.42'84'0924   List, Julie Autumn. The day the loving
                       stopped : a daughter's view of her
                       parents' divorce ... c1980.   79-66075

14. 301.43'5   Atchley, Robert C. The social forces in later
                       life : an introduction to social gerontology
                       ... 3rd ed. ... c1980.   79-25726

15. 301.45'19'6073   The American slave : a composite autobiog-
                       raphy : supplement, series 2 / George
                       P. Rawick ... 1979.   79-12456

16. 301.5'92   Pettman, Ralph. State and class : a sociology
                       of international affairs ... 1979.   79-19109

17. 309.1'46'608   Orrantia, Mikel. Por una alternative
                       libertaria y global ... 1978.   79-348423

18. 309.2'233'7305694 Feuerwerger, Marvin C. Congress and
                       Israel : foreign aid decision-making
                       in the House of Representatives,
                       1969-1976 ... 1979.   78-74654

19. 309.2'62'0941   McKay, David H. The politics of urban
                       change ... c1979.   79-309024

20. 329'.0025'73   Election directory ...   78-648244

21. 329'.023'549303   Communist Party of Sri Lanka. Central Com-
                       mittee. Sri Lanka's general election,
                       1977 ... 1977.   78-905578

22. 329'.025'0973   Political finance / edited by Herbert E.
                       Alexander ... c1979.   78-24439

23. 329'.3'09042   Andersen, Kristi. The creation of a Demo-
                       cratic majority, 1928-1936 ... 1979.   78-11660

24. 329.9'43   Wichard, Rudolf. Parteien in der Demokratie :
                       e. Einf. in d. allgemeine Parteienlehre ...
                       1977.   78-391329

25. 332'.02'40941   Elmsford, Francis. The Over-Fifty Club
                       guide to money management ... 1977?   78-326845

26. 362.7'8'2920941   O'Connor, Joyce. The young drinkers:
                       a cross-national study of social and
                       cultural influences ... 1978.   78-318212

27. 382'.42'1282   Fulda, Michael. Oil and international rela-
                       tions : energy trade, technology, and
                       politics ... 1979.   78-22681

Examples of LC Cataloging to Illustrate the Above Exercises
in DDC Number Synthesis

1. 332.4'5   Brown, Brendan. The dollar-mark axis : on currency
power ... 1979.   79-5345

2. 305.4'2   Agnew, Vijay. Elite women in Indian politics ... c1979.   79-903067

3. 307.7'2'0975   Clinton, Charles Anthony. Local success and Federal
failure : a study of community development and
educational change in the rural South ... c1979.   79-55667

4. 361.7   Clifton, Robert L. Grassroots administration : a
handbook for staff and directors of small community-
based social-service agencies ... c1980.   79-26640

5. 306.8'7   Clerget, Joël. Étre père aujourd'hui ... 1979.   79-121690

6. 338.7'6292222   Warnock, C. Gayle. The Edsel affair : ... what
went wrong? : A narrative ... c1980.   80-81129

7. 398.2'08997   Clay, Charles. Swampy Cree legends / as told to
Charles Clay by Kuskapatchees, the Smoky One
... 2nd ed. ... 1978.   80-460162

8. 320'.07'043   Claussen, Bernhard. Aspekte politischer Pädagogik
: Beitr. zu Wissenschaftstheorie, Fachdida ktik u.
Praxisbezug ... 1979.   80-455421

9. 330.9'83'064   Ellsworth, Paul Theodore. Chile, an economy in
transition ... 1979, c1945.   78-10217

10. 362.2'04'25   Community mental health centers: a decade later
/ Naomi Naierman ... 1978.   78-67184

11. 385'.22'0941   British Railways Board. Passenger timetable:
Great Britain inter-city, local and suburban
services, Irish, Channel Island, coastal
services.   79-647224

12. 307'.3   Elliott, Margaret, M.Soc.Sci. Shifting patterns in
multioccupation ... c1978.   80-461518

13. 382'.0972'073   U.S.-Mexico economic relations / edited by Barry
K. Poulson and T. Noel Osborn ... 1979.   79-4186

14. 353.0071'4'06   United States. Office of Management and Budget.
Paperwork and red tape: new perspectives, new
directions. June 1978-   79-647385

15. 331'.0941   Clegg, Hugh Armstrong. The changing system of industrial relations in Great Britain ... c1979.   80-458963

16. 371.1'02   Clarizio, Harvey F. Toward positive classroom discipline ... 3rd ed. ... 1978.   79-22392

17. 332'.024   Broy, Anthony. Managing your money : how to make
the most of your income and have a financially
secure future ... 1979.   79-11367

18. 368'.971   The Brown chart for all lines of general insurance:
provincial results; report ... 1977-   79-649189

19. 361'.001   Watson, David. Caring for strangers : an introduc-
                  tion to practical philosophy for students of social
                  administration ... 1980.   79-41163

20. 363.4'6'09492 Bruijn, Jan de. Geschiedenis van de abortus
                  in Nederland : een analyse van opvattingen
                  en discussies 1600-1979 ... 1979.   80-462763

21. 305.2'3   Rogers, Dorothy. Adolescents and youth ... 1981.   80-19546

22. 327.431043   Bruns, Wilhelm. Deutsch-deutsche Beziehungen
                  : Prämissen, Probleme, Perspektiven ... 1979.   80-462637

23. 365'.45'0924 Buber-Neumann, Margarete. "Freiheit, du bist
                  wieder mein ..." : d. Kraft zu überleben
                  ... 1978.   80-455261

24. 344'.73'044   United States. Congress. Senate. Committee on
                  Human Resources. Subcommittee on Health and
                  Scientific Research. Community mental health
                  centers and biomedical research extension acts
                  of 1978 ... 1978.   78-602749

25. 361.7'63   Buckingham, Clyde E. Clara Barton, a broad humanity
                  : philanthropic efforts on behalf of the armed
                  forces and disaster victims, 1860-1900 ... c1977.   79-49263

26. 342.45'05   Chimenti, Carlo. Gli organi bicamerali nel Parla-
                  mento italiano ... c1979.   80-459740

27. 362.8'3   Roberts, Albert R. Sheltering battered women : a
                  national study and service guide ... c1980.   80-19827

28. 346.931'02   Cheshire, Geoffrey Cavalier. The law of contract
                  ... 5th New Zealand ed. ... 1979.   80-467152

29. 388.4'0974   Cheape, Charles W. Moving the masses : urban
                  public transit in New York, Boston, and Phila-
                  delphia, 1880-1912 ... 1980.   79-15875

30. 333.91'217'09794 California. Dept. of Water Resources.
                  Northern District. Agricultural water pur-
                  chase pian ... 1979.   79-625535

31. 320'.01'8   Chatterji, Rakhahari. Methods of political inquiry
                  ... 1979.   79-903980

32. 381'.3'0973   Regulation of marketing and the public interest : a
                  tribute to Ewald T. Grether on the occasion of
                  his eightieth birthday / edited by Frederick E.
                  Balderston ... 1981.   80-19731

33. 353.97930085'9 Charles Hall Page & Associates, inc. Nevada
                  State historic preservation plan ... 1978.   78-623413

34. 324.2485072   Chatillon, Colette. Social-démocratie : la Suède
                  ... 1978.   79-127089

35. 338.4'76908'09794 California. Legislature. Assembly. Housing
                  Advisory Panel. California State Assembly
                  Subcommittee on Housing Production, Housing
                  Advisory Panel meeting ... 1979.   80-620559

36. 303.6'2   Responding to the terrorist threat : security and crisis management ... 1980.   80-36812

37. 344.41'02   Calvert, Harry G. Social security law ... 2d ed. ... 1978.   80-463650

38. 361.8'0944   Chobaux, Jacques. L'aménagement et la coopération intercommunale ... 1979.   79-121394

39. 378.764'1411   The Campanile ...   79-644218

40. 373.12'19'794   California. Dept. of Education. Division of Financial Services. Local Assistance Bureau. Enrollment in California's private elementary schools and high schools ...   79-623210

41. 353.099'95   United States. General Accounting Office. What rules should apply to post-Federal employment and how should they be enforced? : Report to Congress ... 1978.   78-602561

42. 378.1'98'55   Field, Irving M. Fraternity house financing ... c1978.   78-105624

43. 307.7'6   Clark, John R. Small seaports : revitalization through conserving heritage resources ... c1979.   79-67736

44. 346.73'07'0269   American Bar Association. Section of Litigation. The role of experts in business litigation ... c1979.   79-112497

45. 333.91'15'0978   Andrews, Wade H. Testing social indicators in the Techcom model for water development ... 1979.   79-624190

46. 373.1'2'64   Turner, David Reuben. High school entrance examinations : for private high schools and special academic public high schools ... 4th ed. ... c1980.   79-20652

47. 362.1'9'6994490926   Humphrey, Derek. Jean's way ... 1978.   78-15113

48. 301'.092'2   Totems and teachers : perspectives on the history of anthropology / Sydel Silverman, editor ... 1980.   80-18457

49. 305.4'3'0973   Feulner, Patricia N. Women in the profession : a social-psychological study ... 1979.   78-68455

50. 370'.941   The Study of education : a collection of inaugural lectures / edited by Peter Gordon ... 1980.   80-507647

51. 346.436'064   Fessler, Peter. Österreichisches Vereinsrecht ... 4., erw. u. erg. Aufl. ... 1979.   80-452708

52. 380.5 s [380.5'068]   National Research Council (U.S.) Transportation Research Board. Evaluating transportation proposals ... 1979. (Transportation research record ; 731)   80-12434

53. 343.7305'2044   Sprouse, Mary L. How to survive a tax audit : What to do before and after you hear from the I.R.S. ... 1981.   80-1127

54.	372.6'044	Petty, Walter Thomas. Experiences in language : tools and techniques for language arts methods 3rd ed. ... c1981.	80-21449
55.	364.1'06'073	Petro, Sylvester. Power unlimited : the corruption of union leadership : a report on the McClellan Committee hearings ... 1979, c1959.	79-4432
56.	338.4'762147	Neff, Thomas L. The social costs of solar energy : a study of photovoltaic energy systems ... 1981.	80-23732
57.	371.3'07'8	Soulier, J. Steven. Real objects and models ... 1981. (The instructional media library)	80-21450
58.	355.8'2'0954	Pant, Gayatri Nath. Indian arms and armor ... 1978-	78-903904
59.	371.3'3523	Newman, Michele M. Films in the sciences : reviews and recommendations : selected science and mathematics films for students, college undergraduates, teachers, and general audiences ... 1980.	80-21704
60.	325'.21'097291	Charette, Pierre. Mes dix années d'exil à Cuba ... c1979.	79-127081
61.	372.13'358	Singer, Dorothy G. Teaching television : how to use TV to your child's advantage ... c1981.	80-20775
62.	303.6'09861	Oquist, Paul H. Violence, conflict, and politics in Colombia ... 1980.	80-23141
63.	388.4'1321	Paratransit, 1979 : proceedings of a workshop ... 1979.	79-26306

Reclassification : Suggested DDC 19 Numbers for pre-DDC 19 Assignments

1. 306.9   Charmaz ... [*DC&*, v. 4, no. 2]

2. 302.5   Schelling ...

3. 303.320967827   Varkevisser ...

4. 306.4   Gal ...

5. 303.482   Acculturation ...

6. 304.25   Roberts ...

7. 304.63095195   Coale ...

8. 307   Sussman ...

9. 307.76   Abrahamson ...

10. 305.310973   Avedon ... [*DC&*, v. 4, no. 2]

11. 305.4095332   Makhlouf ...

12. 306.850942   Wachter ...

13. 306.890924 List ...

14. 305.26 Atchley ...

15. 305.896073 The American ...

16. 306.2 Pettman ...

17. 946.608 Orrantia ...
    [324.2466075]

18. 338.917305694 Feuerwerger ...

19. 307.760941 McKay ...

20. 324.602573 Election ...

21. 324.9549303 Communist ...

22. 324.780973 Political ...

23. 324.273609042 Andersen ...

24. 324.243 Wichard ...

25. 332.0240564 Elmsford ...

26. 362.2920941 O'Connor ...

27. 382.42282 Fulda ...

NOTES

[1]For a review of the *DDC 18* changes, see: John Phillip Comaromi, *The Eighteen Editions of the Dewey Decimal Classification* (Albany, NY, Forest Press Division, Lake Placid Education Foundation, 1976), pp. 592-95.

[2]Ann Ethelyn Markley, "Problems Associated with Presenting and Teaching the Schedules: Social Science (300) and History (900)," *The Dewey Decimal Classification: Outlines and Papers Presented at a Workshop on the Teaching of Classification* ... (New York, School of Library Service, Columbia University, 1968), p. 37, is typical of the criticisms.

[3]John P. Comaromi, "Decimal Classification Editorial Policy Committee Report," *Library Resources & Technical Services*, v. 21, no. 1 (Winter 1977): 94.

[4]Melvil Dewey, *Dewey Decimal Classification and Relative Index.* Ed. 19 (Albany, NY, Forest Press, 1979), v. 1, p. xxiii.

[5]See, for instance, Benjamin A. Custer, "DDC 19: Characteristics," *HCL Cataloging Bulletin*, no. 35 (July/August 1978): 10; and *Cataloging Service Bulletin*, no. 4 (Spring 1979): 16.

[6]Francis Miksa, "The 19th Dewey: A Review Article," *Library Quarterly*, v. 50, no. 4 (October 1980): 485.

[7]Ross Trotter, "Dewey 19—A Subjective Assessment," *Catalogue & Index*, no. 59 (Winter 1980): 2.

[8]Peter Butcher, "Dewey? We Sure Do!," *Catalogue & Index*, no. 55 (Winter 1979): 7-8.

[9]Lizbeth Bishoff, "Dewey Decimal Classification, 19th Edition: Its Changes and Their Implications for Libraries," *Illinois Libraries*, v. 62, no. 7 (September 1980): 631.

[10]ALA/RTSD/CCS Subject Analysis Committee. Subcommittee on Racism and Sexism in Subject Analysis, "Summary Report," *RTSD Newsletter*, v. 6, no. 2 (March/April 1981): 22.

[11]Butcher, p. 1.

[12]Butcher, p. 8.

[13]Ibid.

[14]Trotter, p. 2. See similar comments by Russell Sweeney, "The Old, Grey Mare ... ," *Cataloging & Classification Quarterly*, v. 1, no. 1 (Fall 1980): 93.

[15]*Cataloging Service Bulletin*, no. 4 (Spring 1979): 15.

[16]Butcher, p. 8.

[17]Comaromi, *The Eighteen Editions of the Dewey Decimal Classification*, p. 594. Examples of British criticisms may be found in:
Charles D. Batty, "A Close Look at Dewey 18: Alive and Well and Living in Albany," *Wilson Library Bulletin*, v. 46, no. 8 (April 1972): 714.
Antony Croghan, "The Dewey Decimal Classification and Its Eighteenth Edition," *Library Association Record*, v. 74, no. 7 (July 1972): 120.
M. J. Ramsden, "Dewey 18," *Australian Library Journal*, v. 21, no. 3 (April 1972): 117.
James A. Tait, "Dewey Decimal Classification: A Vigorous Nonagenarian," *Library Review*, v. 23, no. 6 (Summer 1972): 228.

[18]*Cataloging Service Bulletin*, no. 11 (Winter 1981): 104.

[19]Trotter, p. 3.

[20]John Phillip Comaromi, *A Survey of the Use of the Dewey Decimal Classification in the United States and Canada* (Lake Placid, NY?, Prepared for Forest Press, Lake Placid Foundation, 1975), p. 253.

[21]Butcher, p. 8.

[22]Melvil Dewey, *Dewey Decimal Classification and Relative Index*. Ed. 19, v. 2, p. 394.

[23]For full development of this observation, see: S. S. Gupta, "Expansion of 355.48 in Dewey Decimal Classification," *Herald of Library Science*, v. 17, no. 4 (October 1978): 308-311.

[24]Markley, p. 40.

[25]Trotter, p. 2.

[26]Miksa, p. 484.

[27]Butcher, p. 1.

[28]Trotter, p. 2.

[29]Ibid.

[30]See, for instance: M. J. Ramsden, "Dewey 18," *Australian Library Journal*, v. 21, no. 3 (April 1972): 117.

[31]Butcher, p. 8.

10

Class 400   Language

Introduction

The 400's are less changed than any of the other nine classes, and the Comaromi survey found no high priority set on their change. In this regard, one classifier says:

> ... Dewey often only half-knowingly, made his greatest contribution in the exploration of the consistent construction of multitopic assemblies. His methods are clearest in the simplest classes, such as *language, literature* and *history*. In 400 *language*, for example, he recognizes that books may be written about two aspects of language (what Ranganathan later called *facets* of language): (1) the general theoretical aspects of language like *structural systems* (*grammar*), and (2) the particular languages, like *English*. He listed the theoretical aspects first, in 410, and the languages after them in 420-499, to achieve an order on the shelves that proceeds from the general to the particular. But then he went on to admit the subdivision of collections on particular languages, by the theoretical aspects, so that 420 *English* might include, for example, *English grammar*, and he arranged for the characteristic notation for 410 to be used to subdivide the language — in this case 5 from 415 *structural systems* (*grammar*) to create 425. This simple example reveals a model that has scarcely changed for one hundred years: the recognition of the characteristic aspects of the subject, the separate listing of those aspects in general-to-specific order, the availability of the detail from general aspect to divide the specific aspects further, the consequent assembly order of specific use of simple notation from the two aspects.[1]

Division summaries read precisely the same in the two most recent editions:

Summary (*DDC 18*)		Summary (*DDC 19*)	
400	LANGUAGE	400	LANGUAGE
410	Linguistics	410	Linguistics
420	English and Anglo-Saxon	420	English and Anglo-Saxon
430	Germanic (Teutonic); German	430	Germanic (Teutonic); German
440	Romance languages; French	440	Romance languages; French

450	Italian, Romanian, Rhaeto-Romanic languages		450	Italian, Romanian, Rhaeto-Romanic languages
460	Spanish and Portuguese		460	Spanish and Portuguese
470	Italic languages; Latin		470	Italic languages; Latin
480	Hellenic languages; Classical Greek		480	Hellenic languages; Classical Greek
490	Other languages		490	Other languages

As in the case of class 200, general options are cited at the beginning of this class (v. 2, p. 598) to allow preferential reorganization:

> The following options give preferred treatment to, or make available more and shorter numbers for the classification of, any specific language that it is desired to emphasize
> A.   Class in 410, where full instructions appear
> B.   Give preferred treatment by placing before 420 through use
> of a letter or other symbol. Full instructions appear under 420-490

Three distributive changes apply throughout the class. First, the pattern numbers for "Prosody" are discontinued under each language, i.e., for bracketed section numbers [416] through [486] and -[6] in Table 4. Systematic study of versification and metrical structure no longer carries the literary warrant it once enjoyed. Its places in the scheme are reduced and relocated to 808.1 (Rhetoric of poetry). Only the first [416] of the above series carries a cross-classification note. All the others, e.g., [426], are merely captioned "unassigned," although they, too, were Prosody numbers in *DDC 18*. Cf. Example 10 in chapter 3. Only the broad language number without further specification is now available to those who wish to keep Prosody with linguistics.

The second change adds "dictionaries" to the scope notes for non-standard languages (i.e., dialects and regional variations) in 17 schedule locations from 427 to 495.17, and at *lang. sub.*-7 of Table 4. The intent is to avoid unduly long notation which use of *ss*-03 would require. The third change adds the now-popular term "Prescriptive" to applied linguistics pattern numbers from 428 to 488, and -8 of Table 4.

Distributive Add references to Table 4 are explained under centered heading 420-490 (Specific languages). Footnotes refer to these instructions for each starred language. There is also a warning that the 400 schedule does not precisely correspond to notations in class 800 or in Table 6. The user should borrow those sequences only upon special instruction. Besides the potential expansion from Table 4, which is designed exclusively to get needless detail out of class 400, there are 16 references to Table 2, 8 to Table 6, and occasional special instructions for the use of Table 1.

Since the distributive changes and faceting opportunities are the most significant features of class 400, it would be a waste of time to enumerate each section separately. Particular points of interest will be mentioned in the divisional discussions.

Division 400   Standard Subdivisions of Language

New introductory notes say to class comprehensive works on language and literature in section 400, but to put rhetoric in 808 and literature alone in 800.

DC& has already made two further changes. At 401.9, "Psycholinguistics" is extended to include "Sociolinguistics." Under the new 404.2 (Bilingualism) a long cross-classification note is added.

Division 410   Linguistics

A new 413.1 provides for special types of polyglot dictionaries, e.g., abbreviations or acronyms. Discontinued [416] has already been discussed. A Class here note at 418.02 relocates machine translation materials out of the moribund [029.756]. The first issue of *DC&*, v. 4 updates terminology in both caption and notes at 419 (Structured verbal language other than spoken and written).

Division 420   English and Anglo-Saxon

Other than the distributive alterations cited in the chapter introduction, the only notable change is a new note including "standard Canadian spelling and pronunciation" at 421.52 (Spelling and pronunciation of standard English).

Division 430   Germanic (Teutonic) Languages; German

Following Table 6 usage, vernacular names are added in parentheses at 439.82 (Norwegian) and 439.83 (New Norse). *DC&* has added an asterisk to "Modern Icelandic," making it divisible as instructed under 420-490.

Division 440   Romance Languages; French
Division 450   Italian, Romanian, Rhaeto-Romanic Languages
Division 460   Spanish and Portuguese Languages
Division 470   Italic Languages; Latin
Division 480   Hellenic Languages; Classical Greek

The only changes in these five divisions are the three distributive ones cited in the introduction to this chapter.

Division 490   Other Languages

Besides the class-wide changes, there are a few specific differences from the *DDC 18* version of this schedule. "Cornish," "Balto-Slavic," and "Chaldee" are relocated. "Commercial African languages" disappear, but the reduction was already underway in *DDC 18*, and there is no practical classificatory change involved.

Conclusion

Since there are no disruptive changes in class 400, the exercises appended were chosen to give practice in selecting appropriate numbers and facets rather than to alert the user to reclassification pitfalls. General suggestions and explanations accompanying the exercises in previous chapters have equal force here. See particularly those in chapter 5 for the use of auxiliary tables 4 and 6.

Exercises in the Use of Class 400

A. Analysis

401'.9 s [401'.9]	Speech and talk / edited by B. Butterworth ... 1980. [Language production ; v. 1)	80-505326
428'.00973	Safire, William L. On language ... 1980.	80-5145
428.2'4'91851	Kaczmarski, Stanislaw P. A glossary of Polish and English verb forms ... 1978.	79-345099
430'.7'12485	Arvidsson, Mai. Die Prädikatskongruenz im Deutschen auf den drei Stufen des schwed- ischen Gymnasiums ... 1978.	79-364002
437'.01'003	Blech, Ulrike. Germanistische Glossenstudien zu Handschriften aus französischen Biblio- theken ... 1977.	79-360443
439.3'183421	Chérel, Albert. Dutch without toil ... 1979.	80-462445
440'.711'714	Joachim, Sébastien. Le français au collège ... 1978.	79-355667
447'.9'66	Kwofie, Emmanuel N. La langue française en Afrique occidentale francophone ... 1977.	79-355117
448'.007'12713	MacNab, Grace Lowe. A cost analysis model for programs in French as a second lan- guage ... 1978.	79-307160
448'.1	Pouradier Duteil, Françoise. Trois suffixes nomi- nalisateurs ... 1978.	79-360667
478'.2'421	Jenney, Charles. First year Latin ... 1979.	78-55872
483'.81	Ficino, Marsilio. Lessico greco-latino : Laur. Ashb. 1439 ... 1977.	79-337488
489'.3'82421	Tofallis, Kypros. A textbook of modern Greek : for beginners up to GCE "O" Level ... 1977.	79-302918
492.4'3'21	Gesenius, Friedrich Heinrich Wilhelm. Gesenius' Hebrew and Chaldee lexicon to the Old Testa- ment Scriptures ... 1979.	79-104123
494'.511'341	Eckhardt, Sandor. Magyar-francia szotar ... 1978, c1958.	79-337569

B. Synthesis: Examples from LC records are given on pp. 217-18.

1. A dissertation on exceptons in Dutch phonology.

2. The study and teaching of pronunciation.

3. A textbook of business English for foreigners.

4. An introduction to sign language for children.

5. A Russian phrase book for English tourists.

6. A two-way English-Norwegian dictionary.

7. A philosophic investigation of formal semantics and pragmatics for natural languages.

8. An exercise book in Chinese for English-speaking students.

9. A dictionary of South African English.

10. A study of the sociolinguistic aspects of language teaching and learning.

11. A general introduction to Figian language, customs, vocabularies, idioms, etc.

12. A work on teaching English in British secondary schools.

13. Remedial diagnosis and teaching for students with reading disabilities in English.

14. A review of French Creole dialects.

15. The psychological foundations of linguistic analogies.

16. A defense of structuralism against transformationalism in the study of the Rumanian verb system.

17. A two-way Catalan-French dictionary.

18. A directory of Canadian institutions offering adult training courses in French and/or English.

19. A study of the Maghrib Arabic dialects.

20. A systematic study of interlingual European dialects.

21. A survey of errors frequently made by Chinese writers of English.

22. A series of papers on the special idioms and usages of Canadian speakers of French.

23. A Hebrew grammar for English speakers.

24. An investigation into the development of American English.

25. A reference book on dialectical English and unusual customs.

26. The proceedings of a conference on teaching English to illiterates.

27. A work on translating from various languages into modern Hebrew.

28. A French reader for native English-speaking students.

29. A glossary of the French dialect spoken in the Nivernais region of France.

C. Reclassification: Suggested solutions are offered on page 219.

    1. The following numbers from Library of Congress records appear to have clerical or other errors. What class numbers would you assign from *DDC 19*?

422'.045	Classical monologues / edited by Stefan Rudnicki ... 1979.	79-16079
423'.02'03	Mayhew, Anthony Lawson. Concise dictionary of Middle English from A.D. 1150 to 1580 ... 1978.	78-3583
423'.028	Burkett, Eva Mae. American dictionaries of the English language before 1861 ... 1979.	78-11677

    2. These materials were classed before *DDC 19*. Using it, what numbers would you select?

401	Southwest Areal Language and Linguistics Workshop (7th : 1978 : University of Colorado) Bilingual and biliterate perspectives ... proceedings ... 1978.	78-112697
429'.6	Bliss, Alan Joseph. An introduction to Old English metre ... 1978.	78-8129

Examples of LC Cataloging to Illustrate the Above Exercises in DDC Number Synthesis

B. Synthesis

1. 414	Zonneveld, Wim. A formal theory of exceptions in general phonology ... 1978.	78-325582
2. 418'.007	MacCarthy, Peter Arthur Desmond. The teaching of pronunciation ... 1978.	77-84809
3. 428.2'4	Abrams, Sharon. Special English for business ... 1977.	77-20091
4. 419	Sullivan, Mary Beth. A show of hands : say it in sign language ... 1980.	80-15997
5. 491.783'421	Davidson, Pamela. Russian phrase book ... 1980.	80-504613
6. 439.8'2'321	Dietrichson, Jan W. English-Norwegian, Norwegian-English ... 7th ed. ... 1978.	78-387531
7. 401	Formal semantics and pragmatics for natural languages / edited by F. Guenthner and ... 1979.	78-13180
8. 428'.2'4951	Chang, Tao-chen. (Lien hsi yü ta an) [title transliterated]; Title in English on cover: Exercises and answers ... 1978.	79-842965
9. 427'.968	Branford, Jean. A dictionary of South African English ... New enl. ed. ... 1980.	80-505715
10. 401'.9	Sociolinguistic aspects of language learning and teaching / [edited by] J. B. Pride ... 1979.	80-504644

11. 499'.5   Hazelwood, David. A Fijian and English and an
                English and Figian dictionary ... 2d ed. with
                map ... 1979.   75-35119

12. 420'.7'1241 Teaching English across the ability range
                / [edited by] Richard W. Mills ... 1977.   79-301695

13. 428.4'2   Spache, George Daniel. Diagnosing and correct-
                ing reading disabilities ... 2d ed. ... 1980.   80-16010

14. 447'.9   Chaudenson, Robert. Les Creoles français ... 1979.   80-462706

15. 401'.9   Thumb, Albert. Experimentelle Untersuchungen
                über die psychologischen Grundlagen der sprach-
                lichen Analogiebildung ... 1978.   79-348446

16. 415   Juilland, Alphonse G. Transformational and structural
                morphology : about two rival approaches to the
                Rumanian verb system ... 1978.   79-100260

17. 449'.9341   Castellanos i Llorenç, Carles. Diccionari
                catala-frances, frances-catala ... 1979.   79-125113

18. 418'.007'15 Canada. Dept. of the Secretary of State.
                Where to learn French or English ... 1979.   80-464769

19. 492'.77   Zavadovskii, IUrii Nikolaevich. The Maghrib
                Arabic dialects ... 1978.   79-338921

20. 417'.2   Weijnen, Antonius Angelus. Outlines for an inter-
                lingual European dialectologie [sic] ... 1978.   79-304073

21. 428.2'4951 Chin, Ling, fl. 1976-   An analytical study
                of common errors in English compositions
                committed by Chinese college students ...
                / Burt L. King ... 1978.   80-835033

22. 447'.9'71 s Office de la langue française. Vocabulaire
    [629.4'03'41] de l'astronautique ... 1971-1972. (Cahiers
                de l'Office de la langue française ; no.
                10-12)   77-551072

23. 492.4'82'421 La Sor, William Sanford. Handbook of Bib-
                lical Hebrew ... 1978.   78-113168

24. 420'.973   Tibbetts, A. M. What's happening to American
                English? / by Arn Tibbetts ... 1978.   78-10349

25. 427'.09   Stem, Thad. Ransacking words and customs, from
                A to Izzard ... 1977.   77-88204

26. 420'.7   Perspectives on Literacy Conference (1977 : Minne-
                apolis, Minn.) Perspectives on literacy : pro-
                ceedings ... 1978.   79-101906

27. 492.4'8'02 Toury, Gideon. (Normot shel tirgum, veha-
                tirgum ha-sifruti le-'Ivrit ba-shanim
                1930-1945) ... 1930-   79-951428

28. 448.2'421   Halioua, Jean-Pierre. Aventures en ville
                ... 1980.   79-63579

29. 447'.56   Chambure, Eugene de, b. 1813. Glossaire du
                Morvan ... 1978.   80-463586

C. Reclassification.

    1. 822.045 Classical ...

        427.0203 Mayhew ...

        423.0973 Burkett ...
        [423.09034]

    2. 404.2 Southwest ...

        808.1 Bliss ...
        [429]

NOTES

[1]David Batty, "Library Classification: One Hundred Years after Dewey," *Major Classification Systems: The Dewey Centennial*, edited by Kathryn Luther Henderson (Urbana-Champaign, IL, University of Illinois Graduate School of Library Science, c1976), p. 3.

11

Class 500   Pure Sciences

Introduction

The basic organization of class 500 is traditionally disciplinary and predictable, both on the macro- and micro-levels. Any scientist familiar with the classical pedagogical organization of a particular topic or topics can navigate the schedule, although he/she may not always agree with the principle of arrangement. Divisional summaries of the two must recent editions are identical:

Summary (*DDC 18*)		Summary (*DDC 19*)	
500	PURE SCIENCES	500	PURE SCIENCES
510	Mathematics	510	Mathematics
520	Astronomy and allied sciences	520	Astronomy and allied sciences
530	Physics	530	Physics
540	Chemistry and allied sciences	540	Chemistry and allied sciences
550	Sciences of the earth and other worlds	550	Sciences of the earth and other worlds
560	Paleontology; Paleozoology	560	Paleontology; Paleozoology
570	Life sciences	570	Life sciences
580	Botanical sciences	580	Botanical sciences
590	Zoological sciences	590	Zoological sciences

A British reviewer says:

> The 500s and 600s continue as before, but with some useful expansions.... These [chemistry and physics], like the life-sciences, are good examples of problem-oriented disciplines where the process is in general more important than the entity. This is reflected strongly in the literature, but not in DDC.[1]

Criticisms of the life science divisions have long been audible. Nearly 20 years ago we were told:

> The science sections in the Dewey Classification ... with the emphasis on paleontology, fit American science in the later 19th century like a shoe. Unfortunately, the creature wearing the shoe turned out to be a millipede — a situation with which Dewey's successors were never able to cope.[2]

Division 570 was tenth most in want of revision, as reported by the Comaromi survey. In fact, a phoenix schedule was prepared and announced for all the life sciences (560-590), but it was sacrificed at the eleventh hour to concentrate on other changes, particularly those in the 300's. The most conspicuous remnants of that abortive effort are 567.9 (Fossil reptilia [*formerly* 568.1]) and 597.9 (Reptilia [*formerly* 598.1]). These numbers are cited among the 11 instant reuses in v. 1, pp. xxiv-xxv.

The sciences constitute the third most extensive class, having 3,144 entries, next after 6,089 in class 600 and 4,321 in class 300. They are also third in expandable entries, with 897, compared to 1,080 in the 300's and 1,021 in the 600's. Over 100 Add instructions refer to spans in the same class. Five use spans from other classes, and 35 or so take their faceting from Table 2. While science is not essentially regional or local, living organisms, minerals, and other data frequently require a facet for place.

The fairly common references to Table 1 result from schedule tailoring or the addition of cross-classification notes. The first are particularly common from division 530 to the end of the class. For instance, *ss*-01 is modified in 20 places, from 510.1 to 575.01. Fifteen applications of *ss*-0212 (Tables, formulas, specifications, etc.) between 523.30212 to 539.0212 move "Tables" out to a nearby shorter notation. Similar splitting is frequent for *ss*-0222 (Pictures, charts, designs), especially in section 523. *Ss*-028 (Techniques, procedures, apparatus, etc.) is modified 17 times, from 502.8 to 591.028. Special topics are spelled out at 10 locations from 541.04 through 599.004, and in the Add table under 547. There are numerous variations on *ss*-07 and its sub-facets. especially the nine from 531.076 to 539[.076] which qualify or relocate "Review and exercise."

One prevalent pattern in sections 580-590 gives double zero notation to all standard subdivisions, then applies single zeros to "General principles" of the topic. Within this framework, *ss*-009 retains its full Table 1 meaning, while -09 is limited to "Geographical treatment" alone. Examples may be seen from 582 through 599, with variations from 551.6 through 591. Internal tables for distributive expansion, with or without asterisks and footnotes, are presented under 546-547 (Inorganic and organic chemistry), centered heading 582-589 (Specific plants), and centered heading 592-599 (Specific animals). Most of the other changes are straightforward subdivisions of familiar topics. There are a few discontinuances, but not many.

Division 500   Pure Sciences

This division is patterned on Table 1, but the usual reasons for spelling out all section numbers hold true, as we saw in classes 100, 200, and 400.

Section 500 loses two numbers for lack of literary warrant. Both are bracketed.

Sections 501-507 are unchanged and largely undeveloped. "Microscopy," with an Add note, appears as a mutation of *ss*-028 at 502.8. Section [504] remains unassigned.

Sections 508 and 509 are in a state of transition. The DDC editor says, "We have changed the meanings of 508 and 509. *DC&* 4:2 will announce it."[3]

Division 510 Mathematics

The 510's were completely revised in *DDC 18*. Although the phoenix schedule did not win universal accolades, *DDC 19* shows surprisingly infrequent changes.

> This has been expanded, but not all that much, and no really significant change has been made. The schedule has been very heavily criticised in Australia, but not in the U.S., so the Editors have had little incentive to change. I personally have found it very difficult to use, which I ascribe to two causes. Firstly, maths is not my subject — I often haven't any idea what the author is talking about! But even subject experts have found it posed problems, and I think this is because maths is taught and studied differently in different places, and the way it is studied in the U.S., and the way that books from the U.S. are written, does not chime with the British way. So we have difficulty finding a fit, because we are not looking at it in the American way. An example of this is precalculus, a common topic in America, but unknown as such here. That said, it is a pity the schedule was not modelled on the American Mathematical Society's scheme.[4]

Section 511 (Generalities) has a few new scope notes and two extensions under "Sets," with a discontinuance and shift of "Numerical analysis" to 511.

Section 512 (Algebra) adds the descriptor "pedagogical" to 512.1, presumably to distinguish it from centered heading 512.2-.5 (Subdivisions of abstract algebra). More specific designations are added to four notes. The caption at 512.943 inverts "determinants" and "matrices," each of which gets a new extension. *DC&*, v. 4, no. 1 (June 1980): 17 discontinues 512[.904] and its two subdivisions.

Section 513 (Arithmetic) is unchanged except that a note under 513.93 tells us that "Interest and discount tables" are gone off to 332.80212.

Section 514 (Topology) has a new cross-classification note and two extensions, for differential topology and global analysis, under 514.7.

Section 515 (Analysis) is considerably longer than the preceding sections. Number 515[.242] (Sequences) has disappeared without a trace. Two extensions for "Differential equations" are added, with analogous extensions under "Operator theory." There are also new numbers for Banach spaces and Hilbert spaces. The other changes are occasional refinements in captions and notes.

Section 516 (Geometry) shows only a new Class elsewhere note at 516.3 (Analytic geometries).

Sections [517-518] remain unassigned.

Section 519 (Probabilities and applied mathematics) has six new subtopics. Two distinguish the analysis of variance and covariance from factor analysis. Two others separate decision theory from estimation theory. "Time series analysis" and "Statistical hypothesis testing" are also new. Captions and notes show minor updating.

Division 520 Astronomy and Allied Sciences

Section 520 makes only those standard subdivision changes alluded to in the introduction to this chapter.

Section 521 (Theoretical astronomy and celestial mechanics) substitutes "Theoretical astronomy" for "Theory of planets, stars, galaxies" at 521.5. An Inclusion note mentions quasar and pulsar theory. Subtopic 521.54 changes "Theory of planets" to "Theory of solar system," with mention of solar wind and zodiacal light. "Meteors" transmutes to "Meteoroids," to represent technical usage more closely. "Meteoroids" are falling space debris; "Meteors" are the phenomena they produce when they enter the earth's atmosphere. "Meteorites" are the material they deposit on the earth's surface. All three terms can be found in the Relative Index, but *DDC 19*'s schedule is cleaner. The one or two other note or caption changes are minor.

Section 522 (Practical and spherical astronomy) removes the concept "optical" from 522.2 (Telescopes and their use), to mention it negatively at 522.68. A new extension for particle astronomy shows up.

Section 523 (Descriptive astronomy) partially reduces 523.01 (Astrophysics) by moving cosmochemistry to 523.02. Frequent *ss* modifications bring out the special nature of materials in this section. Solar wind is recognized at 523.58, as we saw in Example 6 of chapter 3.

Section [524] is unassigned.

Sections 525-529 show only rudimentary development, and are essentially unaltered.

Division 530 Physics

This division is surprisingly unmodified. Special standard subdivisions, particularly *ss*-01, *ss*-02, and their sub-facets, appear in most sections. There are occasional shifts of terminology, with a few added concepts and notes.

Section 530 (Physics in general) uses double zeros for its standard subdivisions, with an interesting analogue for its primary divisions. "Transport theory" is new in the schedule, though not in the Relative Index. "Physical units, dimensions, constants" get three new scope notes and subdivisions, e.g., 530.812 (Metric system). But one must consult the Index to learn that there is a general location for "Adoption of the metric system" at 389.16.

Sections 531-533 (Mechanics) show only minor change. There is some *ss* adjustment. "Waves, vortex motions, cavitation" at 532.59 and 533.29 are now subdivided. "Types of flow" at 533.21 is given similar treatment to that existing at 532.052. Some people find the 532/533 split between mechanics of fluids and gases undesirable.[5] The relatively limited development of each section makes merger plausible, and would release a section for future advances in physics. On the other hand, disciplinary integrity would probably require such materials to class near 539 (Modern physics).

Sections 534-538 (Sound, Optics, Heat, Electricity, and Magnetism) are barely touched except for their revised Table 1 usages. Comprehensive works on temperature measurement take the long notation 536.5028. "Magnetic properties and phenomena" divides into three subtopics.

Section 539 (Modern physics) is less revised than its classical counterparts. Only a bit of standard subdivision juggling takes place.

Division 540   Chemistry and Allied Sciences

Increasing attention to the history of science gives literary warrant to some development at 540.1.

Sections 541 (Physical and theoretical chemistry) and 542 (Chemical laboratories, apparatus, equipment) are changed by a single number reduction for stable iostopes.

Section 543 (Analytical chemistry) develops nearly two pages of extensions for Instrumental and separation methods. Not all are new techniques, but the literature is growing rapidly enough to make subdivisions, and more Relative Index detail, helpful. Butcher criticizes the "unfortunate split" between 543-545 and 547.3 (Analytical organic chemistry).[6] His is an alternative view of disciplinary integrity.

Section 544 (Qualitative chemistry) has similar, although much briefer, development at 544.9 (Other methods of analysis). Former divisions of Chromatographic analysis are replaced by an Add note. Four new topics appear at the same hierarchical level, some with subtopics.

Section 545 (Quantitative chemistry) retracts a former Add note under 545.01-.07, substituting specific captions. But the change is formal, not substantive. "Chromatographic analysis" is inserted at 545.89, with the same Add note used at 544.92.

Section 546 (Inorganic chemistry) splits "hydrogen" and "water" each into "theoretical" and "physical" subtopics, with identical Add instructions.

Section 547 (Organic chemistry) introduces a distributive table of specific *ss*-04 facets. New numbers from 547.053-.05728 tag specific organometallic compounds, all accompanied by Add instructions. At 547.5, the caption "Alicyclic and heterocyclic compounds" is pruned to "Cyclic compounds," but the subtopics are the same. *DC&*, v. 4, no. 1 (June 1980): 17 adds distributive asterisks to "alicyclic compounds" and "hormones." "Nucleic acids" are relocated to 547.79.

Sections 548-549 (Crystallography and Mineralogy) show no change.

Division 550   Sciences of the Earth and Other Worlds

Section 551 (Geology, meteorology, general hydrology) has its final note revised in *DC&*. It should read "For astronomical geography, [not 'geology'] see 525...." Russell Sweeney foresees inadvertent difficulties from the renaming of this section: There is a change at 550 Sciences of the earth and other worlds

> which may not be desirable. In 18th edition there was a note given at this point "class here geology." This has been removed in 19th edition and class 551 is now labelled "Geology, meteorology, general hydrology," where formerly it was labelled "Physical and dynamic geology." There is surely a danger that less experienced classers will attempt to place general works on Geology at 551 although the index directs to 550.[7]

Four subtopics are added under 551.11 (Interior structure and properties of earth and other worlds). "Plate tectonics (Continental drift)" makes its DDC debut. A pageful of subtopics replace the former Add note at 551.41-.45 (Specific land forms). The user is now encouraged to subdivide "Submarine geology" by region. "Runoff" is moved to 551.488. "Floods and their forecasts" go in under "Hydrology." The span for "Specific aspects of earth temperatures affecting atmosphere" is discontinued. Under "Precipitation," historical treatment is split away from "Distribution" (i.e., geographic treatment). Historical geology gets three new period numbers.

Section 552 (Petrology) has three added subtopics under 552.2 (Volcanic products and rocks).

Section 553 (Economic geology) stands a long way from 622.18 (Prospecting for specific minerals), from 669 (Metallurgy), and from 333.8 (Subsurface resources). The class 600 locations are noted, but only the Relative Index reveals the class 300 numbers. Even there the cross classification is not readily apparent. The 553's, together with the 551's, are the most extended of the *DDC 19* geology division. There are 18 new subtopics here.

Sections 554-559 (Treatment by continent, country, etc.) substitute a distributive Add note at a centered heading for the former instructions under individual sections. It is merely a technical consolidation.

Division 560   Paleontology; Paleozoology

This division initiates the "life sciences" portion of class 500. It was here that the abortive phoenix schedule was to have begun, but we are told that it "was inadequately thought-out and researched, and had to be returned for revision."[8] As it stands, there is about the same amount of change, mostly expansion, as we saw in mathematics.

Section 560 (Standard subdivisions of paleontology) expands 560.172 (Paleozoic paleontology) and 560.176 (Mesozoic paleontology). Paleoecology and Zoological paleoecology are relocated from notes in other divisions to special topic numbers.

Section 561 (Paleobotany) has a single correction from *DC&*, restoring the "9" that was inadvertently dropped from the "fossil plants" example at 561.09.

Section 562 (Fossil invertebrates) upgrades a former Inclusion note to make a single subtopic for "Conodonts."

Section 563 (Fossil Protozoa ...) expands 563.1 (Protozoa; Plasmodroma), and adds "Blastoidea" under Echinodermata.

Section 564 (Fossil Mollusca) is innocent of any significant tampering.

Section 565 (Other fossil invertebrates) shifts Branchiura to a new 565.31. The word "Thysanoptera" at 565.73 is misspelled and should be corrected.

Section 566 (Fossil Chordata ...) is unpartitioned. Only its cross-classification note is changed.

Sections 567 and 568 change their captions and share the most important relocation in this division. Section 567 (Fossil cold-blooded vertebrates; Fossil fishes) used to be "Fossil Anamnia; Fossil fishes," with a subtopic "Urodela" at 567.9. Section 568 (Fossil birds; Fossil Neornithes) was "Fossil Sauropsida (Fossil reptiles and birds)," with a subtopic Reptilia at 568[.1]. In a phoenix single-number change, Reptilia goes to 567.9, getting its subtopics rearranged in the process. Urodela is parenthesized after "Caudata" in an Inclusion note at 567.6 (Amphibia). See the corresponding shift from 598[.1] to 597.9.

Section 569 (Fossil Mammalia) has only two new subsections under "Glires."

Division 570   Life Sciences

This division ranked tenth among the requests for revision on the Comaromi survey. It was already part of the predicted phoenixing, but its changes are as blandly inconsequential as most others in class 500.

There has been much support for the idea that biologists now study processes rather than organisms, and that the Life sciences schedule should be organised to take account of this. Greg New of LC Decimal Classification Division spent the best part of two years working out a phoenix on these lines, but for various reasons it was not accepted. The idea has now come to the fore once more, and a project to consider a phoenix is presently under way at Preston Polytechnic.[9]

Section 570 has only the unspecified possibility of Table 1 expansion.
Section [571] is unassigned.
Section 572 (Human races) shows no change in its four extended subtopics.
Section 573 (Physical anthropology) has seven subtopics, but they, too, are unextended and unchanged. A major transfer of comprehensive works on anthropology and all its social science aspects from the 570's to 301.2 (now 301) caused some consternation when *DDC 18* was published, but the disciplinary distinctions are fairly clear. Only the shelf distance between these two related topics is burdensome for many users.
Section 574 (Biology), in addition to its Table 1 modifications, introduces "Regional physiology" and "Control processes." "Biological rhythms" goes in, as was mentioned in chapter 4. A "meaningless context" number is discontinued (Cf. Example 8 in chapter 3). Trotter commends the potential for expressing organic compounds by faceting at 574.1924, but the numbers will be quite long.[10] Ecology (574.5) is repeatedly expanded with some 35 new subtopics. Only one number is discontinued by reduction.
Section 575 (Organic evolution and genetics) transfers "Physiological genetics" to Inclusion under 574.87322 (Chromosomes). Darwin and Lamarck's names are used as eponyms under 575.01.
Section 576 (Microbes) makes three extensions, including a span with an Add note. *DC&* has relocated "Interferons" from 576.64 (Viruses) to 591.295 (Immune reactions in pathology).
Sections 577-579 are unaltered.

Division 580   Botanical Sciences

Section 581 (Botany), in an Add note based on 574.8, relocates "Physiological genetics" as a subtopic of 581.8 (Tissue, cellular, molecular botany). "Biological rhythms," as in section 574, gets its own number. But a problem similar to that posed in section 553 makes it increasingly hard to distinguish what should class in 581.6 (Economic botany) from what belongs in 333.7 (Natural resources), or from what fits into certain Agriculture subdivisions. For example, "Weeds" is made a legitimate scientific term at 581.652, but without definition or scope note to support it. Heretofore it was used only at 632.58, and parenthetically at 632.954 (Herbicides).

Section 582 (Spermatophyta) does nothing innovative.

Section 583 (Dicotyledones) drops an "Arrange" (a kind of option) note, but that is all.

Sections 584-588 remain virtually intact.

Section 589 (Thallophta) adds two extensions under 589.222 (Agaricales), and one each under "Ascomycetes" and "Phycomycetes." "Schizophyta" is reduced.

Division 590 Zoological Sciences

Section 591 (Zoology) adds its own "Biological rhythms." "Skeletal organs" shows up under 591.4 (Anatomy and morphology of animals). Nearly a page of development takes place at 591.5 (Ecology of animals), but zoological paleoecology is lost to the 560's.

Sections 592-599 (Specific animals) expand the 09 portion of the distributive Add table under their centered heading.

Sections 592-594 (Invertebrates; Protozoa, etc.; Mollusca, etc.) repeat *DDC 18* except for *ss* extensions of 592 and 594 by the use of an Add note.

Section 595 (Other invertebrates) inadvertently omits the asterisk at 595.3 (*Crustacea, etc.). It is restored by *DC&*. Additional taxonomic specifications are "Syncarida," "Ricinulei," "Uropygi," "Collembola," and "Polyphaga."

Section 596 (Chordata; Vertebrata) places "Tunicata" in parentheses after "Urochordata" at 596.2. It then adds a second subtopic, "Cephalochordata (Lancelets)."

Section 597 (Cold-blooded vertebrates) relocates the geographic subdivisions of "Hydrographic zoology" to shorter notation. "Salientia" now has five partitions. "Urodela" is replaced by "Reptilia" at 597.9, and becomes a second caption with "Caudata" at 597.65. This phoenix change has been discussed several times.

Section 598 (Aves [Birds]) now classes "Shore birds" with "Charadriiformes," which gets one subtopic, "Lari." "Galliformes" now divides into six species; "Falconiformes" into five.

Section 599 (Mammalia) transfers "Tubulidentata (Aardvarks)" to its own number, as we saw in Comparison C-8 of chapter 4. Three extensions are added to 599.884 (Ponginae) to separate Orangutans from Chimpanzees and Gorillas. But complaints are still heard.

> ... Mammals at 599 has not been expanded nearly as much as it should have been—there are still no specific numbers for such common animals as deer, lions, tigers, wolves or otters—all of which have a sizeable literature.[11]

Conclusion

Adjustments in class 500 are for the most part cautious expansions of existing topics, to accommodate increased literature on scientific methodology, instrumentation, and taxonomic refinements. However useful, they are superficial rather than structural. We have heard that the British classifiers try to revive the aborted phoenix schedule for the life sciences. The Decimal

Classification Editorial Policy Committee seems more concerned with unresolved phoenix schedule problems, as in 302-307 (Sociology), and with proper application of standard subdivisions to multiply-captioned topics and Inclusion note topics.[12] The ultimate effect of these countervailing thrusts on the classification scheme remains to be seen.

Exercises in the Use of Class 500

A. Analysis

507'.1059	Regional Centre for Education in Science and Mathematics. Task force. Report of the third Task Force meeting of the SEAMEC Regional Centre ... [1968?]	78-311454
510'.7'1173	Kline, Morris. Why the professor can't teach : mathematics and the dilemma of university education ... c1977.	76-62777
519'.02'461	Atlani, Robert. Probabilités & [i.e. et] statistiques : rappels de cours, exercises et annales corrigés ... c1976.	77-560811
523.01'5'84	Blanchard, Paul A. Atoms in astronomy : a curriculum project of the American Astronomical Society ... 1976.	77-602592
523.8'01'4	Limburg, Peter R. What's in the names of stars and constellations ... c1976.	76-13637
531'.01'51	Kardestuncer, Hayrettin. Discrete mechanics : a unified approach ... 1975.	77-368677
547'.1'39	Epiotis, N. D. Theory of organic reactions ... 1978.	77-17405
547'.308'7	Baiulescu, George. Application of ion-selective membrane electrodes in organic analysis ... 1977.	77-80262
551.4'614'6	Alexander, James E. Chemical properties ... 1979.	77-624522
553.7'9'0976311	Case, H. L. Ground-water resources of Washington Parish, Louisiana ... 1979.	79-624546
561'.13'09486	Pahlsson, Ingemar. A standard pollen diagram from the Lojsta Area of Central Gotland ... 1977.	78-358305
573'.6'09541	Das, Bhuban Mohan. Variation in physical characteristics in the Khasi population of north east India ... 1978.	78-902304
581.1'924	Karrer, Walter. Konstitution und Vorkommen der organischen Pflanzenstoffe (exklusive Alkaloide) : Ergänzungsband ... 1977-	77-579583
581.5'267'099432	Clifford, Harold Trevor. The vegetation of North Stradbroke Island, Queensland ... 1979.	80-456990

582'.01'33	Kluge, Manfred. Crassulacean acid metabolism : analysis of an ecological adaptation ... 1978.	78-12658
591.1'9285	International Symposium on Quantitative Mass Spectrometry in Life Sciences (1st : 1976 : State University of Ghent) Quantitative mass spectrometry in life sciences : proceedings ... 1977.	77-3404
592'.09'213 s [595'.35]	Nilsson-Cantell, Carl August. Cirripedia Thoracica and Acrothoracica ... 1978. (Marine invertebrates of Scandinavia ; no. 5)	79-300616
596'.01'16	Cardiac Muscle Symposium (1977 : Pahlavi University) Biophysical aspects of cardiac muscle : proceedings ... 1978.	78-17025
597'.05'908	Sound production in fishes / edited by William N. Tavolga ... c1977.	76-28352
599'.01'826	Chemoreception in the carotid body / edited by H. Acker ... 1977.	77-13691

B. Synthesis: Examples from LC records are given on pp. 231-34.

1. A layman's introduction to the physical sciences.

2. The use of computers in chemical research, education, and technology.

3. The College Board Achievement test in chemistry.

4. A reference book with short, alphabetically arranged entries about topics in physics and mathematics.

5. A history of mathematical progress from 1600 to 1750.

6. A book of sky charts for amateur star gazers.

7. A symposium on the structure of non-crystalline materials for a glass manufacturers' convention.

8. A collection of papers on mutagenesis.

9. The proceedings of a conference on the color of the ocean.

10. A FORTRAN programming manual for use with calculus courses.

11. A study of cooperative equilibria in physical biochemistry.

12. A vocational guidance survey of careers in chemistry.

13. A children's book about giraffes.

14. Radiationless transitions of electrons, including the Auger effect.

15. A layman's introduction to the earth sciences.

16. A history of the mathematical sciences.

17. The annual water quality inventory taken by the Water Resources Control Board in the state of California.

18. A basic computer supplement to a linear algebra text.

19. A series of monographs issued by the Geological Survey of India on economic geology.

20. A periodical devoted to cytology, and cell biophysics in particular.

21. The effects of the pipeline on caribou movements in Alaska.

22. A collection of essays on teaching arithmetic, algebra, and geometry in the elementary school.

23. A set of lectures on mathematical principles as applied to biology.

24. A guide to the application of mathematical analysis in physics.

25. A description and analysis of the properties of supernovae.

26. A series of bulletins on the climatic conditions in the vicinity of Hong Kong.

27. Molecular bonding in the organic chemistry of silicon, phosphorus, and sulphur.

28. Symposium papers on mammalian ingestion and digestion.

29. A collection of essays on the chemistry of lignans.

30. A book on fossil plants in Sweden.

31. A work on behavioral complexities and adaptations among animals.

32. Basic physical chemistry for biologists.

33. The physiology of leucocytes in the blood of mammals.

34. The effects of climatic change on the Canadian prairie provinces.

35. The report of a field expedition to collect fossil mollusks in Tegelen, Netherlands.

36. A guide to the identification of British aquatic earthworms.

37. Fossil hominid remains in central Africa.

38. The physiology of Angiosperms (flowering plants).

39. Diseases and injuries in animals caused by pollutants.

40. Mathematical models of allosteric protein building in living organisms.

41. Monthly tables of meteorological observations in Canada.

42. A college text in basic arithmetic and algebra.

43. A book on Stonehenge as a huge astronomical instrument for the observation of eclipses of the moon.

44. An encyclopedia of the space sciences.

45. Mathematics for modern business managers.

46. The microbiology of airborne infections.

47. An index to the chemistry and math handbooks published by the Chemical Rubber Company.

48. A workbook for practicing skills in basic arithmetic, algebra, and geometry.

49. A series of investigative reports published by the North Dakota Geological Survey.

50. A history of Islamic mathematics from the eighth to the fifteenth century.

51. A popular history of maps.

52. The use of dimensional analysis to solve chemical problems.

53. Oceanographic research at La Jolla, California.

C. Reclassification: The following records carry pre-*DDC 19* number assignments by the Library of Congress. What adjustments would you make? Suggested solutions are offered on pp. 234-35.

1. 500.9'022'2	Grillone, Lisa. Small worlds close-up ... c1978. [Microscope and microscopy--Pictorial works-- Juvenile literature]	77-15860
2. 500.9'08 s [595'.44]	Platnick, Norma I. A review of the spider genus Anapis (Araneae, Anapidae) ... 1978. (American Museum novitates ; no. 2663 ISSN 0003-0082)	78-113115
3. 512.9'042	Auvil, Daniel L. Intermediate algebra ... c1979.	78-18643
4. 540'.28	Vlassis, C. G. A laboratory guide for chemistry ... c1978.	76-49572
5. 542'.08 s [542]	Chemical experimentation under extreme condi- tions / edited by Bryant W. Rossiter ... c1980. (Techniques of chemistry ; v. 9)	79-10962
6. 543'.01'82	Validation of the measurement process : a symposium ... 1977.	77-15555
7. 547'.1'2230183	Davis, Henry W. Computer representation of the stereochemistry of organic mole- cules : with application to the problem of discovery of organic synthesis by computer ... 1976.	77-366704
8. 547'.0028	Linstromberg, Walter William. Organic experiments ... 4th ed. ... c1978.	77-156013
9. 574.8'732	Rees, Hubert. Chromosome genetics ... 1977.	77-16211

Examples of LC Cataloging to Illustrate the Above Exercises in DDC Number Building

1. 500.2   Thurber, Walter A. Exploring physical science ... c1977. 75-41824

2. 542'.8   International Conference on Computers in Chemical
                 Research, Education, and Technology (1976 : Caracas)
                 Computers in chemical education and research : [pro-
                 ceedings ...] ... c1977.   77-9473

3. 540'.76   Spector, Leo. CBAT, College Board Achievement test
                 in chemistry ... 1978.   76-47486

4. 530'.03   McGraw-Hill dictionary of physics and mathematics
                 ... c1978.   78-8983

5. 510'.9'032   Griffiths, P. L. Mathematical discoveries, 1600-
                 1750 ... 1977.   78-310242

6. 523.8'903   Jobb, Jamie. The night sky book : an everyday
                 guide to every night ... c1977.   77-24602

7. 530.4'1   The Structure of non-crystalline materials : proceed-
                 ings of the symposium held in Cambridge ... 1977.   78-303674

8. 575.2'92   Mutagenesis / edited by W. Gary Flamm ... c1978.   77-26342

9. 551.4'601   The Color of the ocean : report of the conference
                 on August 5-6, 1969, held at Woods Hole Oceano-
                 graphic Institution ... 1969?   73-611946

10. 515'.028'5   Fuller, William Richard. FORTRAN programming :
                 a supplement for calculus courses ... c1977.   77-12129

11. 574.1'9283   Poland, Douglas. Cooperative equilibria in physical
                 biochemistry ... 1978.   77-30538

12. 540'.23   Taylor, L. B. Chemistry careers ... 1978.   77-21313

13. 599'.7357   Brown, Louise C. Giraffes ... c1979.   79-52037

14. 539.7'2112   Burhop, E. H. S. (Eric Henry Stoneley) The
                 Auger effect and other radiationless tran-
                 sitions ... 1980, c1952.   79-23744

15. 550   Burrus, Thomas L. Earth in crisis : an introduction
                 to the earth sciences ... 2d ed. ... 1980.   79-19596

16. 510'.9   Cajori, Florian. A history of mathematics ... 1980.   70-113120

17. 553.7'09794 California. State Water Resources Control Board.
                 Surveillance and Monitoring Section. Annual
                 water quality inventory ...   80-640260

18. 512'.5   Caton, Gerald. A computer supplement to Linear
                 algebra : basic ... c1980.   79-21280

19. 553'.0954 s Chakravarty, S. C. The geology and manganese-
    [553.4'629' ore deposits of the maganese belt in Madhya
    09543]   Pradesh and adjoining parts of Maharashtra
                 ... 19-   (Bulletins of the Geological Sur-
                 vey of India : Series A - economic geology ;
                 no. 22)   80-465692

20. 574.87'6041 Cell biophysics. v. 1- Mar. 1979-   79-647796

21. 599.73'57   Cameron, Raymond D. Third interim report of the effects of the Trans-Alaska Pipeline on caribou movements ... 1978.   79-625960

22. 513'.142   Frand, Jason L. Theory and applications of mathematics for teachers ... 2nd ed. ... c1978.   77-7591

23. 574'.01'51   Canadian Mathematical Congress (Society) Mathematics and the life sciences : selected lectures ... 1977.   77-11151

24. 515'.02'453   Potter, Merle C. Mathematical methods in the physical sciences ... c1978.   77-11192

25. 523.8'446   Clark, David H. Superstars ... 1979.   80-456507

26. 551.6951'25 s [551.5'185]   Chen, Tin-ying. Wind shear at Hong Kong International Airport in four squally shower situations ... 1978. (Technical note - Royal Observatory, Hong Kong ; no. 46)   79-111792

27. 547'.1'224   Kwart, H. D-orbitals in the chemistry of silicon, phosphorus, and sulfur ... 1977.   77-1555

28. 599'.01'32   International Symposium on Food Intake and Chemical Senses (1st : 1976 : Fukuoka, Japan) Food intake and chemical senses: [papers] ... c1977.   77-28509

29. 547'.613   Chemistry of lignans / editor-in-chief, C. B. S. Rao ... 1978.   79-912164

30. 561'.19'485   Florin, Maj Britt. Late-glacial and Pre-boreal vegetation in Southern Central Sweden ... 1977.   78-309280

31. 591.5   Chauvin, Rémy. Behavioral complexities ... c1980.   79-20944

32. 541'.3'024574   Marshall, Alan G. Biophysical chemistry : principles, techniques, and applications ... c1978.   77-19136

33. 599'.01'13   Leukocyte chemotaxis : methods, physiology, and clinical implications / edited by John I. Gallin ... c1978.   76-58053

34. 551.6'9'712   Longley, Richmond Wilberforce. Climatic change as it affects Alberta and the other prairie provinces ... 1977.   77-374873

35. 564'.09492'4   Freudenthal, M. Preliminary report on a field campaign in the continental Pleistocene of Tegelen (The Netherlands) ... 1976.   77-376918

36. 595'.146'0942   Brinkhurst, Ralph O. A guide for the identification of British aquatic Oligochaeta ... 2d ed. rev. ... 1971.   79-854117

37. 569'.9'0967   Early hominids of Africa / edited by Clifford J. Jolly ... 1978.   78-54136

38. 582'.01   Raab, Carl M. Budding wonders : the flowering plants ... 1979.   78-11715

39.	591.2'4	Hanford Biology Symposium (17th : 1977 : Richland, Wash.) Developmental toxicology of energy-related pollutants : proceedings ... 1978.	78-606139
40.	574.1'9245	Levitzki, Alexander. Quantitative aspects of allosteric mechanisms ... 1978.	79-302021
41.	551.6971'02'12	Canada. Atmospheric Environment Service. Monthly record; meteorological observations in Canada. Supplement ... v. 62- 1977-	79-648317
42.	513'.123	Hockett, Shirley O. Basic mathematics : what every college student should know ... c1977.	76-27302
43.	523.3'8'028	Hoyle, Fred, Sir. On Stonehenge ... 1977.	78-312276
44.	500.5'03	The Illustrated encyclopedia of astronomy and space / editor, Ian Ridpath ... 1976.	77-374874
45.	510'.2'4658	Dean, Burton Victor. Mathematics for modern management ... 1978, c1963.	77-27927
46.	574.909'6	Aerobiology : the ecological systems approach ... c1978.	78-23769
47.	540'.2'02	Composite index for CRC handbooks ... 2d ed. ... c1977.	77-10770
48.	513'.142'076	Haldi, John F. Basic mathematics : skills and structure ... c1978.	77-73943
49.	557.84 s [551.7'31'0978482]	Carroll, W. Kipp. Depositional environments and paragenic porosity controls, upper Red River Formation, North Dakota ... 1979. (Report of investigation - North Dakota Geological Survey ; no. 66)	79-625010
50.	510'.917'671	Ĩŭshkevich, Adol'f Pavlovich. Les mathématiques arabes : VIIIe-XVe siècles ... 1976.	78-342570
51.	526'.09	Brown, Lloyd Arnold. The story of maps ... 1979, c1949.	79-52395
52.	540'.1'5308	Loebel, Arnold B. Chemical problem-solving by dimensional analysis : a self-instructional program ... 2d ed. ... c1978.	77-78565
53.	551.46'007'2079498	Scripps Institution of Oceanography. Scripps Institution ... 1976/77-	79-643881

C. Reclassification: Suggested *DDC 19* numbers for pre-*DDC 19* records.

1. 502.820222   Grillone ...
   [535.3320222]

2. 508   Platnick ... [American Museum of Natural History]

3. 512.9   Auvil ... [See *DC&*, v. 4, no. 1 (June 1980): 17]

4. 542   Vlassis ...

5. 542   Chemical ...

6. 543.0028   Validation ...
    [543.0072]

7. 547.1223072   Davis ...

8. 547.0076   Linstromberg ...

9. 574.873224   Rees ...

NOTES

[1]Peter Butcher, "Dewey? We Sure Do!," *Catalogue & Index*, no. 55 (Winter 1979): 8.

[2]Phyllis A. Richmond, "The Future of Generalized Systems of Classification," *College and Research Libraries*, v. 24, no. 5 (September 1963): 399.

[3]John Phillip Comaromi, in a communication to the publisher dated April 29, 1981.

[4]Ross Trotter, "Dewey 19—A Subjective Assessment," *Catalogue & Index*, no. 59 (Winter 1980): 3. Some of the Australian criticism can be read in the following articles, although they are not all negative:
David Batty, "A Close Look at Dewey 18: Alive and Well and Living in Albany," *Wilson Library Bulletin*, v. 46, no. 8 (April 1972): 714.
Peter W. Donovan, David C. Hunt, and John M. Mack, "Mathematics in a Major Library Using the Dewey Decimal Classification," *Australian Academic and Research Libraries*, v. 6, no. 2 (June 1975): 87-91.
Peter W. Donovan, David C. Hunt, and John M. Mack, "Professional Developments Reviewed: DDC and Mathematics," *Wilson Library Bulletin*, v. 48, no. 3 (November 1973): 220-22.
John McKinlay, "Dewey and Mathematics," *Australian Academic and Research Libraries*, v. 4, no. 3 (September 1973): 105-111.
Barbara K. Schaefer, "The Phoenix Schedule 510 in Dewey 18," *Library Resources & Technical Services*, v. 19, no. 1 (Winter 1975): 46-59.

[5]Butcher, p. 8.

[6]Ibid.

[7]Russell Sweeney, "The Old, Grey Mare ... ," *Cataloging & Classification Quarterly*, v. 1, no. 1 (Fall 1980): 94.

[8]Butcher, p. 8.

[9]Trotter, p. 4.

[10]Ibid.

[11]Ibid.

[12]Margaret E. Cockshutt, "Annual Report of the Decimal Classification Editorial Policy Committee, July 1, 1979-June 30, 1980," *Library Resources & Technical Services*, v. 25, no. 1 (January/March 1981): 123-24.

12

Class 600 Technology (Applied Sciences)

Introduction

This largest of all classes in number of entries (6,089), and second largest in the number of expandable entries (1,021), embodies the enormous growth of technology during the century since Dewey first presented his system. One classifier calls it:

> ... an unpredictable disarray of "disciplines" and/or subjects ...
> an arbitrary arrangement of a heterogeneous mass.[1]

Only classes 620 and 610 were targeted for revision on the Comaromi survey, but they ranked second and third in the overall order of urgency. A major readjustment in the contemplated phoenix schedule 560-590 (Life sciences) would have moved both Human anatomy from section 611, and Human physiology from section 612, into section 591, partially to relieve the congestion in the 610's, but also to affirm their relationship to the anatomy and physiology of animals. As we know, it was withdrawn, after receiving criticisms such as the following:

> ... It appears that "veterinary anatomy" will continue to be classified under a separate notation, 636.089 with the appropriate numbers following 61 in 610-619 added and not under 591 like "human anatomy" and "physiology" ... Another argument for the proposed shifting of concepts under 611 and 612 to 591 appears to be that "anatomy" and "physiology" are *pure sciences* and should not be classified under medicine which is an applied science.... Even granting the feasibility of the exact demarcation of *pure* and *applied sciences*, it can be argued ... that pharmacodynamics is now a pure science, but it is proposed to continue its classification under 615.7. The editors would have done well to avoid so far-reaching a change, bound as it is to affect extensively the existing classification of the holdings of numerous libraries, particularly medical libraries.[2]

Nearly one-half of the 340 relocations above and beyond the *DDC 19* phoenix changes took place in classes 300 and 600.[3] They are listed in *DDC 18* order under *Relocations and Schedule Reductions* (v. 1, pp. 453-60). A generally sympathetic British writer says dourly:

The 660s, 670s and 680s remain an inscrutable hotchpotch — a further illustration of the need for summary tables at the beginning of each class.... Construction ... is still split between 624 and 690.[4]

Divisional summary captions changed very little between editions:

Summary *(DDC 18)*		Summary *(DDC 19)*	
600	TECHNOLOGY (APPLIED SCIENCES)	600	TECHNOLOGY (APPLIED SCIENCES)
610	Medical sciences; Medicine	610	Medical sciences; Medicine
620	Engineering and allied operations	620	Engineering and allied operations
630	Agricultural and related techniques	630	Agriculture and related technologies
640	Domestic arts and sciences (Home economics)	640	Home economics and family living
650	Managerial services	650	Management and auxiliary sciences
660	Chemical and related technologies	660	Chemical and related technologies
670	Manufactures	670	Manufactures
680	Miscellaneous manufactures	680	Manufactures of products for specific use
690	Buildings	690	Buildings

Division 600   Standard Subdivisions of Technology

Except for section 608 (Inventions and patents), this division follows a fairly predictable Table 1 pattern. Two bracketed numbers carry cross-classification notes. The study and teaching of technology in areas or regions, and in the ancient world, goes under 607.01-.03, but for specific places of the modern world it falls under 607.4-.9, for slightly shorter notation.

Division 610   Medical Sciences; Medicine

This discipline, as noted above, was considered the third most in need of revision in the Comaromi survey. It barely escaped a major reduction of its 611-612 portions. As it stands, 89 schedule pages make it one of the longest divisions in *DDC 19*. Custer claimed "substantial adjustment and expansion," but what there is occurs chiefly in section 614.[5]

Section 610 (Standard subdivisions of the medical sciences) moves statistics on illness and somatology out to 312.3 (Data on social morbidity) and 312.6 (Comparative anthropological measurements). An instruction at 610.695 to "class here medical missionaries" was mentioned under section 266. A note at 610.724 distinguishes between "Experimental research in medicine" and "Experimental medicine." The latter should be classed 619. "Nursing as a profession" and "Services of medical technicians" relocate to nearby numbers. A new subtopic, "Relationships of nurses," is inserted, as is "Intensive (Critical) etc. nursing."

Section 611 (Human anatomy, cytology, tissue biology) adds numbers for Cytopathology and Physiological genetics. There are a couple of scope notes added under "Arteries." The aborted shift of human anatomy and physiology has been criticized on still further grounds than those cited in the chapter introduction:

> The arguments advanced in support of the shifting of all concepts from 611 and 612 to 591 appear unconvincing. The shifting is sought to be justified on the basis that the present trend is to class the "anatomy" and "physiological processes" of specific organisms with the processes rather than the *individual organism*. But under 611 and 612 as well as 591 classification is already in terms of processes and not in terms of species. The editors and the Committee have further set a limit to the preparation of this principle, that it will be applied only up to the Kingdom level.[6]

Section 612 (Human physiology) has limited expansion. "Biochemistry" gets a brief *ss* development chiefly for the housing of cross-classification notes. "Thermal forces" acquires three subtopics. "Blood plasma" is added, and "Biological immunity" now divides into "Antigens," "Antibodies," and "Immune reactions."

Section 613 (General and personal hygiene) drops its "middle-aged" category, presumably for lack of literary warrant. Nobody in the United States is middle-aged anymore. "Health resort areas" show up at 613.122, but they cannot be accessed through the Relative Index. Vegetarianism gets its own number, but all subtopics for specific beverages are reduced. Hatha yoga joins a seemingly unrelated span at 613.7046. We are told to class sex education of children in the home at 649.65. Manuals of sexual technique are relocated here out of the old sociology schedule.

Section 614 (Public health and related topics) has 1 of the 11 "phoenix numbers" cited in the editor's introduction (v. 1, p. xxv). Forensic medicine (Medical jurisprudence) replaced "Registration and certification," of which it was originally a subtopic. Much, but not all, of the old 614.1 content is now affiliated with Public administration in 351. Other parts are relocated to 363, as we saw in chapter 9. First aid moves out to the 616's.

> 614 is left looking rather empty — 614.4 and 614.5 remain, of course, for actual disease control measures, and you will still be able to class in 614.6 a work on how to embalm a body — but not much else goes there.[7]

The *Relocations and Schedule Reductions* list is helpful. The only fresh material is the extension of 614.57 (Bacterial and viral diseases).

Section 615 (Pharmacology and therapeutics) has 13 new numbers and two discontinuances in nine pages. Additions include "Drugs derived from bryophytes," "Special interactions from pharmacodynamics," and subtopics under "Hypnotic drugs," "Activity therapies," and "Other therapies" (including Acupuncture). *DC&* does some tidying up at 615.9 (Toxicology).

Section 616 (Diseases) is nearly 30 pages long, with some 65 additions, not counting expanded possibilities for synthetic number building. We shall not take the space to itemize them all. They cover "Myocardial infarction," "Sickle cell anemia," "Hemophilia," "Bronchitis," "Diarrhea," "Colitis," "Gout," "Hermaphroditism," "Arthritis," "Suicidal compulsions," "Zoonoses," and the like. A distributive Add table under 616.1-.9 (Specific diseases) has several facets not available in *DDC 18*. Nine relocations are bracketed. Psychologists will not be pleased that this section retains such cross-disciplinary materials as "Mental deficiency." Cf. our chapter 7 review of division 150.

Section 617 (Surgery and related topics) starts with a distributive Add table in which extensive new facets appear. It includes double zero standard subdivisions and single zero special aspects, but there are at least 17 places in the 14-page schedule where *ss* modification occurs. New numbers extend coverage for surgery of the capillaries, the palate and throat, the back and hips, and intraocular lenses, as well as internal parts of the ear. Discontinuances signal relocations for Thyroid and parathyroid surgery, Eye banks, and Tissue and organ banks.

Section 618 (Other branches of medicine) starts off with a new distributive table for 618.1-.8 (Gynecology and obstetrics). It is based in part on a *DDC 18* table at 616.1-.9 (Specific diseases) which, as we saw, is considerably extended in *DDC 19*. This new table differs from those at 616 and 617 chiefly in being more compact, with Add notes of its own to provide patterned expansions. There are new specific entries for Fetal diseases of specific systems and organs, Diseases of the placenta and amniotic fluid, and Special branches of pediatric medicine. Two of the six bracketed relocations are carried over from *DDC 18*.

Section 619 (Experimental medicine) is brief and unchanged.

Division 620   Engineering and Allied Operations

In 1975, the DDC editor predicted very substantial expansion "as always" for this largest of all divisions.[8] Together, sections 621, 623, and 629 occupy 74 of its 127 pages. It was second choice for urgent reorganization in the Comaromi survey, but there is nothing innovative here—merely a baroque ornamentation of a creaking edifice. Not only do its sections follow little discernible logic, but many are internally heterogeneous. Hierarchies are ignored, disciplinary relationships violated with abandon, or out of reluctance to inconvenience established practice. Piecemeal attempts to integrate our rapidly diversifying literature of engineering only highlight basic inconsistencies. Slotification, the only viable solution under the circumstances, shows its weaknesses in their worst light. Because of their length and multiplicity, changes in the following sections will not be itemized. Rather, an attempt is made to give some sense of their nature and direction.

Section 620 (Standard subdivisions and special aspects of engineering) makes some shifts in Table 1 facets. "General concepts" replaces "Special topics ... " and receives some half-dozen extensions. The Add table under 620.12-.19 (Specific engineering materials) is essentially a re-writing of *DDC 18* instructions. "Testing and measurement" and "Properties and tests" account for 21 new numbers under 620.1. Seven topical entries, e.g., "Zinc and cadmium," are new under 620.18 (Nonferrous metals and alloys). Architectural acoustics is moved to 690. Some cross-classification dilemmas are posed, such as the following:

All of 600 is of course a marvelous illustration of ... the wide separation of subjects by discipline, i.e., engineering materials from their processing and their manufactured products, e.g. aluminum in 620, 699, 673.[9]

One need only look in the Relative Index under "Aluminum" to find 19 separate class 600 locations, not to mention 3 each in classes 500 and 700. While several have clear disciplinary grounds, others are harder to distinguish. The price of choosing "disciplinary" over "subject" integrity is dramatically portrayed. The 620's are modified in a dozen places by a widespread terminological change in *DC&*, v. 4, no. 1 (June 1980). "Illustrations," "Models," "Scale models," or combinations thereof, expand in every case to include "Miniatures."

Section 621 (Applied physics) may be theoretically and hierarchically justified in its placement, being fundamental to most of the rest of engineering. Still it is closely related to division 530. Unfortunately, most of the 500's and two sections of 600's intervene. Starting with adapted standard subdivisions for mechanical engineering, it puts "Energy engineering" in 621.042. "Plasma engineering" in 621.044 is "unhappily perched between dictionaries and serials on applied physics." [10] *Ss* shifts recur frequently throughout this section to reduce potentially long numbers for such common topics as "Mathematical principles," "Physical principles," "Maintenance and repair," "Safety measures," "Standards," and "Testing and measurement." The subtopics show little or no orderly progression. Not even the branches of classical physics, as given in division 530, are echoed, for there Heat precedes Electricity and magnetism. It is of course the "Electromagnetic" 621.3 which is the bulkiest, extending over 23 of the section's 34 pages. Sweeney points out:

> ... at 621.312 the various means employed to generate electricity (electrochemical, thermoelectrical, solar, nuclear) have been moved from other parts of the classification.[11]

Magnetic engineering is at 621.34; "Applied electrochemistry" moves to 621.31242. Thermoelectricity and the generation of electrical energy by solar radiation and by nuclear power are relocated. Laser technology, technological photography, and other branches of applied optics add four subtopics. There are five new 10-digit numbers under "Semiconductor (Crystal) devices" and "Circuits," with five extensions under "Manufacture, maintenance, repair of TV receivers." "Tape records and recorders" is new, as is "Hi-fi" and its stereophonic and quadraphonic offspring. Changes in the remaining primary subtopics are spotty. "Shielding" in the design and construction of nuclear reactors wins a number. "Factory operations engineering" and its former subtopic "Packaging technology" go to different locations, at 670.42 and 688.8, respectively. "Numerical control" and "Knives" are new under 621.9 (Tools and fabricating equipment). *DC&* adds specific thermometer readings for 621.59 (Cryogenic temperatures).

Section 622 (Mining engineering and related operations) surely has its strongest cross-disciplinary ties to the 550's, but its sequencing here shows none of that. Specific numbers are added for Gold, Silver, and Platinum at 622.342. A couple of note corrections can be found in *DC&*. This is a comparatively short four-page section.

Section 623 (Military and nautical engineering) is awkwardly distant from 355 (Military art and science), as was noted in chapter 9. They form a classic example of the sometimes irreconcilable strictures of linear disciplinary classification. As for its internal placement in the 620's, historians tell us that, at least in its formal guise, military engineering preceded most other branches (the first engineering classes in the United States were taught at West Point). Its placement after "Mining" but ahead of "Civil" engineering may reveal no editorial bias, but gives pause for thought. We should also be mindful of a note added by *DC&* under 660 (Chemical and related technologies) to class military applications of that "discipline" in 623. Added in this section are "Land transportation technology," three numbers under "Heavier-than-air aircraft," Add instructions under "Design of naval craft," seven subtopics for "Nautical engineering," and two under "Seamanship." Nine bracketed discontinuances are readily visible in its 20 pages. There is occasional special treatment of Table 1 notation, as at 623.892 (Geonavigation). *DC&* has also made seven revisions under "Nautical craft."

Section 624 (Civil engineering) has only six pages. Its changes, however, are analogous to those for Military engineering. Some classifiers find its relationship to the 690's not always clear. A new span opens under "Rock and soil mechanics." "Embankments" and "Retaining walls" are added to "Supporting structures." "Earthquake engineering," "Beams and girders," "Shells," and "Plates" are all new. "Reinforced concretes" now come "Prestressed" and "Precast." "Foundations" and "Floor systems" recur under various subdivisions of Bridges, while "Truss" exchanges a span for a single number. There are three other discontinuances.

Section 625 (Engineering of railroads, roads, highways) shows mostly adaptations of Table 1, although there are specific new numbers for "Surveying," "Design," and "Culverts."

Section [626] is unassigned in this longest of all divisions.

Section 627 (Hydraulic engineering) carries only new injunctions against using *ss*-0299 for "Maintenance and repair." It covers only five pages.

Section 628 (Sanitary and municipal engineering) ought to be next door to civil engineering. It is nine pages long, an increase from less than four in *DDC 18*. Sweeney comments:

> Widespread provision for waste control and pollution has been made throughout the classification.... It seems a pity that this topic hasn't been provided with a consistent Standard Subdivision so that the constant enumeration with different class numbers could be avoided. Such a standard subdivision is available at -028 so the question must be asked, "Why is this not expanded and used for this topic?"[12]

See the entries under "Sources of water supply," "Saline water conversion," "Pollution and counter-measures," "Sewerage systems, treatment, and disposal," "Public sanitation," "Pollution and industrial sanitation," "Fire safety technology," and "Control of animals and plant pests." The literary warrant occasioned by today's environmental concerns is quite evident.

Section 629 (Other branches of engineering), like section 623, is 20 pages long, although only five of its primary subdivisions have content. The first four deal chiefly with various kinds of land, air, and space vehicles. They would be more useful alongside the 623-625 block, e.g., in the vacant [626] if that could be arranged. "Automatic control engineering" has certain affinities for "Machine engineering" and "Tools and fabricating equipment," although its attraction to

"Electronic engineering" is also strong. "Transportation engineering" and "Aerospace engineering" get new subtopics, but the familiar 629.13 (Aeronautics), which takes eight pages, loses nearly as much as it gains (seven bracketed numbers contrasted to eight new ones). Its most interesting additions are "Operation of various specific types of aircraft" and "Helicopters." "Motor land vehicles, and cycles" covers five pages, with some caption revisions and a centered heading from *DC&*. There are new numbers for "Tires," "Emission control devices," and extensions of "Parts and auxiliary systems of internal combustion engines." "Astronautics" adds only "Space shuttles" and two kinds of auxiliary power systems. "Servomechanisms" is added under "Automatic control engineering." Overall, the section has 14 bracketed entries, most of which move important *ss* facets to shorter notation.

Division 630   Agriculture and Related Technologies

The DDC editor promised "clarification and correction of scientific terminology" here.[13] What he seems to have had in mind was a single caption/scope note switch at 631. All other changes are expansive, or superficial. This division is better received than many others by the faceters. One calls it "exemplary."

> For example, in 630 Agriculture the method of facet analysis is clearly at work. We have the energy facet stated at 631-632 under operations and problems in agriculture. The crop facet follows at 633-635, with the ability to qualify certain crops by operation and problem. This is pure facet analysis.[14]

The former editor explained:

> When Edition 17 appeared ... it extended the application of the principles of faceting, e.g., at ... 630 where specific crops in 633-635 could be subdivided by the production and pathology topics considered in general in 631-632.[15]

There are other signs of user approval:

> Latin American countries are characterized by a special predilection for the Dewey Decimal Classification (DDC), as shown by the survey carried out by the Inter-American Institute of Agricultural Sciences, IICA.... The reason for this tendency is perhaps to be found in the adoption of the DDC by the Inter-American Institute of Agricultural Science Library, which has always been, and still is, the leader of and advisor on the Latin American agricultural librarians' activities.[16]

Section 630 (Standard subdivisions and scientific principles of agriculture) changes its mode of presentation slightly, but not its content.

Section 631 (Crops and their production) inverts the *DDC 18* caption and scope note, placing emphasis on "crops" rather than "techniques, procedures, etc." It is to improve disciplinary terminology, and does not disturb the subordinate arrangement or wording. The critics do not approve of everything in this division, in spite of their general satisfaction:

> *Agricultural soil* science is classed inside agriculture, at 631.4. Curiously, the subject is then interrupted in 631.5, where *Cultivation and harvesting* appears, to be continued, however, in 631.6 with *Soil improvement*, at .7 with *Irrigation*, and at .8 with *Fertilizers and soil conditioners*.
> *Soil Chemistry* and *Soil physics* are separated from *Soil biology* by concepts that do not seem to be of the same category, such as *Soil classification* and *Soil erosion and its control*.[17]

The potential confusion over use of Table 2 under "Soil science and conservation" has been explained as follows:

> 631.47 Soil and land use surveys vs. 631.49 Historical and geographical treatment of soils and soil conservation: Both numbers involve the use of the area table. Soil surveys usually involve small areas (the size of a county or less), are quite detailed, and are accompanied by numerous detailed maps. Historical and geographical treatment usually covers much larger areas (the size of a state or province) and is not detailed.[18]

"Soil fertility" is new. "Grading" and "Storing" are now subdivisions of "Other harvesting and subsequent operations." "Controlled-environment agriculture" and "Organic farming" form a new duo. Four old subdivisions of "Irrigation farming" disappear. "Revegetation" is inserted.

Section 632 (Plant injuries, diseases, pests) gives "Bacterial diseases" a longer number. There are no other changes in this short section, whose dependence on sections 589.2 (Fungi) and 592-599 (Specific animals and groups of animals) is attested by three Add instructions.

Sections 633-635 (Specific plant crops) expand "Fertilizers and soil conditioners" in the Add table by reference to the 631.8 subdivisions.

Section 633 (Field crops) now includes a number for "Forage crops." "Specific grasses" fall into a nearby span, of which the last three divisions are new. The catch-all 633[.59] (Other fibers) is discontinued. Cassava (Manihot) and Marihuana (Cannabis sativa) are added.

Section 634 (Orchards, fruits, forestry) reneges on the linear hierarchical principle of grouping broad topics just ahead of their subdivisions. It places "Citrus fruits" at 634.35, after particular varieties, thus avoiding a reclassification scramble in evicting "Oranges" from 334.31. "Moraceous fruits," on the other hand, fare better, because 634.36, preceding their various subdivisons, was vacant.

Section 635 (Garden crops [Horticulture]; Vegetables) has only a few extensions added under "Flowers and ornamental plants." "Annuals" and "Biennials" subdivide "Groupings by life duration." "Turf" and "Lawns" do the same for "Groupings for ground cover." "Controlled-environment gardening" is divided into "Greenhouse" and "Terrarium." "Bonsai" gets a number, as do "Pot" and "Organic" gardening.

Section 636 (Animal husbandry) has a *DC&* warning about misuse of *ss*-0277 (Ownership marks). A few extensions show up under "Generalities," e.g., "Auxiliary care of sick and disabled animals." "Eggs," "Hide," and "Feathers" are added under "Animals for special products." The extensions for special orders or families of domesticated animals are little changed. "Arabian," "Thoroughbred," and "American quarter horse" graduate from Inclusion notes to dedicated numbers. "Game bird culture" shows up. One critic uses Add instructions from this section to illustrate the long synthetic notation which is caused by using zero as a facet separator:

> Screams of anguish over lengthy notation may perhaps be tempered to mild whimpers or even faint expressions of pleasure when the synthesis is desired for one's own local needs.... Consider the precise topic specification, as well as the intellectual gamesmanship of 636.59201-.59208 *turkeys--general principles*, which permits synthesis from 636.01-.08 *animal husbandry--general principles* or of 636.089 *veterinary sciences--veterinary medicine* which permits additional synthesis from 610-619 *medical sciences--medicine*.[19]

Section 637 (Dairy and related technologies) adds *ss*-028 (Techniques, etc.) to 637.124 so the user can be warned that milking machinery and equipment belong in 637.125. There is a reduction of "Cheese by-products."

Section 638 (Insect culture) is brief and has no alterations.

Section 639 (Nondomesticated animals and plants) has new numbers for "Marine" and "Freshwater" fish culture under 639.34. *DC&* changes the notes at 639.1 and 639.2 to read "Methods, equipment, catches; techniques of locating resources."

Division 640   Home Economics and Family Living

There is some change of focus in this division, as indicated by the new caption (Cf. the summary tables in the chapter introduction). Most of the number shifts were in place prior to *DDC 19*, however. The Class-here note now includes "Management of home and personal life," and "Related services."

Section 640 (General subdivisions of home economics and family living) adds a new special topic, "Management of time and energy."

Section 641 (Food and drink) becomes more diet-conscious with "Calories   Including calorie counters." A second cultural reflection is the broadening of 641.2 from "Alcoholic beverages" to "Beverages (Drinks)." The old caption now fits into 641.21. Added subtopics are "Grape wines" and "Nonalcoholic beverages." The latter were formerly implied under "Foods and foodstuffs," but the Pepsi generation has antiquated that assumption. On the other hand, "Health foods   Including organically grown foods" come into their own. And some epicures will welcome "Reptiles, amphibians, insects as meat." Under "Preservation, storage, cookery," a special place is made for "Storage." Cookbooks and similar works are subdivided into those for "Beginners," "Children," and "Gourmet cookery." But where are the manuals for the merely competent? Cooking for health and appearance now has provision "for sick persons," and there is a number for seasonal cookery. Outdoor cookery is divided into "Camp" and "Barbecue." Slow and fireless cookery splits into "Microwave" and "Electric slow." Cookery with beverages has three new alcoholic particulars.

Section 642 (Meals and table service) has been criticized for including "catering" and "how to run a restaurant."[20] But it is quite short so has plenty of room, with comfortably short notation, and seems consonant with the disciplinary stance underlying the new *ss*-068 scatter by topic rather than process. "Special kind" spans are discontinued under meals "for social occasions" and "for public eating places and institutions."

Section 643 (Housing and household equipment) shows two new primary extensions. "Housing" has subdivisions for "possession" and "security." "Special kinds of housing" is not yet subdivided, but has scope and cross-classification notes covering such modern forms as mobile homes, prefabricated houses, and condominiums. Indexing for these concepts is inadequate, however. The Relative Index entry for the first reads "Mobile homes *see* Trailers--automobile--dwellings," but the reference entry has no 643 number. Similarly, none of the three Index subentries under "Prefabricated materials" leads to 643.2. Nor can this location be reached using the Index reference "Condominiums--law *see* Horizontal property law." Going back to the schedule, how do the principles of disciplinary integrity apply for "Kitchens and their equipment"? We are told to put kitchen linen here, but dishwashers in 648.56. Installation of dishwashers and garbage disposal units is covered under 696.184. And how does all this fit with 643.6 (Appliances and laborsaving installations)? A similar dilemma comes up at 643.52 (Bathrooms Including toweling). Can a distinction be preserved between this number and 696.182 (Design and installation of lavatories and bathrooms)?

Sections 644 (Household utilities) and 645 (Furnishing and decorating the home) continue the questions. The disciplinary difference between sections 644 and 696 (Utilities) may be valid, but do library materials follow it? Overlapping occurs between 644.1 (Heating) and 697 (Heating, ventilating, air-conditioning engineering), and also between 644.3 (Lighting) and 621.3228 (Lighting of residential buildings). If it is the "decoration" aspect which belongs in 645.5 (Lighting fixtures), might there not be more affinity for 728 (Residential buildings)? See the scope note at 729 (Design and decoration of structures and accessories). What about 747 (Interior decoration)? If it is "use" which the 640's should emphasize, how can it be separated from design and construction? Both of the sections covered here are extremely short, giving some evidence of redundancy. Two *ss*-04 "Special topics" are added to section 645.

Section 646 (Sewing, clothing, management of personal and family living) substitutes "personal and family living" for "grooming" in its caption. We were told that this section would expand to include both concepts.[21] But Grooming was already at 646.7, with a single zero *ss* span. It is now preceded by a double zero *ss* span for "personal and family living." "Home hairdressing" is no longer distinguished from "Professional." "Care of the hair" now absorbs "Care of men's hair." Four new subdivisions provide guides to charm, dating, family living, and old age.

The earlier "sewing" portion of this section relocates basic sewing operations, with subtopics for "hand" and "machine" sewing. "Patterns" and "Fitting and alterations" are new. Topics formerly in notes under "Outer house garments," "Outdoor garments," and "Garments for special purposes" receive their own numbers. *DC&*, v. 4, no. 1 (June 1980): 20 transfers clothing materials from 646.1 to 646.3.

Section 647 (Management of public households [Institutional housekeeping]) has no significant changes.

Section 648 (Housekeeping) is very short, with a reduced span and a "Moving" subtopic added for our mobile population.

Section 649 (Child rearing and home care of sick and infirm) substitutes "care of sick and infirm" for the DDC 18 "nursing" in the caption. Under "Works on home care of children" there is a category added "for older children in the family." There are a half-dozen minor caption changes for subtopics, a new list of subdivisions under "Training," and a Class elsewhere note appended to "Clothing and health."

Division 650   Management and Auxiliary Services

The DDC editor promised "extensive adjustment and clarification throughout," but not much happens anyplace other than section 658.[22]

Section 650 has only one subtopic, to whose caption the word "Personal" has been added.

Section 651 (Office services) has four discontinuances and five additions. Three of the latter are a hierarchical group at 651.504, to provide a place for "Medical records management." Two others are specific forms of correspondence under 651.75.

Sections 652 (Processes of written communication) and 653 (Shorthand) cover special aspects of the office communication theme broached in 651.7-.8 (Communication and Record processing). Communication will be picked up again in another context at 658.45 under "Executive management." There is also a soft link to sections 383-384 (Specific kinds of communication), although their discipline is "mass communications." This short section has some expansion, with one reduction, under "Typewriting."

Section 653 (Shorthand) is only slightly longer, and has no changes. "Gregg," "Pitman," and other handwritten systems have their own numbers, but the more contemporary "Stenotypy" is not in the schedule or Relative Index. It presumably goes under 653.3 (Machine systems).

Sections [654], [655], and [656] are unassigned.

Section 657 (Accounting) rearranges the precedence table at 657.1-.9 (Elements of accounting). There is some expansion under "Financial reporting," and "Specific fields of accounting."

Section 658 (General management) is where the action is. By far the longest section in this division (24 pages), it carries the brunt of the ss-068 scatter (see the Table 1 discussion in chapter 5). The change was a response to criticisms documented in the Comaromi survey. A new precedence table appears at 658.401-.409 (Specific management activities). Psychologists cry foul at the continuance of "Performance rating (Evaluation)" at 658.3125. There are 17 bracketed numbers, including 658[.809], 658[.838], and 658[.89], which were bracketed in DC&, v. 4, no. 1. The over 40 extensions include 658.805 (Marketing to foreign buyers) from DC&, but its short happy life will be terminated by issue number 2 according to the DCD editorial office.

Section 659 (Advertising and public relations) is unchanged except for the addition of "Social aspects of advertising" under 659.1042.

Division 660   Chemical and Related Technologies

Here starts the three-division sequence which has been termed "an inscrutable hotchpotch." (See page 237.) The DDC editor claimed "expansion and adjustment," but there appears to be more of the former than the latter.[23] Preoccupations with waste control give literary warrant to nine new numbers. *DC&* appends the cross-classification note already mentioned in the 623 discussion.

Section 660 (Standard subdivisions and special aspects) creates two subtopics under "Precipitation, filtration, solvent extraction." Other changes are confined to Table 1 modifications under "Chemical engineering."

Sections 661 (Technology of industrial heavy chemicals) and *662 (Technology of explosives, fuels, related products)* have no alterations in their total of six pages.

Section 663 (Beverage technology) trades an Add note under "Special topics of general applicability to grape wines" for a reduction of "Wines from other fruits."

Section 664 (Food technology) is the most "adjusted." "Waste control" joins "Packaging" at three subdivisions, but there is no reference to 688.8, the new location for packaging technology in general. Standard subdivisions often have double zero notation; *ss*-028 (Techniques, etc.) is sometimes dropped for shorter notation. In other locations it carries special instructions, as under "Fruits and vegetables," "Meats and allied foods," and "Red meats." "Preservation techniques" sometimes, but not always, have an Add or a cross-classification note. "Bakery goods" are diversified into "Breads" and "Pastries." Add notes expand "Cane sugars and syrups," "Specific fruits," and "Specific vegetables."

Section 665 (Technology of industrial oils, fats, waxes, and gases) inverts Table 1 order to insert 665.0287 (Maintenance and repair) ahead of the previously established 665.0288 (Tests, analyses, quality controls). By such practical compromises is the faceting principle diluted. Other additions are three dealing with wastes and six dealing with storage, transportation, and distribution under "Petroleum" and "Industrial gases."

Section 666 (Ceramic and allied technologies) also makes a place for waste control, changes the 666.13 caption into "Auxiliary procedures," giving it three subtopics, and adds "Bottles" in lonely spendor under "Glass products."

Section 667 (Cleaning, color and related technologies) has a single new number for "Waste control."

Section 668 (Technology of other organic products) adds "Waste control," plus three "Auxiliary procedures for plastics." Its four other additions are "Polyurethanes," "Containers," "Bactericides," and "Polymers."

Section 669 (Metallurgy) splits 669.5 into "Zinc" and "Cadmium," adding other specific numbers for "Titanium" and "Nickel."

Division 670   Manufactures

Like its neighbors, this division shows moderate expansion and a few reworkings of Table 1 facets, but there is no reduction, and almost no basic change. The DDC editor cites the relocation of "Factory operations engineering" from 621.7 to 670.42 as the major adjustment.[24]

Section 670 adds three specific concepts to the factory operations number cited above.

Section 671 (Metal manufactures) subdivided "Specific methods of casting." "Forging," "Sintering," "Bonding," "Pipes," and "Wires" are all new. Under

"Welding," 671[.520287] should be bracketed since it moves testing and measurement elsewhere.

Section 672 (Ferrous metals manufactures) is unchanged and unpartitioned except for already established Add instructions.

Section 673 (Nonferrous metals manufactures) follows the pattern used in 669 by giving specific numbers to zinc, cadmium, titanium, and nickel.

Sections 674 (Lumber, cork, wood-using technologies) and 675 (Leather and fur technologies) make some general standard subdivision adjustments, but nothing else changes.

Section 676 (Pulp and paper technology) is reminiscent of the 660's in its increased emphasis on waste control. Two new numbers join the already established 787.26 in its short three pages.

Section 677 (Textiles) also offers a new location for waste control. "Techniques, etc." frequently relocate, as "Testing and measurement" did in 676. Under ss-028 extensions, Weaving, Knitting, Fibers, and Textile chemicals are all new. So is 677.8 (Surgical gauze and cotton). "Nonwoven felt hats" move out to 687.4 (Headgear).

Sections 678 (Elastomers and elastomer products) and 679 (Other products) show no significant change.

Division 680   Manufacture of Products for Specific Uses

The DC& note to class military applications in 623, which was cited for divisions 660 and 670, applies here as well.

Section 681 (Precision instruments) adds "Lenses," "Mirrors," and "Pressure vessels."

Section 682 (Small forge work) keeps its two lone subtopics without alteration, or even subdivision.

Section 683 (Hardware and household appliances) juggles "Maintenance and repair of small firearms," and finds specific numbers for Rifles, Shotguns, Pistols, and Revolvers. The National Rifle Association will be glad.

Sections 684 (Furnishings and home workshops) and 685 (Leather and fur goods) similarly juggle ss-0288, but make no other changes.

Section 686 (Printing) adds "Color printing."

Section 687 (Clothing) moves "Generalities" into ss-04. The old "Men's clothing" at 687.11 loses its sexist terminology for "Outer garments," except at 687.11042. But 687.12 is now called "Women's house garments," so the new 687.112-.117 span demonstrates a kind of ambivalent unisexism. Considering the developments under "Outdoor garments for specific classes of people," "Underwear for specific classes of people," and "Headgear," it seems clear that DDC and the clothing trade still agree on the unique differences between men, women, and children. There is a new, neutral number for "Nightclothes," but the old subtopics under 687.3 are gone. "Hosiery" is reduced; "Sweaters" become a type of specific outdoor garment at 687.146. Hasn't DDC heard of the fuel shortage?

Section 688 (Other final products, and packaging technology) now captions 688.1 "Models and miniatures." For more detail on the terminology change, see the introductory remarks for division 620. Under "Smokers' supplies" the sole subtopic is "Pipes." Compare this caption with its homonym at 671.832 for a good illustration of the principle of disciplinary classification. New are "Dolls,"

"Puppets and marionettes," "Equipment for equestrian sports and animal racing," and the previously cited "Packaging technology."

Section [689] is unassigned.

Division 690   Buildings

The difficult disciplinary split between the 624's and the 690's has been discussed, as has the incipient overlap with portions of sections 643-645, and division 720.

Section 690 adjusts some Table 1 usages, and makes a place for "Structural analysis." The scope note under "Construction of specific types of buildings" carries a *DC&* addition to the effect that buildings for defense against military action belong in 623.1.

Sections 691 (Building materials) and 692 (Auxiliary construction practices) are short and unaltered.

Section 693 (Construction in various specific materials and for specific purposes) introduces "Miscellaneous materials" with an Add instruction.

Section 694 (Wood construction; Carpentry) is short, and getting shorter. There is no longer literary warrant for subtopics under "Rough carpentry (Framing)" or "Finish carpentry (Joinery)."

Sections 695 (Roofing), 696 (Utilities), 697 (Heating, ventilation, air-conditioning engineering), and 698 (Detail finishing) have no changes except some standard subdivision polishing. Perhaps the DDC staff hesitates to develop this part of the schedule until broader disciplinary questions have been decided.

Section [699] is unassigned.

Conclusion

The problems of illogical arrangement, disciplinary overlap, and overcrowding in this class are widely recognized. What to do about them is less obvious. Recent questions from the field focus on increasing financial hazards attached to issuing new revisions:

> Is a new edition, on the lines with which we are familiar, probable? And if it is, do we want it? Well, I should think that on one plane (not the economic one, that is) we most certainly do. The classification has (as any classification will have) many areas where radical change is needed. Medical Sciences come at once to mind, and the Fine Arts.... In his recent review of DC19 Peter Butcher has reminded us of the difficulties we experience with the 720/Architecture — 624/Civil engineering — 690/Building split (A huge task, this, to rectify and rationalise this field — but one which should give great satisfaction when done). Life Sciences, 560, 70, 80 and 90 plus 611 and 612, stand greatly in need of rewriting.[25]

If, when, and how such rewriting will be accomplished can be seen only as through a glass, very darkly. The Decimal Classification Editorial Committee plays its cards close to its collective chest until enough time has elapsed to give some firm indication of *DDC 19*'s reception.[26] Classifiers in local institutions have some obligation to do their grumbling in public, and to accompany it with concrete, workable suggestions.

Exercises in the Use of Class 600

A. Analysis

604'.7'024649	Center for Science in the Public Interest. The household pollutants guide ... 1978.	77-76262
614.5'73'2'094551	Cipolla, Carlo M. Faith, reason, and the plague in seventeenth-century Tuscany ... 1979.	79-2479
615.9'5292223	Champignons toxiques : compte rendu de la réunion du Groupement français des centres anti-poisons ... c1978.	80-455382
616.9'94'06	Cancer treatment / edited by Charles M. Haskell ... 1980.	79-3926
618.9'28'553	Critchley, Macdonald. Dyslexia defined ... 1978.	79-102133
620.4'16'2	Ship Technology and Research (STAR) Symposium (3rd : 1978 : New London, Conn.) Proceedings ... 1978.	78-107613
621.3819'58'3	Coffron, James. Understanding and troubleshooting the microprocessor ... c1980.	79-20950
623.82'0028'54	International Conference on Computer Applications in the Automation of Shipyard Operation and Ship Design (2d : 1976 : Gothenburg, Sweden) ... 1976.	76-44279
623.89'29716	Canadian Hydrographic Service. Instructions nautiques : Nouvelle Écosse (Côte SE) et Baie de Fundy ... 8ème éd. ... 1979.	79-119192
629.45'4'09730740153	Bruno, Leonard C. We have a sporting chance : the decision to go to the moon : an exhibition at the Library of Congress, July 16-September 16, 1979 ... 1979.	79-603047
636.7'08'3	Mulvany, Mollie. All about obedience training for dogs ... 2nd ed. ... 1978.	79-304124
639.9'797358	American pronghorn antelope : articles published in the Journal of Wildlife management, 1937-1977 / compiled by James D. Yoakum ... 1979.	79-89207
646.4'04	Goldsworthy, Maureen. New fashion from old ... 1978.	79-303025
647'.954436'0924 [B]	Coffe, Jean Pierre. Gourmandise au singulier ... 1979.	80-457314
650.1'4'024658	Career management for the individual and the organization / [edited by] Marian Jelinek ... 1979.	78-65578
658'.05'4	Gore, Marvin. Elements of systems analysis for business data processing ... 1975.	74-19663

669'.96'722	Altenpohl, Dietrich. Un regard à l'intérieu de l'alumninium : une introduction à la métallurgie structurale et à la transformation de l'alumin--ium ... c1976.	77-451585
673'.722'33	Centre technique de l'aluminium. L'Emboutissage de l'aluminium et de ses alliages ... 1976.	77-561707
686.2'172	Harvey, Machael. Letters into words ... 1973.	75-316356
690'.1'1	Brown, Robert Wade. Residential foundations : design, behavior, and repair ... c1979.	78-12069
690'.1'8	Community of the European Lock and Fittings Industries ... Specification for overhead closing devices ... c1975.	77-560612

B. Synthesis: Examples from LC records are given on pp. 254-57.

1. A general work on the theory and management of organizations.

2. A pounds-off program based on the partnership or group reinforcement approach.

3. A book about windmills in Sussex, England.

4. A study of the techniques of process control in chemical engineering.

5. A checklist for computer center security routines.

6. Geriatric psychosocial nursing care.

7. Engineering and seamanship for sailing craft of Australia.

8. Radioisotope scanning in cardiovascular medicine.

9. A case study of foreign trade promotion and export marketing in India.

10. A textbook on medical diseases for physiotherapists.

11. Industrial heavy chemical technology.

12. A discussion of the various dog breeds.

13. Statistical methods for decision-making in management.

14. Feedback amplifiers and electric circuitry analysis.

15. A collection of papers from a symposium on hemodialysis and artificial kidneys.

16. A Corvette automobile repair and tune-up guide.

17. Hatha yoga for older people.

18. The principles and practices of sugar-cane farming.

19. Water cooling systems for nuclear reactors.

20. A history of enamel advertising signs.

21. A series of handbooks on asphalt technology.

22. A how-to book on applying and interviewing for a job.

23. A domestic history and collectors guide for American kitchen utensils.

24. A book on kitchen equipment for interior decorators.

25. How to make and fly kites.

26. Conference proceedings on water-born plastic coatings and emulsion paint.

27. Refrigeration and air-conditioning technology.

28. A guide to the use of Standard International metrics in heating, air conditioning, and refrigeration.

29. An engineering analysis of air pollution control technology.

30. A history of patents on American handguns.

31. A series of papers on dynamical methods in soil and rock mechanics.

32. A vocational guide to the clothing trade and the world of fashion.

33. A do-it-yourself carpentry guide.

34. A catalog of tools for clock and watch making.

35. A collective biography of steam locomotive designers.

36. Power tool carpentry.

37. An identification manual for aquarium fishes.

38. Abstracts of papers on the ground wood process of pulp and paper manufacture.

39. A book of German motorized combat vehicles in World War II.

40. A manual of home plumbing and heating.

41. The chemistry of the Hall-Héroult process in aluminum electrolysis.

42. A collection of articles on the selection and fabrication of aluminum alloys.

43. A case study of employee representation in management in the aluminum industry in Toronto, Ontario.

44. Studies in type design and type making.

45. Preparing camera-ready pasteups for advertising layouts.

46. A catalog of printing press machinery and supplies.

47. Analytical methods for testing coal and coal products.

48. Environmental aspects of coal liquification.

49. Reclamation of strip-mined land in Illinois.

50. Industrial processing of sheep's wool.

51. Engineering graphics and drafting techniques.

52. A book for tourists on shopping in Europe.

53. A self-instructional program for learning every aspect of safe boating.

54. Grafting and pruning ornamental plants.

55. American cookery.

56. A journal (periodical) of fluid engineering.

C. Reclassification: What *DDC 19* numbers would you assign to the following records? Suggestions are offered on p. 257.

1. If your library owned both of the following editions, how would you classify them?

| 621.9'08 | McDonnell, Leo P. The use of hand woodworking tools ... Albany, N.Y. : Delmar Publishers, c1978. | 76-48504 |

| 684'.082 | McDonnell, Leo P. The use of hand woodworking tools ... Rev. ed. - New York : Van Nostrand Reinhold, 1978. | 77-26031 |

2. 604'.2'621381 Kirshner, Cyrus. Electronics drafting workbook ... c1977. 77-7872

3. 614.7'12'09784 Schock, Martin R. ND-REAP air quality network : final report to North Dakota Regional Environmental Assessment Program ... 1977.
[Air quality monitoring stations--North Dakota] 78-623597

4. 616.8'52 Cognitive therapy of depression / Aaron T. Beck ... c1979. 79-19967

5. 621.7'57 United Parcel Service. Packaging for the small parcel environment ... 2d ed. ... c1971. 75-314234

6. 623.82'07'26 Sims, Ernest H. Boatbuilding in aluminium alloy ... 1978. 78-316898

7. 629.1'08 s AIAA/NASA Conference on "Smart" Sensors (1978 : [621.36'7] Hampton, Va.) Remote sensing of earth from space ... c1979. (Progress in astronautics and aeronautics ; v. 67) 79-18200

8. 641.5'55 Good Housekeeping Institute, London. Good Housekeeping freezer recipes ... 1974.
[Frozen foods--Cookery] 75-309029

9. 658.4'51 Allen, Sylvia. A manager's guide to audiovisuals ... c1979. 79-19303

10. 658.8'09'0705730973 Duke, Judith S. Children's books and magazines : a market study ... c1979.
[Cf. *DC&*, v. 4, no. 1 (June 1980): 20] 78-24705

11. 658.89'687 Mathisen, Marilyn Purol. Apparel and accessories ... c1979.
[Cf. *DC&*, v. 4, no. 1 (June 1980): 20] 78-12321

12. 658'.91'36210182   Broyles, Robert W. Statistics in health
administration ... c1979-   79-23280

13. 658'.96'972206541172   Drummond, G. Gordon. The Invergordon
smelter : a case study in management ... 1977.
[Aluminum industry and trade--Scotland--
Management--Case studies]   78-302595

14. 659.11'125'0681   Association of National Advertisers. Agency
compensation : a guidebook ... c1979.   79-129709

Examples of LC Cataloging to Illustrate the Above Exercises
in DDC Number Synthesis

1. 658.4   Brown, Warren B. Organization theory and management
: a macro approach ... c1980.   79-18709

2. 613.2'5   Brownell, Kelly D. The partnership diet program :
the do-it-together pounds-off program that doesn't
feel like a diet ... c1980.   79-64200

3. 621.4'5'094225   Brunnarius, Martin. The windmills of Sussex
... 1979.   80-463251

4. 660.2'84   Buckley, Page S. Techniques of process control ...
1979, c1964.   78-10782

5. 658.4'78   Browne, Beter. Security : checklist for computer
center self-audits ... c1979.   79-56012

6. 610.73'65   Burnside, Irene Mortenson. Psycholosocial nursing
care of the aged ... 2d ed. ... c1980.   79-13044

7. 623.8'22'0994   Campbell, Peter. The observer's book of sailing craft of Australia and New Zealand ...
1979.   80-459329

8. 616.1'07'575   Cardiovascular nuclear medicine ... 1979-   80-107444

9. 658.8'48'0954   Cases in international marketing : Indian
experience ... c1979.   79-906088

10. 616'.002461   Cash, Joan Elizabeth. Cash's Textbook of medical conditions for phsysiotherapists / edited
by Patricia A. Downie ... 6th ed. ... c1979.   78-71655

11. 661   Chalmers, Louis. Chemical specialities : domestic and
industrial ... 2nd ed. / revised by Peter Bathe ...
1978-1979.   78-317465

12. 636.7'1   Chandler, Jennie. Best loved dogs of the world ...
1979.   80-456996

13. 658.4'033   Chao, Lincoln L. Statistics for management ... c1980.   79-22706

14. 621.3815'3   Chen, Wai-kai. Active network and feedback
amplifier theory ... c1980.   79-16997

15. 617'.461   Chronic replacement of kidney function / Fernando
Villarroel ... 1979.   79-9185

16.	629.28'722	Chilton Book Company. Chilton's repair & tune-up guide, Corvette, 1963 to 1979, 327, 350, 396, 427, 454 ... c1979.	78-20255
17.	613.7'046	Christensen, Alice. Easy does it yoga for older people ... c1979.	78-784755
18.	633'.61	Clements, Harry F. Sugarcane crop logging and crop control : principles and practices ... c1980.	79-9894
19.	621.48'336	Cohen, Paul. Water coolant technology of power reactors ... c1980.	79-57306
20.	659.13'42	Baglee, Christopher. Street jewellery : a history of enamel advertising signs ... 1978.	79-302722
21.	665'.5388 s [625.8'5]	Asphalt Institute. A basic asphalt emulsion manual ... 1979.	79-50450
22.	650'.14	Dickhut, Harold W. Professional resume / job search guide ... 4th ed. ... 1978.	78-2513
23.	683'.82'0973	Franklin, Linda Campbell. From hearth to cook-stove : America in the kitchen : an American domestic history of gadgets and utensils made or used in America from 1700 to 1930 : a guide for collectors ... 2d ed. ... c1978.	78-54417
24.	643'.3	Conran, Terence. The kitchen book ... 1977.	77-7059
25.	629.133'32	Moulton, Ron Godfrey. Kites ... c1978.	78-321484
26.	667'.9	Chemical Coatings Conference (2nd : 1978 : Cincinnati) Water-borne coatings session : technical papers / presented at ... c1978.	79-100971
27.	621.5'6	Air-Conditioning and Refrigeration Institute. Refrigeration and air-conditioning ... c1979.	77-25335
28.	697	Stoecker, W. F. (Wilbert F.) Using SI units (Standard International metric) in heating, air conditioning, and refrigeration ... 1977 ed. ... 1977.	77-12467
29.	628.5'3	Bethea, Robert M. Air pollution control technology : an engineering analysis point of view ... c1978.	77-27563
30.	683'.43'0272	Macewicz, Joseph John. American handgun patents, 1802-1924 ... 1977.	79-302436
31.	624'.1513 s [624'.1513]	NATO Advanced Study Institute (1977 : University of Karlsruhe) Dynamic response and wave propagation in soils / edited by B. Prange ... 1978. (Its Dynamical methods in soil and rock mechanics ; 1)	79-303800
32.	687'.023	Fashion Group. Your future in the new world of American fashion / by 15 famous members of the Fashion Group, inc. / Christine LeVathes, editor ... 1979.	78-11905
33.	694'.028	Carpentry ... c1976. (Do it yourself guides)	78-100102
34.	681'.113'028	Wyke, John. A catalogue of tools for watch and clock makers ... 1978.	77-12219

35. 625.2'61'0922   Westwood, J. N. Locomotive designers in the
age of steam ... 1978, c1977.   77-90502

36. 684'.083   Black & Decker power tool carpentry / consultant
editors, George Daniels and ... 1978.   77-90840

37. 639'.34   Schmitz, Siegfried. Aquarium fishes ... 1978.   78-326833

38. 676'.122   International Mechanical Pulping Conference (1973 :
Stockholm, Sweden) International ... Conference,
June 18-21, 1973 : abstracts ... 1973.   78-309496

39. 623.74'75'0943 Ellis, Chris. German tanks & fighting vehicles
of World War II ... 1976.   78-315769

40. 696'.1   Adams, Jeannette T. Complete home plumbing and
heating handbook ... c1977.   76-28519

41. 669'.722   Aluminium electrolysis : the chemistry of the Hall-
Héroult process / K. Grjotheim ... c1977.   77-372003

42. 673'.722   American Society for Metals. Publications Development. Sourcebook on selection and fabrication of
aluminum alloys : a comprehensive collection of
outstanding articles ... c1978.   78-18869

43. 658.31'52'09713541 Mansell, Jacquelynne. Workers' participation : a case study of Supreme Aluminum
Industries Limited ... 1976.   77-375403

44. 686.2'24   Goudy, Frederic W. (Frederic William) Typologia :
studies in type design and type making, with comments on the invention of typography, the first
types ... 1977.   78-305196

45. 659.13'24   Graham, Walter B. Simplified techniques for preparing camera-ready pasteup ... 1977.   78-303824

46. 681'.62   Campbell Press Works, New York. Illustrated catalogue, Campbell Press Works ... 1974.   78-311442

47. 662.6'22   Analytical methods for coal and coal products /
edited by Clarence Karr, Jr. ... 1978-   78-4928

48. 662'.6622   Environmental, health, and control aspects of coal
conversion : an information overview : prepared
for the Energy Research and Development Administration ... 1977.   77-604030

49. 631.6   Our reclamation future : the missing bet on trees / by
W. Clark Ashby ... [et al.] ... 1978.   78-623281

50. 677'.31   Fletchall, Gale Frederick. Oregon wool and natural
dyeing ... c1977.   78-322580

51. 604'.2'4   Poole, Jerome D. Engineering drawing for technician
engineers ... 1978.   77-13235

52. 658.87'0094   The News, New York, 1919- European round trip
... 1960.   60-26688

53. 623.88'8   United States. Coast Guard. Simple guide to safer
sailing and boating ... 1974.   75-314345

54.	635.9'1'541	Allen, Oliver E. Pruning and grafting ... c1978.	78-15795
55.	641.5'973	American dainties and how to prepare them / by an American lady ... [190?]	75-314153
56.	620.1'06	Journal of fluids engineering. v. 95- Mar. 1973-	74-644131

Reclassification: Suggested DDC 19 Numbers

1. 684.082   McDonnell ...

2. 621.3810221   Kirshner ...

3. 363.73926309784   Schock ...

4. 616.8527   Cognitive ...

5. 688.8   United ...

6. 623.8207   Sims ...

7. 629.105 s   AIAA/NASA ...
   [621.3678]

8. 641.6153   Good Housekeeping ...

9. 658.45   Allen ...

10. 070.5730688   Duke ...

11. 687.0688   Mathisen ...

12. 362.1068   Broyles ...
    [312.3068]

13. 669.722068   Drummond ...

14. 659.11250681   Association ...

NOTES

[1]Margaret Kaltenbach, "Problems Associated with Presenting and Teaching the Schedules: Science (500) and Technology (600), *The Dewey Decimal Classification: Outlines and Papers Presented at a Workshop on the Teaching of Classification* ... (New York, School of Library Science, Columbia University, 1968), p. 47. Similar views are expressed by Marty Bloomberg and Hans Weber, *An Introduction to Classification and Number Building in Dewey*, edited by John Phillip Immroth (Littleton, CO, Libraries Unlimited, 1976), p. 114.

[2]I. N. Sengupta, "Some Observations on the Forthcoming 19th Edition of the Dewey Decimal Classification (DDC) Scheme," *International Classification*, v. 6, no. 3 (November 1979): 171.

[3]Benjamin A. Custer, "DDC 19: Characteristics," *HCL Cataloging Bulletin*, no. 35 (July/August 1978): 10. See also his "Dewey Decimal Classification One Hundred Years After," *Catalogue & Index*, no. 39 (Winter 1975): 3.

[4]Peter Butcher, "Dewey? We Sure Do!," *Catalogue & Index*, no. 55 (Winter 1979): 8.

[5]Custer, "DDC 19: Characteristics," p. 10.

[6]Sengupta, p. 171.

[7]Ross Trotter, "Dewey 19 — A Subjective Assessment," *Catalogue & Index*, no. 59 (Winter 1980): 3.

[8]Custer, "DDC 19: Characteristics,", p. 10.

[9]Kaltenbach, p. 47.

[10]Butcher, p. 8.

[11]Russell Sweeney, "The Old, Grey Mare ... ," *Cataloging & Classification Quarterly*, v. 1, no. 1 (Fall 1980): 94.

[12]Ibid., pp. 94-95.

[13]Custer, "DDC 19: Characteristics," p. 11.

[14]James A. Tait, "Dewey Decimal Classification: A Vigorous Nonagenarian," *Library Review*, v. 23, no. 6 (Summer 1972): 227.

[15]Benjamin A. Custer, "The Responsiveness of Recent Editions of the Dewey Decimal Classification to the Needs of Its Users," *General Classification Systems in a Changing World....* (The Hague, Fédération Internationale de Documentation [FID], 1978), p. 82.

[16]Milton Nocetti, "Agricultural Soil Science in Universal Classification Systems: A Comparative Analysis," *International Classification*, v. 5, no. 1 (March 1978): 15.

[17]Ibid., p. 16.

[18]Trotter, p. 5.

[19]Margaret E. Cockshutt, "Dewey Today: An Analysis of Recent Editions," *Major Classification Systems: The Dewey Centennial* (Urbana-Champaign, IL, University of Illinois Graduate School of Library Science, 1976), p. 39.

[20]John Phillip Comaromi, *A Survey of the Use of the Dewey Decimal Classification in the United States and Canada* (Lake Placid, NY?, Prepared for Forest Press, Lake Placid Foundation, 1975), p. 256.

[21]Custer, "DDC 19: Characteristics," p. 11.

[22]Ibid.

[23]Ibid.

[24]Ibid.

[25]Marjorie Jelinek, "Twentieth Dewey: An Exercise in Prophecy," *Catalogue & Index*, no. 58 (Autumn 1980): 1-2.

[26]Margaret E. Cockshutt, "Annual Report of the Decimal Classification Editorial Policy Committee, July 1, 1979-June 30, 1980," *Library Resources & Technical Services*, v. 25, no. 1 (January/March 1981): 124 says, "The committee considered reviews of edition 19 and their implication for the DCEPC's future work."

13

Class 700   The Arts:
Fine and Decorative Arts

Introduction

The Dewey decimal system is used successfully by several large art libraries, although it is designed primarily as a comprehensive scheme for general collections. A well-known art librarian says:

> While other approaches to classification systems have been pioneered by art librarians in the United States and abroad, e.g. the faceted classification for fine arts devised by Peter Broxis and special systems prepared by other English art librarians, most art libraries in the United States use the Dewey decimal classification system (DDC) or the Library of Congress system (LC), or systems modified from the Dewey or LC systems. For example, the systems used in the libraries of the Metropolitan Museum of Art and the Art Institute of Chicago are derived from the notation principles used in Dewey....
>
> Dewey remains a popular system in American libraries, and may be satisfactory in smaller art library collections where close classification is not considered an important factor.
>
> Neither system may be as successful as faceted classification systems in analysing complex works. However, as Wolfgang Freitag has observed: "A detailed enumerative system, in spite of all its errors and shortcomings, will meet the practical requirements of libraries far better than the few principles and guidelines provided in a system of faceted classification."[1]

The entire 700 class has been faulted for its fragmentation and overlapping, but criticisms tend to focus on the final two divisions.[2] Immediately after *DDC 18* was published in 1971, a number of phoenix possibilities, including the 700's, were discussed. Eventually, "the fine arts were regarded as too wide an area in relation to other material, and perhaps, more significant subjects.[3] To be sure, the 780's received a more concrete challenge, but in the end the old schedule won out. For *DDC 19*, we are told editorially only of "lots of expansion" in divisions 700-770.[4] Divisional summaries for the two most recent editions are identical:

Summary (*DDC 18*)		**Summary (*DDC 19*)**	
700	THE ARTS	700	THE ARTS
710	Civic and landscape art	710	Civic and landscape art
720	Architecture	720	Architecture
730	Plastics arts; Sculpture	730	Plastic arts; Sculpture
740	Drawing; decorative and minor arts	740	Drawing; decorative and minor arts
750	Painting and paintings	750	Painting and paintings
760	Graphic arts; Print making and prints	760	Graphic arts; Print making and prints
770	Photography and photographs	770	Photography and photographs
780	Music	780	Music
790	Recreational and performing arts	790	Recreational and performing arts

Like the 500's and 600's, class 700 tends to detailed enumeration, with little synthetic faceting except by region, person, and occasionally chronology. References to other schedules are very rare. Only Tables 1 and 2 are invoked with any regularity. "Geographic treatment of museums, etc." and "Individuals associated with the subject" are familiar parts of LC number assignments, but Tables 5 and 7, distinguishing groups of persons, are seldom used.

Division 700 Standard Subdivisions and Generalities of the Fine and Decorative Arts

This introductory division is more elaborately developed than its analogues in other classes. It extends to nine full pages. Divisions 000 and 300 have 7 and 11 pages, respectively, but they cover topical rather than "aspect" categories. The entire 000 class, and the initial divisions of the other seven classes, stick more or less faithfully to an *ss* format. The use of 700.1-.9 for the arts in general, then *ss* section numbers 701-709 for the "fine and decorative" arts, is more ambiguous than similar patterns in classes 200 and 900. There are no scope notes to help. We must assume that sections 701-709 exclude the "recreation" materials of the 790's, but are theater and dance, also located in 791-792, included here? They seem closer to the "fine arts" than to sports.

Section 700 (Standard subdivisions of the arts) introduces a psycho-social "effects" sequence, e.g., "Effects of social conditions and factors on the arts." "Festivals" is made part of the 700.79 caption, where an Add Areas ... note not provided by *ss*-079 appears.

Section 701 (Philosophy and theory of fine and decorative arts) adds a "Special topics" span, but reduces "Use of audiovisual aids" to an Inclusion note.

Section 702 (Miscellany of fine and decorative arts) expands its single hitherto unpartitioned 702.8 (Techniques, etc.). This is the first of a series of special mentions of *ss*-028 throughout the 700 class.

Section 703 (Dictionaries, etc.) is unchanged and unpartitioned.

Section 704 (Special topics of general applicability) has four new numbers, a discontinuance, and a permanently unassigned number, all under 704.9 (Iconography). The new numbers specify iconography of Jesus Christ, apostles, saints, and angels. The permanent option would probably be used with those at

289[.2] (Small Christian denominations, etc.) or at [298] (Less familiar non-Christian religions).

Sections 705 (Serial publications), 706 (Organizations and management), and 707 (Study and teaching) are extremely short, and practically unchanged. "Business organizations" disappears without even a bracketed warning at 706[.5].

Section 708 (Galleries, museums, private collections) is devoted to geographic treatment, with references to Table 2 pointedly including the United Kingdom changes.

Section 709 (Historical and geographical treatment) adds numbers for "Paleolithic" and "Rock" art. Twentieth-century periods, schools, and styles have new Add notes. *DC&*, v. 4, no. 1 (June 1980): 21 says to class a specific school or style in a specific period. The imminent 21st century at 709.05 is a by now familiar insertion throughout the classification, but appears more frequently in a chronologically oriented discipline such as art history.

Division 710   Civic and Landscape Art

This division is only five pages long, with so little change that it is not worthwhile to consider individual sections. "Commercial" and "Industrial" planning now have their own numbers. Bicycles join other kinds of transportation modes, with literary warrant from the energy crunch. A cross-classification note under "Philosophy and theory of landscape design" completes the revisions.

Division 720   Architecture

Architecture remains at 720, still in its ivory tower, divorced from the real world of construction—which, incidentally, is still split between 624 and 690—which is unfortunate since architecture, as rightly reflected in these schedules, is far more concerned with the mechanics of construction than with pretty, useless buildings.[5]

There is also dissatisfaction over the internal split between the 720's and the 740's. It will be further explored in our discussion of divisions 730-740.

Section 720 (Standard subdivisions of architecture) uses the interdisciplinary special topic span at 700.1 by means of an Add note. Under "Techniques, etc.," extensions now cover "Architectural drawing," "Remodeling," etc. Architecture for use by the handicapped, and by the aged and infirm, as well as "Utilization of natural energy sources" are given locations.

Sections 721-729 (Specific aspects of architecture) are grouped under a centered heading with a new distributive Add table resembling the extensions noted in section 720 above.

Section 721 (Architectural construction), like section 720, uses special topic spans from other class 700 locations. It also extends "Other structural elements" with locations for types of openings, elevators, balconies, patios, etc.

Section 722 (Ancient and Oriental architecture) provides numbers for Chinese, Japanese, Korean, and Indian architecture. Its cross-disciplinary note about Saracenic art is extended by *DC&*.

Sections 723 (Medieval architecture) and 724 (Modern architecture) are quite short, without any alterations.

Section 725 (Public structures) has examples of potential translation confusions, e.g., the following one from English to Spanish:

> Other problems, more subtle and difficult to detect, are the shades of meaning and the colloquialisms that only a complete mastery of the two languages can overcome. A specialist in art history translating the 700's believed that "taproom buildings" (725.72) were places people gathered for tap dancing, not drinking, and that "halls for pool" (725.84) were used for swimming and not for billiards.[6]

We noted in chapter 2 that actual caption wordings

> ... may be incomplete, because, from the principle of hierarchy, the heading must be read as part of the larger group that includes it.... [7]

Then why not "Taprooms" instead of "Taproom buildings"? And even a native speaker could be misled by the Victorian euphemism "Halls for pool." The Relative Index is more direct with "Pool hall bldgs." *DDC 19* changes in this section are limited to providing numbers for "Multipurpose" and "Sports" complexes.

Sections 726 (Buildings for religious purposes) and *727 (School buildings)* add two expandable numbers for the design, construction, and decoration of Christian church buildings. See our comments in section 254 concerning overlap.

Section 727 (School buildings ...) has no changes. The overlap continues here. The 727.1-.4 span has much in common with 371.62 (Educational physical plants), and with 690.7 (Construction of educational buildings). Numbers 727.6-.7 share "Museum physical plants" with 069.2. And library building materials shelve in 022.3 as well as in 727.8.

Section 728 (Residential buildings) was mentioned in section 644. The old caption "Urban types" is here broadened to "Conventional housing." Four specific kinds of "Vacation houses, etc." now have numbers, while "Barns" shows up under "Accessory structures." "Single-story houses" relocate internally.

Section 729 (Design and decoration of structures and accessories) is unsullied by *DDC 19* tampering.

Division 730   Plastic Arts; Sculpture

Complaints about divisional sequencing usually start here, e.g.:

> It seems natural to many librarians to rank the art forms in a hierarchy, separating the fine arts from the minor or decorative arts.... If that bias is accepted, then Dewey's disposition of the various decorative arts media is inconsistent and unreasonable. In the 730s, along with "pure" sculpture, there are class numbers for carving in all materials, numismatics, ceramics, and metalwork. The operating principle seems to be the inclusion of three dimensional materials, but other decorative arts are assigned to the later 740s, after drawing,

including not only textiles but also antiques, glassware, furniture, and interior design. The logic of how or why the decorative arts have been split becomes difficult to follow.[8]

This division starts with the *ss* pattern displayed in division 700, with double zero notation for the plastic arts, and single zeros for sculpture. Here, as elsewhere, the use of multiple zeros for facet indicators has been criticized (counting zeros is hard on the eyes).[9]

Section 731 (Processes and representations of sculpture) adds "Direct-metal sculpture," but relocates "Styles" and "Specific types" of sculpture.

Section 732 (Nonliterate, ancient, Oriental sculpture) adds locations which follow those in section 722 nearly to the digit.

Sections 733 (Greek, Etruscan, Roman sculpture), 734 (Medieval sculpture), and 735 (Modern sculpture) are all very short and barely altered, except for a *DC&* shift of the cross-classification note at 733. Chronological development under 735.23 (20th century sculpture) is reminiscent of, if not precisely identical to, that under 709.04.

Sections 736-739 (Other plastic arts) are related to, yet classified apart from, the arts and crafts in 745-749.

Section 736 (Carving and carvings) is quite short (only one page), with additions for Ivory carving and Origami.

Section 737 (Numismatics and sigillography) is slightly shorter, but doubles its former length with specific subdivisions under "Medals, medallions, etc.," and a number for Gold under "Coins."

Section 738 (Ceramic arts) adds general numbers for "Specific varieties and brands" and for "Specific products" of pottery. Under Enameling and enamels are "Cloisonné" and "Surface-painted enamels." Under Mosaics we now have "Used with architecture" and "Applied to portable objects." There is also a general place for "Conservation, preservation, restoration."

Section 739 (Art metalwork) puts in "Conservation, etc." The 739.2-.4 span reactivates the formerly discontinued *ss*-028 (Techniques, etc.) under "Goldsmithing," "Jewelry," "Watch- and clockcases," and "Ironwork." We also get "Monumental brasses," "Swords and sabers," and "Shields."

Division 740   Drawing, and Decorative and Minor Arts

Questions raised over placement of the 730's are equally pertinent to this division, as the following comment shows:

> What is the ideal sequence for subclasses within an art classification outline? Both Dewey and LC place architecture and sculpture immediately after the general numbers, apparently creating no problems. Both systems, however, separate the drawing subclass from the engraving, or print media subclass — an unfortunate split, since both media are essentially linear in character and would logically come one after the other. In the case of Dewey 740s, drawing is also separated from painting by numbers for the decorative and minor arts.[10]

Section 741 (Drawing and drawings) inserts "Techniques of reproduction and conservation" at 741.21, and subdivides it. Its specific topical additions are "Magazines and their covers," "Covers for sheet music and recordings," and a set of four specific numbers for "Calendars," "Postcards," "Greeting cards," and "Trade cards." The nineteenth and twentieth centuries are now distinguished among the "Historical periods." *DC&* converts the 741.6 caption into "Graphic design, illustration, commercial art." There are two relocations.

Section 742 (Perspective) is unchanged and unpartitioned.

Section 743 (Drawing and drawings by subject) reactivates *ss*-028 as the location for comprehensive works, in a move similar to that under 731, but counter to those under 738, 739, and 741.

Section [744] is unassigned.

Section 745 (Decorative and minor arts) subdivides 745.1028 (Techniques, etc., for antiques). It also provides numbers under "Periods of development" for the nineteenth, twentieth, and twenty-first centuries. Plastics gets its own number, as do Papier mâché and Decoupage. Beads are differentiated from "Found objects." Snuffboxes and Egg decorating each win recognition. "Candlesticks" is provided with a subdivision for "Candles." Latin lettering splits four ways. Illuminated manuscripts and books are not grouped by language, using an Add reference to Table 6. Gilding goes in under "Decorative coloring."

Section 746 (Textile arts and handicrafts) starts with a distributive development of *ss*-04 (Special topics). Its precedence table at 746.1-.9 (Products and processes) has a few cosmetic changes, but nothing disruptive. New topics are "Carding and combing," "Dyeing," and three "Laces" extensions. "Needle and handwork" gets 13 new subtopics, 3 having already appeared in *DC&*, v. 3. "Appliqué" is a restoration of a *DDC 18* discontinuance. "Printing, painting, dyeing" has four added divisions.

Section 747 (Interior decoration) raises disciplinary questions relative to 645 (Furnishing and decorating the home), 684 (Furnishings and home workshops), and 698 (Detail finishing). But these do not exhaust the placement problems.

> Neither Dewey nor Class N [LC classification] manages to bridge the gulf in their schedules between the subclasses for architecture and interior design. These closely related topics are widely enough separated in Dewey — 720 and 740 — but in LC they are hopelessly split, from NA to NK. There is probably no satisfactory outline which can pull together related subclasses in one ideal sequence, for what may be gained in one set of reasonable juxtapositions will require compromise elsewhere.[11]

New entries are Decoration "under specific limitations," "with color," and "with houseplants." A list of specific centuries appears for periods of development. Two specifics with Add notes are now available under "Decoration of specific types of buildings."

Section 748 (Glass) makes the by now familiar *ss*-028 expansion under Glassware, and Stained, painted, leaded, mosaic glass. Bottles, Drinking glasses, and Paperweights now have their own numbers.

Section 749 (Furniture and accessories) presents disciplinary integrity problems similar to those noted in section 747. Again *ss*-028 is developed under "Antique furniture." "Chairs" now have a dedicated number.

Division 750   Painting and Paintings

There are several related objections to the divisional arrangement: 1) that its principles (subject, period, area) are heterogeneous, 2) that the nationality of a painter and the treatment of his style cannot be reconciled, and 3) that artists working in more than one medium cannot be contained at any one location.[12]

Section 751 (Processes and forms) gives "Techniques, etc." four more entries. Two carry Add instructions for expanding "Water color" and "Oil" techniques by subject. The other two separate "Ink painting" into "Chinese" and "Japanese." "Mosaic painting" is relocated to 738.5. "Conservation, etc." splits into "Preservation and restoration" and "Routine care."

Section 752 (Color) and the span 753-758 (Iconography) are extremely short and unchanged except for an Add note at 758.9.

Section 759 (Historical and geographical treatment) adds specific time spans under "Periods of development." This extension, as we have seen, is characteristic of several 700 sections. Art schools or movements, formerly lumped into Inclusion notes, now have extensive expansion, e.g., for "Kitsch (Trash)." Altogether, chronological, topical, and geographic development make this schedule about twice its former size.

Division 760   Graphic Arts; Printmaking and Prints

Not just criticism, but literary warrant, seems lacking for this division. It is quite short, particularly in its interior schedules. Sections [762] and [768] are unassigned. The sections under centered heading 761-767 (Printmaking and prints) are mostly limited to two or three unpartitioned subtopics.

Section 760 (Standard subdivisions of graphic arts; Generalities of printmaking) adds only explanatory ss assignments such as 760.044 (Iconography of graphic arts).

Section 769 (Prints) relocates "Collecting" within the section, and gives it six subtopics such as "Techniques of reproduction," "Conservation," and "Routine maintenance and repair." "Postage stamps and related devices" are carefully captioned to show that they belong in the "Prints" discipline. It includes "Philately," which some classifiers would like to see located with 790.13 (Hobbies). This most fully developed of any subtopic in the section has new numbers for U.N. postage stamps, "Covers, postal stationery, postmarks," and "Stamps other than for prepayment of postage."

Division 770   Photography and Photographs

Section 770 (Standard subdivisions of photography) spells out ss-02 (Miscellany) in some detail. "Use of specific types of cameras" is new. A caption change at 770.283 turns "Preparation of negatives" into "Darkroom and laboratory practice." DC& has revised the note under 770.92 (Photographers).

Sections 771 (Apparatus, equipment, materials) and 772-774 (Special processes) show a single addition, for Silver processes.

Sections [775-777] are unassigned.

Section 778 (Specific fields, etc.) adds "Special kinds" and "Related activities" to the caption, but other changes are few in this longest (five pages) of the photography sections. "Ultra" disappears from "High-speed photography." "Generalities of motion-picture and television photography" now has an Add note. "Cinematography and editing" gets new subtopics, such as "Darkroom and laboratory practice." "Television recording and recorders" is now partitioned.

Section 779 (Photographs) loses its restrictive "Collections of," along with the old "Class here ... " note. The Add instruction to provide subject separation remains intact.

Division 780 Music

Librarians agree that DDC is the most widely used classification for music collections, especially those in general libraries.[13] In spite of that fact—possibly because of it—the 780's were an iffy affair during the preparation of *DDC 19*. Complaints from the field had been long-standing, e.g.:

> The most obvious fault in the treatment of music in DC is ... failure to recognise the fundamental difference between the physical nature of books and of music with, consequently, no allowance made for such a difference in the scheme such as exists in LC, BC [Bliss Bibliographic Classification] and BCM [British Catalogue of Music Classification]. The most it does is to provide a separate number for each within the same division:
> 787.1   Literature on the violin
> 787.15   Music for the violin
> There is also an option that M can precede a number for a score. Yet, curiously, bibliographies of books about music are preferred at 016.78 or, following the alternative offered at 016, at 780.16 from table 1, while bibliographies of music are classed either at 016.78 for preference or at 781.97. It would seem useful to have all bibliographies of the subject in one place, especially as many cover both books and music.[14]

Other difficulties have been documented, such as the following list:

> a.   Oriented toward the performer rather than musicologist or historian
> b.   Troublesome overlapping of categories ("Theater music," 782.8, versus "Music for small ensembles," 785.4; "Oratorios," 783.3, versus "Complete choral works," 784.2)
> c.   Incomplete treatment of works for early and primitive instruments
> d.   Combination of "study and teaching" with music scores for various instruments.[15]

DDC 18 "was not changed to any great extent."[16] Indeed, the Comaromi survey found no overwhelming ground swell for change, although Music was eleventh (last) on its list of schedules "needing extensive revision most urgently."[17] British music librarians were less complacent, as this account shows:

There had been much criticism in Britain of 780, so we were given the chance to so [sic] something about it. A project headed by Russell Sweeney created a new Music schedule which recognised that whereas for scores the primary facet is the executant, for books it is the composer (see Example 9).

1) SCORES: Executant — Form — Character — Techniques — Elements
   e.g. Bach cello sonatas 787.4183 = 787.4   Cello (executant)
                                      781.83   Sonata (form)

2) BOOKS: Composer — Executant — Form — Character — Techniques —
   Elements e.g. Counterpoint in Beethoven's orchestral music
   789.151421286 or 789.BEE421286 = 789.15   Beethoven (composer)
   or 789.BEE
      784.2   Symphony orchestra (executant)
      781.286 Counterpoint (element)

Example 9.   Facet order in Music phoenix — proposed. The new schedule is brilliant, allowing precision in expressing complex topics without overlong numbers by using both zero and one as facet indicators. Unfortunately it took longer to prepare than expected, and there were some misgivings in America over the treatment of composers using mixed notation, which meant it was not possible to incorporate it in DC19. It will be issued as a separate publication by Forest Press sometime in 1980, and will probably be used by BCM, but not in BNB. If is [sic] proves acceptable it should later become part of the Classification. So again the DC19 schedule is based on the structure of the previous edition. There is some expansion — I particularly like the new section at 784.5 for Popular songs, giving numbers for Blues, Rock and Soul — but it of course embodies the structural faults of the DC18 schedule.[18]

The scheme, a fruitful collaboration between library and subject specialists, was largely the work of Eric J. Coates, on the staff of the British National Bibliography, in consultation with members of the United Kingdom branch of the International Association of Music Libraries. In 1975, Forest Press had offered the Decimal Classification Sub-Committee of the Library Association $7,500 to do the job.[19] Russell Sweeney and John Clews completed the draft at Leeds Polytechnic Institute in 1975, "introducing the basic structure of the BCM faceted scheme into the DC enumerative schedules without too great a wrench."[20] There was much talk of its being published in *DDC 19*, but reports of Decimal Classification Editorial Policy Committee meetings are laden with questions, discussions, and referrals — to the Music Library Association and the IAML-UK for comments, and back to the authors for revision.[21] Eventually time ran out.

The position in regard to 780 Music was [in 1976] still uncertain. Much of the text of the 19th edition was in an advanced state of preparation. A phoenix of 780 could be published as a separate; it was a subject which had the least interrelationship with other parts of the classification.[22]

In the spring of 1979, two years after excluding it from *DDC 19*, DCEPC made six substantive recommendations.[23] As predicted, it is now available, published separately by Forest Press.[24]

As for the *DDC 19* division 780, a well-nigh ubiquitous feature is the relocation of *ss*-019 (Psychological principles) to a recaptioned *ss*-015 (Appreciation). "Scientific principles," the Table 1 caption for *ss*-015, reduces to *ss*-01. "Festivals, etc.," which we met at 700.79, keeps bobbing up in most 780 sections.

Section 780 (Standard subdivisions and Generalities of music) has four bracketed numbers, of which two are new. For instance, we learn that music price lists and trade catalogs belong now in 016.78, with other music bibliographies. One librarian's quibbles over the 016 location were quoted in our division introduction. The fourth (1959) edition of the Library of Congress class Z schedule, under "Subject bibliography," carried an optional Z6810-6820 span with the note "In general, prefer classification in ML111-158. Extra copies may be classed here."[25] The fifth (1980) edition schedule eliminates the option with a direct reference to *"see* ML111 + ." In *DDC 19*, music scores and parts among specific racial, etc., groups are sent to section 781. However, treatment among groups of specific kinds of persons is still in 780. The imminent twenty-first century is included here, as elsewhere, under "Periods of development."

Section 781 (General principles and consideration of music) shows no change in its four pages except the unannounced disappearance of former option 781[.97] (Bibliographies, etc., of scores and parts). Mr. Redfern may find some comfort in the change.

Section 782 (Dramatic music and production) gets notes on synchronization and scoring from *DC&* for "Incidental film music" and "Incidental television music."

Section 783 (Sacred music) has almost no changes except two shifts for "Psychological principles."

Section 784 (Voice and vocal music) now has a place for Madrigals. *DC&* has inserted "Words to be sung or recited" into the distributive table at 784.1-.7 (Specific kinds of vocal music). Popular songs is split into "Country," "Blues," "Rock," and "Soul," so Trotter's pleasure in the phoenix 784.5's is not utterly dissipated.

Section 785 (Instrumental ensembles and their music) shows format and caption changes in the distributive table under "Specific kinds of music." The subdivided "Scores and parts" permits synthetic number building to replace two specific *DDC 18* numbers.

Section 786 (Keyboard instruments and their music) makes no unique changes. The distributive table under "Other instruments and their music" is considerably expanded, largely along lines already observed in previous sections.

Section 787 (String instruments and their music) loses its page and a half of schedule development under 787.1 (Violin) in favor of new faceting possibilities from the 787-789 table. The only topical addition is "Dulcimer."

Sections 788 (Wind instruments and their music) and *789 (Percussion, mechanical, electrical instruments)* receive new topics "Bagpipe" and "Electronic music," with some special instructions at other points for standard subdivisions.

Division 790   Recreational and Performing Arts

As Mark Twain said about the weather, everyone complains, but no one does anything about, the incongruities of disciplinary relationship in this division. Yet the arrangement is less disturbing than the pseudo-hierarchies implied by the notation. The "performing arts" do shelve between music (a performing art), and sports (also performance oriented, in America anyway). Unfortunately, lots of extraneous matter falls in between.

Section 790 (Standard subdivisions and Generalities) is all recreation until it reaches 790.2 (The performing arts). The tyranny of DDC notational conventions is nowhere more evident than in its isolation of the 790.01-.1 span. "Collecting as a recreation," "Passive (Spectator) activities," and the like would fit better with the 793-799 schedules.

Section 791 (Public performances) shows very minor change except for the *DC&* addition of "Cheerleading." This topic was mentioned in our chapter 4 examination of Berman's "Dance drill teams, etc." A patterned split into "Single" and "Multiple" recurs under Descriptions, critical appraisals, etc., "for motion pictures," "for radio," and "for television."

Section 792 (Theater and stage presentation) adds "Special effects" analogues to 778.5345 and 778.8. However, there is no entry in the Relative Index under "Special effects" for their treatrical uses, as there is for their photographic uses. "Tragedy" and "Comedy" are spelled out under 792.1-.2. The "single/multiple" split that we saw in section 791 occurs here for "Ballets" and "Stage presentations."

Sections 793-795 (Indoor games and amusements, etc.) are untouched except for three additions: "Checkers," "Darts," and "Snooker."

Section 796 (Athletic and outdoor sports and games), while considerably longer than the three preceding sections (slightly over 13 pages), shows no more adjustment proportionally. *DC&* changes "Toys" to "Devices," with an Inclusion note under "Play with kites, etc." *Ss*-068 (Management) becomes -069 at such places as 796, 796.332 (American football), 796.4 (Athletic exercises and gymnastics), 796.42 (Track and field athletics), and 796.72 (Automobile racing). "Football competitions and awards" is relocated within the section. "Jumping" and "Vaulting" are now separately identified. There is a misspelled "Rock climbing." "Racing" and "Snowmobiling" appear, as do six subtopics under "Ice hockey." "Katsu" is moved out to 616.0252. And *DC&* respells "T'ai chi ch'uan."

Sections 797 (Aquatic and air sports) and 798 (Equestrian sports and animal training) add little more than "Race tracks" in their two pages.

Section 799 (Fishing, hunting, shooting) is a bit longer (four pages), but adds only "Blowpipes, boomerangs, etc.," and moves the hunting of reptiles from the synthetic 799[.2581] to 799.279, as a corollary of the phoenix change in the 597-598 schedules. Some ambiguity surfaces here. If the Add note under 799.254-.259 is followed, numeric synonyms are available which may possibly be justified on hierarchical grounds, but they overlap dangerously, e.g.:

799.2579   Hunting of reptiles (small game other than birds)

799.279   Hunting of reptiles (specific kinds of big game other than birds)

Conclusion

The aborted phoenix class 780 and its subsequent publication as an alternative classification is the most important event in the *DDC 19* fine arts, and possibly sets a precedent for future revisions of other areas and topics. In fact, it is not the first straw in the wind, as a British writer indicates:

> If a regular new edition, with all mod. cons. [sic], would be beyond our means to adopt, what could we have instead? One possibility we could call "Alternative Dewey," which could go like this: DC 19 remains, unchanged, as the standard text. Meanwhile, alternative schedules are under construction, in those fields most in need of radical revision.... The programme could continue over a period of years; new Alternative Schedules would be published at intervals; any of them could be adopted by libraries who wanted to do so.... The national bibliographies would continue to use the standard classification. There would have, of course, to be a dateline; for there would come a point at which DC 19 was becoming badly out-of-date, a point at which a decision would have to be made, in the light of the use made of the published Alternative Schedules, to take them, or not to take them, into the body of the classification in a new edition. Meanwhile, should Alternative numbers appear in the MARC record, along with DC 19 numbers?
>
> ... One should remember that the foundations for it were laid some years ago—in 1974, in fact, when the Area Tables -41 and -42 were published as separates.... [26]

It is not only the British who construct such possible scenarios. At the Ninety-Ninth annual Conference of the American Library Association in New York City, June 30, 1980, the topic was on at least one agenda:

> ... The Subject Analysis Committee had discussed the idea that two or more "phoenixes" (complete revisions of numbers for certain fast developing disciplines) strung out in the interval between editions would be easier for most libraries to accommodate than the "double whammy" changes with the appearance of new editions every eight to ten years. It was pointed out that revisions between editions would create indexing complications and would involve "ripple effects" where changes in one discipline mandated changes in related disciplines.[27]

An example of the "ripple effect" alluded to might have occurred in section 799 above. Separate construction and publication of a phoenix Life sciences schedule, such as the aborted 560-590 one, could cause unexpected relocations to result from the application of Add notes, or alternatively, could preserve obsolete sequences in different but related disciplines.

As was suggested at the close of chapter 1, the coming decade will be crucial for the Dewey Decimal Classification. Probably its longevity is not so much at stake as the ultimate significance of its evolution. Mutation and survival of the fittest affect the continuing success of any species. One influential factor here has never been discerned in the origin and endurance of biological species, however.

Conscious intellect, applying reliable methods of observation and self-correction, should be able to evaluate trends and adjust responses. That is, mutation need not be altogether random. With something a little better than luck, Forest Press and the Editorial Policy Committee may find the means to keep the scheme alive and well through another century, or longer.

Exercises in the Use of Class 700

A. Analysis

704.948'9'44	Sūtradhāramandana, 16th cent. Jaina iconography in Rūpamandana of Sūtradhara Śri Mandana, son of Ksetra of Medapata ... 1978.	78-904245
707'.4'02753	Port sunlight, Eng. Lady Lever Art Gallery. Treasures from the Lady Lever Art Gallery ... [catalogue] ... 1977.	79-304634
707'.4'02132 s [730'.074'02132]	Sotheby, firm, auctioneers, London. Works of art which will be sold at auction ... 1978. (Its The Robert von Hirsch Collection ; v. 2)	79-300833
709'.794'074019496	California perceptions, light and space : selection from the Wortz Collection ... c1979.	79-55768
728.3'09392'2	Ramage, Andrew. Lydian houses and architectural terracottas ... 1978.	78-15507
730'.094'0740321	Dresden. Grünes Gewölbe. The Green Vault : an introduction ... 3., rev. ed. ... 1977.	79-344396
737.4'9'17671	Mitchiner, Michael. The world of Islam ... c1977.	79-348130
741.9'492'07402733	Brussells. Musées royaux des beaux-arts de Belgique. Landscape in Flemish and Dutch drawings of the 17th century ... [Catalogue] ... 1976.	77-364963
743'.8'36	Borgman, Harry. Landscape painting with markers ... 1977.	77-9345
745.4'07'1242	Design in general education : eight projects / edited by John Harahan ... 1978.	79-304786
745.4'49'24	Hanks, David A. The decorative designs of Frank Lloyd Wright ... c1979.	78-55777
745.59'23'09034	Jacobs, Flora Gill. Victorian dolls' houses and their furnishings ... 1978 ed. ... c1978.	78-62816
746.7'965'1	Authentic Algerian carpet designs & motifs / edited by June Beveridge ... 1978.	78-1174
748.2'904	Arwas, Victor. Glass : art nouveau to art deco ... 1977.	76-62548
758'.1'094207402142	London. University. Courtauld Institute of Art. English landscape drawings and watercolours from ... [catalogue] ... 1977.	78-307280

769'.4'32	Reiterszenen aus dem alten England : d. Jagd auf Fuchs, Hase, Hirsch u. Rehbock : colorierte Stiche aus d. 19. Jh. ... 1977.	78-356756
779'.4'0978	Woodall, Ronald. Taken by the wind : vanishing architecture of the West ... c1977.	77-77332
779'.9973926	An Album of the American family, 1980 : the search for pride--the joy of caring ... c1979.	79-91905
781.7'2'98	Hornbostel, Erich Moritz von. Music of the Makuschí, Taulipáng and Yekuaná ... 1969.	73-12701
782.1'079'4331	Bayreuth in der deutschen Presse : Beitr. zur Rezeptionsgeschichte Richard Wagners u. seiner Festspiele ... 1977-	79-343145
784'.1'00938	Calame, Claude. Les choeurs de jeunes filles en Grèce archaïque ... 1977.	78-347199
787'.1'0712	Domington, Robert. String playing in Baroque music ... c1977.	76-62621
790.2'07'2073	Dimaggio, Paul. Audience studies of the performing arts and museums : a critical review ... 1978.	78-26884
791.43'028'0922	Mulholland, Jim. The Abbott and Costello book ... 1977.	79-105959
792.8'025'0903	Clarke, Mary. Design for ballet ... c1978.	77-93100
796.32'306'04435	Canque, Michel. Rebonds ... c1976.	78-363158

B. Synthesis: Examples from LC records are given on pp. 276-79.

1. A book for children on trout fishing.

2. A book of Buddhist paintings from Asia done by a modern Hungarian painter.

3. A book on the Mormon Tabernacle Choir.

4. A printmaker's collected wood engravings.

5. The collected drawings of a modern British artist.

6. A periodical devoted to rock music.

7. A story of a balloon ascension.

8. Running as sport and as exercise.

9. Nineteenth- and twentieth-century triumphal arches.

10. A manual on the restoration and conservation of sculptures.

11. A directory of architects in South Carolina.

12. Planning and maintaining your home garden.

13. A light-hearted, ironic book on sports.

14. A catalog of an exhibition of eighteenth-century European white porcelain.

15. A plan for restoring and using the Frank Lloyd Wright home and studio in Oak Park, Illinois.

16. A study of an opera conductor and regisseur, his techniques and accomplishments.

17. An introduction to the study of musical pitch and scale intervals.

18. A guide to Virginia's ante-bellum churches.

19. A handbook about collecting art objects.

20. A collection of heroic fantasy illustrative paintings by British painters.

21. An auction price guide for collectors of bronzes and sculptures.

22. The uses of trees in English landscape design.

23. A casting director's hints to actors on how to audition.

24. The catalog of an exhibit at Queensborough Community College, New York, of sculptures by modern American artists.

25. An exhibition at the Newark, New Jersey Museum of Arshile Gorky's aviation murals.

26. A biography for children of a young circus aerialist.

27. A study of modern pop art and its effect on culture and society.

28. A stage history of a touring Shakespearean company in Africa.

29. A book on folk music and folk dancing in Ireland.

30. A description of the logistics of moving a circus by train.

31. Plans for central city malls.

32. A study with photographs of a famous glass collection.

33. A manual on cinematic design.

34. Case studies of housing and city planning in Belfast, Ireland.

35. A guide to U.S. coin and paper money valuations.

36. A book about ornamental design in Germany.

37. Hunting decoys from Martha's Vineyard, Massachusetts.

38. Historical criticism of drama, the theater, and society.

39. A critical study of music of the baroque period.

40. A catalog of an exhibit of French drawings, watercolors, and pastels from 1800 to 1950, shown in the Cincinnati Art Museum.

41. A discussion of images and ideas in seventeenth-century Spanish painting.

42. A biography and "illustrated history" of Bob Dylan.

43. Neoclassicism and Gothic revival in the architecture of a manor house in North Wiltshire, England.

44. A book on electronic music in Sweden.

45. A book of plans for building homes in and on hillsides.

46. A critical study of the chamber music of Antonin Dvorak.

47. A catalog of Charles Dickens' mementos and art collections sold at auction.

48. A children's book on disco dancing.

49. A book about a well-known organ maker.

50. A field guide for rock climbing at Devil's Lake, Wisconsin.

51. A study of British theories of design during the nineteenth century.

52. High school football rules for officials, coaches, players, and spectators.

53. A treatise on note-separation in musical performance.

54. A book of sports photographs.

55. A book on dance forms in Trinidad and Tobago.

56. Paintings of the World War II years: catalog of an exhibition at the Canadian War Museum.

57. Primitive art in black Africa.

58. The sculpture and bronze casting of equestrian statues.

59. A study of the moral and religious values inherent and potential in movies.

60. Extraterrestrial space as represented in art.

C. Reclassification: Suggested solutions are offered on pages 279-80.

1. Can you suggest a location in a different DDC location which seems equally appropriate for the following works?

a. 704.94'9'78	Mirimonde, Albert P. de. Astrologie et musique ... 1977.	78-392160
b. 709'.2'4	Clair, Jean. Duchamp et la photographie : essai d'analyse d'un primate technique sur le dévelope-ment d'une oeuvre ... 1977.	78-397583
c. 741.9'24	From naked to nude : life drawing in the twentieth century / [compiled by] Georg Eisler ... 1977.	77-359515

2. The DDC numbers on the following records do not, for one reason or another, appear to fit *DDC 19*. What adjustments would you make?

a. 706'.5 [B[	Heuvel, Arthur de. Souvenirs d'un expert en tableaux ... 1977. [The biography of a Belgian art dealer]	79-339229
b. 709'.01'1097010740176579	American Indian art : form and tradition ... 1972. [An exhibition catalog from the Walker Art Center, Minneapolis, Minnesota]	72-90701

c. 711.0621   International Housing and Town Planning Congress
(11th : 1928 : Paris) ... 1977.   agr 29-505

d. 722'.4   Jacob, Samuel Swinton. Jeypore portfolio of architectural details ... 1977-   77-911998

e. 728.9   Radford, William A. Practical plans for barns, car-
riage houses, stables & other country buildings
... c1978.   78-60318

f. 732'.9'3928 Childs, William A. P. The city-reliefs of
Lycia ... c1978.   78-51159

g. 745.59'4   Ukrainian Easter eggs and how we make them /
by Anne [i.e. Ann] Kmit ... [et al.] ... c1979.   79-8477

h. 751.4'8   Fischer, Peter, fl. 1969-   Mosaic history and
technique ... 1971.   72-178870
74-148984

i. 792'.029   Joseph, Bertram Leon. Elizabethan acting ...
2d ed. ... 1979.   78-31950

j. 796.6'06'241 Oakley, William. Winged wheel : the history
of the first hundred years of the Cyclists'
Touring Club ... 1977.   78-326670

k. 797.3'2'0954 Pant, Gayatri Nath. Indian archery ... 1978.   78-904149

3.   The following record has appeared with two different DDC numbers as
shown below. Which number do you prefer? Give your reasons.

a. From the *National Union Catalog* 1979, v. 11, p. 75:

720'.952'074013 A New wave of Japanese architecture, September 25,
1978 to November 14, 1978 ... 1978.   78-63442

b. From the MARC tape data base:

722'.12'074013 A New Wave of Japanese architecture, September 25,
1978 to November 14, 1978 ... 1978.   78-63442

Examples of LC Cataloging to Illustrate the Above Exercises in DDC Number Building

1. 799.1'7'55   East, Ben. Trapped in the devil's hole / as told to
Ben East ... c1979.   79-53773

2. 759.39   Brunner, Elizabeth, artist. A painter's pilgrimage :
Elizabeth Brunner's Buddhist paintings from India,
Nepal, Burma, Sri Lanka, and Thailand ... 1978.   79-903106

3. 783.8'09'792'23 Calman, Charles Jeffrey. The Mormon Tabernacle
Choir ... c1979.   79-1656

4. 769.92'4   Campbell, Duine. From the wood : engravings ...   80-460915

5. 741.942   Christian, Andy. Megaliths and water : Andy Christian's drawings / with poems by Peter Scupham ...
1978.   80-460189

6. 784.5'4'005   Circus weekly. no. 192-   Oct. 3, 1978-   80-640497

7. 797.5   Clark, Chatham. The wayward balloon : a true story ... c1979.   79-129223

8. 796.4'26   Fixx, James F. The complete book of running ... c1977.   77-5984

9. 725'.96'09034   Westfehling, Uwe. Triumphbogen im 19. [i.e. neunzehnten] und 20. Jahrhundert ... 1977.   79-346974

10. 731.4'8   André, Jean Michel. Restauration des sculptures ... c1977.   77-572201

11. 720'.25'757   State of South Carolina roster of registered architects, firms, corporations, and partnerships ...   78-645592

12. 712'.6   Weber, Nelva M. How to plan your own home landscape : how to organize your outdoor space and how to utilize it for maximum pleasure and minimum maintenance all year round ... c1976.   75-33535

13. 796'.02'07   Rushton, William George. Pigsticking, a joy for life : a gentleman's guide to sporting pastimes ... 1977.   78-304560

14. 738.2'7   Winifred Williams (Firm). Exhibition of eighteenth century European white porcelain ... 1976.   77-374256

15. 728.3'7'0924   Frank Lloyd Wright Home and Studio Foundation. Restoration Committee. The plan for restoration and adaptive use of ... 1978.   78-67224

16. 782.1'071   Irmer, Hans-Jochen. Joachim Herz, Regisseur im Musiktheater : Beiträge zu Theorie und Praxis des Musiktheaters ... 1977.   77-553783

17. 781'.22   Young, Robert William. Making sense out of cents : a table relating frequency-to-cents, with deviations from the equally tempered scale based on A-440 Hz. ... c1976.   77-360536

18. 726'.5'09755   Perdue-Davis, Vernon. Virginia's ante-bellum churches : an introduction with particular attention to their furnishings ... 1978.   79-100708

19. 707'.5   Collector's Symposium (1978 : Cincinnati Art Museum) Collector's handbook : published in conjunction with the Collector's Symposium ... c1978.   78-112775

20. 759.2   Achilleos, Chris. Beauty and the beast : a collection of heroic fantasy illustrations ... c1978.   78-4394

21. 730'.75   Bronzes and sculptures at auction, around the world ... 1977. [Spine title: Bronze and sculptures price guide]   77-644341

22. 715'.2'0942   Edwards, Paul Francis. Trees and the English landscape ... 1962.   77-375163

23. 792'.028   Hunt, Gordon. How to audition : a casting director's guide for actors ... c1977.   78-111837

24. 730'.973'0740147243   The Department of Art and Design and CAPA
present Outdoor sculpture and works inside
by Alice Adams, Jerry Jones ... c1978.   78-111150

25. 759.13   Gorky, Arshile. Murals without walls : Arshile Gorky's
aviation murals rediscovered / Ruth Bowman, guest
curator ... 1978.   78-13898

26. 791.3'4'0924   Krementz, Jill. A very young circus flyer /
[B]   written and photographed by Jill Krementz ...
1979.   78-20546

27. 700'.1   Taylor, Roger. Art, an enemy of the people ... 1978.   79-302498

28. 792.95   Fraser, John. The bard in the bush ... 1978.   78-326192

29. 781.7'415   Breathnach, Breandán. Folk music and dances of
Ireland ... Revised ed. ... 1977.   79-300462

30. 791.3'028   Parkinson, Tom. The circus moves by rail ... c1978.   78-23457

31. 711'.552   Rubenstein, Harvey M. Central city malls ... c1978.   78-7536

32. 748.8   The Cinzano glass collection / [texts by Peter Lazarus
; photos. by Derek Balmer] ... c1978.   79-300221

33. 778.5'3   Hacker, Leonard. Cinematic design ... 1978, 1931.   77-11375

34. 711'.4'094167   Northern Ireland. Planning Appeals Commission.
Poleglass area public inquiry : reports ...
1977.   78-325770

35. 737.4'9'73   Wilhite, Robert. Standard guide to U.S. coin and
paper money valuations ... 4th ed. ... c1977.   77-93060

36. 745.4'49'43   Wichmann, Heinrich. Die Ornamentfibel : Stile-
pochen ... 1977.   78-390072

37. 745.59'3   Murphy, Stanley. Martha's Vineyard decoys ... c1978.   78-58592

38. 792'.09   Drama and society ... 1979.   78-54723

39. 780'.903'2   Borroff, Edith. The music of the baroque ... 1978.   77-17401

40. 741.9'44'074017178   Cincinnati. Art Museum. French drawings,
watercolors, and pastels, 1800-1950 : a
catalogue raisonné ... 1978.   78-75226

41. 759.6   Brown, Jonathan. Images and ideas in seventeenth-
century Spanish painting ... 1978.   78-52485

42. 784'.092'4   Gross, Michael. Bob Dylan : an illustrated history
[B]   ... c1978.   77-87808

43. 728.8'3'0942312   Ladd, Frederick J. Architects at Corsham Court
: a study in Revival style architecture and
landscaping, 1749-1849 ... 1978.   79-304658

44. 789.9   Sweden. Elektronmusikutredningen. Elektronmusik i
Sverige : betänkande ... 1977.   77-572851

45. 728.3   Hillside home plans / selected by Hudson home guides /
Home Building Plan Service ... 1978.   78-112898

46. 785.7'0092'4   Šourek, Otakar. The chamber music of Antonín
                    Dvořák ... 1978.   78-17848

47. 745.1   Dickens memento / with introd. by Francis Phillimore
                    and "Hints to Dickens collectors" by John F. Dexter.
                    Catalogue with purchasers' names & prices ... 1978. 78-16479

48. 793.3   Van Ryzin, Lani. Disco ... 1979.   78-24078

49. 786.6'3   Blewett, P. R. W. Antony Duddyngton, organ maker
                    ... 1977.   79-302781

50. 796.5'22'0977576   Widule, William. Climbers' guide to Devil's
                       Lake ... 1979.   79-1514

51. 745.4'49'41   Bøe, Alf. From Gothic revival to functional form :
                    a study in Victorian theories of design ... 1979,
                    c1957.   78-31194

52. 796.33'2'02022 National Federation of State High School Associa-
                    tions. Official high school football rules
                    simplified and illustrated for officials, coaches,
                    players, spectators ...   78-648353

53. 781.6'3   Babitz, Sol. Note-separation in musical performance,
                    and other matters ... c1977.   77-376779

54. 796'.022'2   Leifer, Neil. Sports ! / Photos. by Neil Leifer
                    ; text by George Plimpton ... 1978.   78-7166

55. 793.3'19729'83 Ahye, Molly. Golden heritage : the dance in
                    Trinidad and Tobago ... c1978.   78-113431

56. 759.11   Canadian War Museum. Charles Fraser Comfort, the
                    war years ...   80-462733

57. 732'.2'0966   Lauzinger, Elsy. The art of Black Africa ... 1977,
                    c1976.   76-62892

58. 731'.81   Bossrand, Germain. Sculpture and casting of eques-
                    trian statues ... 1974.   78-312262

59. 791.43'013   Adler, Mortimer Jerome. Art and prudence ... 1978,
                    c1937.   77-11371

60. 704.94'9'999   Miller, Ron. Norman Jacobs & Kerry O'Quinn present
                    Space art ... c1978.   79-101645

C. Reclassification: Suggested *DDC 19* numbers for pre-*DDC 19* or other
    records:
    1. a. 133.5878   Mirimonde ...

        b. 770.924   Clair ...

        c. 704.9421   From naked to nude ...
            [741.9242]

    2. a. 338.76170924   Heuvel ...
            [381.457]

        b. 709.011089970740176579   American Indian art ...

    c. 711.0601   International Housing ...

    d. 722.444   Jacob ...

    e. 728.922   Radford ...

    f. 732.928   Childs ...

    g. 745.5944   Ukrainian Easter eggs ...

    h. 738.5   Fischer ...

    i. 792.0280942   Joseph ...

    j. 796.6060411   Oakley ...

    k. 799.320954   Pant ...

NOTES

[1]William B. Walker, "Art Books and Periodicals: Dewey and LC," *Library Trends*, v. 23, no. 3 (January 1975): 452, 469.

[2]Doralyn J. Hickey, "Problems Associated with Presenting and Teaching the Schedules: Philosophy (100); Religion (200); and the Fine Arts (700)," *The Dewey Decimal Classification: Outlines and Papers Presented at a Workshop on the Teaching of Classification* ... (New York, School of Library Science, Columbia University, 1968), p. 34.

[3]Joel C. Downing, "The Role of the Editorial Policy Committee in the Development of the Dewey Decimal Classification," *Dewey International: Papers Given at the European Centenary Seminar* ... (London, The Library Association, 1977), p. 39.

[4]Benjamin A. Custer, "DDC 19: Characteristics," *HCL Cataloging Bulletin*, no. 35 (July/August 1978): 11.

[5]Peter Butcher, "Dewey? We Sure Do!," *Catalogue & Index*, no. 55 (Winter 1979): 8.

[6]Carmen Rovira, "The Present Spanish Translation of the Dewey Decimal Classification," *Dewey International: Papers Given at the European Centenary Seminar* ... (London, The Library Association, 1977), p. 89.

[7]Melvil Dewey, *Dewey Decimal Classification and Relative Index*. Ed. 19 (Albany, NY, Forest Press, 1979), v. 1, p. xli.

[8]Walker, p. 457.

[9]P. Dhyani, "DDC 18: Critical Appraisal of Some Auxiliary Tables," *International Library Review*, v. 9, no. 2 (April 1977): 178.

[10]Walker, p. 457.

[11]Ibid., pp. 457-58.

[12]See, for instance, Hickey, p. 35. The general tenor of her criticisms is pursued by M. J. Ramsden, "Dewey 18," *Australian Library Journal*, v. 21, no. 3 (April 1972): 117.

[13]See, for instance, Malcolm Jones, *Music Librarianship* (London, Clive Bingley, 1979), p. 97; and Kathi Meyer-Baer, "Classifications in American Music Libraries," *Music Review*, v. 12, no. 2 (February 1951): 76.

[14]Brian Redfern, *Organising Music in Libraries, Volume 1: Arrangement and Classification* (London & Hamden, CT, Clive Bingley & Linnet Books, 1978), p. 56.

[15]Hickey, p. 35.

[16]John Phillip Comaromi, *The Eighteen Editions of the Dewey Decimal Classification* (Albany, NY, Forest Press Division, Lake Placid Education Foundation, 1976), p. 596.

[17]John Phillip Comaromi, *A Survey of the Use of the Dewey Decimal Classification in the United States and Canada* (Lake Placid, NY?, Prepared for Forest Press, Lake Placid Foundation, 1975), p. 74 gives diverse perceptions of the lack of logical order in the 780's. Sixty percent of the correspondents said they used the division to classify musical scores and parts (p. 132). See also his "Decimal Classification Editorial Policy Committee Report," *Library Resources & Technical Services*, v. 21, no. 1 (Winter 1977): 93-94.

[18]Ross Trotter, "Dewey 19 — A Subjective Assessment," *Catalogue & Index*, no. 59 (Winter 1980): 4.

[19]Russell Sweeney, "The Decimal Classification in Britain and the Role of the Library Association Dewey Decimal Classification Sub-Committee," *Dewey International: Papers Given at the European Centenary Seminar ...* (London, The Library Association, 1977), p. 27. See also Ann Hobart, "The Work of the Dewey Decimal Classification Sub-Committee, 1968-1979," *Catalogue & Index*, no. 58 (Autumn 1980): 6.

[20]Redfern, p. 58.

[21]The DCEPC reports are available in *Library Resources & Technical Services*, v. 21, no. 1 (Winter 1977): 93-94; v. 22, no. 1 (Winter 1978): 88-89; and v. 23, no. 1 (Winter 1979): 86-87.

[22]Benjamin A. Custer, "How an Edition of the Dewey Decimal Classification Is Prepared," *Dewey International: Papers Given at the European Centenary Seminar ...* (London, The Library Association, 1977), p. 49.

[23]John P. Comaromi, "Decimal Classification Editorial Policy Committee Report, *Library Resources & Technical Services*, v. 24, no. 2 (Spring 1980): 179-80.

[24]*Cataloging Service Bulletin*, no. 11 (Winter 1981): 104. For those who wish a concise overview, the following two articles will help:
Russell Sweeney, "Music in the Dewey Decimal Classification," *Catalogue & Index*, no. 42 (Autumn 1976): 4-6.

John P. Clews, "Revision of DC 780: The phoenix schedule," *Brio*, v. 12, no. 1 (Spring 1975): 7-14.

[25]Library of Congress. Processing Department, *Classification. Class Z. Bibliography and Library Science*, 4th ed. (Washington, The Library, 1959), p. 99; 5th ed. (Washington, The Library, 1980), p. 143.

[26]Marjorie Jelinek, "Twentieth Dewey, an Exercise in Prophecy," *Catalogue & Index*, no. 58 (Autumn 1980): 2.

[27]Gregory New, "Dewey Decimal Classification Edition 19," *Library of Congress Information Bulletin*, v. 39, no. 34 (August 22, 1980): 319-20.

14

Class 800 Literature (Belles-Lettres)

Introduction

Disciplinary logic led Dewey to view "belles-lettres" as an art with such overwhelming literary warrant that it required a class of its own between the fine and decorative arts on one side, and the cultural frame of history and geography on the other. Users lament its separation from class 400 (Language), which DDC treats as a communication science linking the social and the hard sciences. The DDC approach is not without logic. Modern linguists, with their tape recorders, their etymological probings, their structural grammars, and their rules of phonetic change, often have but peripheral interest in literature. Literati are usually less concerned with the nuts and bolts of language than with social observation, aesthetic sensitivity, and elegant or pungent expression. For our purposes, however, the argument is academic. Classes 400 and 800 remain externally divorced, but morphologically linked by ancestral ties too strong to be ignored. Both have short schedules; both depend on auxiliary tables (in many cases the same tables); both employ the same hierarchical arrangement of linguistic families, giving precedence and emphasis to the Indo-European group, and starting with English.

We have been told that Dewey's early contributions to the principle of faceting were evident in language (the 400's), literature (the 800's), and history/geography (the 900's).[1] Class 800 intricacies multiplied through the years, showing substantive changes, particularly in its auxiliary tables, and instructional changes in the schedules. Most criticisms address its formal presentation rather than its content. However, a critique of its assumptions concerning literary forms appeared at the time *DDC 18* was published.

The most common problems are the following.
   1. problems encountered by the catalogers:
      (a)   the difficulty in application caused by the lack of clear, workable definitions of the forms;
      (b)   the problems of treating works of mixed forms or uncertain forms; and
      (c)   some of the forms that are questionable in their nature as literary forms.
   2.   Problems encountered by the users:
      (a)   inconvenience resulting from the separation and scattering of works written by and about single authors; and
      (b)   confusion caused by the seemingly arbitrary decisions made by the catalogers as regards the forms of certain literary works.[2]

Bloomberg and Weber give special attention to the analysis of long DDC class 800 numbers.

> This approach is most appropriate in this class because of the many different possible subdivisions and elements represented in each number. These elements include the base number for the language, a possible number for literary form (poetry or drama, for example), a possible number for the time or period of the work, a number for collections or history and criticism, and, finally, a number for specific themes.[3]

Table 3 (Subdivisions of Individual Literatures) made its first appearance in *DDC 18* (1971). Not surprisingly, it proved hard to apply, although it was a move toward synthetic faceting.

> In theory, synthesizing a literature number was quite simple. The classifier found a base number for a literature from the Schedules, turned to Table 3 and found the appropriate number there. If necessary, the Schedules could be checked again for a period number for the literature in question. In practice steps one and three were not difficult, but the second step was. The classifier had to choose from a variety of citation orders, depending, of course, upon the work being classified.... Directions were correspondingly complex, and all of the above considerations had to be kept in mind as one solved the puzzle.[4]

Still, the Comaromi survey showed that 89% of the classifiers claimed to handle literature according to the prescribed method.[5] *DDC 19* polished up its instructions. As one reviewer says:

> *Table 3* has comprehensible instructions at last, and has sprouted a sub-table which appears to provide even more scope for synthesis than in DDC 18. It is intriguing to reflect that DDC still goes overboard for far more synthesis in the horribly named "belle-lettristic arts" than in any other area: is it really logical to be able to say "criticism of the treatment of gardens in 19th century French drama written in Belgium" but to be unable to say "employment services for the mentally ill"?[6]

The new features are introduced, together with examples of their application, in our chapter 5 discussion of Table 3. They will be examined in greater detail under centered heading 810-890 below. But first let us compare the two most recent divisional summaries. No change at all occurred in *DDC 19*.

Summary (*DDC 18*)		Summary (*DDC 19*)	
800	LITERATURE (BELLES-LETTRES)	800	LITERATURE (BELLES-LETTRES)
810	American literature in English	810	American literature in English
820	Literatures of English and Anglo-Saxon languages	820	Literatures of English and Anglo-Saxon languages
830	Literatures of Germanic (Teutonic) languages	830	Literatures of Germanic (Teutonic) languages

840	Literatures of Romance languages; French literature	840	Literatures of Romance languages; French literature
850	Literatures of Italian, Romanian, Rhaeto-Romanic languages	850	Literatures of Italian, Romanian, Rhaeto-Romanic languages
860	Literatures of Spanish and Portuguese languages	860	Literatures of Spanish and Portuguese languages
870	Literatures of Italic languages; Latin literature	870	Literatures of Italic languages; Latin literature
880	Literatures of Hellenic languages; Classical Greek literature	880	Literatures of Hellenic languages; Classical Greek literature
890	Literatures of other languages	890	Literatures of other languages

Division 800   Standard Subdivisions of Literatures in General; Rhetoric and Collections

The class opens with a full page of notes. The third note describes the basic pattern, and complements instructions in the Practical Guide to the Use of the Classification (v. 1, p. xxxvii). It replaces a now defunct illustrative table of synthesized numbers appended to the *DDC 18* schedule. The table of precedence for literary forms which follows is changed slightly to show consistent subordination under "Miscellaneous writings" with Table 3. The option note, like analogous ones for classes 200 and 400, is unrevised. A cross-classification note for folk literature and song texts is new.

Section 801 (Philosophy and theory) follows *DDC 18* exactly except for restoration of the initial "a" in "Aesthetics" and inclusion of "Parody" under Satire and humor.

Section 802 (Miscellany about literature) incorporates a Table 1 aspect "Procedures, apparatus, etc.," omitting "Techniques," which relocate to 808.

Sections 803-807 (Standard subdivisions of literature) represent the kind of redundant spelling out of Table 1 facets that was discussed under division 100 in chapter 7.

Section [804] is unassigned.

Section 808 (Rhetoric and collections) now houses all the "Prosody" materials relocated from sections [416], [426], etc. The definition of "Rhetoric" is expanded, as are other introductory notes, partly from *DC&*, v. 4, no. 1 (June 1980): 22, which also discontinues "Literature for learning rhetoric." Writing abstracts and summaries relocates here, though abstracting techniques is in 025.4 (Subject analysis and control). While this sacrifice to disciplinary integrity is plausible, it is the kind of split which disturbs strict subject constructionists like James Duff Brown. An option disappears at 808.066, while the Add note expands for greater clarity. A page and a half of extensions drop out under 808.801-.803 (Collections from various literatures displaying specific features), but there is no real notational change. The new auxiliary Table 3-A only slightly revises and generalizes those features. Similar schedule reductions are achieved at 808.81-.83, 808.85, and 808.89. A sample synthesis of 808.89973 (Literary collections for and by U.S. residents) can be studied on page 128.

Section 809 (History, description, critical appraisal of more than one literature) has a relocation from schedule to Table 3-A at 809.89 similar to that at 808.89.

Divisions 810-890   Literatures of Specific Languages

Like divisions 420-490 (Specific languages), this portion is so monolithic that it may be considered as a bloc. Eight notes, of which two are new, precede the instructions for building numbers (v. 2, pp. 1398-1400). The sixth note offers a new option, and the seventh warns that literature/language notation used in the 400's, the 800's, and Table 6 is not always identical. One of the 11 phoenix changes cited in v. 1, p. xxv is a relatively minor reduction of 879[.99] (Osco-Umbrian literatures).

Schedule instructions for building class numbers are identical with those given at the head of auxiliary Table 3. They offer a semi-programmed approach "which simplifies synthesis of numbers."[7] Still, technical writing is an art, not a science. The following, admittedly bulky program is offered as an alternative which may find favor with some users, or serve as a working paper for further flow charting.

Number Synthesis for Literatures of Specific Languages

These instructions cover only works in or about specific literatures or groups of literatures. For works in or about more than one literature or group, see the 800 division. It is understood that many libraries choose not to extend numbers to maximum expressivity. These instructions, although given in imperatives, may be applied with local discretion.

I.   Select the literature number for the work at hand, e.g., 810 (American literature in English).

    A.   Explore all 810-899 resources, including the Relative Index.

        1.   Note those literatures named in Inclusion notes, e.g., "Ainu" under 894.6 (Paleosiberian literatures). The group-of-literatures number under which each falls is its literature number.

        2.   Note references to Table 6, e.g., 895.95 (Munda literature).

    B.   If you must use, or if you prefer, a group-of-literatures number, do you choose the option in the sixth note under 810-890 (Literatures of specific langues) in v. 2, p. 1398?

        1.   If yes, add 04 and go to step IV.
            Examples: 891.604....   (Celtic literatures to be divided by Table 3)
                        896.04....   (African literatures to be divided by Table 3)

        2.   If no, go to step I. C.

C. Do you give local emphasis to a literature not emphasized in the schedule, e.g., to Canadian French literature?

1. If yes, choose your option before going to step II.

Option A: a. Class the preferred literature in 810.
   b. Class American literature in English in 820.
      Examples: 810 (Brazilian literature in Portuguese)
      810 (Breton literature)

Option B: a. Class the preferred literature ahead of 810 by interpolating a letter or other symbol in place of the second digit.
      Examples: 8A0 (Arabic [Australian] literature)
      8F0 (Finnish [French] literature)
   b. Use the first two symbols as base number.[8]
      Examples: 8A.... (Base for Arabic [Australian] literature)
      8F.... (Base for Finnish [French] literature)

Option C: Where two or more countries share the same language:
   C-1: Use initial letters to distinguish.
      Examples: C810   (Canadian literature in English)
      US810 (United States literature in English)
      A821   (Australian poetry in English)
      C842   (Canadian drama in French)
      M865   (Mexican speeches in Spanish)

   C-2: Use the appropriate bracketed number in the schedule.
      Examples: 819.1 (Canadian literature in English)
      819.3 (United States literature in English)
      828.99341 (Australian poetry in English)
      848.9922 (Canadian drama in French)
      868.99215 (Mexican speeches in Spanish)

2. If no, go to step II.

II.   Is a base number given for the literature of the work at hand?[9]
      Examples: 84....   (Base for French literature)
                    859....   (Base for Romanian literature)
                    895.4.... (Base for Tibetan literature)

      A.   If yes, retain it and go to step III.

      B.   If no, use the schedule number for the literature, or one synthesized
           from instructions, and go to step III.
           Examples: 869....   (Base for Portuguese literature)
                         894.83.... (Base for Brahui literature)
                         898.3....   (Base for the literatures of Andean-
                                     Equatorial languages)

III. Is the literature of the work at hand starred?[10]

      A.   If yes, go to step IV.
           Examples: 820   (Literatures of *English and Anglo-Saxon
                               languages)
                         829   (*Anglo-Saxon [Old English] literature)
                         839.83 (*New Norse [Landsmal, Nynorsk] literatures)
                         896.332 (*Ibo literature)

      B.   If no, do you wish to use a standard subdivision?

           1.   If yes, are there special instructions for Table 1 use?
                a.   If yes (e.g., at 891.43), add as instructed.
                     Examples: 891.43007   (Study and teaching of Western
                                               Hindi literatures)
                                   895.40025   (Directories of Tibeto-Burman
                                               literary societies)
                b.   If no, add the appropriate Table 1 facet to your base.
                     Examples: 892.603   (Concordances of Canaanite-
                                             Phoenician literatures)
                                   893.0285   (Data processing applications to the
                                              study of Hamitic and Chad
                                              literatures)

           2.   If no, your number is complete unless it requires a zero third
                digit.
                Examples: 840   (All works in and about the Romance
                                    languages)
                              859.9   (All works in and about the Rhaeto-
                                      Romanic literatures)

IV.   Is the work at hand concerned with more than one form by more than one
      author, i.e., does it fall under notations 01-09 in Table 3 (v. 1, p. 389)?

      A.   If it falls under *ss*-01-07, add the appropriate notation from Table 1
           to your base.
           Examples: 820.3   (Encyclopedic works about English literature)
                         895.805   (Burmese literary journals)
                         [optional]   896.071073   (Schools and courses in the
                                      United States on the literatures of all *African
                                      languages)

B. If it is a collection or anthology, add -08 to your base.

> *Examples*: [optional] 822.993608 (South African literature in English, and in more than one form, by more than one author)
>
> 896.39208 (Collections of Swahili literature in several literary forms and by several authors)

1. If it is a collection of American literature in English for or by persons resident in Hawaii, class in 810.8099 (Cf. v. 2, p. 1401).

2. Class here works giving equal attention to collections of literary texts and to history, description, critical appraisal of the specific literature.

> *Examples*: 839.208 (Frisian literature collections including texts, history, description, and critical appraisal)
>
> 895.9108 (Siamese literary texts in several forms, by several authors, balanced with history and description)

3. If you wish further subdivision, add -080 to your base and then add appropriate notations from Table 3-A.

   a. If your work is limited to a specific time period, i.e., if it falls under notations 01-09 in Table 3-A, go to step IX.

   b. If it displays specific features or subject values, add appropriate notations 1-4 to your base-plus-080 as instructed.

   > *Examples*: [optional] 810.8908041339 (Bermudan literary collections in English and in many forms, dealing with spiritualism)
   >
   > 820.8033 (Collections of English literature in many forms about holidays)
   >
   > 859.08012 (Collections of realistic Romanian literature)
   >
   > 870.803538 (Collections of Latin erotica)

   c. If it is for or by specific kinds of persons, add appropriate notations 8-9 to your base-plus-080 as instructed.

   > *Examples*: 840.80896 (Collections of French literature by Africans and persons of African descent)
   >
   > [optional] 863.99233080920544 (Anthologies of Spanish literature from the Dominican Republic, designed for use in the elementary schools)

4. If it is history and description of a subject among groups of persons, go to step IV. C. 3.

5. If it is a collection by an individual author, go to step V. D.

C.   If it is about works of more than one form by more than one author, add -09 to your base.
Examples: 839.709   (Collected biography of Swedish authors from more than one period)
839.709
894.81109   (History, description, critical appraisal of Tamil literature)

1.   If it is limited to a specific time period, i.e., if it falls under notations -09001-09009 in Table 3, go to step IX.

2.   If it is history, description, critical appraisal of American literature in English for or by persons resident in Hawaii, class in 810.999 (Cf. v. 2, p. 1401).

3.   If it concerns specific features or subject values, add appropriate notations 1-4 from Table 3-A to your base-plus-09 as instructed.
Examples: 830.9351   (History and descriptive appraisal of German literature on Faust)
840.9142   (History of classicism in French literature)
870.93538   (Critical appraisal of Latin erotica)
895.10942   (History and criticism of Chinese religious works as literature)

4.   If it concerns specific kinds of persons, add appropriate notations 8-9 from Table 3-A to your base-plus-09 as instructed.
Examples: [optional] 868.9923109920824   (Descriptive analysis of Cuban Spanish literature written for and by emotionally disturbed persons)
889.098895   (History and criticism of modern Greek literature written for or by Cypriots)
895.7099287   (History and description of Korean literature written by women)

V.   Is the work at hand in or about a specific literary form, i.e., does it fall under notations -1-8 in Table 3?
Examples: 821   (English poetry)
839.312   (Dutch drama)

A.   If it is in or about a specific kind of literary form, go to step VIII.
Examples: 821.01....   (Dramatic English peotry)
891.4420527....   (Bengali melodrama)
891.992807   (Collections and/or critical treatment of nonformalized Albanian works from more than one period) Cf. step VI. B.

B.   If it is a comprehensive work relating to the form, add the appropriate form digit to your base.
Examples: 839.364   (Comprehensive works relating to Afrikaans essays)
891.76   (Comprehensive works relating to Russian letters)

C. Is it description, critical appraisal, biography, or single or collected works of an individual author?

   1. If the author is William Shakespeare, see the optional arrangement in the schedule under 822.33.

   2. If you choose the option to class all works by and about individual authors regardless of form under -8 (Miscellaneous writings), go to step VI.[11]

   3. If you follow recommended DDC practice, go to step VII. F.

VI. Is the work at hand in the form of miscellaneous writings, i.e., does it fall under notation -8 in Table 3?
   Examples: 848   (Miscellaneous writings in French)
      892.48   (Miscellaneous writings in Hebrew)
      [optional]   897.8   (Miscellaneous writings in North American native languages)

   A. If a standard subdivision applies, i.e., if it falls under notations -8001-8009, add to your base as instructed.
      Examples: 818.007154   (Correspondence courses on miscellaneous writings in American English)
         828.0016   (Indexes to miscellaneous English writings)
         839.48009896   (Critical appraisal by Africans of miscellaneous writings in Plattdeutsch from more than one period)
         891.798008091734   (Collections of miscellaneous writings by rural Ukrainians)

   B. If it is history, description, critical appraisal, biography, or collections of specific kinds of works of authors from more than one period, add appropriate notations -802-808 without further subdivision to your base.
      Examples: 828.02   (Collections of English quotations from more than one period)
         891.5803   (Histories of Iranian diary-keeping through many periods)
         891.799807   (Critical appraisals of Belorussian jokes)
         891.819808   (Anthologies of miscellaneous prose literature forms in Macedonian)
         891.87808   (Collected biography of Slovak prose writers in many forms)

   C. Class individual authors of all periods who are not limited to or chiefly identified with one specific form in -8.
      Examples: [optional] 848.999621108 (Works by or about a French-language Tahitian author of any period, and not identified with any one literary form)
         891.648 (Individual Manx authors of any period, not identified with any specific form of literature)

   D. If it is limited to a particular time period, go to step IX.

E. It is optional to class here description, critical appraisal, biography, single and collected works of all individual authors regardless of form; prefer step VII. F.[12]

Examples: 828   (Spenser's *Faerie Queene*)
            828   (Critical biographies of Spenser)
            848   (Balzac's *La cousine Bette*)
            848   (Collections of Balzac's shorter novels)

VII. Is the work at hand in or about a specific literary form, but not a specific kind-of-form, i.e., does it fall without further form subdivision under notations -1-7 in Table 3?[13]

Examples: 813   (American fiction in English)[14]
            889.2   (Drama in modern Greek)

A. If it combines two or more literary forms, see the table of precedence under -1-8 (Specific forms), v. 1, p. 390.

Examples: 822....   (English poetic drama)
            843....   (French fiction in the form of a letter exchange)

B. If it is a comprehensive work relative to the form, add the appropriate form digit to your base without further subdivision.

Examples: 831   (Comprehensive works relative to German poetry)
            892.45   (Comprehensive works relative to Hebrew speeches)

C. If it falls under notations -x001-x007 (Standard subdivisions of specific forms), add to your base-plus-form from Table 1 as instructed under -1001-1007, v. 1, p. 391.

Examples: 839.3250016   (Indexes to Flemish speeches)
            842.00202   (Synopses of French plays)
            849.7003   (Dictionaries for use with Provençal satire and humor)
            895.81005   (Burmese poetry journals)

D. If it is a collection or anthology of the form by more than one author from more than one period, add -x008 to your base-plus-form and then add appropriate notations 1-9 from Table 3-A, as instructed under -1008 in v. 1, p. 391.

Examples: 821.0080356   (Collections of English poetry on scientific or technical themes)
            822.008091734   (Collections of English drama by rural authors)
            [optional]   828.99364008   (English essays by South Africans)
            839.2600809275   (Anthologies of letters by Frisian painters)
            844.0080358   (Collections of French essays about war)

E. If it is history, description, critical appraisal of writings in the form, or of authors associated with the form, from more than one period, add -x009 to your base-plus-form, and then add appropriate notations from Table 3-A, as instructed under -1009 in v. 1, p. 391.

Examples: 821.00915 (History of symbolism, allegory, and fantasy in English poetry)
            849.94009952 (Critical appraisal by persons resident in Japan of Catalan essays of more than one period)
            881.009 (Collected biography of classical Greek poets)

F. If it is description, critical appraisal, biography, single or collected works of an individual author chiefly identified with one literary form, add the appropriate form digit to your base and go to step IX (Cf. step V. C.).
    Examples: 821.... (Spenser's *Faerie Queene*)
                821.... (Critical biographies of Spenser)
                843.... (Balzac's *La cousine Bette*)
                843.... (Collections of Balzac's shorter novels)

G. If it represents a specific kind or type of literary form, go to step VIII.

VIII. Is the work at hand limited to a specific kind of literary form, i.e., does it fall under -102-108, -202-205, -301-308, or -501-506 in Table 3?
    Examples: 811.07 (Satirical and humorous poetry in American English by more than one author regardless of period)
           891.5520516 (Farsi religious and morality plays by more than one author from more than one period)

A. If it is a work by or about an individual author, return to step V. C.

B. Is the specific kind-of-form starred?

    1. If yes, add notations 01-09 from the table under centered heading -1-8 in Table 3 (v. 1, p. 390).

        a. If it falls under *ss*-01-07, add the appropriate notations from Table 1 to your base-plus-type-of-form.
            Examples: 821.03016 (Indexes to English narrative, including epic, poetry)
                      832.0205 (Serial publications devoted to German radio and television drama)
                      891.6650107073 (Works on the study and teaching in the United States of Welsh oratory)

        b. If it is a collection by more than one author regardless of period, add 08 to your base-plus-kind-of-form, and then add appropriate notations 1-9 from Table 3-A.
            Examples: 822.04108896 (One-act plays in English by Africans)
                      831.04408 (Collections of German ballads from all periods)
                      831.04408 (Anthologies of German ballads giving equal attention to texts and to critical appraisal)

831.0440832 (Collections of German ballads
dealing with places)
896.33330108 (Yoruba short story collections)

c. If it is history, description, or critical appraisal of more than
one author regardless of period, add 09 to your base-plus-
kind-of-form, and then add appropriate notations 1-9 from
Table 3-A.
Examples: 821.04209 (Histories of the sonnet form in
English)
839.8210509 (Biographies of didactic Norwegian poets)
894.5112045099282 (Critical appraisal of
dramatic monologues by
Hungarian children)

2. If the specific kind-of-form is not starred, add the appropriate
notation to your base without further subdivision.
Examples: 812.04 (American English drama of restricted
scope by various authors regardless of
period)
[optional] S822.05 (Specific kinds of drama in
English by Scotch authors of various periods)
839.7308 (Specific types of fiction by Swedish
authors of any and all periods)

C. Do not subdivide specific kinds or types of literary forms
chronologically.
Examples: 821.04 (English lyric poetry of the Elizabethan period)
821.04 (Nineteenth-century English lyric poetry)
895.1506 (Chinese collections of Middle Epoch
conversations)

D. If the work falls under -1-7 (Specific literary forms) rather than
under a specific kind-of-form, return to step VII.

E. If it falls under -8 (Miscellaneous writings), return to step VI.

IX. Is the work at hand limited to a particular time period?

A. Is there a period table in the schedule for the literature? See, for
instance, the period table for Modern Icelandic under 839.69.

1. If yes, can the table be used?[15]

a. If yes, go to step IX. B.

b. If no, your base-plus-standard subdivision, or base-plus-
form number is complete.[16]
Examples: 822 (Twentieth-century English drama by
New Zealanders)
861.016 (Indexes to nineteenth-century Spanish poetry by Chileans)
869.4 (Brazilian essays in Portuguese from
the late eighteenth century)

891.43007 (Study and teaching of Western Hindi literatures of the eighteenth century)

2. If no, your base-plus-standard-subdivision, or base-plus-form number is complete.
   Examples: 891.8195 (Macedonian speeches from the renaissance period, ca. 1550-1700)
   892.8025 (Directories of post-World War II Ethiopic literary societies)
   893.0285 (Data processing applications to the study of post-1945 Hamitic and Chad literatures)
   894.55808 (Twentieth-century Lapp prose literature)[17]

B. Is the work at hand in or about more than one form of a specific literature of a given period?

1. If it is a collection by more than one author, add -080 to your base, and then add the appropriate digits for the period (cf. notations 01-09 from Table 3-A).
   Examples: 820.80091 (Collections of twentieth-century English literature)
   [optional] A820.8003 (Collections of later twentieth-century Australian writings in English)
   891.8108001 (Collections of pre-1850 Bulgarian literature in many forms by many authors)

2. If it is history, description, critical appraisal of more than one author, add -0900 (Literature from specific periods) and then add the appropriate period notation for the literature.
   Examples: 810.9003 (Canadian English literary history of the colonial period to 1867)
   839.709002 (Collected biography of Swedish authors of the Reformation, 1520-1640)
   894.81109005 (History, description, critical appraisal of early twentieth-century Tamil literature, 1895-1920)

C. Is the work by or about an individual author?

1. If you prefer the option under -8 (v. 1, p. 396), go to step IX. E.

2. If you follow recommended DDC practice, go to step IX. D.

D. If the work relates to a specific literary form of a specific period, i.e., if it falls under notations -11-19, -21-29, -31-39, -41-49, -51-59, -61-69, or -71-79 in Table 3, add the appropriate period digits to your base-plus-form number.
   Examples: 813.5 (Twentieth-century Canadian fiction in English)
   821.3 (Elizabethan English poetry)

    842.914 (Post-1945 French drama in France)
    [optional] B842.34 (Post-1945 French drama in
    Belgium)
    894.54552 (Post-1861 Estonian speeches)

1. If it is by or about an individual author who is chiefly identified with one form, your number is complete.
    Examples: 821.3 (Spenser's *Faerie Queene*)
              821.3 (Critical biographies of Spenser)
              843.7 (Balzac's *La cousine Bette*)
              843.7 (Collections of Balzac's shorter novels)

2. If it is by or about more than one author associated with one form and one period, and can be extended with standard subdivisions, add the appropriate numbers following -10 in -1001-1009 (v. 1, p. 391) to your base-plus-form-plus-period number.
    Examples: 821.309 (History, description, critical appraisal
                       of Elizabethan English poetry)
              821.30913 (Critical appraisal of idealism in
                       Elizabethan poetry)
              821.9108 (Collections of twentieth-century
                       English poetry)
              821.91080351 (Collections of twentieth-century
                       English poetry about individuals,
                       e.g., King Arthur)

E. If the work falls among miscellaneous writings of specific periods, i.e., under -81-89 in Table 3, add -8 to your base, and then add appropriate notations from the correct period table.
    Examples: [optional] A868.44 (Miscellaneous post-1945 Span-
              ish literature from one or more American countries)
              868.64 (Miscellaneous post-1945 Spanish literature
                    from Spain)
              895.185 (Miscellaneous twentieth-century Chinese
                    literature)

1. If it is by or about an individual author, add further appropriate notation 01-09 from the table under -81-89 (v. 1, pp. 397-98) without further subdivision.
    Examples: 818.108 (Critical appraisal of miscellaneous prose
                    writings in English by a colonial Mary-
                    land writer)
              828.403 (Critical appraisals of Pepys' *Diary*)
              858.702 (Quotations from an early nineteenth-
                    century Italian writer using miscellaneous
                    literary forms)
              [optional] M868.307 (An experimental work of
                    unidentifiable form, in Spanish, by a Mexican
                    writing from 1888 to 1910)
              894.838709 (Biographies of a contemporary
                    Brahui writer not limited to or
                    identified with one specific form)

2. If it is by or about more than one author, add appropriate notation -020-080 from the table to your base-plus-form-plus-period number, and then add further from the notation following -100 in -1001-1009 (v. 1, p. 391).

    Examples: [optional]   C818.540705   (Serial publications devoted to contemporary experimental Canadian works in English)

    828.403080478   (Collections of post-Elizabethan journals and reminiscences in English written primarily for musicians)

    838.91407079   (Surveys of upcoming competitions, awards, prizes, etc., for experimental literary works in German)

    [optional]   Co868.4407080358   (Collections of jokes about political themes by post-1945 Colombian writers in Spanish)

    891.86850708025   (Anthologies of contemporary Czech stream-of-consciousness writings)

    895.6810808   (Collections of Japanese prose literature by more than one author living between 1185 and 1603)

Conclusion

Apart from the major bodies of sacred scripture, as was noted in chapter 8, the only literary collections specifically classed in *DDC 19* are the works of William Shakespeare (822.33), the Anglo-Saxon poets Caedmon and Cynewolf, and the epic *Beowulf* (all in section 829). A similar abstention from subject classifying in what DDC calls belles-lettres has long been an article of faith, to underscore their aesthetic function.

> In class 8, subject is disregarded for works of literature (belles-lettres), e.g. a play about Julius Caesar and Roman history is a piece of imaginative literature, and belongs in the appropriate part of 800 instead of under history or biography. Arrangement of individual works of belles-lettres is first by the discipline literature, then by original language, then by literary form, then by period of composition.[18]

Nevertheless, Table 3-A, once we get past its introductory 01-09 chronological span, is by and large a subject faceting tool. It travels so far in the rear of the number building process that most classifiers never get to it. Still, its topical presence and purpose are emphasized by the *DDC 19* format. Rules are written so that it applies to collections and general criticism rather than to single works or individual authors, but it does make subject content a part of literary classification.

A frequently mentioned 800's problem is the scattering of works by and about single authors.[19] A guiding principle confines most single-author numbers to relatively broad configurations reflecting, along with literature and period, the "form with which he [i.e., the author] is chiefly identified."[20] Facet -8 (Miscellaneous writings) in Table 3 raises dubious intricacies with its topsy-turvy number building. As lines of formal differentiation blur, the demand for precise placement intensifies. Its fourth, kind-of-form, facet is not new. We saw similar development under poetry, drama, fiction, and speeches. But these specifics have an inverted relationship to period faceting. And a "non-specific prose literature" facet -8x08 (where x stands for period) is supplied for description, criticism, and collected works of individual authors, although individual works of identifiable form, not to mention "description, critical appraisal, biography," are remanded, presumably for those same authors, to the form "with which he [the author] is chiefly identified," as we saw above. The disarray is compounded by a -8x09 facet, but it claims at least to apply only to works by and about "authors not limited to or chiefly identified with one specific form."[21]

Pitfalls of synthesis and the opacity of the instructions are nearly all traceable to these mysteries. They are also affected by implicit assumptions about literary form. The fault is of course not entirely that of the DDC editors. Art, as we well know, defies definition. So long as artists, including literary artists, strive for new vision and new modes of expression, classes 700 and 800 will be hard put to provide simple, logical, universally accepted typologies.

Exercises in the Use of Class 800

A. Analysis

808'.0461'75	Cuban consciousness in literature, 1923-1974 : a critical anthology of Cuban culture ... 1978.	78-53265
808.8'004	In the wake of the wake / edited by David Hayman and Elliott Anderson ... 1978. [Joyce's influence on modern literature]	78-53285
809'.933'51	McConnell, Winder. The Wate figure in medieval tradition ... c1978.	78-325555
811'.54	Hamilton, Randi. Eula, a southern story and collected poems ... c1979.	79-92565
812'.5'4	Durang, Christopher. A history of the American film ... 1978.	78-53965
813'.5'2	Eberhard, Mignon Good. Nine o'clock tide ... 1979, c1977.	79-13136
814'.5'408	The Human elements . critical essays / edited by David Helwig ... c1978. [On Canadian literature in both French and English]	79-308089
820'.8'0091	The Bell House book : celebrating sixty years of a literary agency, 1919-1979 ... 1979.	79-308051
820'.9'00912	Muir, Edwin. The present age from 1914 ... 1978.	78-18714
821'.008'0356	The Poetry of railways / edited by Samuel Carr ... 1978.	79-306039

821'.009'15	Steadman, John M. Nature into myth : medieval and Renaissance moral symbols ... c1979.	77-25397
821'.3'09354	Mayr, Roswitha. The concept of love in Sidney and Spenser ... 1978.	79-303630
821'.9'1080351	A Selection from Poems for Shakespeare, volumes 1 to 6, with original drawings / edited by Roger Pringle ... 1978.	79-308152
823'.8	Dickens, Hard times, Great expectations, and Our mutual friend : a casebook / edited by Norman Page ... 1979.	80-456036
823'.9'109	Trivialliteratur / Hrsg., Hans-Jürgen Diller ... et al.] ... 1977.	79-364700
828'.9'1407	Brandreth, Gyles Daubeney. A joke-a-day book ... c1979.	78-66298
830'.8'094355	Autoren in Nordrhein-Westfalen : [bio.-bibliograf. Daten, Fotos u. Texte / hrsg. von Hugo Ernst Kaufer ...] 1974-1977.	76-516388
832'.009'351	Fiesser, Wilhelm. Christus-Motive in Revolutions-dramen ... 1977.	79-347732
832'.6'09352	Lea, Charlene A. Emancipation, assimilation and stereotype : the image of the Jew in German and Austrian drama (1800-1850) ... 1978.	79-305499
840'.9'001	Di Stefano, Giuseppe. Essais sur le moyen français ... 1977.	79-346842
842'.4'0917	Greene, Edward Joseph Hollingsworth. Menander to Marivaux : the history of a comic structure ... 1977.	79-306284
843'.914	Drucker, Michel. La chaîne : roman ... c1979.	80-452138
848'.8'07	Tulou, François, b. 1848. Mille et un calembours ... 1978.	79-348718
848'.91'407	Drachline, Pierre. De l'apprentissage du dégoût ... c1979.	80-452316
871'.04'08	Renaissance Latin verse : an anthology / compiled and edited by Alessandro Perosa and John Sparrow ... 1979.	78-10969
891.7'08'0044	Straight from the heart / [translated from the Russian ; compiled by I. Sobolev ...] c1977.	79-350836
891.8'2'104	Rootham, Helen, tr. Kossovo, heroic songs of the Serbs / translated from the original ... 1979.	78-74518
895.1'1'2	Ku shih shih chiu shou. The nineteen ancient poems / translated and with an introd. by ... 1977.	79-100429
895.6'1'008'0354	Japanese love poems / translated by Howard S. Levy ... 1977-1980.	78-670065
895.9'2'21008	The Heritage of Vietnamese poetry / edited and translated by Huỳnh Sanh Thông ... 1979.	78-17092

B.   Synthesis: Examples from LC records are given on pp. 303-307.

1.   A book of ballads from the Kentucky highlands.

2.   An anthology of Latin poetry from 350-600 A.D. translated into English, with critical notes.

3.   An anthology of Petrarch's poetry translated by English poets from Sir Thomas Wyatt to John Milton.

4.   An anthology of twentieth-century Irish literature in English from the files of the literary agent John Farquharson, Ltd.

5.   The diaries of Bertolt Brecht from 1920 to 1922.

6.   Early English poems from the Pearl manuscript, including *Sir Gawain and the Green Knight*, recently edited by Malcolm Andrew and Ronald Waldron.

7.   A selection of American poems for nature lovers.

8.   Essays by Walter Pater devoted to history and criticism of English literature.

9.   A guide to critical theory and practice of English composition and rhetoric.

10.   A study of the Deirdre legend as handled in Anglo-Irish literature.

11.   Selections from classical Sanskrit literature, accompanied by English translations and critical notes.

12.   Studies of rural scenery and society as depicted in English poetry from 1630.

13.   Biography, history, and criticism of the nineteenth-century French symbolist poets.

14.   A study of Charles Churchill and other satirical English poets from 1750 to 1800.

15.   A collection of medieval middle high German lyric poetry in English translation.

16.   An anthology of twentieth-century American and English poetry.

17.   A collection of English translations of Oriental poetry.

18.   Poems in English by seven Irish poets coming after William Butler Yeats.

19.   The Sanskrit plays of the early twentieth-century author V. Krishnan Tampy, with introductory matter in English.

20.   An anthology of English war poetry from 1914 to 1918.

21.   A handbook by Robert Graves on English prose composition.

22.   An anthology of post-1945 Irish poetry in English.

23.   An anthology of twentieth-century French poetry.

24. A memorial volume of 7 poems by the twentieth-century British poet Andrew Young, plus 13 poems by admirers in homage to him.

25. A historical and critical study of German literature during the period from 1688 to 1789.

26. Interpretative essays on nineteenth- and twentieth-century English and American poetry.

27. An anthology of twentieth-century regional and German dialect literature from Germany, Switzerland, and Austria.

28. A study of humor in late eighteenth- and early nineteenth-century English poetry.

29. A series of essays on Italian literature of the thirteenth and fourteenth centuries.

30. An anthology of English and American poetry.

31. A study of the Spanish picaresque novel *La vida de Lazarillo de Tormes*, first published around 1553.

32. A critical and interpretative study of the Welsh poet Dylan Thomas.

33. A collection of translations by Ezra Pound from more than one literature.

34. A book about the influence of the classics on Matthew Arnold's poetry.

35. A comparative study of French and English poetry.

36. A post-1945 collection of English poetry by Irish authors.

37. An investigation into themes of social isolation and exclusion in medieval European literatures.

38. A collection of twentieth-century Welsh poetry in English.

39. The writings of a twentieth-century critic of Chinese literature.

40. Italian studies of three English poets killed in World War I.

41. A study of poetic structure in English and American poetry.

42. A study of tradition and experiment in English poetry.

43. An anthology of twentieth-century Catalan poetry.

44. An examination of the romantic self in Victorian English prose literature.

45. Short stories by the nineteenth-century New Englanders Sarah Orne Jewett and Mary Wilkins Freeman.

46. Feminist essays on English and American women poets.

47. A study of the eighteenth-century French novel *Les liaiasons dangereuses*, by Laclos.

48. A French look at English drama from 1660 to 1800.

49. A semi-classic early twentieth-century American western novel.

50. A critical study of the Victorian English novelist George Meredith.

51. A collection of French satire about post-1945 election promises.

52. A critical study of the plays of the post-1945 British writer Edward Bond.

53. A study of class consciousness in English novels from Walter Scott to David Storey.

54. A bio-critical review of the early twentieth-century Swiss-French novelist, poet, and librettist for Stravinsky's *Une Histoire du Soldat*, Charles Ferdinand Ramuz.

55. A new edition of Charles Dickens' *A Christmas Carol*.

56. A comparative study of the early twentieth-century British novelists John Cowper Powys and David Jones.

57. A collection of William S. Merwin's translations of foreign-language poetry into English.

58. A thematic anthology of French-Canadian drama of the nineteenth century.

59. An anthology of Canadian English poetry and English translations of French-Canadian poetry.

60. Teaching outlines and study notes on twentieth-century French-Canadian literature.

61. A history of French literature from 1940 to 1978.

62. A collection of fiction in French from the Franche-Comté region.

63. A study of the Don Juan motif in seventeenth-century French and Italian drama.

64. A critical examination of twentieth-century French drama and theatre.

65. An anthology of French wit and humor.

66. A collection of twentieth-century French science fiction.

67. Studies of eighteenth-century French literature.

68. A review of the terminology of love in literature.

69. Studies of the nineteenth-century French writer Stendhal, and of the twentieth-century French writer Proust.

70. A collection of famous English poems with biographical notes of the authors and aids for interpretation.

71. English translations of the twentieth-century Chinese poet T. C. Lai's flower and tree poetry.

C. Reclassification: Suggested solutions are offered on page 307.

1. 809'.933'1   Ivasheva, Valentine Vasil'evna. On the threshold
   of the twenty-first century : the technological
   revolution and literature ... c1978.   79-304351

2. 821'.5'07   Nicolson, Marjorie Hope. Newton demands the muse :
   Newton's Opticks and the eighteenth century poets
   ... 1979, c1946.   78-13146

3. 831'.008'031 Bräutigam, Kurt. Zugänge zum sozialkritischen
   und politischen Gedicht ; e. didakt. Einf. mit
   Modellinterpretationen für d. Sekundarstufe ...
   1977. [History and criticism of German political
   poetry]   79-362358

4. 840   Écrits louisianais du dix-neuvième siècle : nouvelles,
   contes et fables ... c1979. [Afro-American tales and
   other French-American literature from 19th century
   Louisiana]   78-24295

5. 842'.009   Borgerhoff, Joseph Leopold. Nineteenth century French
   plays / edited by ... 1978, c1933.   77-27470

6. 843'.03   Turnell, Martin. The rise of the French novel :
   Marivaux, Crèbillon fils, Rousseau, Stendhal, Flaubert,
   Alain-Fournier, Raymond Radiguet ... c1978.   77-26792

**Examples of LC Cataloging to Illustrate the Above Exercises in
DDC Number Building**

B. Synthesis

1. 811'.04   Fuson, Henry Harvey. Ballads of the Kentucky
   highlands ... 1977.   77-19283

2. 871'01   Lindsay, Jack. Song of a falling world : culture during
   the break-up of the Roman Empire (A.D. 350-600)
   ... 1979.   78-59028

3. 851'.1   Petrarch in England : an anthology of parallel texts from
   Wyatt to Milton / edited with an introduction ...
   1979.   79-306515

4. 820'.8'0091 The Best from the Bell : great Irish writing / edited
   by Sean McMahon ... 1979.   79-112295

5. 838'.9'1203 Brecht, Bertolt. Diaries 1920-1922 ... c1979.   78-21345

6. 821'.1   British Museum. Manuscript. (Cottonian Nero A. x)
   The poems of the Pearl manuscript : Pearl, Cleanness,
   Patience, Sir Gawain and the Green Knight / edited
   by ... 1979, c1978.   78-64464

7. 811'.008'036 Grover, Edwin Osgood. The nature lover's knapsack :
   an anthology of poems for lovers of the open road
   ... 1979.   78-73488

8. 820'.9   Pater, Walter Horatio. Appreciations, with an essay on
   style ... 1978.   78-27473

9. 808'.042   Watson, George. The discipline of English : a guide to
                  critical theory and practice ... 1979.   78-12695

10. 820.9'351   Fackler, Herbert V. That tragic queen : the Deirdre
                  Legend in Anglo-Irish literature ... 1978.   79-307824

11. 891'.2'08   Brough, John. Selections from classical Sanskrit liter-
                  ature / with English translation and notes by ... 1978.   79-345809

12. 821'.4'09321734 Turner, James G. The politics of landscape :
                  rural scenery and society in English poetry
                  1630-1660 ... c1979.   78-11027
                                                                             79-306778

13. 841'.009'15   Richard, Noël. Profils symbolistes ... 1978.   79-347540

14. 821'.6'09   Lockwood, Thomas. Post-Augustan satire : Charles
                  Churchill and satirical poetry, 1750-1800 ... c1979.   78-4366

15. 831'.2'08   Thomas, John Wesley. Medieval German lyric verse in
                  English translation ... 1978.   78-27834

16. 821'.9'1208   Mikels, Rosa Mary Redding. Poetry of to-day : an
                  anthology ... 1979.   78-73491

17. 890   The Elek book of Oriental verse / general editor
                  Keith Bosley ... 1979.   79-313822

18. 821'.9'1208   Irish poetry after Yeats : seven poets / Austin
                  Clarke ... [et al.]; edited by ... 1979.   79-308056

19. 891'.2'2   Krsnantampi, Vataśśeri, 1890-1938. Sanskrit plays of
                  V. Krishnan Tampy / edited by N. P. Unni ... 1977.   78-900957

20. 821'.9'1208035 Gardner, Brian. Up the line to death : the war
                  poets, 1914-1918 : an anthology ... 2nd ed.
                  ... 1978.   79-303629

21. 808'.042   Graves, Robert. The reader over your shoulder : a hand-
                  book for writers of English prose ... 2d ed., rev.
                  ... 1979.   78-21368

22. 821'9'1408   Castle poets. -- Limerick : Limerick Poetry Circle,
                  1977-   79-306629

23. 841'.9'108   Belloc, Gabriel. Les chemins de la poésie française
                  au XXe [i.e. vingtième] siècle ... c1978.   79-357954

24. 821'.9'108   Andrew Young, remembrance & homage / compiled and
                  introduced by Leslie Norris ... 1978.   78-575150

25. 830'.9'005   Wilke, Jürgen. Literarische Zeitschriften des 18.
                  Jahrhunderts : (1688-1789) ... 1978-   79-364070

26. 821'.009   San Juan, Epifanio. Poetics : the imitation of action
                  : essays in interpretation ... c1979.   78-4345

27. 830'.8'00914 Literatur im alemannischen Raum : Regionalismus u
                  Dialekt / hrsg. von Jochen Kelter ... 1978.   79-363111

28. 821'.7'0917   Storey, Mark. Poetry and humour from Cowper to
                  Clough ... 1979.   78-23875

29. 850'.9'001   Buck, August. Studien zu den "Volgarizzamenti" römischer Autoren in der italienischen Literatur des 13. und 14. Jahrhunderts ... 1978.   78-396223

30. 821'.008   Zeitlin, Jacob. Types of poetry ... 1979.   78-57868

31. 863'.3   Sieber, Harry. Language and society in *La vida de Lazarillo de Tormes* ... c1978.   78-8425

32. 821'.912   Davies, Aneirin Talfan. Dylan, druid of the broken body ... New ed. ... 1977.   79-302549

33. 808.8   Pound, Ezra Loomis. Translations / Ezra Pound ; with an introd. by Hugh Kenner ... 1978, c 1963.   78-13153

34. 821'.8   Houghton, Ralph Edward Cunliffe. The influence of the classics on the poetry of Matthew Arnold ... 1977.   77-28050

35. 809.1   Stewart, Jean Margaret. Poetry in France and England ... 1978.   78-2182

36. 821'.9'1408   Poetry of the Cuchulainn country / edited by Donal Ó Cathasaigh ... 1978.   79-304444

37. 809'.02   Exclus et systèmes d'exclusion dans la littérature et la civilisation médiévales ... 1978.   79-339289

38. 821'.9'108   Rhys, Keidrych, ed. Modern Welsh poetry ... 1979.   78-73499

39. 895'.1'09005   Ragvald, Lars. Yao Wenyuan as a literary critic and theorist : the emergence of Chinese Zhdanovism ... 1978.   78-398757

40. 821'.9'1209   Mullini Zanarini, Roberta. Killed in action : saggi sulla poesia di Wilfred Owen, Edward Thomas e Isaac Rosenberg ... 1977.   79-357553

41. 808.1   Lawlor, Justus George. Celestial pantomime : poetic structures of transcendence ... 1979.   78-21964

42. 821'.009   Hobsbaum, Philip. Tradition and experiment in English poetry ... 1979.   79-308080

43. 849'.9'15   Modern Catalan poetry : an anthology : poems / selected and translated from the Catalan by ... 1979.   78-71541

44. 820'.9'007   Interspace and the inward sphere : essays on Romantic and Victorian self / edited by ... c1978.   78-58247

45. 813'.01   Short fiction of Sarah Orne Jewett and Mary Wilkins Freeman : including The country of the pointed firs / edited and with an introd. by ... c1979.   79-84605

46. 821'.009   Shakespeare's sisters : feminist essays on women poets / edited, with an introd. by ... c1979.   78-9510

47. 843'.6   Rosbottom, Ronald C. Choderlos de Laclos ... 1978.   78-18722

48. 822'.009   Dulck, Jean. Le théâtre anglais de 1660 [i.e. seize cent soixante] à 1800 [i.e. dix-huit cent] ... c1979.   80-464351

49. 813'.5'2   Guthrie, A. B. (Alfred Bertram) These thousand hills / A. B. Guthrie, jr. ; with a new introd. by ... 1978.   79-16716

50. 823'.8	Peel, Robert. The creed of a Victorian pagan ... 1978, c1931.	78-1327
51. 848'.91402	Halimi, André. Demain on rase gratis : 25 ans de pro-messes électorales ... c1978.	80-463047
52. 822'.914	Donahue, Delia. Edward Bond : a study of his plays ... c1979.	80-452583
53. 823'.009'355	Eagleton, Mary. Attitudes to class in the English novel from Walter Scott to David Storey ... c1979.	80-451200
54. 848'.91209	Dunoyer, Jean Marie. C. F. Ramuz, peinture vaudois ... 1978.	79-125694
55. 823'.8 [Fic]	Dickens, Charles. A Christmas carol : in prose, being a ghost story of Christmas ... 1979.	79-65390
56. 823'.9'12	Hooker, Jeremy. John Cowper Powys and David Jones : a comparative study ... 1978.	79-313827
57. 808.81	Merwin, W. S. (William Stanley). Selected translations, 1968-1978 ... 1979.	78-55021
58. 842	Anthologie thématique du théâtre québécois au XIXe siècle [compilée par] Étienne-F. Duval ... c1978.	79-353731
59. 808.81	The Poets of Canada / edited by John Robert Colombo ... c1978.	79-304944
60. 840.9	Writers' Development Trust. Quebec Work Group. Quebec literature ... 197-?	79-304437
61. 840'.9'0091	Brenner, Jacques. Histoire de la littérature française : de 1940 à nos jours ... 1978.	79-359978
62. 843'.008	Contes et nouvelles du pays contois / [textes choisis et présentés par Daniel Bouvier] ... 19	79-352631
63. 809'.933'51	Spaziani, Marcello. Don Giovanni dagli scenari dell' arte alla foire : quattro studi con due testi forains inediti e altri testi italiani e francesi ... 1978.	79-355533
64. 842'.9'109	Simon, Alfred. Le théâtre à bout de souffle? ... c1979.	79-358913
65. 847'.008	Guillois, Mina. Encyclopédie des bonnes histoires ... c1978.	79-351176
66. 843'.0876	La France fantastique 1900 [i.e. dix-neuf cent] : choix de textes / [présenté par] ... 1978.	79-349687
67. 840'.9'005	Studies in the French eighteenth century : presented to John Lough by colleagues, pupils ... 1978.	79-306395
68. 809'.933'54	Barthes, Roland. Fragments d'un discours amoureux ... c1977.	77-482684
69. 843'.009	Vigneron, Robert. Études sur Stendhal et sur Proust ... 1978.	79-345766
70. 821'.008	Barbe, Waitman. Famous poems explained : helps to reading with the understanding, with biographical notes of the authors represented ... 1979.	78-73480

71. 895.1'1'5   Lai, T'ien-ch'ang. Noble fragrance : Chinese flowers
                & trees / T. C. Lai ... c1977.   78-106334

C. Reclassification: Suggested *DDC 19* numbers for certain LC cataloging
records.

   1. 809.93356 Ivasheva ...

   2. 821.509 Nicolson ...

   3. 831.0080358 Bräutigam ...

   4. 840.9763 Écrits louisianais ...

   5. 842.709 Borgerhoff ...

   6. 843 Turnell ...

NOTES

[1]David C. Batty, "Library Classification One Hundred Years after Dewey," *Major Classification Systems: The Dewey Centennial* (Urbana-Champaign, IL, University of Illinois Graduate School of Library Science, 1976), p. 3. The cited passage in this text is on page 212.

[2]Lois Mai Chan, "The Form Distinction in the 800 Class of the Dewey Decimal Scheme," *Library Resources & Technical Services*, v. 15, no. 4 (Fall 1971): 458.

[3]Marty Bloomberg and Hans Weber, *An Introduction to Classification and Number Building in Dewey*, edited by John Phillip Immroth (Littleton, CO, Libraries Unlimited, 1976), p. 151.

[4]John Phillip Comaromi, *The Eighteen Editions of the Dewey Decimal Classification* (Albany, NY, Forest Press Division, Lake Placid Education Foundation, 1976), pp. 587-88.

[5]Mary Ellen Michael, "Summary of a Survey of the Use of the Dewey Decimal Classification in the United States and Canada," *Major Classification Systems: The Dewey Centennial* (Urbana-Champaign, IL, University of Illinois Graduate School of Library Science, 1976), p. 54.

[6]Peter Butcher, "Dewey? We Sure Do!," *Catalogue & Index*, no. 55 (Winter 1979): 7.

[7]John Phillip Comaromi, "Decimal Classification Editorial Policy Committee Report," *Library Resources & Technical Services*, v. 21, no. 1 (Winter 1977): 93.
Benjamin A. Custer, "Dewey 19," *Catalogue & Index*, no. 53 (Summer 1979): 2; also in *Cataloging Service Bulletin*, no. 4 (Spring 1979): 16.

[8]See step II for determination of a literature's base number.

[9]See the explanations of base number in v. 1, p. xlvii (Section 8.545) and p. lxxvii.

[10]Groups of literatures are usually not starred; individual literatures are usually starred. Schedule divisions of a starred literature, e.g., 821 (English poetry), though not individually starred in the schedule, fall under the instructions for the starred literature.

[11]Cf. the option note under -8 in Table 3, v. 1, p. 396.

[12]It is not clear from the optional instruction under -8 (v. 1, p. 396) whether period subdivisions may be used for works by and about all individual authors regardless of form. Presumably they may. Apply the instructions in step IX. E.
Examples: 828.3 (Spenser's *Faerie Queene*)
    828.3 (Critical biographies of Spenser)
    848.7 (Balzac's *La cousine Bette*)
    848.7 (Collections of Balzac's shorter novels)

[13]Note that Latin and Classical Greek sections 873-874 and 883-884 as spelled out in the schedules do not precisely agree with form notation -3-4 in Table 3.

[14]For other options in arranging works of fiction, see v. 1, pp. lxix-lxx, Section 13.23 (Types of works not classified).

[15]Some period tables not available with recommended DDC practice may be used with certain optional literature assignments.
Examples: 8N2.... (New Zealand drama in English from a specific period, e.g., 8N2.1 for pre-1907 drama)
    NZ822.... (New Zealand drama in English from a specific period, e.g., NZ822.2 for twentieth-century drama)
    828.993321 (Pre-1907 New Zealand drama in English)

[16]If the work at hand is devoted to a specific kind or type of literary form, note the warning against chronological subdivision in step VIII. C.

[17]Note the instruction at the end of Table 3 (v. 1, p. 398) on classing miscellaneous writings when there is no period table.

[18]Melvil Dewey, *Dewey Decimal Classification and Relative Index*. Ed. 19 (Albany, NY, Forest Press, 1979), v. 1, p. xxxvii.

[19]Chan, p. 458.

[20]Dewey, v. 1, p. 390.

[21]Ibid., v. 1, p. 398.

15

Class 900 General Geography and History

Introduction

The broad outline of this final DDC class stays relatively stable in spite of its sizeable enumerative reductions. Comaromi says its original structure "was in general well-conceived."[1] There are nonetheless perennial complaints that it subordinates geographical to historical considerations, as evidenced by its captive 910 division, its organic split of ancient from modern history, and, formerly, its local place enumerations, to which all other geographic arrangements throughout the schedules were referred. *DDC 17* (1965) relocated much of its notation to a separate Area Table, now called Table 2, which grows with each passing edition, and presently occupies nearly five times as many pages in volume 1 as the other six auxiliary tables combined. Proliferation of local chronologies is probably the most visible class 900 development in *DDC 19*, although other, more fundamental restructuring, barely mentioned in official discussions, has taken place. Reviewers stress its importance, e.g.:

> 900 has—wrongly, I think—subsumed 309, but with no instructions on what to do with the sort of material we used to class at 309.[2]

> This edition provides for a general relocation of social and cultural history materials into the history section per se. Works on social situation and conditions (formerly 309.1), political history (formerly a part of 320.9), and social and cultural history (including archeology, but excluding travel) formerly in 910 and 913-19 are now to be placed in 909 and 930-90. The relocations bring the DDC more in line with the collocation pattern of the Library of Congress classification, although without the particular numbers that the latter scheme uses to differentiate kinds of treatment.... These changes represent the most significant and widespread of all the changes made in the present edition.[3]

Before we consider specific features, let us make our usual comparison of division captions from the last two editions. "Extraterrestrial worlds" in the 990 caption looks new, but it represents section 999, which was part of *DDC 18*. The "Western Europe" in the 940 caption was a 1974 *DC&* insertion. Most of the post-*DDC 18* alterations took place at that time. Both the Library of Congress and the *British National Bibliography* applied them forthwith to their cataloging records.[4]

Summary (*DDC 18*)		Summary (*DDC 19*)	
900	GENERAL GEOGRAPHY AND HISTORY AND THEIR AUXILIARIES	900	GENERAL GEOGRAPHY AND HISTORY AND THEIR AUXILIARIES
910	General geography; Travel	910	General geography; Travel
920	General biography, genealogy, insignia	920	General biography, genealogy, insignia
930	General history of the ancient world to ca. 500 A.D.	930	General history of the ancient world to ca. 499
940	General history of Europe	940	General history of Europe; Western Europe
950	General history of Asia; Orient; Far East	950	General history of Asia; Orient; Far East
960	General history of Africa	960	General history of Africa
970	General history of North America	970	General history of North America
980	General history of South America	980	General history of South America
990	General history of other parts of the world; Pacific Ocean islands (Oceania)	990	General history of other parts of the world; of extraterrestrial worlds; Pacific Ocean islands (Oceania)

Division 900   General Geography and History and Their Auxiliaries

The *DDC 17* caption was "General geography and history and related disciplines." One classifier lodged a complaint which is still valid:

> ... A meaningless title, therefore instructions to subdivide it are equally meaningless.... *Recommendation*: Avoid rambling generalities in titles and avoid suggesting subdivisions unless literary warrant supports the suggestion.[5]

Subdivision possibilities increased, however, with the growing enthusiasm for faceting. Section 900 was undeveloped until *DC&* in 1975 set a double *ss* pattern of "meaningless" subdivisions. It resembled those in divisions 200-209 and 700-709. The 900.1-.9 span applies to works combining geography and history; Sections 901-907 do the same for works limited to general history.

Section 901 (Philosophy and theory of general history) contains one of the special phoenix numbers cited in the editor's introduction. The 1975 *DC&* changes included a switch at 901.9 from "Civilization" to "Psychological principles." "Civilization" relocated to 909 (General world history).

Sections 902-907 (Standard subdivisions of general history) introduce a note under 904 to "class travel events and accidents in 910." *DC&*, v. 4, no. 1 (June 1980): 22 struck the "events and accidents." Presumably the accidents go to 363.12 (Transportation hazards), although nothing is said to that effect. Surely invocation, incantation, and taboo lurk in this ambivalence over linking accidents with travel literature. A second change at 904.7 turns "events induced by man" into "events induced by human activity."

Section [908] is unassigned, having lost its "Collections" function during the Table 1 overhaul of *ss*-08.

Section 909 (General world history) absorbs materials on civilization in general from both 901.9 and 910[.03]. See also the discussion of Section 913. Questions and suggestions such as the following are still coming in from the field.

> ...The editors of the DDC would render a distinct service to classifiers were they to explain more clearly what is meant by and what is specifically included in and excluded by the term "civilization."[6]

This section is also now the preferred location for elementary general history texts, which were formerly classed with education, under 372.89.

Division 910   General Geography; Travel

The enumerative classifier of the "meaningless standard subdivisions" comments:

> This division suffers from lack of identity. The editors have wavered between *Geography* and *Description and travel* since the 14th edition.... Recommendation: Use this whole division for physical and economic and cultural geography. Leave travel out of it.[7]

If the suggestion were acted upon, where would travel go? Finding easy bench-marks to distinguish the science of geography from the products of man's wanderlust acting upon his reportorial instincts is difficult. The Library of Congress classification makes "manners and customs in general" a subclass GT of its Geography class. It scatters "civilization" and "culture" to subclass CB, "archeology" to subclass CC, works of "description and travel," usually to history classes D-F, and those on "social life and customs," often to subclass HQ (Social groups) or HT (Communities). The 1975 DDC redistribution of social and cultural history out of Geography into History proper was cited in our chapter introduction for its analogies to LC collocation. It will be further examined in our discussion of centered heading 914-919.

Section 910 spells out *ss*-014 (Languages [Terminology] and communication) to distinguish linguistic study of place names from gazetteers, which class in 910.3. The disadvantages of such splits were discussed generally under Table 1 in chapter 5. Disappearance of 910[.03] (Man and his civilization) without a bracketed warning was mentioned under Section 909. Another phoenix number is 910.8 (Travel by specific kinds of persons). Its old "Collections or original accounts of travel" meaning moves to 910.4. The old caption "Historical treatment" at 910.9 is more explicitly directed to "geography as a discipline."

Sections 911 (Historical geography) and 912 (Graphic representations of the surface of the earth ...) house atlases, maps, charts, and plans. Their separation from 526.8 (Map drawing and projections) is reminiscent of the technique/product splits we observed between 242 (Christian devotional literature) and 248.3 (Christian worship), and again between 328 (Legislation) and 340 (Law). The only novelty in these sections is a cryptic note at 914.014 to "class languages (terminology) in 912.01."

Centered heading 913-919 (Geography of and travel in the ancient world; specific continents ...) poses a hierarchical format failure. It is logically superordinate to centered heading 914-919, but nothing in the schedule arrangement makes the hierarchy clear. Close proximity and overlapping functions mislead neophyte classifiers, who overlook the implicit relationships and differences. Omission of this broader heading would improve comprehension even if it meant repetition of notes under 913 and 914-919.

Section 913 (Geography of and travel in ancient world), like section 910, discontinues its former -03 subdivision. Archaeology has been transferred to 930.1, where subtopics are reduced by both natural and artificial means. A -01 division for prehistoric geography shows up here and in the Add table under 913.1-.9, which is part of a 913[.3] transformation. The final note under that Add table replaces, but does not contradict, a 1972 *DC&* reminder to class Biblical archaeology in 220.93.

Centered heading 914-919 (Geography of and travel in specific modern areas) drops divisions [03] (Man and his civilization) and [06] (Civilization of specific ethnic, etc. groups) from its Add table in a distributive transfer into the 940-990 schedules. "Area studies" are similarly distributed. The long [040202] (Travel guides) reduces to plain 04 (Travel). Starred captions for sections 914 through 919 now refer by means of a footnote to the Add table, but their basic functions are unchanged.

Division 920   General Biography, Genealogy, Insignia

A humanities librarian from the Comaromi survey could not distinguish reminiscences, as presented in literature Table 3 under -8 (Miscellaneous writings), from autobiographies, which usually are classed with other individual biographies in specific disciplines or subjects, or, optionally, here.[8] Berwick Sayers earlier voiced similar problems.

> We are told in the important note under 920 "autobiography, diaries, personal narratives, eulogies, biographic dictionaries, etc." But by one of the curious anomalies of the Decimal System "letters" are not included. As "the man's life in the letters of the man" is much more important than a mere formal account of his life, this makes Dewey's biography class defective. Letters, as we have seen, are placed at 816, 826, 836, etc., under Literature merely by language, and are thus separated from the man and his work.[9]

DDC 19 phrasing of the note, "Class here autobiographies, diaries, reminiscences, correspondence" compounds the problem by setting the 920 "correspondence" against the 8x6 "letters." A note under 920.7 (Biographies of persons by sex) accommodates individual biographies of persons not associated with a specific discipline or subject. Equal opportunity librarians may now class individual lives of men in 920.71, as distinct from those of women in 920.72.

Sections [921] through [928] remain optional, with some minor adjustments. A new option appears for Sikhs, but it is synthetic. The sequence follows an established pattern from section 294 (Religions of Indic origin). At 923[.4], the old caption "Persons in law, and criminals" is inverted, apparently to reflect the notational placement of criminals ahead of persons in law. Hot pursuit, rather than social value, appears to inspire the imagery.

Section 929 (Genealogy, names, insignia) adds subtopics "Surnames" and "Forenames." Their distance from materials on place names looks farther notationally than it really is, because of all the bracketed numbers between. Still, any separation of these interrelated materials is regrettable. Other new numbers in the section are subtopics of "Awards, orders, etc." and "Other forms of insignia and identification." In the former, as in "Heraldry," *DC&* has already inserted terminological additions.

Centered heading 930-990 (General history of ancient world; of specific continents, etc.) makes more format sense in comparison to its companion 940-990 heading than does its 913-919 counterpart vis-à-vis 914-919. Here the generalized Add table falls under the superordinate group, so that overlooking the subordinate group heading would cause relatively little confusion. The faceting principle is congruent to, though less intricate than, that used in class 800. The schedule provides a base number, to which area notations from Table 2 are attached. A third segment comes in most cases from a period table in the schedule proper. Other situations require *ss* notation, or special Add instructions. Although number building is basically simpler in geography and history than in literature, neophytes find the instructions less helpful. A set of steps after the fashion of those offered under centered heading 810-890 might help. New notes cover conceptual and notational shifts which have already been for the most part examined. *DC&* adds advice on classing war-related groups to the last note under 004 in the Add table.

Section 930 (General history of the ancient world) is notable for its absorption of archaeology. Local prehistoric and modern archaeology moves out of 914-919 into the 940-990's.

Sections 931 (China to 420), 932 (Egypt to 640), and 933 (Palestine to 70) all introduce or considerably expand period tables.

Sections 934 through 938 had extensive chronological development. Only a few alterations can be found. The Asoka period in India gets its own number, but cannot be located through the Relative Index. A new 936.1 distinguishes early Northern from Southern Britain and England. Standard and Area subdivisions of 938 (Greece to 323) are relocated out of the schedule into their respective auxiliary tables. The generalized Add table under 930-990 gives instructions.

Section 939 (Other parts of the ancient world) still has minimal chronological development. Crete to 323 is now separated from the Aegean Sea islands. Option notes under -39 in Table 2 permit the classing of *all* history for these areas together in *areas*-4, -5, and -6, if that approach is locally preferred.

Centered heading 940-990 (General history of the modern world) suggests obvious analogies to specific literature divisions 810-890, but they obscure certain theoretical distinctions to which custom makes experienced classifiers blind, while confusing beginners. Both spans have an immediate disciplinary affiliation, but works of "history," by DDC interpretation, include comprehensive treatments dealing with diverse aspects of a given area in addition to its history. For students trying to keep their disciplinary integrity straight, it is baffling to find that an *area* number from Table 2 or the Relative Index must be attached to a base 9 if there is no more obvious discipline, such as geography, to which the work at hand belongs. As for true histories, one of the official predictions for *DDC 19* was its "precise instructions for using the 940-990 numbers as options to 930 for the ancient history of specific places."[10] Every section but 947 (History of

Eastern Europe) now has one or more bracketed options for early history. *DC&* repeatedly closes out captions for the decade of the seventies, and opens new ones for the 1980s.

Section 940 (General history of Europe; Western Europe) offers an optional phoenix 940[.11] (Ancient history of Europe to ca. 499). "Invasions and rise of new nations, ca. 476-799," which it ousts, goes next door. Sub-periods are inserted for "Feudalism" and "the Crusades." The major portion of this section is devoted to the two world wars. Both were highly subdivided prior to *DDC 19*, and undergo no change. Later twentieth-century European history is now partitioned into decades. All time numbers reflect popular rather than arithmetic grouping of decades and centuries, as was noted on pages 124-25.

Section 941 (British Isles) is radically affected by the *DC&* changes of the mid-1970s. Its caption had been "Scotland and Ireland." It still contains Scottish and Irish history, but the Scotland chronology shifts to formerly vacant 941.1, leaving the 940.0x notation for works on Great Britain and the United Kingdom. A third phoenix number in the 900 class, at 941.081, substitutes "Victoria's reign" for "Twentieth century Scottish history." Irish period notation shifts from 941[.51-.59] to 941.501-.508. Ulster and the Republic of Ireland get their own chronologies.

Section 942 (England and Wales) shows a slightly altered caption, with disappearance of the schedule entries for the union of England and Scotland in favor of an Add instruction.

Section 943 (Central Europe; Germany) adds periods for post-1945 German, and post-1919 Austrian history, as well as for Czech, Polish, and Hungarian history.

Sections 944 (France) and 945 (Italy) are slightly expanded chronologically. Two geographic changes can be adduced from Table 2. Lyon now has its own notation, and the Alpes-Maritime department of France now includes Corsica, which was formerly classed under Italy.

Section 946 (Iberian Peninsula; Spain) has new period numbers for recent political developments in both Spain and Portugal.

Section 947 (Eastern Europe; USSR) adds subdivisions to every historical period from 1462 to the late twentieth century. Works on Finland are relocated from 947[.1] to the formerly vacant 948.97.

Section 948 (Northern Europe; Scandinavia), in addition to receiving Finland, has new places for post-1905 Scandinavian, Norwegian, and Swedish history, and for post-1906 Danish history.

Section 949 (Other parts of Europe) has similar twentieth-century expansions for the Northwestern Islands, Holland, Belgium, Luxembourg, Switzerland, Greece, Yugoslavia, and Crete. Spelled out only in Table 2 is the shift of "Turkey in Europe" from this section to 956.3. Serbia, which was formerly listed only in Table 2, now has its own schedule chronology.

Division 950   General History of Asia; Orient; Far East

There are no big surprises in this division, but a lot of modern expansion, e.g., for India, Iran, Singapore, etc. Optional early history numbers are bracketed here and there.

Section 950 (History of Asia in general) adds decade numbers for developments since 1945.

Section 951 (China and adjacent areas) adds a number for the Sung dynasty. Unlike the Asoka period of early India, this insertion appears in the Relative Index. There are new numbers with subdivisions for the East China Sea area and for Hong Kong. At 951.05, the People's Republic has added decade divisions.

Section 952 (Japan and adjacent islands) extends its feudal periods (1185-1868) and its post-1945 periods. Table 2 provides a new number for the Osaka prefecture and city.

Section 953 (Arabian Peninsula and adjacent areas) is still very short, but subdivides the post-1926 period. Oman and the United Arab Emirates can now be distinguished by means of Table 2, which gives additional jurisdictions not written into the schedule proper.

Section 954 (South Asia; India) grows to three times its former length, with added history periods from 997 A.D. through post-1971 India. *DC&* has since recognized Indira Gandhi's second prime ministership. Chronologies for Pakistan and Bangladesh appear. Mizoram and Sikkim have numbers in Table 2. The latter is relocated.

Section 955 (Iran) is short and only slightly expanded. The next issues of *DC&* may have to catch up.

Section 956 (Middle East) adds modern notations for Turkey, Iraq, Syria, Lebanon, Israel, and Jordan. A whole series of option notes in Table 2 remind us that the ancient history of this region preferably classes in section 939.

Section 957 (Siberia) has only three subdivisions, none of which are altered.

Section 958 (Central Asia) expands only post-1919 Afghanistan in its short scope. It will be interesting to see how literary warrant affects the future classing in this and related areas.

Section 959 (Southeast Asia) adds a general introductory sequence of single zero subdivisions for regional history. All three former Thailand numbers are extended in *DDC 19*. Malaysia and the Commonwealth of Nations territories gain new subdivisions for the post-1963 Federation and the Brunei protectorate. Singapore numbers were revised by *DC&*. A post-1975 Vietnam division adds to its already intensively developed chronology. There are decade numbers added for the Indonesian Republic, and numbers for each executive administration in the Philippine Republic.

Division 960   General History of Africa

When predicting many new class 900 chronologies, the DDC editor stressed those for precolonial Africa.[11] A quick survey of this division corroborates his claim, especially for the west, central, and southern regions. The continent's many rapid political changes are reflected not only in *DDC 19* but in the June 1980 issue of *DC&*.

Section 961 (North Africa) introduces a general chronology. Its two existing subdivisions for Tunisia and Libya are unchanged.

Section 962 (Egypt and Sudan) introduces post-1922 head-of-government administration numbers.

Section 963 (Ethiopia) expands later nineteenth- and early twentieth-century spans, with an Inclusion note to cover the deposition of Haile Selassie in 1974.

Section 964 (Northwest African coast, etc.) inserts a triple-zero *ss* span for the coast in general, as distinct from the double-zero span for Morocco. The Canary Islands have a new chronology.

Section 965 (Algeria) makes minor adjustments in its four non-extended period numbers.

Section 966 (West Africa, etc.) does not show it, but Table 2 provides expansions for Anglophone and Francophone West Africa. General history periods appear for the Mali, Upper Volta, and Niger regions. New "Independence" notation is available for Guinea-Bissau and the Cape Verde Islands. "Benin" replaces the older "Dahomey." A double-zero span under Nigeria reminds the user of the Add table at 930-990. Nigeria's chronology is also extended, as is that for Fernando Po.

Section 967 (Central Africa and offshore islands) adds a local history table for Equatorial Guinea. "Independence" numbers appear for Angola, and are realigned under Rwanda and Burundi to accommodate Add instructions. The Congo Republic is rechristened "Zaire," and acquires local place notation. So does Angola, through reference to Table 2. "Djibouti" replaces the old "Somaliland," with its independence number added. Mozambique likewise has independence recognized, and gets local place extension from Table 2.

Section 968 (Southern Africa ...) shows extensive chronological expansion for all specific localities. The former high commissioner territories are divided into Botswana, Swaziland, and Lesotho, all with period subdivisions. The Transvaal, Natal, the Orange Free State, the Cape of Good Hope, and Namibia are similarly subdivided. So are Zimbabwe (*DC&* drops "Rhodesia"), Zambia, and Malawi.

Section 969 (South Indian Ocean islands) adds period numbers for Madagascar, Réunion, and Mauritius.

Division 970   General History of North America

Much has been said about the tyranny of decimal notation (cf. the discussion in this text under section 790), but it has its defenders:

> Decimal notation rarely inhibits proper division; there are many classes that do not use all of the ten notational divisions available, and others that use them as major groupings in classes with more than ten members — the class 970 (North America) is an example of both cases.[12]

In the geographic updates of 1975, this division lost its 970[.1-.5] span to other, distributed locations. Those heavily used numbers for Indians of North America are now bracketed as options. The only other change puts decade numbers under 970.053, and a pre-history sequence under 970.01.

Section 971 (Canada) shows two schedule changes. The Northern territories, formerly classed with the prairie provinces, move to 971.9, reflecting phoenix *area*-719, and ousting Labrador, which goes next door to 971.82. In the other shift, the French and Indian War is now classed under 973.26 (Extension of English rule). The old number is bracketed as optional. *DC&* expands 971.064 to provide for the Clark and the second Trudeau prime ministries.

Section 972 (Middle America; Mexico) is most notable for its local pre-history extensions for Mexico, Central America, Panama, the West Indies, Cuba, Jamaica, the Dominican Republic, Haiti, Puerto Rico, and Trinidad and Tobago. A triple-zero *ss* span for Middle America now precedes the double-zero one for Mexico. Post-1917 Mexican history is subdivided for each presidential administration. Central America has a twentieth-century partition. Panama was relocated in a 1975 *DC&* issue from South to Middle America. The Canal Zone went with it. States, provinces, districts, and departments for Mexico, Central America, and Cuba can now be specified by reference to Table 2.

Section 973 (United States) was already extensively developed. Only two minor changes occur. A 973.1 reduction sends early North American history to 970.01, where chronology is available through an Add note for subdividing the now more specific 973.1. Since time marches on and American presidents change at least once every eight years (recently more often), new divisions identify the incumbencies of Gerald Ford and Jimmy Carter.

Sections 974-979 (Specific states of the U.S.) merely have their chronologies expanded since the Civil War, the turn of the Century, or statehood, depending on the region or state. There is no point in enumerating what can be easily spotted.

Division 980   General History of South America

Changes in this division are all the mixture as before, since South American history unfolds much like that of North America, at least in many of its chronologies. The relocation of general history and civilization numbers for native races from 980[.1-.5] into Table 5 facets of 980.004 is similar to that cited in the introduction to division 970. Specific nineteenth- and twentieth- century time divisions are inserted, and pre-history numbers are added for Argentina, Chile, Bolivia, Peru, Venezuela, Paraguay, and Uruguay. The loss of Panama was noted under section 972. Table 2 provides extended local place divisions for all South American countries.

Division 990   General History of Other Parts of the World; Extraterrestrial Worlds; Pacific Ocean Islands

New Zealand and Australia already had their early and pre-history numbers, but both receive twentieth-century extensions. The north central Pacific acquires triple-zero *ss* numbers, distinguishing it from the double-zero Hawaii span. The rest of the action is tucked away in Table 2, where local Australian states have local extensions.

Conclusion

We must expect continuing expansion of class 900. New chronology, with realigned jurisdictional notation, is mandated by global change, particularly since World War I. Far-flung reporting, cheap and rapid transportation, massive population shifts from urbanization and political displacement, and of course the international aspirations of DDC, all stimulate a gazetteer-like coverage of local places. Socio-political developments in the Third World and elsewhere provide literary warrant for close classification.

The other, more disruptive *DDC 19* changes are relocation of general civilization, culture, and archaeology materials, plus the shifting of regional and local pre-history out of Geography into the history schedules. They aim at better disciplinary integrity, along with better collocation for geographers, historians, and the public at large. Libraries should, however, weigh carefully the costs of full reclassification against those of anachronistic or inconsistent distributions before deciding how soon and how far to adopt all possible number extensions and placement shifts.

Exercises in the Use of Class 900

A. Analysis

909'.04927'070492 Brugman, J. Arabic studies in the Netherlands
... 1979.   80-457962

912'.133373'097945 California. Resources Agency. Sacramento River
environmental atlas, 1978 ... 1978?   79-620695

914.25'9'0485   Burden, Vera. Walks in Buckinghamshire ... c1978.   79-300543

915.1'0458   Malloy, Ruth Lor. Travel guide to the People's Republic
of China ... Rev. ed. ... 1980.   80-16428

917.94'610453   Bailey, John. San Francisco insider's guide : a unique
guide to Bay Area restaurants, bars ... c1980.   80-81305

919.8'04'0924   Tilman, Harold William. Triumph and tribulation ...
1977.   77-367704

920'.009'04   Wintle, Justin. Makers of modern culture ... 1981. 80-20199

929'.2'0945   Dumon, George. Les Albizzi : histoire et généalogie
d'une famille à Florence et en Provence du onzième
siècle à nos jours / George-Dumon ... 1977.   79-337051

939.4   Coon, Carleton Stevens. The seven caves : archaeological explorations in the Middle East ... 1981, c1956. 80-24503

941'.009'92   Dewhurst, Jack. Royal confinements ... 1980.   80-52921

954'.3035   Baker, D. E. U. (David E. U.). Changing political
leadership in an Indian province : the Central
Provinces and Berar, 1919-1939 ... 1979.   80-900122

967.8'26004963   Thornton, Robert J. Space, time and culture among
the Iraqw of Tanzania ... c1980.   79-6793

970.004'97   Cartin, Hazel. Elijah ... 1981.   80-21662
[B]

973'.0495   Perrin, Linda. Coming to America : immigrants from
the Far East ... 1980.   80-65840

975.5'365'00496073 Fitzgerald, Ruth Coder. A different story : a
Black history of Fredericksburg, Stafford,
and Spotsylvania, Virginia ... c1979.   79-67534

981'.004'96   Nascimento, Abdias do, 1914- O genocídio do negro
brasileiro : processo de um racismo mascarado ...
1978.   79-339211

996.9'004'956   Ogawa, Dennis M. Kodomo no tamme ni - For the
sake of the children : the Japanese American
experience in Hawaii ... c1978.   77-18368

B.   Examples from LC records are given on pp. 322-24.

1. Genealogical data on some Virginia families.

2. The account of a post-World War II trip across Siberia by train.

3. Bio-history of C. A. Buckley, boss of San Francisco in the late nineteenth century.

4. A book of photographs of Australia's scenic coastline.

5. The memoires of a lady-in-waiting to Marie Antoinette.

6. Description and travel in the island of Bali.

7. A selection from the historical writings of Arnold Toynbee.

8. A collection of essays by archaeologists on ancient civilizations.

9. A study of the effects of Byzantine and Islamic cultures on medieval western Europe.

10. A study of the Irish element in medieval European culture.

11. A book on technology, civilization, and forecasting the twenty-first century.

12. A periodical devoted to the history of Clark County, Ohio.

13. A physical and economic geography of present-day Hungary.

14. A general review of western civilization to the year 1715.

15. The biography of a twentieth-century rafter on the rivers of the western United States.

16. An account of Oak Ridge, Tennessee during the World War II years.

17. Politics, life, and labor in Petersburg, Virginia from 1874 to 1889.

18. A book of Arizona's ghost towns and historical haunts.

19. The life of Salmon P. Chase, a nineteenth-century governor of Ohio, President Lincoln's Secretary of the Treasury, and later Chief Justice of the U.S. Supreme Court.

20. A study of the Mappilas of Malabar, an Islamic society on the south Asian frontier from 1498 to 1922.

21. A modern commentary on Arrian's history of Alexander.

22. A recent auto travel guide to the coast of Oregon.

23. Historiography for eignteenth-century Europe.

24. A contemporary travel guide to Hawaii.

25. A list of archival sources for British political history from 1900 to 1951.

26. A general historical introduction to the Greek and Roman worlds.

27. An index to western story magazines.

28. A history of Renaissance Florence.

29. A book on the archaeology of New England.

30. A history of the Lincoln Battalion in the Spanish Civil War.

31. An account of the Russian Revolution and the influence of Marx and Lenin.

32. A travel account of crossing Siberia by rail followed by a month in Japan.

33. A look at post-World War II European politics and government.

34. A biographical story of a Jewish immigrant to Canada.

35. A study of the impact of Europe on the North American Indian societies.

36. A study of immigrants from the British Isles in the United States.

37. Essays on the Chinese unrest and Boxer Rebellion of the turn of the century.

38. The story of the Washington Peace Conference of 1861.

39. A selection of wartime photographs of German aerial operations over Russia in World War II.

40. Personal narratives of mercenaries in Angola in the 1961-1975 Revolution.

41. The memoires of a Napoleonic soldier in the 1812 invasion of Russia.

42. A new historical perspective on the War between the States.

43. A chronology of American history.

44. An interpretation and bibliography of medieval historiography.

45. A collection of views of the Appalachian mountains.

46. A book of Giza, the Great Pyramid of Cheops.

47. A description of the daily activities of two young members of the Masai tribe in Kenya.

48. A personal account of the 1975-1976 Civil War in Lebanon.

49. A biography of Thomas Jefferson.

50. A study of the interaction of western Republican senators with the New Deal.

51. The 1841-1859 letters of a traveler around the Horn to California and on to Hawaii.

52. A history of the relations of the Delhi Sultanate with Rajasthan from 1206 to 1526.

C. Reclassification: Suggested solutions are offered on page 325.

1. Different editions of the following books have received different DDC numbers. What number do you prefer, according to *DDC 19*?

a. 909.008   Stavrianos, Leften Stavros, comp. The epic of modern man : a collection of readings ... 1966.   66-10710

    901.9   Stavrianos, Leften Stavros. The epic of modern man : a collection of readings ... 2d ed. ... 1971.   77-138472

b. 914.59'5'0483   Carrington, Dorothy. Granite island : a portrait of Corsica ... 1971.   72-179861

    914.4'945'0483   Carrington, Dorothy. Corsica : portrait of a granite island ... 1974, c1971.   73-17015

c. 301.24'3   Hunter, Robert, 1940 or 41- The enemies of anarchy : a gestalt approach to change ... 1973, c1970.   72-9739 MARC

    309.1'04   Hunter, Robert, 1940 or 41- The enemies of anarchy : a gestalt approach to change ... 1973, c1970.   72-9739 NUC

    901.94   Hunter, Robert, 1940 or 41- The enemies of anarchy : a gestalt approach to change ... 1970.   71-879425 NUC

2. 309.1'82'06   Boris, Dieter. Argentinien : Geschichte u. polit. Gegenwart ... 1978.   79-347162

3. 901.93'3   American Society for Eighteenth-Century Studies. Irrationalism in the eighteenth century ... 1972.   73-240

4. 901.94   Anshen, Ruth Nanda, ed. Our emergent civilization ... 1971, c1947.   70-134048

5. 912'.427'46   Geographia Ltd. Sheffield & Rotherham street by street; with the national grid ... [Rev. ed.] ... [1972?]   73-153662

6. 912'.595'2   Singapore. Ministry of Culture. Singapore guide and street directory, with sectional maps ... [10th ed. ... 1972.]   74-150819

7. 913'.031   Branigan, Keith. Reconstructing the past : a basic introduction to archaeology ... 1974.   74-81006

8. 913.362   Laing, Lloyd Robert. Orkney and Shetland : an archaeological guide ... [1974.]   74-76182

9. 913.3'8'03   Carpenter, Rhys. The humanistic value of archaeology ... [1971, c1933]   72-138582

10. 914'.03'253   Fritz, Paul Samuel. City & society in the 18th century ... 1973.   73-93037

11. 914.27'46   South Craven Centre Local History Group. Sutton-in-Craven, the old community : a study of village life in the 19th and early 20th centuries ... 1973.   74-163876

12. 914.29'8   Carmarthen Rural District : official guide ... [1970]   70-565001

13. 914.71'03'30222 De Biasi, Mario. Meet the Finns / Pictures:
                     Mario de Biasi; Text ... 1969.   70-248053

14. 915.49'7'04   Edgar, John Ware. Report on a visit to Sikhim
                  and the Thibetan frontier in October, November,
                  and December 1873 ... 1969.   76-911533

15. 938'.07'2   Pavan, Massimiliano. Antichità classica e pensiero
                  moderno ... 1977.   78-383318

16. 914.6'1   Budge, Ian. Belfast : approach to crisis; a study of
                  Belfast politics, 1613-1970 ... 1973.   72-85194

17. 959.5'2'004'951 Wu, Te-yao. The cultural heritage of Singapore :
                  the essence of the Chinese tradition ... 1975.   77-940836

Examples of LC Cataloging to Illustrate the Above Exercises in DDC Number Building

B. Synthesis

1. 929'.2'0973   Brown, Dakota Best. Data on some Virginia families
                  / collected and compiled by ... c1979.   80-106627

2. 915.7'048   Bruckner, Pascal. Nostalgic express : le voyage dans
                  le Trans-sibérien ... 1978.   80-459547

3. 979.4'61'040924 Bullough, William A. The blind boss & his city
                  : Christopher Augustine Buckley and nineteenth-
                  century San Francisco ... c1979.   78-64468

4. 919.4'0022'2   Burt, Jocelyn. Australia's scenic coastline ...
                  1978.   80-458743

5. 944'.035'0924 Campan, Jeanne Louise Henriette Genet, 1752-1822.
                  Mémoires de Madam Campan, première femme de
                  chambre de Marie-Antoinette ... c1979.   80-458902

6. 959.8'6   Delcourt, Jérôme. Bali, matin du monde ... c1978.   79-341276

7. 907'.2   Toynbee, Arnold Joseph. Arnold Toynbee, a selection
                  from his works ... 1978.   78-40203

8. 930'.1   Ancient civilizations / [editor, Frances M. Clapham] ...
                  1978.   78-50676

9. 909.07   Geanakoplos, Deno John. Medieval Western civilization
                  and the Byzantine and Islamic worlds : interaction of
                  three cultures ... c1979.   78-52827

10. 943'.0004'9162 Zimmer, Heinrich. The Irish element in mediaeval
                  culture ... 1978, c1891.   78-1573

11. 909.83   Vajk, J. Peter. Doomsday has been cancelled ... 1978.   78-62300

12. 977.1'49'005 Yester year in Clark County, Ohio. v. 1-
                  1947-   78-649078

13. 914.39'04'5   Pécsi, Márton. Physical and economic geography of
                  Hungary ... 1977.   79-303320

14. 909'.09'821   Kagan, Donald. The Western heritage, to 1715 ... c1979.   78-16636

15. 917.8'04'30924   Clark, Georgie White. Georgie Clark : thirty years of river of running ... [1977]   77-25448

16. 976.8'73   Johnson, Charles W. City behind a fence : Oak Ridge, Tennessee, 1942-1946 ... c1980.   80-15897

17. 975.5'581   Henderson, William D. Gilded age city : politics, life, and labor in Petersburg, Virginia, 1874-1889 ... 1980.   80-1385

18. 979.1   Heatwole, Thelma. Ghost towns and historical haunts in Arizona ... c1981.   80-26433

19. 973.7'092'4 [B]   Hart, Albert Bushnell. Salmon P. Chase ... 1980, 1899.   80-21705

20. 954'.83   Dale, Stephen Frederic. Islamic society on the South Asian frontier : the Màppilas of Malabar, 1498-1922 ... 1980.   79-41666

21. 938'.07   Bosworth, A. B. A historical commentary on Arrian's History of Alexander ... c1980.   79-40885

22. 917.95'0443   Blood, Marje. Exploring the Oregon coast by car ... c1980.   80-25484

23. 940.2'53'072   Anderson, Matthew Smith. Historians and eighteenth-century Europe, 1715-1789 ... 1979.   78-40319

24. 919.69'04'4   Key, Thelma Bennett. Hawaii's best and how to find it ... 1978.   78-111164

25. 941.082'072   Cook, Chris, 1945- Sources in British political history, 1900-1951 ... 1975-1978.   75-321564

26. 938   Walton, Brian G. The Greek and Roman worlds ... c1980.   80-5791

27. 978'.005   Western publications index : America's largest source of true stories of the Old West ... c1980.   80-82436

28. 945'.5105   Trexler, Richard C. Renaissance Florence : the public life of a complex society ... 1980.   80-22061

29. 974   Snow, Dean R. The archaeology of New England ... 1980.   80-982

30. 946.081   Rosenstone, Robert A. Crusade of the Left : the Lincoln Battalion in the Spanish Civil War ... 1980.   80-5703

31. 947.084'1   Luxemburg, Rosa. The Russian Revolution, and Leninism or Marxism? ... 1981, c1961.   80-24374

32. 915   Lamplugh, Barbara. Trans-Siberia by rail and a month in Japan ... 1979.   80-510422

33. 940.55   Jones, R. Ben. The making of contemporary Europe ... 1981.   80-21063

34. 971'.004924   Horowitz, Aron. Striking roots : reflections on
                  five decades of Jewish life ... 1979.   80-481509

35. 970.004'97   Hecht, Robert A. Continents in collision : the
                  impact of Europe on the North American Indian
                  societies ... 1980.   80-1381

36. 973'.042   Blumenthal, Shirley. Coming to America : immigrants
                  from the British Isles ... 1980.   80-65841

37. 951'.03   Hart, Robert, Sir, Bart. These from the land of Sinim :
                  essays on the Chinese question ... 1981, 1903.   79-2826

38. 973.7'1   Gunderson, Robert Gray. Old gentleman's convention
                  : the Washington Peace Conference of 1861 ...
                  1981, c1961.   80-24747

39. 940.54'4943   German fighters over Russia : a selection of wartime
                  photographs from the Bundesarchiv, Koblenz
                  ... 1980.   80-507382

40. 967'.303'0922 Dempster, Chris. Fire Power ... 1981.   80-51902

41. 940.2'7'0924 Bourgogne, Adrien Jean Baptiste Françoise. The
    [B]   memoires of Sergeant Bourgogne, 1812-1813
                  ... 1980.   80-453231

42. 973.7   Barney, William L. Flawed victory : a new perspective
                  on the Civil War ... 1980.   80-68972

43. 970'.002'02   The Timetables of American history ... c1980.   80-36860

44. 940.1   Sterns, Indrikis. The greater medieval historians :
                  an interpretation and a bibliography ... 1980.   80-5850

45. 917.4'0022'2 Smith, Clyde H. Appalachian mountains ... c1980.   80-65134

46. 932   Seiss, Joseph Augustus. The Great Pyramid : a miracle
                  in stone ... 1981.   80-19801

47. 967.6'2   Schachtman, Tom. Growing up Masai ... c1981.   80-25017

48. 956.92'044   Raburn, Terry. Under the guns in Beirut ... c1980.   80-65308

49. 973.4'6'0924 Morse, John Torrey. Thomas Jefferson ... 1980.   80-23357
    [B]

50. 973.917   Feinman, Ronald L. Twilight of progressivism :
                  the western Republican senators and the New Deal
                  ... c1981.   80-20124

51. 917.94'04'3   Gleason, James Henry, 1823-1861. Beloved Sister :
                  the letters of James Henry Gleason, 1841-1859,
                  from Alta California and the Sandwich Islands,
                  with a brief account of his voyage in 1841 via
                  Cape Horn to Oahu and California ... 1978.   78-111643

52. 954'.4'02   Ahluwalia, Manjeet Singh. Muslim expansion in
                  Rajasthan : the relations of Delhi Sultanate
                  with Rajasthan, 1206-1526 ... c1978.   78-904124

C. Reclassification

    1. a. 909 Stavrianos ...

        b. 914.4'945'0483 Carrington ...

        c. 909.82 Hunter ...

    2. 982.06 Boris ...

    3. 909.7 American Society ...

    4. 909.82 Anshen ...

    5. 912.42821 Geographia, Ltd. ...

    6. 912.5957 Singapore ...

    7. 930.1 Branigan ...

    8. 936.101 Laing ...

    9. 930.1 *or* 938.01 Carpenter ...

  10. 940.253 Fritz ...

  11. 914.42841 South Craven ...

  12. 914.2965 Carmarthen ...

  13. 948.970330222 De Biasi ...

  14. 915.416704352 Edgar ...

  15. 938.0072 Pavan ...

  16. 941.67 Budge ...

  17. 959.57004951 Wu ...

NOTES

[1]John Phillip Comaromi, *The Eighteen Editions of the Dewey Decimal Classification* (Albany, NY, Forest Press Division, Lake Placid Education Foundation, 1976), p. 82.

[2]Peter Butcher, "Dewey? We Sure Do!," *Catalogue & Index*, no. 55 (Winter 1979): 9.

[3]Francis Miksa, "The 19th Dewey: A Review Article," *Library Quarterly*, v. 50, no. 4 (October 1980): 485.

[4]*Cataloging Service*, bulletin 112 (Winter 1975): 16-17. The same news release was published for the benefit of British librarians in: *Catalogue & Index*, no. 36 (Spring 1975): 16.

[5]Anne Ethelyn Markley, "Problems Associated with Presenting and Teaching the Schedules: Social Science (300) and History (900)," *The Dewey Decimal Classification: Outline and Papers Presented at a Workshop* (New York, School of Library Science, Columbia University, 1968), p. 41.

⁶Miksa, p. 486.

⁷Markley, p. 42.

⁸John Phillip Comaromi, *A Survey of the Use of the Dewey Decimal Classification in the United States and Canada* (Lake Placid, NY?, Prepared for Forest Press, Lake Placid Foundation, 1975), p. 257.

⁹W. C. Berwick Sayers, *An Introduction to Library Classification, Theoretical, Historical and Practical*, 9th ed., with corrections (London, Grafton, 1958), pp. 280-81.

¹⁰Benjamin A. Custer, "DDC 19: Characteristics," *HCL Cataloging Bulletin*, no. 35 (July/August 1978): 11.

¹¹Ibid.

¹²David C. Batty, "Library Classification One Hundred Years after Dewey," *Major Classification Systems: The Dewey Centennial* (Urbana-Champaign, IL, University of Illinois Graduate School of Library Science, 1976), p. 3.

16

The Abridged DDC, Eleventh Edition

Introduction

It is curious how reticent the Forest Press has always been about its abridgments of DDC. *Abr 1* first appeared in 1894, in the wake of *DDC 5*, but one must search the full DDC editions carefully to find references to abridgments. In his extensive history of the Dewey classification, John Comaromi devotes considerable space to foreign versions, but barely mentions the abridged editions.[1] They are entirely ignored in his index. Benjamin Custer says they are "intended mainly for small North American public and school libraries."[2]

The *DDC 19* editor's introduction repeats what *DDC 18* said of *Abr 10*, without indicating the significant change about to occur in *Abr 11*.[3] The original change was in *Abr 10*, but neither was it recorded in *DDC 18*. Only from the work itself did we learn:

> ... As well as having shorter numbers, the present abridged edition in some places presents different classification policies and slightly different numbers from those in Edition 18.... Recent abridged editions have been developed from the respective full editions upon which each was based on the premise that all libraries will grow in size indefinitely, and that, therefore, even the smallest library using the abridged Dewey should be able, as it grows, to expand and deepen its classification simply by lengthening the class numbers used.... The present edition abandons that position, and is addressed to the thousands of general libraries that have no expectation of ever growing very big. It is not, therefore, in the strictest sense an *abridgment* of the full 18th edition, but a close *adaptation* of it.[4]

The idea was sound, but it foundered on a dilemma of universal classification. Standardization offered economic advantages to local libraries, using ready-prepared class numbers, which they could not afford to forego. Small libraries found the segmentation marks on Library of Congress records widely accessible and easy to adapt, but when they referred to their *Abr 10*'s, they stumbled over variant forms. One of the most vital life-signs of this centenarian classification is its 20-20 vision for handwriting on the wall. We have, therefore, in *Abr 11* a reversion, rather than a change.

Edition 10 of the Abridged Dewey Decimal Classification represented a departure from the traditional literal abridgment of the full edition.... The editors made an attempt to produce a modified edition expecting that it would be easier to use and better adapted to the needs of small libraries.

Experience has shown that, in fact, a literal abridgment meets these needs better....[5]

Abr 11, like all previous abridgments, crops numbers. The practice, plus certain conventions for selecting index terms from the schedules, results in a few apparently contradictory index entries, as the following examples show:

DDC 19 Index		*Abr 11 Index*	
Abdias--Bible	224.91	Abdias--Bible	224
Babies *see* Infants		Babies *see* Children	
CENTO--mil. sci.	355.0310956	CENTO *see* Mutual defense & security	
Deeside Clwyd Wales	*area*-42936	Deeside Scot.	*Area*-412
Ethnic groups		Ethnic groups	
& state	323.11	& state	323.1
history	909.04	history	909
law--status	346.013	legal status	342
Franco-German War--history	943.082	Franco-German War--history	943.08
Gestalt--psychology	150.1982	Gestalt psychology	150.19
Mutual		Mutual	
defense		defense & security	
internat. law	341.72	internat. law	341.7
security pacts			
internat. law	341.72		
mil. sci.	355.031	mil. sci.	355

Increased use of boldface type in various sizes makes *Abr 11* look more like its parent and improves its readability. Dhyani's recommendation, cited on page 168, that section numbers which merely duplicate standard subdivisions, area notation, or other faceting devices, should be curtailed, is followed here. See, for instance, 101-107 (Standard subdivisions of philosophy), 314-319 (General statistics by specific continents, etc.), 421-425 (Description and analysis of standard English), and 811-818 (Specific forms of American literature). Unassigned section numbers, e.g., [132], [134], and [136], are simply omitted. Use of standard subdivision is reduced, particularly in places where *DDC 19* requires multiple zeros. The editors say:

It should be noted that many entries carry the instruction "Do not use standard subdivisions." In Edition 10, which was not a literal abridgment, standard subdivisions frequently appeared with a single 0 where the full edition used two or more. Literal abridgment dictates that these now be moved back into the double- or triple-zero position, even though there is no need for this in the abridged schedule. In such cases it seemed better to dispense entirely with standard subdivisions.[6]

For instance, in *DDC 19*, 352.0001-.0009 (Standard subdivisions of local governments in general) precedes 352.002-.009 (Generalities of local government) and 352.03-.09 (Treatment of local government by specific continents, etc.). In *Abr 11*, the only zero notation at this point is the 352.03-.09 span.

One criticism of *Abr 10* was its lack of expansion for minority groups.[7] *Abr 11* is not much better. The only two obvious additions are an Inclusion note at 338.6 (Organization of production ... Including ... specific kinds of industries ... minority enterprises) and a new entry at 371.97 (Special education for students exceptional because of racial, ethnic, national origin). Both are represented in the Relative Index, but the latter is erroneously numbered 391.97. There is also a new Index entry under "Minority groups—ed. soc." The schedule 370.19 (Social aspects of education) already covered segregation and integration.

A critic of *Abr 10* suggested that citation orders would be very helpful.[8] The need was not just in the abridged version, but general to the entire scheme. Tables of precedence were increased in *DDC 19*, as we saw in chapter 2. Abr 11 follows them at such locations as the beginning of auxiliary Table 1 (slightly curtailed and reshuffled), centered heading 012-016 (Special bibliographies and catalogs), and the like.

The editor's introduction is superficially refurbished, but essentially unchanged. It is based on the pattern established for the unabridged edition, only simpler and shorter. It says nothing about variation from recommended practice or alternative methods for classing fiction. Biography options are mentioned in Section 2.1 (p. 10); options for serials in Section 6.1.2.2.8 (p. 25). The glossary is cut from 77 terms to 60. It is followed by a similarly abbreviated index to the editor's introduction and glossary.

Significant auxiliary table and schedule changes are listed in *Abr 10* numeric order in *Relocations and Schedule Reductions* (pp. 89-91). Phoenix changes for Sociology, the Political Process, and the British Isles are indexed alphabetically in *Lists of Changed Numbers* (pp. 92-98). Class, division, and section summaries precede the schedules proper.

Auxiliary Tables

New Table 1 numbers are -029 (Commercial miscellany), -04 (Special topics of general applicability), and -068 (Management of enterprises engaged in specific fields of activity, etc.). Facets for "Tabulated and related materials" and for "Collections" are newly bracketed. *DDC 19* still uses both -021 and -08, but italicizes the latter as warning of a phoenix change not shown in *Abr 11*. There are almost no subdivisions of the basic 10 *ss* facets except under -02 (Miscellany), -07 (Study and teaching), and -09 (Historical and geographic treatment).

Table 2 has 19 changes cited in the list of *Relocations and Schedule Reductions* (pp. 87-91) besides 36 British Isles entries in the *Lists of Changed Numbers* (pp. 97-98). *DDC 19* shifts are copied for ancient Britain, Finland, the Ottoman Empire, and the Northern Territories of Canada. They are reduced for the Aegean islands, Crete, Asia Minor, Cyprus, Corsica, Sikkim, Socotra, and Labrador. *Abr 11* also reduces its own former notation for Sicily, Malta, Sardinia, Albania, Bulgaria, and Crete. It reopens spans for Norway, Sweden, Turkey, and the Sudan.

Table 3 brings its notation for collections by, and history and description of, more than one author into line with *DDC 19* usage by converting *lit. sub.*-[108]

through -[808], and -[109] through -[809] into -x008-x009. It does not recognize the specific kinds of literary form included in *DDC 19*. There is nothing analogous to Table 3-A.

Table 4 shows only one change—the *DDC 19* shift of -[6] (Prosody of the standard form of the language) into class number 808.1.

Tables 5-7 are missing. Their application tends to produce longer numbers than small libraries need or want. A few schedule comparisons may be illuminating. For example, *DDC 19* use of Table 5 is dropped in *Abr 11* at the following location:

> 323.1   Relation of state to nondominant aggregates   (*DDC 19*)
> .11   Racial, ethnic, national aggregates
>   Add "Racial, Ethnic, National Groups" notation
>   from Table 5 to base number 323.11 ...

* *

> 323.1   Relation of state to racial, ethnic, national   (*Abr 11*)
>   aggregates
>   Class here comprehensive works on relation of
>   state to social aggregates
>   If preferred, class relation of state to North
>   American native races in 970.5
>   Class women of, socioeconomic classes among
>   racial, ethnic, national groups in 323.3, sla-
>   very in 326

Not only is Table 6 by-passed at 494.1-.3, for instance, but none of the *DDC 19* divisions under 494 are retained. *DDC 19* references to both Tables 5 and 7 are missing from such positions as section number 704.

> 704   Special topics of general applicability in fine and   (*DDC 19*)
>   decorative arts
>   .03   Treatment among specific racial, ethnic, national
>   groups
>   Add "Racial, Ethnic, National Groups" notation
>   01-99 from Table 5 to base number 704.03 ...
>   .04-.87   Treatment among other groups of specific kinds
>   of persons
>   Add "Persons" notation 04-87 from Table 7 to
>   base number 704 ...

* *

> 704   Special topics of general applicability in fine and   (*Abr 11*)
>   decorative arts
>   Including persons occupied with art, e.g. patrons
>   Class art dealers in 338.7; description, critical
>   appraisal, works, biography of artists in 709.2

Class 000   Generalities

Relocations and Schedule Reductions lists 24 changes in this class. Three relate to 016 (Bibliographies and catalogs of specific disciplines and subjects).

Nineteen are in the 020's (Library and information sciences). Specific government libraries can be identified at 027.53-.59, as can specific academic libraries at 027.73-.79, but school libraries miss the 027.82 subdivisions of *DDC 19* for specific levels and libraries. Transfers of general Scottish and Irish organizations from 068 to 062, and of Scottish and Irish newspapers and journalism from 079 to 072, are modelled on more specific *DDC 19* shifts.

Class 100   Philosophy and Related Disciplines

Most of the 13 changes recorded in *Relocations and Schedule Reductions* originate from *DDC 19* revisions, but with shorter notation. Sections 111 (Ontology) and 135 (Dreams and mysteries) lose *Abr 10* subtopics.

Class 200   Religion

The 19 changes in this class are tied to *DDC 19* changes, although again they tend to involve broader notation than that in the unabridged edition.

Class 300   Social Sciences

As might be expected, there is more revision here than elsewhere. Apart from the phoenix changes of 301 and 329, there are 77 *Relocations and Schedule Reductions* entries. Twenty-nine are discontinued numbers or spans, of which 20 are total reductions. The other 9 are relocations for various reasons. Two expansions reflect *DDC 19* shifts. Seven illustrate the reversion of *Abr 11* from adaptation to abridgment. Let us review them briefly.

Abr 10 located "Labor union organization" in 331.88 rather than the 331.87 of the full edition. It is now restored. Centered heading 333.7-.9 (Utilization of specific natural resources) appears only in *Abr 11* (not in *DDC 19*). Under it, a note reminds us to "Class pollution and its control [*both formerly* 333.7-333.9] in 363.7."

At 342.2-.9 (Constitutional and administrative law), *Abr 10* used type-of-law subtopics that followed neither *DDC 17* nor the phoenix law schedule in *DDC 18*. In fact, it conflicted with the "Specific jurisdictions and areas" span 342.3-.9 in *DDC 18*. Both *DDC 19* and *Abr 11* follow *DDC 18* usage. Similar *Abr 10* subdivisions were made for "Miscellaneous public law," "Social law," "Criminal law," "Private law," and "Civil procedure," but all now have their content reduced to broad section numbers.

Abr 10 used 351[.04] (Executive branch of central governments). The materials are now distributed to 320.4 (Structure, functions, activities of government), 321.8 (Democratic forms of governments and states), and 351.003-.009. *Abr 10* took the initiative in shifting a pattern sequence out of 350 (Public administration) into 351 (Central governments). Both *DDC 19* and *Abr 11* retain the shift. But *Abr 10* classed "Merit system (Civil service)" in 351.1, not the 350.6 of *DDC 18*. *Abr 11* follows the *DDC 19* relocation to 351.6.

Abr 10 reduced 368.5-.8 (Casualty insurance) to a single 368.5, and changed the content of 368.8 to "Miscellaneous forms of insurance" from "Other casualty insurance." *Abr 11* restores the unabridged sequence, but without its *DDC 19* subdivisions.

Class 400   Language

Only two changes are cited for this class. The first is the transfer of "Prosody" from [416], etc., into 808.1 (Rhetoric of poetry). The second reflects a *DDC 19* Table 6 relocation of Negrito languages from -[9911] into -9593 (Mon-Khmer and Austroasiatic languages). *Abr 11* generalizes the shift, from broad section 499 to 495. Its Relative Index fails to follow through, however. There is a *see* reference from "Negrito" to "Austroasiatic," but the "Austroasiatic" entry is missing.

Class 500   Pure Sciences

Of the 16 changes in this class, only 2 restore *Abr 10* adaptations. There, Anseriformes and Perching birds had been reduced into 598.2 (Birds and ornithology). The specific notations are used in *Abr 11*, but at 598.2 the caption is now "Environmental treatment of birds," as distinct from *DDC 19*'s "General principles and geographic treatment of birds."

Abr 11 follows eight *DDC 19* revisions. The most significant were described in chapter 11, and include the "Reptilia" relocations. Reduction of both *Abr 10* and *DDC 19* notation occurs for "Theories of electricity," "Electrostatics," "Specific human races," and "Insular biology." "Physiological genetics" moves from 575.2 (unabridged 575[.21]) to 574.87 (unabridged 574.87322).

Class 600   Applied Technology (Applied Sciences)

The 59 changes in this class include 25 in division 610 (Medical sciences) and 22 in the 620's (Engineering). Five, including the much-discussed dispersion of management of specific enterprises, from section 658 to *ss*-068, are taken wholesale from *DDC 19*. Thirty-seven are based on unabridged changes, but carry broader notation. *Abr 10* adaptations are eliminated as follows. "Mental illness" is consolidated in 362.2, leaving 614.5 free to assume its "Control of specific diseases" meaning. The unabridged span 618.3-.8 (Diseases, etc. of pregnancy), which *Abr 10* eliminated in favor of 618.2 (Obstetrics), is now back. "Specific instruments and apparatus of radiotelephony" returns to 621.3846, after being moved to 621.3845. "Wire telephone terminal equipment" is similarly returned to 621.387. "Ballistics and gunnery" was lumped with "Ordnance" in *Abr 10*, but is now back in 523. And 630.1, formerly covering "Scientific principles of agriculture," has given them over to 630.2.

Class 700   The Arts: Fine and Decorative Arts

Thirty-three changes in the fine arts are scattered rather evenly through all of its divisions except 710 (Civic and landscape art). As in other classes, the majority follow or reduce *DDC 19* changes. There are five reversions from previous adaptations. *Abr 10* had put temporary and traveling art exhibits with all galleries, museums, etc. *Abr 11* restores its own 707.4. Collections of drawings by subject from a specific period or place were lumped with all subject drawings in 743. *Abr 11* says to use 741.9. Specific glasswares were classed in 748.2, although *DDC 18/19* and *Abr 11* use 748.8. Displacements under 786 (Keyboard instruments and their music) are restored in *Abr 11*.

One entry in the *Abr 11 Relocations and Schedule Reductions* is gratuitous. A schedule note at 753 (Abstractions, symbolism, etc.) reads "For religious symbolism, see 755." The note is useful, but not new. It appeared in *Abr 10* exactly the same.

Class 800   Literature (Belles-Lettres)

Two of the three *Relocations and Schedule Reductions* changes for this class are related to those in class 400, for Prosody and the Negrito languages. "Research authorship," formerly at 808 (808.023 in *DDC 18*), is gone off to 001.4. Table 3 is regularly invoked, but it is a tame Table 3, with no Table 3-A to complicate matters, and some significant reductions. No literary chronologies chase the user from schedule to table, back again to the schedule, and possibly once more to the auxiliary facets.

Class 900   General Geography and History and Their Auxiliaries

The seven *Relocations and Schedule Reductions* changes in this class are nearly verbatim transfers from major *DDC 19* readjustments. Only 901[.9], from which "Civilization" departs for 909, is discontinued rather than reclassified, with no hint of its *DDC 19* meaning. Chronological tables are fairly frequent in the 940-990 portions, but are less detailed than in the unabridged edition. Instructions under 930-990 for building numbers are essentially the same, but the Add table is shorter. Even so, the off-again-on-again classing of the *Abr 10/11* experiment can be especially troublesome in this class.

> Libraries trying to follow the latest abridged DC will see a pendulum in operation: they will have classed the history of Oslo in 948.2, then in 948.1, then again in 948.2. My frustration only reflects that of the suffering librarians caught in the middle between the equally noisy sets of partisans.[9]

Conclusion

It would be interesting to know the comparative sales of *DDC 19* and *Abr 11*, with their type-of-use breakdown. We might find that most library classification can proceed quite well with *Abr 11* alone. This possibility would not invalidate use of the unabridged DDC for classed catalog and indexing projects, but DDC has always been regarded as primarily designed for shelf arrangement. Most DDC libraries rely on LC segmentation. Yet *Abr 11* notation is by no means restricted to the traditional two places beyond the decimal point. Six of the 10 classes have a few longer numbers spelled out in the schedules. Add notes at many places, referring most often to auxiliary tables 1 and 2, also encourage longer notation.

Examples of Abridged *DDC 11* Extended Schedule Notation

025.4028	Techniques, procedures, apparatus, equipment, materials for subject analysis and control of library materials
180.1-.8	Standard subdivisions of ancient philosophy; Notations from Table 1
274-279	Treatment by specific continents, etc. in the modern world
	Class geographical treatment of a specific subject with the subject, using "Standard Subdivisions" notation 09 from Table 1, e.g., persecutions in France 272.0944
324.27104	The Progressive Conservative political party of Canada
491.7	East Slavic languages *Russian
	*Add to base number as instructed under 420-490
523.3022	Illustrations of the moon
621.3841028	Techniques, procedures, apparatus, equipment, etc. for radio
796.332028	Apparatus, equipment, materials for American football
808.81-.87	Collections of miscellaneous literary writings.
	Add to base number 808.8 the numbers following 808 in 808.1- 808.7, e.g., collections of essays 808.84, of debates 808.853
941.50824	Post-1970 Irish history

Not only are sales potentially indicative of use and value, but questionnaire and case study could be applied to the problem. Are successive septennial or octennial unabridged editions justifiable in the face of escalating costs of production and marketing? Possible compromises have been suggested. One involves a "Basic Dewey" that would be, in essence, an abridgment designed for the entire DDC clientele, not just for "North American public and school libraries."

> A basic edition provides the structure of the whole classification in details, but not in great depth. Depth is provided, for those who want it, in expanded editions of individual classes which are published from time to time. However, since the prerequisite of this form of publication would be that the basic structure as defined in Basic Dewey must of necessity be fixed at the outset, the choice to libraries would be a choice, not of structure (as in Alternative Dewey), but of depth.... The new structures would have to be built into the basic schedules, with all the problems their adoption would pose to libraries in terms of costs and resources.[10]

Whether the abridged DDC format could, or would ever be permitted to, furnish a launching pad for a "Basic Dewey" remains at present with the inscrutable deliberations of the Decimal Classification Editorial Policy Committee.

NOTES

[1]John Phillip Comaromi, *The Eighteen Editions of the Dewey Decimal Classification* (Albany, NY, Forest Press Division, Lake Placid Education Foundation, 1976), p. 610.

[2]Benjamin A. Custer, "The View from the Editor's Chair," *Library Resources & Technical Services*, v. 24, no. 2 (Spring 1980): 103.

[3]Melvil Dewey, *Dewey Decimal Classification and Relative Index*. Ed. 19 (Albany, NY, Forest Press, 1979), v. 1, pp. xxxvi, lxii.

[4]Melvil Dewey, *Abridged Dewey Decimal Classification and Relative Index*. Ed. 10 (Lake Placid Club, NY, Forest Press, 1971), pp. 1, 3.

[5]Melvil Dewey, *Abridged Dewey Decimal Classification and Relative Index*. Ed. 11 (Albany, NY, Forest Press, 1979), p. 9.

[6]Ibid., pp. 11-12.

[7]Lois Mai Chan, "The Tenth Abridged DDC ... and Children's Room/School Library Collections," *School Library Journal*, v. 20, no. 1 (September 15, 1973): 43.

[8]Ibid.

[9]Custer, p. 103.

[10]Marjorie Jelinek, "Twentieth Dewey: An Exercise in Prophecy," *Catalogue & Index*, no. 58 (Autumn 1980): 2.

17

Special Considerations

Introduction

Certain aspects of DDC's impact on library classification must be omitted from a discussion already grown too long. There is no room to compare it with other systems or to discuss the DDC-to-LC stampede, though a section on "Arguments for Using DDC" will be offered later in this chapter, more in the spirit of balance than in any effort to prove DDC the answer to every classifier's prayer. A few supplementary themes will be developed for practicing catalogers who use the system daily. To give an overview of available recent literature, a topical bibliography has been appended.

Book Numbers

Unlike Library of Congress call numbers, Dewey class numbers on LC bibliographic records are incomplete for most shelving, if not indexing, purposes. Successful classification starts with collocation, but ends with differentiation. Users want similar materials together in some sort of logical order, but they frequently need to locate a particular author, title, edition, volume, or copy. As early as *DDC 2* (1885), Melvil Dewey experimented with ways to turn his class numbers into complete call numbers. Without deciding which of several competing methods best fit his purpose, he was interested in "translation systems by which a name is represented by the initial with the rest translated into numbers."[1] Charles A. Cutter did not propose the "translation" technique. He even at first opposed it, but he soon capitulated. His *Alfabetic-order table* first appeared in 1886. Historians agree that Dewey's endorsement of Cutter's book numbers "certainly influenced their success."[2]

DDC 19 says relatively little about book numbers, but touches upon their uses in large collections, and for distinguishing works related to other works, such as translations, abridgments, commentaries, criticisms, reviews, indexes, and concordances.[3] It also suggests standard sources of information, including Barden's *Book Numbers*, the Cutter and Cutter-Sanborn *Author Tables*, and the system of *Author Numbers* used by the Library of Congress.[4] Most manuals on DDC number-building include a section on selecting book numbers.[5] In response to requests from the field, the *DDC 19* editor says:

It has sometimes been proposed that Library of Congress catalog cards should include a book number along with each Dewey Decimal Classification number, but this has not been considered feasible, because (1) different existing libraries use different book numbering systems; (2) even newly established libraries, which might be expected to find this service most useful, class and number works not covered by printed cards, and in so doing may be expected, in a given class, to preempt book numbers that would later appear on printed cards for other titles in the same class.[6]

The second difficulty cited above is familiar to every librarian who has tried for any length of time to use LC call numbers. Until standardized catalog services become more comprehensive, or develop a simple, acknowledged set of rules for assigning book numbers, ready-made call numbers will give a false sense of security to the copy cataloger. Centralized and cooperative cataloging agencies usually prefer the first one-to-three letters of the main entry. Cutter and Dewey would find them reactionary. Both felt that only compact, decimalized letter-number combinations gave the flexibility needed to keep a growing collection in reasonable order.

Is cuttering necessary, or worth its cost? Public service librarians say that full book numbers, judiciously extended with work marks, dates, and volume and copy numbers, are important especially for biographies and the types of materials named in the *DDC 19* discussion. A recent book on the subject says:

> The four basic purposes of book numbers are to:
> 1. Subarrange the materials with the same classification number in a systematic and logical order.
> 2. Assign to each item a distinctive group of symbols, that is, a call number, that will distinguish it from all others in the collection.
> 3. Provide a call number that facilitates finding a particular item among all others in the collection and returning it to the same relative location.
> 4. Maintain an accurate record of loaned items, or items that are temporarily away from their normal position....

There are three rudiments which must be followed in the formation of book numbers:

> 1. It is necessary to consult the shelflist before assigning a book number in order to avoid the problem of having different publications with identical call numbers. Also, by consulting the shelflist it is easier to assign the simplest, but yet the most appropriate book number in relation to all other materials already classified with the same classification number.
> 2. The length and detail of each book number depends on the number of items with the same classification number....
> 3. Book numbers are always considered as decimals. In this way, new numbers can be intercalated indefinitely and an alphabetical order is always maintained.[7]

The DC Editorial Policy Committee continues to chew on the possibility of having LC supply full DDC call numbers.

> The committee agreed that it did not favor at this time the assignment of book numbers, to complete the call number, by the Decimal Classification Division (DCD) of the Library of Congress. However, the DCEPC recognized the usefulness of subjects not adequately represented by the regular notation. It recommended that the DCD prepare a paper on the practicality of assigning such subject cutters for further consideration by the DCEPC.[8]

Classifying Non-print Materials

Opinion on whether DDC, or any general classification scheme, serves equally well for print and non-print depends upon whom you ask. Negative replies focus on difficulties of physical integration and arrangement, but they usually admit that there are extenuating arguments.

> ... The various forms which media now take ... means that some items seem to defy reliable classification, or at least that we need several "parallel" classified sequences in the library....
> One basic problem concerning order on the shelves is that a classified library consumes more shelf space than an unclassified one of the same size.... But Ranganathan has remarked that the conservation of space on the shelves is by no means the primary purpose of librarianship.[9]

School librarians object to separating works on the same subject. They are probably the strongest advocates of fully integrated collections.

> It is not necessary to introduce new cataloguing, classification and indexing systems solely in order to deal with NBM [non-book materials]. Users have adjusted to classified or alphabetical catalogs.[10]

Some libraries classify all materials, to get the benefits of topical analysis and a unified shelflist, but they maintain separate shelf arrangements for the various formats. Location symbols or color coding can help control such split collections, although the latter, once popular, is now in disrepute. Media librarians often prefer broad classification because their patrons are multidisciplinary in approach. Much of their distrust of traditional library classification centers on this issue.

> ... Many libraries ... have arranged themselves according to the Dewey Decimal Classification. But the artificial subject divisions pose problems, and particularly in the case of NBM. For example, a slide of a diamond may be of use to the chemist studying crystallography, the student learning to cut glass, the mathematician concerned with volume, the art lecturer concerned with shape, or the economist interested in forms of wealth. The librarian must consider each of these needs and decide to what extent the library retrieval system can meet them.[11]

This cross-disciplinary orientation tends to foster the classification "by attraction" which crept into early editions of DDC until it reached its peak in Edition 16. Under Benjamin Custer's editorship, it was then reversed, as we saw in chapter 1. Media librarians are today the most vocal critics of disciplinary integrity.

> The major problem in using DC (or any other conventional classification) is that the broad topics studied in schools often do not conform to the subject analysis in classification schemes. For example material may be required on "water," which in DC may be classified at several places including 333.339 (Economic control of water), 333.91 (Utilization of water), 338.456281 (Economics of the water supply industry), 338.76281 (Organizations in the water supply industry), 352.6 (Local government control of water supply), 386 (Inland waterway transportation), 387 (Water, air, space transportation), 546.22 (Chemistry of water), 551.4 (Geomorphology), 551.524 (Water temperature), 574.92 (Marine biology), 581.92 (Marine botany), 591.92 (Marine zoology), 614.772 (Public health aspects of water pollution), 614.81 (Water safety), 628.1 (Water supply), 631.7 (Irrigation and water conservation), 714 (Water features in landscape design), 797 (Aquatic and air sports) and 910.02 (Physical geography).
>
> Similarly, schools may initiate projects on countries, scattered by subject in all classification schemes, and on periods such as the Renaissance or the nineteenth century.[12]

The ghost of James Duff Brown must rejoice at such observations. But media librarians recognize the dangers, and try solutions such as the following:

> Limit the classification headings and provide the user with plenty of help before he consults the catalogue. It does lay the librarian open to the accusation that he has omitted to classify an item under an obvious heading, but that is a charge that he is professionally required to bear, particularly if he has provided good reference tools to back up his catalogue.[13]

Professional help and "good reference tools" may turn out to be quite inventive.

> One solution to this problem is the preparation of charts showing the interrelationships of DC class numbers within broad themes. Another is to regard classification purely as a shelving device, relying on detailed subject indexing for information retrieval. Another method used to overcome the problem of "broad themes" and "distributed relatives" is the publication of "materiographies" on such subjects as Power and Energy, Africa, the United States of America, Birds, Environmental experience, and Community help.[14]

Limiting the classification headings to broad themes takes the following form in one British school library which still uses *Abr 7*, supplemented by *Abr 10*, for all materials:

The major problem of DC for school libraries — that of "distributed relatives" — is solved by collecting all aspects of a topic at one class number: for example, everything on transport is collected at 625 (385 being unused), everything on the role of women at 301.424 (396 being unused), everything on children at 302 (362.7 and 649 being unused) and everything on geography at 910. 380.9 (Commercial geography) is unused and the following additions are made at 910:

910.1   Commodities
910.2   Distribution

Some adjustments are also made in the shelving of material, with the use of broken order to collocate related topics: 910 (Geography) is followed by 909 (General history) and 940-999 (Modern history by locality), and Ancient history (930) is shelved with Classical mythology (290).[15]

Hints are supplied on how to choose the correct "reduced" class number from among competing disciplines. Other ideas abound in the literature. A polytechnic institute in England facilitates topical browsing by hanging classified slides in filing cabinets in pocketed transparent sheets.[16] Australian map librarians suggest direct classification by Dewey areas from Table 2, with a zero added to two-digit notation, and a decimal point after the third digit in longer notation. A colon could introduce a subject aspect, e.g., 940:55 for a geologic map of Australia.[17] However, the Dewey establishment, although it supplies official options, continues to stress the dangers of local manipulation.

Such a simple and ingenious notation system as the Decimal Classification enjoys is highly adaptable and, far more than any other system, Dewey has been subjected to very many unofficial shifts and grafts of its numbers in order to achieve real or fancied advantages. Among the real advantages have been the preempting of short notations, officially assigned to American, Anglo-Saxon, or Western cultural topics such as language, literature, religion, and public administration, and instead using them for topics favored in other cultural situations. Unfortunately, this notation, the Decimal Classification's great strength, has also been its great weakness: the temptation to play with it becomes nearly irresistible, and many libraries that have not resited have later found themselves blocked off from taking proper advantage of the cultural services and so have chosen to throw out both baby and bath water by giving up the Decimal Classification altogether. This was another of the reasons for the shift to the Library of Congress system in the 1960's by some.[18]

In the United States, the ALA/RTSD/CCS Ad Hoc Subcommittee on the Subject Analysis of Audiovisual Materials discussed the inadequacy of the Dewey Decimal Classification in treating some of the subjects covered by those formats.[19] It recommended assigning both Dewey and LC numbers "even though they may not be used in actual storage of materials."[20] The Library of Congress has wrestled with the problem in various ways. After publication in 1975 of AACR revised chapter 12 (Audiovisual Media and Special Instructional Materials), it polled its clientele. The results were never reported in the

Cataloging Service Bulletin, but *LC Catalogs: Audiovisual Materials* still includes numbers from both the LC and the DDC classifications.

Assignment of Dewey decimal numbers was temporarily discontinued in November 1963 and resumed in October 1967. Numbers are taken from the 10th abridged edition of the Dewey list.[21]

LC experiments in automated subject retrieval of all types of materials have implications for the classifying of audio-visual formats.

The desirability of giving complete Dewey coverage to MARC titles was pointed up by the finding of the Technical Processes Research Office study on the relative efficiency of DC and LC numbers for machine retrieval. It showed that, in the present state of the MARC retriever DC numbers are significantly more efficient than LC numbers for searching a broad topic.[22]

Pitfalls of DDC

There is an old adage that "you pays yer money and takes yer cherce." Its latent scepticism applies to the choice of a classification system, although studies such as the one cited above give straws in the wind. No system is perfect, or answers all needs under all circumstances. The most successful ones undergo constant revision, but Janus-like, revisions look two ways. Although Bakewell's study, cited on pages 339-40, was done in the mid-1970s, 8 of the 33 DDC class numbers included in those citations have their meanings changed, or cannot be found, in *DDC 19*. Yet many librarians question the necessity for reclassifying works with obsolescent numbers, as the following comment shows:

How many libraries will be able to afford to reclassify the United Kingdom? Many changes will cost libraries much money and/or make librarians look foolish. Is there a real need to have an absolutely consistent classification? Aside from aesthetics, what purpose does a "neat" Dewey serve? We are not organizing knowledge, we are retailing books.[23]

Such comments raise the old spectre of "slot-ification," and so we go, round and round. And if schedule revision has its pros and cons, so does DDC's buffet of options. They appeal to special interests, but can become a Pandora's box. Moreover, they proceed from an ambivalent donor, as Custer's comments in the *Encyclopedia of Library and Information Science* indicated. In offering them, *DDC 19* warns:

Libraries following such options will continue to sacrifice the benefits to be derived from numbers assigned by centralized classification services.[24]

Custer spoke of the "nearly irresistible" temptation to play with the notation. The comfortable feeling of mastery can make a classifier rash in "adjusting" for local idiosyncrasies. In the labyrinthine Library of Congress and Bliss classifications fewer of these temptations seem to lurk.

Arguments for Using DDC

In 1959, after deploring "the librarian's distrust of the importance of classification," Jesse Shera asserted:

> The D.C. may be "a 'ell of a 'ole," but we seem unable to discover any other that is sufficiently superior to justify the risk of migration.[25]

Speaking at a time when the flight from Dewey to LC was just starting, Shera seemed for the next decade or so to have been wrong, but DDC partisans were never vanquished. They once again appear to be gaining ground.[26] Access to standardized records is a boon, as is user familiarity, and periodic revision.

> When it was decided to reclassify the library of Bedford College in 1969, DC was preferred to other possible contenders ... largely because it came nearest to satisfying the five features suggested ... as being desirable ... a) it is reasonably up-to-date; b) apart from the separation of language and literature, its order of main subjects is acceptable; c) its notation displays order clearly and is practical, memorable, easily expansible and adaptable; d) it has a useful relative index; e) it is familiar to library staff and, through their use of public libraries, to users.
>
> Apart from these points ... the use of DC in the British national bibliography was considered a powerful argument....[27]
>
> The City of London Polytechnic was formed in 1970 by the amalgamation of a number of colleges which between them used several different classification schemes.... It was decided that the library and learning resource service should use the DC 18 for a number of reasons, most notably the fact that it would allow the use of the UK MARC services with a minimum of amendment. Other attractive features of DC were familiarity to users, frequency of revision.... This contrasted strongly with the two most viable alternatives, Bliss and UDC.[28]

DDC Numbers on LC Bibliographic Records

Much has been said about the joys and economies of ready-made, standardized, easily copied call numbers. Users rely heavily on finding such numbers in their national bibliographies or MARC services. For American, and indeed for much English-language, publication, that means using Library of Congress records. In chapter 1 we learned that by mid-1980 LC had supplied a total of 2,253,731 records with DDC numbers. Recent production is shown in Table 6.

Table 6
Library of Congress Records with DDC Numbers

Year	Records	Increase/Decrease
1970	73,525	
1971	68,155	[7.3%]
1972	80,463	18.0%
1973	80,474	0.0%
1974	90,793	12.8%
1975	100,302	10.5%
1976	94,020	[6.3%]
1977	100,797	7.2%
1978	104,721	3.9%
1979	120,678	15.2%

Most of the statistics in Table 6 come from the *Annual Report of the Librarian of Congress*, which until recently used fiscal years ending June 30th, then changed to years ending September 30th. Production decreases were usually caused by abnormal staff turnover or cutbacks in funds for overtime. In 1975, when records with DDC numbers first topped 100,000, LC claimed that they accounted for virtually all titles in English and French, plus a growing number in German, Spanish, and Portuguese, and 8,400 audiovisual records. The Dewey Decimal Division revises proposed drafts of phoenix schedules, performs most of the editorial preparation of new editions, exchanges operating personnel with BNB and other national libraries for mutual in-service benefits, and sends a staff member "on occasional visits" to 1600 Pennsylvania Avenue to catalog, classify, and maintain the White House Library.

Conclusion

The phoenix schedule technique introduced in *DDC 16* was a defensive change of direction from abrupt, system-wide, to controlled, selective revision. *DC&* appeared in the wake of *DDC 16*, evidence of further official effort at gradual revision and improved communication with the clientele. The clientele, unaccustomed to such pampering, more or less ignored it at first, but as knowledge developed, book publishing increased, and libraries grew, they learned to consult it for insights into the state of the art and the shape of things to come. Most significant was its announcement of mid-edition changes in area numbers for the British Isles, and other far-reaching adjustments.

Post-*DDC 19* developments include Marjorie Jelinek's provocative speculations on the format of *DDC 20*.[29] The ALA/RTSD/CCS Subject Analysis Committee examined similar proposals at its ALA Conference meeting on June 30, 1980.

It was reported that the Subject Analysis Committee had discussed the idea that two or more "phoenixes" (complete revisions of numbers for certain fast developing disciplines) strung out in the interval between editions would be easier for most libraries to accommodate than the "double whammy" changes with the appearance of new editions every eight to ten years. It was pointed out that revisions between editions would involve "ripple effects" where changes in one discipline mandated changes in related disciplines.[30]

Separate publication in 1981 of the alternative 780 (Music) schedule points in the same direction. So do the DCEPC plans to continue revision of phoenix 301-307, and the recommendations of the RTSD/CCS Subcommittee on Racism and Sexism in Subject Analysis:

> Specific recommendations ... for Decimal Classification Editorial Policy Committee:
> 1. Use of recommended changes to 305-306 for creation of an alternative schedule.
> 2. Breakup of indiscriminate groupings of women, slaves, and ethnic groups.[31]

In chapter 2 we examined DDC guidelines for citation order among competing aspects of a complex topic. Tucked away in the editor's introduction to *DDC 19* is a new piece of common-sense advice for cross-classification situations of all kinds.

> Sometimes the classifier's life will be made more difficult by his realization that none of the foregoing rules reflects the author's intention and emphasis, and he will be faced with the temptation to flout the rules. Given adequate reason, he should do so. (v. 1, p. xlix)

Successful classifiers develop a forte of intuitive responses to the materials they organize, and, like many professionals, tend to acquire a little hubris in the process. They are sometimes annoyed by advice from their public service colleagues, or even from interested laypersons, who often have personal axes to grind. Such comments may reveal new insights, but their chief value is in their encouragement of dialog. The deeper understanding which hopefully results should, and can, be mutual. For example, a linguist, taking a pot-shot at Wilson Follett's *Modern American Usage*, makes one point by use of a library analogy:

> If I were in charge of library classification, I would never assign Mr. Follett's book to the language section. I might be tempted to put it among the autobiographies (because it is, after all, a book about Mr. Follett), but I would probably put it alongside the works of Emily Post, Amy Vanderbilt, and other specialists in proper behavior.[32]

Any experienced cataloger could tell that linguist that he would be labeling, not classifying. Yet his whole article is an essay on the distinctions between factual truth and value judgments. Lucia Rather, defending Library of Congress handling of the controversial works of Carlos Castaneda, explains:

> In subject cataloging, the general policy is to follow the statements of the author and publisher as long as the item has been issued as a legitimate work on the subject. Reclassification would not be undertaken without a statement from the author and/or publisher

that a misrepresentation had occurred, although others may have determined that the work is one of the imagination. The basic goal in book classification is to bring similar works together on the shelves. Such an arrangement best serves the library user when browsing through the book stacks in search of material of interest. The cataloger fulfills his role by identifying the topics of particular works and placing them with other works on the same topics. While some of these works may be outstanding contributions, others may be poor in quality, based on inaccurate research, or even outright frauds. The cataloger does not and should not place value judgments on these works.[33]

Sandy Berman, the Lyncaeus of cataloging ethics, in his comments on *DDC 19*, takes exception, not so much to Rather's principles, perhaps, as to their implementation. He feels that the makers of classification schemes, being slow to incorporate new concepts and terminology, blunt their tools so that the classifier is inadvertently forced into a kind of labeling. The challenge to reflect accurately the constant changes in literary warrant creates a healthy tension in all information retrieval. We cannot always predict what tomorrow's classification categories will be, and we should be well aware that there is no such thing as a perfected, definitive, static system. Yet the quest for better classification will continue, with success measured by step-wise advances along an open scale.

NOTES

[1]Melvil Dewey, *Decimal Classification and Relative Index.* Ed. 2 (Boston, Library Bureau, 1885), pp. 35-37.

[2]Donald J. Lehnus, *Book Numbers: History, Principles, and Application* (Chicago, American Library Association, 1980), p. 28.

[3]Melvil Dewey, *Dewey Decimal Classification and Relative Index.* Ed. 19 (Albany, NY, Forest Press, 1979), v. 1, p. lx.

[4]The Library of Congress adaptation of Cutter's *Author Tables* appeared in its most recent published version in "Book Numbers and Shelflisting the Various Editions of a Work," *Cataloging Service Bulletin*, no. 3 (Winter 1979): 19-23.

[5]See, for example, Marty Bloomberg and Hans Weber, *An Introduction to Classification and Number Building in Dewey* (Littleton, CO, Libraries Unlimited, 1976), pp. 181-85; *or* J. McRee Elrod, *Classification*, 2nd ed. (Metuchen, NJ, Scarecrow Press, 1978), pp. 44-62.

[6]Dewey, *Dewey Decimal Classification and Relative Index*, Ed. 19, v. 1, p. lxvii.

[7]Lehnus, pp. 75-77.

[8]Margaret E. Cockshutt, "Annual Report of the Decimal Classification Editorial Policy Committee, July 1, 1979-June 30, 1980," *Library Resources & Technical Services*, v. 25, no. 1 (January/March 1981): 123.

[9]W. C. Berwick Sayers, *Sayers' Manual of Classification for Librarians*, 5th ed. [rev. by] Arthur Maltby (London, André Deutsch, 1975), pp. 25, 286.

[10]Richard Fothergill and Jan Butchart, *Non-book Materials in Libraries: A Practical Guide* (London & Hamden, CT, Clive Bingley & Linnet Books, 1978), p. 187.

[11]Ibid., p. 46.

[12]K. G. B. Bakewell, *Classification and Indexing Practice* (London & Hamden, CT, Clive Bingley & Linnet Books, 1978), p. 27.

[13]Bernard Chibnall, *The Organization of Media* (London & Hamden, CT, Clive Bingley & Linnet Books, 1978), p. 64.

[14]Bakewell, pp. 27-28.

[15]Ibid., pp. 31-32.

[16]Philip Pacey, "Handling Slides Single-handed," *Art Libraries Journal*, v. 2, no. 3 (Autumn 1977): 22-30.

[17]P. A. G. Alonso and D. F. Prescott, "Deweying Maps," *Australian Library Journal*, v. 26, no. 3 (May 18, 1977): 47-52.

[18]Benjamin A. Custer, "Dewey Decimal Classification," *Encyclopedia of Library and Information Science* (New York, Marcel Dekker, 1972), v. 7, p. 137.

[19]Suzanne Massonneau, "Developments in the Organization of Audiovisual Materials," *Library Trends*, v. 25, no. 3 (January 1977): 680.

[20]Edward J. Blume, "Cataloging and Classification Section Report," *Library Resources & Technical Services*, v. 22, no. 1 (Winter 1978): 85.

[21]Library of Congress. *Library of Congress Catalogs: Audiovisual Materials, July-September 1980* (Washington, The Library, 1980), p. v.

[22]Library of Congress. *Annual Report of the Librarian of Congress for the Fiscal Year Ending June 30, 1974* (Washington, The Library, 1975), p. 23.

[23]"Dewey Drops (Mostly) .08," editor's note in the *U*N*A*B*A*S*H*E*D Librarian*, no. 32 (1979): 4. See also on the same page quotations from: Maurice J. Freedman, "Better Latent Than Never—A Few Short Comments on the Proposed DDC 19 and the Custer/Comaromi Statements in HCLCB #35," *HCL Cataloging Bulletin*, no. 37 (November/December 1978): 6-10.

[24]Dewey, *Dewey Decimal Classification and Relative Index*, Ed. 19, v. 1, p. xxiii.

[25]Jesse H. Shera, "What Lies Ahead in Classification," *The Role of Classification in the Modern American Library* (Champaign, IL, distributed by the Illini Union Bookstore, 1959), p. 116.

[26]One of the latest salvos in this waning war was fired, of all places, over the heads of school librarians. *See* Ahmed Fouad Gamaluddin, "Dewey Decimal Classification: A Quagmire," *School Library Journal*, v. 26, no. 8 (April 1980): 32-35.

[27]Bakewell, p. 19.

[28]Ibid., p. 24.

[29]Marjorie Jelinek, "Twentieth Dewey: An Exercise in Prophecy," *Catalogue & Index*, no. 58 (Autumn 1980): 1-2.

[30]Gregory New, "Report on the Dewey Decimal Classification Edition 19," *Library of Congress Information Bulletin*, v. 39, no. 34 (August 22, 1980): 319-20.

[31]ALA/RTSD/CCS Subject Analysis Committee. Subcommittee on Racism and Sexism in Subject Analysis, "Summary Report," *RTSD Newsletter*, v. 6, no. 2 (March/April 1981): 22.

[32]James C. Bostain, "Wishing Will Not Make It So: A Linguist Takes on the Grammarians," *Today's Education*, v. 70, no. 2 (April/May 1981): 39GS.

[33]Lucia J. Rather, letter to Richard de Mille quoted in "Cataloging Castaneda," *HCL Cataloging Bulletin*, no. 37 (November/December 1978): 2.

Bibliography

ALA/RTSD/CCS Subject Analysis Committee. Subcommittee on Racism and Sexism in Subject Analysis. "Summary Report." *RTSD Newsletter*, v. 6, no. 2 (March/April 1981): 21-22.

Alonso, P. A. G., and Prescott, D. F. "Deweying Maps." *Australian Library Journal*, v. 26, no. 3 (May 18, 1977): 47-52.

Anglo-American Cataloging Rules. North American Text. Chicago, American Library Association, 1967.

Anglo-American Cataloguing Rules. 2nd ed. Chicago, American Library Association, 1978.

Bakewell, K. G. B. *Classification and Indexing Practice.* London & Hamden, CT, Clive Bingley & Linnet Books, 1978.

Balling, Eigil. "Cataloguing in Denmark." *International Cataloguing*, v. 8, no. 3 (July/September 1979): 28-30.

Batty, David C. "A Close Look at Dewey 18: Alive and Well and Living in Albany." *Wilson Library Bulletin*, v. 46, no. 8 (April 1972): 711-717. *Pakistan Library Bulletin*, v. 5, no. 3/4 (March-June 1973): 1-13.

Berman, Sanford. "Cataloging Castaneda." *HCL Cataloging Bulletin*, no. 37 (November/December 1978): 1-3.

Berman, Sanford. "DDC 19: An Indictment." *Library Journal*, v. 105, no. 5 (March 1, 1980): 585-89.

Bishoff, Lizbeth. "Dewey Decimal Classification, 19th Edition: Its Changes and Their Implications for Libraries." *Illinois Libraries*, v. 62, no. 7 (September 1980): 625-31.

Bloomberg, Marty, and Weber, Hans. *An Introduction to Classification and Number Building in Dewey.* Littleton, CO, Libraries Unlimited, 1976.

Blume, Edward J. "Cataloging and Classification Section Report." *Library Resources & Technical Services*, v. 22, no. 1 (Winter 1978): 83-86.

Bostain, James G. "Wishing Will Not Make It So: A Linguist Takes on the Grammarians." *Today's Education*, v. 70, no. 2 (April/May 1981): 34GS-39GS.

Broadus, Robert N. "Dewey and Religion." *Library Resources & Technical Services*, v. 14, no. 4 (Fall 1970): 574-78.

Butcher, Peter. "Dewey? We Sure Do!" *Catalogue & Index*, no. 55 (Winter 1979): 1, 7-8.

"Canadian and British Librarians to Serve on Dewey Decimal Classification Editorial Policy Committee." *Library Resources & Technical Services*, v. 15, no. 1 (Winter 1971): 95.

Cataloging Service, bulletins 1-125. 1945-1978.

Cataloging Service Bulletin no. 1- . Summer 1978- .

Chan, Lois Mai. "Dewey 18: Another Step in the Evolutionary Process." *Library Resources & Technical Services*, v. 16, no. 3 (Summer 1972): 383-99.

Chan, Lois Mai. "The Form Distinction in the 800 Class of the Dewey Decimal Scheme." *Library Resources & Technical Services*, v. 15, no. 4 (Fall 1971): 458-71.

Chan, Lois Mai. "The Tenth Abridged DDC ... and Children's Room/School Library Collections." *School Library Journal*, v. 20, no. 1 (September 15, 1973): 38-43.

Chibnall, Bernard. *The Organization of Media*. London & Hamden, CT, Clive Bingley & Linnet Books, 1976.

Classification in the 1970's: A Second Look. Rev. ed. London & Hamden, CT, Clive Bingley & Linnet Books, 1976.

Clews, John P. "Revision of DC 780: The Phoenix Schedule." *Brio*, v. 12, no. 1 (Spring 1975): 7-14.

Cockshutt, Margaret E. "Annual Report of the Decimal Classification Editorial Policy Committee, July 1, 1979-June 30, 1980." *Library Resources & Technical Services*, v. 25, no. 1 (January/March 1981): 123-24.

Comaromi, John Phillip. "DDC 19: The Reclass Project." *HCL Cataloging Bulletin*, no. 35 (July/August 1978): 12-15.

Comaromi, John Phillip. "Decimal Classification Editorial Policy Committee Report." *Library Resources & Technical Services*, v. 21, no. 1 (Winter 1977): 93-94; v. 24, no. 2 (Spring 1980): 179-80.

Comaromi, John Phillip. *The Eighteen Editions of the Dewey Decimal Classification*. Albany, NY, Forest Press Division, Lake Placid Education Foundation, 1976.

Comaromi, John Phillip. *A Survey of the Use of the Dewey Decimal Classification in the United States and Canada*. Lake Placid, NY?, Prepared for Forest Press, Lake Placid Foundation, 1975.

Comaromi, John Phillip. "Use of the DDC in the US and Canada." *Library Resources and Technical Services*, v. 22, no. 4 (Fall 1978): 402-408

Croghan, Antony. "The Dewey Decimal Classification and Its Eighteenth Edition." *Library Association Record*, v. 74, no. 7 (July 1972): 120-21.

Curwen, Anthony G. "Revision of Classification Schemes: Policies and Practices." *Journal of Librarianship*, v. 10, no. 1 (January 1978): 19-38.

Custer, Benjamin A. "Changes in Application." *Catalogue & Index*, no. 36 (Spring 1975): 16; *International Cataloguing*, v. 4, no. 2 (April/June 1975): 2; *Library Association Record*, v. 77, no. 5 (May 1975): 114.

Custer, Benjamin A. "DDC 19: Characteristics." *HCL Cataloging Bulletin*, no. 35 (July/August 1978): 9-11.

Custer, Benjamin A. "Dewey Decimal Classification." *Encyclopedia of Library and Information Science* 7: 128-42.

Custer, Benjamin A. "Dewey Decimal Classification One Hundred Years After." *Catalogue & Index*, no. 39 (Winter 1975): 1, 3.

Custer, Benjamin A. "Dewey Lives." *Library Resources & Technical Services*, v. 11, no. 1 (Winter 1967): 51-60.

Custer, Benjamin A. "Dewey 19." *Cataloging Service Bulletin*, no. 4 (Spring 1979): 15-17; *Catalogue & Index*, no. 53 (Summer 1979): 1-2.

Custer, Benjamin A. "Dewey 17: A Preview and Report." *Indian Librarian*, v. 19, no. 3 (March 1965): 191-97; *Library Association Record*, v. 67, no. 3 (March 1965): 79-83; *Wilson Library Bulletin*, v. 39, no. 7 (March 1965): 555-59.

Custer, Benjamin A. "The View from the Editor's Chair." *Library Resources & Technical Services*, v. 24, no. 2 (Spring 1980): 99-105.

"D.C. Numbers on L.C. Cards." *Library Journal*, v. 50, no. 17 (October 1, 1930): 786.

Davison, Keith. *Classification Practice in Britain*. London, Library Association, 1966.

Dewey, Melvil. *Abridged Dewey Decimal Classification and Relative Index*. Eds. 10-11. Lake Placid Club and Albany, NY, Forest Press, 1971, 1979.

Dewey, Melvil. *Decimal Classification*. Standard (15th) ed. Lake Placid Club, NY, Forest Press, 1951.

Dewey, Melvil. *Dewey Decimal Classification and Relative Index*. Eds. 16-19. Lake Placid Club and Albany, NY, Forest Press, 1958-1979.

Dewey Decimal Classification: Additions, Notes, and Decisions. v. 1- . 1959- .

The Dewey Decimal Classification: Outlines and Papers Presented at a Workshop on the Teaching of Classification. New York, School of Library Service, Columbia University, 1968.

"Dewey Drops (Mostly) .08." *The U*N*A*B*A*S*H*E*D Librarian*, no. 32 (1979): 4.

Dewey International: Papers Given at the European Centenary Seminar on the Dewey Decimal Classification. London, Library Association, 1977.

Dhyani, P. "DDC 18: Critical Appraisal of Some Auxiliary Tables." *International Library Review*, v. 9, no. 2 (April 1977): 175-81.

Donovan, Peter W., Hunt, David C., and Mack, John M. "Mathematics in a Major Library Using the Dewey Decimal Classification." *Australian Academic and Research Libraries*, v. 6, no. 2 (June 1975): 87-91.

Donovan, Peter W., Hunt, David C., and Mack, John M. "Professional Developments Reviewed: DDC and Mathematics." *Wilson Library Bulletin*, v. 48, no. 3 (November 1973): 220-22.

Duckett, R. J. "Philosophy and Religion in Dewey 19." *Bulletin of the Association of British Theological and Philosophical Libraries*, n.s., v. 18 (June 1980): 12-16.

Eaton, Thelma. "Epitaph to a Dead Classification." *Library Association Record*, v. 57, no. 11 (November 1955): 428-30.

Elrod, J. McRee. *Classification.* 2nd ed. Metuchen, NJ, Scarecrow Press, 1978.

Encyclopedia Americana. 1980 International ed. Danbury, CT, Americana Corporation, 1980.

Fothergill, Richard, and Butchart, Jan. *Non-book Materials in Libraries: A Practical Guide.* London & Hamden, CT, Clive Bingley & Linnet Books, 1978.

Freedman, Maurice J. "Better Latent Than Never—A Few Short Comments on the Proposed DDC 19, and the Custer/Comaromi Statements in HCLCB #35." *HCL Cataloging Bulletin*, no. 37 (November/December 1978): 6-10.

Friedman, Joan, and Jeffreys, Alan E. *Cataloguing and Classification in British University Libraries.* Sheffield, University of Sheffield Postgraduate School of Librarianship, 1967.

Friis-Hansen, J. B. "Library Classification Systems in Denmark." *International Classification*, v. 3, no. 2 (1976): 91-93.

Gamaluddin, Ahmed Fouad. "Dewey Decimal Classification: A Quagmire." *School Library Journal*, v. 26, no. 8 (April 1980): 32-35.

Gangadhara Rao, P. "Homonyms in Dewey Decimal Classification Edition 18: Case Studies." *Library Science with a Slant to Documentation*, v. 14, nos. 3-4 (September-December 1977): 120-23.

General Classification Systems in a Changing World: Proceedings of the FID Classification Symposium Held in Commemoration of the Dewey Centenary. The Hague, Fédération Internationale de Documentation (FID), 1978.

Guide to Use of Dewey Decimal Classification, Based on the Practice of the Decimal Classification Office at the Library of Congress. Lake Placid Club, NY, Forest Press, 1962.

Gupta, S. S. "Expansion of 355.48 in Dewey Decimal Classification." *Herald of Library Science*, v. 17, no. 4 (October 1978): 308-311.

Harris, Jessica L. Milstead, and Clack, Doris H. "Treatment of People and Peoples in Subject Analysis." *Library Resources & Technical Services*, v. 23, no. 4 (Fall 1979): 374-90.

Hickey, Doralyn J. "Subject Analysis: An Interpretive Survey." *Library Trends*, v. 25, no. 1 (July 1976): 273-91.

Hobart, Ann. "The Work of the Dewey Decimal Classification Sub-Committee, 1968-1979." *Catalogue & Index*, no. 58 (Autumn 1980): 5-6.

Hudson, Judith A. "Searching MARC/DPS Records for Area Studies: Comparative Results Using Keywords, LC and DC Class Numbers." *Library Resources & Technical Services*, v. 14, no. 4 (Fall 1970): 530-45.

Jelinek, Marjorie. "Dewey 18: A British View." *Catalogue & Index*, no. 28 (Winter 1972): 8-10.

Jelinek, Marjorie. "Twentieth Dewey: An Exercise in Prophecy." *Catalogue & Index*, no. 58 (Autumn 1980): 1-2.

Jones, Malcolm. *Music Librarianship*. London, Clive Bingley, 1979.

Kumar, P. S. G. "Dewey through a Century." *Herald of Library Science*, v. 12, no. 1 (January 1973): 38-43.

LaMontagne, Leo E. *American Library Classification, with Special Reference to the Library of Congress*. Hamden, CT, Shoe String Press, 1961.

Langridge, Derek. *Approach to Classification for Students of Librarianship*. London & Hamden, CT, Clive Bingley & Linnet Books, 1973.

Lehnus, Donald J. *Book Numbers: History, Principles, and Application*. Chicago, American Library Association, 1980.

Library of Congress. *Annual Report of the Librarian of Congress....* Washington, The Library, 1975.

Library of Congress. *Library of Congress Catalogs: Audiovisual Materials*. Washington, The Library, 1980.

Library of Congress. *Library of Congress Catalogs: Monographic Series*. Washington, The Library, 1975- .

Library of Congress. Processing Department. *Classification. Class Z. Bibliography and Library Science*. 5th ed. Washington, The Library, 1980.

Library of Congress Information Bulletin. v. 1- . 1942- .

McKinlay, John. "Dewey and Mathematics." *Australian Academic and Research Libraries*, v. 4, no. 3 (September 1973): 105-111.

McKinlay, John. "More on DC Numbers on LC Cards: Quantity and Quality." *Library Resources & Technical Services*, v. 14, no. 4 (Fall 1970): 517-29.

Major Classification Systems: The Dewey Centennial. Urbana-Champaign, IL, University of Illinois Graduate School of Library Science, 1976.

Massonneau, Suzanne. "Developments in the Organization of Audiovisual Materials." *Library Trends*, v. 25, no. 3 (January 1977): 665-84.

Matthews, W. E. "Dewey 18: A Preview and Report." *Wilson Library Bulletin*, v. 45, no. 6 (February 1971): 572-77; *Library Association Record*, v. 73, no. 2 (February 1971): 28-30.

Merrill, William Stetson. *Code for Classifiers*. 2nd ed. Chicago, American Library Association, 1939.

Meyer-Baer, Kathi. "Classifications in American Music Libraries." *Music Review*, v. 12, no. 2 (February 1951): 76-82.

Miksa, Francis. "The 19th Dewey: A Review Article." *Library Quarterly*, v. 50, no. 4 (October 1980): 483-89.

The Nature and Future of the Catalog: Proceedings of the ALA's Information Science and Automation Division's 1975 and 1977 Institutes on the Catalog. Phoenix, AZ, Oryx Press, 1979.

New, Gregory. "Dewey Decimal Classification Edition 19." *Library of Congress Information Bulletin*, v. 39, no. 34 (August 22, 1980): 319-20.

Nocetti, Milton. "Agricultural Soil Science in Universal Classification Systems: A Comparative Analysis." *International Classification*, v. 5, no. 1 (March 1978): 15-20.

Pacey, Philip. "Handling Slides Single-Handed." *Art Libraries Journal*, v. 2, no. 3 (Autumn 1977): 22-30.

Parkhi, R. S. *Decimal Classification and Colon Classification in Perspective.* New York, Asia Publishing House, 1964.

Paul, André, "DDC 18: A Review." Association Canadienne des Bibliothécaires de Langue Française *Bulletin*, v. 18, no. 4 (December 1972): 276-79.

Prescott, Dorothy F. "The Dewey Decimal Classification and AACR as Applied to Maps—A Criticism." *Cataloguing Australia*, v. 3, nos. 1-2 (January-June 1977): 12-17.

Problems in Library Classification: Dewey 17 and Conversion. New York, School of Library and Information Science, The University of Wisconsin—Milwaukee; published in cooperation with R. R. Bowker, 1968.

Ramsden, M. J. "Dewey 18." *Australian Library Journal*, v. 21, no. 3 (April 1972): 116-19.

Redfern, Brian. *Organising Music in Libraries.* London & Hamden, CT, Clive Bingley & Linnet Books, 1978.

Richmond, Phyllis. "The Future of Generalized Systems of Classification." *College and Research Libraries*, v. 24, no. 5 (September 1963): 395-401.

The Role of Classification in the Modern American Library. Champaign, IL, distributed by the Illini Union Bookstore, 1959.

Sayers, W. C. Berwick. *An Introduction to Library Classification, Theoretical, Historical and Practical.* 9th ed., with corrections. London, Grafton, 1958.

Sayers, W. C. Berwick. *Sayers' Manual of Classification for Librarians.* 5th ed. [rev. by] Arthur Maltby, London, André Deutsch, 1975.

Schaefer, Barbara K. "The Phoenix Schedule 510 in Dewey 18." *Library Resources & Technical Services*, v. 19, no. 1 (Winter 1975): 46-59.

Sengupta, I. N. "Some Observations on the Forthcoming 19th Edition of the Dewey Decimal Classification (DDC) Scheme." *International Classification*, v. 6, no. 3 (November 1979): 170-72.

Soudek, Miluse. "On the Classification of Psychology in General Library Classification Schemes." *Library Resources & Technical Services*, v. 24, no. 2 (Spring 1980): 114-28.

Subject Authorities: A Guide to Subject Cataloging. New York & London, R. R. Bowker, 1981. 3 volumes.

Sultana, John B. "The DDC Centenary Seminar—Banbury 1976." *Catalogue & Index,* no. 44 (Spring 1977): 3-5.

Svenonius, Elaine. "Directions for Research in Indexing, Classification, and Cataloging." *Library Resources & Technical Services,* v. 25, no. 1 (January/March 1981): 88-103.

Sweeney, Russell. "Dewey 18: A Review." *Catalogue & Index,* no. 26 (Summer 1972): 10-12.

Sweeney, Russell. "Dewey in Britain." *Catalogue & Index,* no. 30 (Summer 1973): 4-6.

Sweeney, Russell. "Music in the Dewey Decimal Classification." *Catalogue & Index,* no. 42 (Autumn 1976): 4-6.

Sweeney, Russell. "The Old, Grey Mare ... ," *Cataloging & Classification Quarterly,* v. 1, no. 1 (Fall 1980): 91-96.

Tait, James A. "Dewey Decimal Classification: A Vigorous Nonagenarian." *Library Review,* v. 23, no. 6 (Summer 1972): 227-29.

Trotter, Ross. "Dewey 19—A Subjective Assessment," *Catalogue & Index,* no. 59 (Winter 1980): 1-5.

Trotter, Ross. "The New Dewey Area Tables for Great Britain and Their Application." *Catalogue & Index,* no. 38 (Autumn 1975): 1, 3-4.

Vann, Sarah K. "Dewey Abroad: The Field Survey of 1964." *Library Resources & Technical Services,* v. 11, no. 1 (Winter 1967): 61-71.

Vann, Sarah K. *Field Survey of DDC Use Abroad.* Albany, NY, Forest Press, 1965.

Walker, William B. "Art Books and Periodicals: Dewey and LC." *Library Trends,* v. 23, no. 3 (January 1975): 451-70.

Webster's New International Dictionary of the English Language. 2nd and 3rd unabr. eds. Springfield, MA, G. & C. Merriam, 1958-1969.

Welsh, William J. "The Processing Department of the Library of Congress in 1968." *Library Resources & Technical Services,* v. 13, no. 2 (Spring 1969): 175-97.

Williams-Wynn, Brenda. "Nearly 100 and Still Going Strong: A Review of Dewey 18." *South African Librarian,* v. 40, no. 2 (October 1972): 92-99.

World Book Encyclopedia. Chicago, World Book-Childcraft International, 1981.

"The Year's Work in Cataloging." [Annual feature in *Library Resources & Technical Services*].

Author/Title/Subject Index

Bibliographic footnotes are not indexed, but there are a few citations of substantive matter in the chapter notes. All references to DDC editions are indexed except those to *DDC 18* and *DDC 19*, which are too numerous. Similarly, references to the many DDC auxiliary table and instruction references in the text are exemplary rather than exhaustive.